GRAIN
CARRIAGE BY SEA

By

Tom Sewell, MA

Foreword by
THE LORD PLUMB OF COLESHILL DL MEP

|L|L|P|

LONDON HONG KONG

1999

LLP Reference Publishing
69–77 Paul Street
London EC2A 4LQ
Great Britain

EAST ASIA
LLP Asia
Sixth Floor, Hollywood Centre
233 Hollywood Road
Hong Kong

First published in Great Britain 1999

British Library Cataloguing in Publication Data
A catalogue record for this book is
available from the British Library

ISBN 1–85978–886–6

Text set in 10pt Century Schoolbook by
Mendip Communications Ltd, Frome, Somerset
Printed in Great Britain by
MPG Books, Bodmin, Cornwall

For Jennifer, Alex and Jono

About the Author

After study at Oxford, Lausanne and Stockholm Universities where he read languages and economics, Tom Sewell joined the senior branch of the Diplomatic Service, serving in Moscow, Madrid and South America before becoming Head of the American Department of the Foreign Office. He later transferred to the Ministry of Agriculture and took part in the negotiations for UK entry to the EEC. As Assistant Secretary in charge of the External Relations and Cereals Divisions of the Ministry, he was UK Representative to the International Grains Council for eight years, Council Member of the Flour Milling and Baking Research Association, and also represented the UK on the InterGovernmental Grains Group and Rice Group Meetings of the Food and Agriculture Organisation of the United Nations in Rome, being elected Chairman of the InterGovernmental Rice Group.

Tom Sewell subsequently founded an international grains and media consultancy business and was appointed EC Consultant to the United Kingdom Agricultural Supply Trade Association Ltd. In 1985 he held a Visiting Fellowship at the Hubert H. Humphrey Institute of Public Affairs and the Department of Agricultural and Applied Economics at the University of Minnesota, USA. He is a travel writer as well as being the author of two previous works on grain—"Famine and Surplus" published by the European Parliament, and "The World Grain Trade", published by Simon and Schuster International. He currently farms 300 acres in Surrey with his wife, Jennifer, a livestock expert.

Foreword

It gives me great pleasure to provide a Foreword to this book on the subject of the international maritime commerce in grains.

Tom Sewell, whom I first met when he was a senior diplomat working in the Foreign Office, has chosen the right moment to write it. Agriculture continues to occupy a prominent position in the context of world trade. On the one hand, the European Union is busily debating the fundamental reform of its Common Agricultural Policy in the context of the year 2000, while attempting to reach an accommodation in disputes with powerful trading partners and competitors on the other, both inside and outside the disputes settlement mechanisms of the World Trade Organisation. We shall shortly be witnessing the start of another round in what are certain to be bitter and protracted negotiations on the question of trade liberalisation within the WTO, and at the same time the EU will be continuing to seek a solution to the insistent desires of the Central and Eastern European nations to join the Union. In the recent Uruguay Round success or failure hung for two years on whether or not agreement could be found on the terms of the agricultural chapter.

In these circumstances there is urgent need for informed and expert knowledge of the trade on which these negotiations turn. Every stage of the production, processing, sale and transportation of cereals and rice is an intricate affair. A number of books have been written on these subjects, ranging from the academic to the unashamedly journalistic; but I dare say that this is the first book in which so many aspects including the vital conditions of seaborne trade have been brought together and analysed concisely, yet in sufficient detail to provide the reader with the essential background information to form a balanced opinion on the many issues which confront us. If the result is to improve the flow of trade and help to stabilise markets, the work involved will have been well worth while.

Tom Sewell and his wife, Jennifer, a livestock expert, are farmers. Jennifer is the first woman to have been elected to the Central Council of the National Farmers' Union, the first to have won the Farmers' Club Cup for her paper on European Agriculture, and was chosen *Vogue*

Woman of the Year for her services to agriculture. In the circumstances, it is not surprising that when the pair felt that their children's education took precedence over overseas postings, Tom was invited by the late Freddie Kearns at the Ministry of Agriculture, as an experienced negotiator and fluent French and German speaker amongst other languages, to assist in Britain's entry negotiations to the EEC. Much of his time thereafter was spent in commuting to Brussels each week representing British interests in the Cereals and Rice Management Committees of the Brussels Commission and in the FAO in Rome; it fell to him to oversee the transformation of the UK from a cereals deficit nation to a major exporting one, thereby benefiting the UK balance of payments to the tune of more than a billion pounds sterling in a matter of five years. Subsequently his interest and his wide circle of friends in the grain trade involved him in consultancy work for the trade and in standing for election to the European Parliament. He also did much for transatlantic understanding over the years through his work as a Visiting Fellow with the Hubert H. Humphrey Institute and the Department of Agricultural and Applied Economics at the University of Minnesota, and the leading role which he played in the International Grain Market Conferences held annually in Brussels under American sponsorship. More recently he has continued to make his experience available through his position as a Contributing Editor with the *International Bulk Journal*, part of the LLP group of publications.

I wish his book every success.

THE LORD PLUMB OF COLESHILL DL MEP
Former President of the European Parliament

Preface

Trade in agricultural commodities is the most important trade known. You can live without material possessions but you cannot feed yourself without the produce of growing crops. Of these crops, the most important are wheat and rice, followed by the coarse grains, which are eaten by humans after conversion into livestock.

The value of grain produced world-wide is very difficult to compute—total wheat and coarse grains grown annually may be worth US$180 billion, at a conservative estimate, and total rice US$150 billion.

The main difficulty with any attempt to describe the world grain trade is its extraordinary complexity. Every country trades in grain—there may be only five major exporters of wheat and coarse grains, but there are a myriad of importers; there are countries which export rice in significant quantities and which also import it. A further complication is that grains are of different varieties and qualities, are processed, and enter into agricultural trade in the form of flour, bran, offals, starch, malt, etc., while also being used for many non-agricultural industrial purposes, ranging from adhesives, paper, board, motor fuel, etc.—all of which have their own trading patterns. In the Brussels tariff headings no fewer than 122 are allotted to wheat and coarse grains and 34 to rice. Moreover, these are just the main headings and do not include the products and by-products, or such items as compound feedingstuffs, substitutes, etc., with which a trader has to be familiar.

Most studies of the grain trade deal with production, transport, exchange, and supply and demand. Some include oilseeds. Some cover political history. Most attempt forecasts and draw conclusions. I cannot do better than follow the general pattern, though bearing in mind the responsibilities I have exercised through two decades in government and trade, I give appropriate importance to rice and soya as well as to wheat and coarse grains.

Throughout I have borne in mind the purpose of the book. Too many textbooks and papers are written by agricultural economists for other agricultural economists: they contain great scholarship and some are of great value, but this book is not intended to be another one of that kind.

Rather, my purpose is to give an introductory education to students of the subject, whether management trainees in the cereals industries, university and college students and academics, general traders or administrative trainees in government departments. I hope that those specialising in particular aspects will also find some general interest.

Although this work is intended primarily as a textbook, the reader will find passages of an anecdotal nature. This is deliberate. Just as bread requires leaven to make it more appetising, so a dry textbook can, I think, be rendered more readable by the occasional reference to personal experience.

One word of advice I would give to young officials and those entering the grain trade is to acquire a good working knowledge of French. This is not solely in tribute to French civilisation but for the very practical reason that owing to the leading role of France in European grain production and trade, and to the early establishment of French influence in the cereals directorates in Brussels, the first working drafts of documents are almost invariably written in French. If you cannot read them, you will always be one step behind. Furthermore, my diplomatic training taught me that the outcome of meetings and conferences is nearly always established before they take place: therefore do not neglect the importance of social contacts and work in the "corridors".

Limitations of space prevent me from dealing with every aspect of each chapter heading: where others have dealt more fully and more expertly than I on particular aspects I have thought it best to make appropriate acknowledgement and direct the student to these sources for further study. Half the task in the search for information lies in knowing what information already exists and where to look for it: I hope this book may have some value as a work of reference.

TOM SEWELL

Surrey, July 1998

Acknowledgements

All authors are pleased when their work meets with a favourable reception, and still more so if they are again invited to put pen to paper.

However little merited it may have been, both my previous essays on grain—*Famine and Surplus*, written for the European Parliament in 1986, and *The World Grain Trade*, published by Simon & Schuster in 1992—were kindly received not only by the critics but also by my colleagues in trade and government. It was therefore doubly appreciated when LLP Ltd approached me with a request to follow these up with a volume on the international maritime commerce in grain, to form part of a new series.

The present work is the response to this request. It is far more than an update of my previous volumes, however necessary this may have been in view of all that has passed since the end of the Cold War, the progress of the developing countries, and the onset of economic problems in many parts of the world. Historical material has been largely retained since I am not in the business of rewriting history, being too familiar at first hand with totalitarian regimes. But much of the book is entirely new and I could not have attempted it without the expertise and long experience of seaborne commerce of Keri Phillips, who found time from his other pressing work to provide me with much material, including the invaluable detailed Appendices.

I am also greatly indebted to colleagues, amongst others Richard Barnes and Mike Conlon of the US Embassy in London, Lindsey Bartlett and Tia Gibbs of the American Waterways Operators, Mary Brown, Librarian of DG VI in Brussels, Peter Brown, Registered Arbitrator and Commodities Consultant, Jim Buckley of the Baltic Exchange, Michel Costes of Champagne Céréales, Jerry Fruin at the University of Minnesota, Pascal Durouchoux of the Louis Dreyfus Group, Pierre Géhanne of Louis Dreyfus Armateurs, Jim Greenfield of the FAO Rome, Susan Hunt of Continental Grain, Pamela Kirby Johnson and Sandra Black of GAFTA, Nick Lawrence, Editor of *The Agronomist*, Monica Mbanefo of the International Maritime Organisation, John Pitchford of the Federal Grain Inspection Service, Adrian Pickett of NIAB

Cambridge, Ruth Rawling of Cargill Europe, Jim Reed of UKASTA, Andrei Sizov of SovEcon, Peter Tesdorpf of André & Cie SA, Doug Thow of LIFFE, and Bernard Valluis and Mark Treadway of Soufflet Négoce. None of them is wholly responsible for anything I have written, least of all for any errors which this work may contain. If I have omitted any of those whose counsel I found so helpful I ask their forgiveness.

Above all I would thank the expert economists of the International Grains Council in London under the direction of Germain Denis, and in particular Bill de Maria and Richard Woodhams, who willingly placed information and statistics at my disposal.

Laura Sharp and Clive Kelly both kept an eye on my computer, and my family constantly relieved me of work on the farm to attend to the time-consuming chores of authorship. To them I shall always be grateful.

TOM SEWELL

Surrey, July 1998

Contents

List of Tables and Figures

Tables

Figures

Conversion Factors

Area	1 acre	= 0.40469 hectare
	1 hectare	= 2.4710 acres
Weight	1 long ton	= 2.240 lb = 1.01605 metric tons
	1 metric ton	= 10 quintals = 1.000 kg = 2204.62 lb
		= 0.984206 long tons
	1 short ton	= 2.000 lb = 0.907185 metric tons
Wheat	1 bushel	= 60 lb = 27.2155 kg = 0.0267857 long tons
		= 0.0272155 metric tons
	1 metric ton	= 36.74371 bushels
	1 long ton	= 37.33333 bushels
	1 bushel per acre	= 0.6725 quintals per hectare
	1 quintal per hectare	= 1.487 bushels per acre
Maize (corn)	1 bushel	= 56 lb = 25.4012 kg
		= 0.025401 metric tons
	1 metric ton	= 39.3682 bushels
Soyabeans	1 bushel	= 60 lb = 27.2155 kg
		= 0.0272155 metric tons
	1 metric ton	= 36.74371 bushels

		Australia	Canada	United States
Barley				
1 bushel	= lb	50	48	48
	= kg	23.6796	21.7724	21.7724
	= metric tons	0.023680	0.021772	0.021772
1 metric ton	= bushels	44.0924	45.9296	45.9296
Oats				
1 bushel	= lb	40	34	32
	= kg	18.1437	15.4222	14.5150
	= metric tons	0.01814	0.01542	0.014515
1 metric ton	= bushels	55.1155	64.8418	68.8944
Rye				
1 bushel	= lb	60	56	56
	= kg	27.2155	25.4012	25.4012
	= metric tons	0.027216	0.025401	0.025401
1 metric ton	= bushels	36.74371	39.368261	39.368261
Sorghum				
1 bushel	= lb	60	—	56
	= kg	27.2155	—	25.4012
	= metric tons	0.027216	—	0.025401
1 metric ton	= bushels	36.74371	—	39.3682

Freight stowage factors in bulk

1 long ton =

Wheat	47 cubic feet
Maize (corn)	49/50 cubic feet
Soyabeans	44 cubic feet
Barley	54 cubic feet
Oats (clipped)	66 cubic feet
(unclipped)	76 cubic feet
Rye	50 cubic feet
Sorghum	50/52 cubic feet

Source: MAFF.

PART 1

Overview—The importance of grain and its derivatives in world trade

CHAPTER 1

Types of cereals and rice: their history

Cereal grains include rice, oats, barley, buckwheat, maize, millet, sorghum, rye, triticale and wheat. Strictly speaking, buckwheat does not belong to the family Gramineae but to Polygonaceae (docks, etc.), but it is traded as a cereal internationally so I include it here. A recent study has shown that wheat forms the staple food in 45 countries, including the whole of Europe, North America and Oceania; rice is the staple food in about 25 countries (including those with the greatest population); while maize (or corn, as it is called in North America) is the principal food in 16 countries, mostly in Latin America and in Africa south of the Sahara. Maize, of course, is also a very important livestock feed in many countries (including the United Kingdom, before that country joined the European Community—see later chapters).

Most authorities seem to agree that nomadic tribes in the Middle East first discovered that the ears of certain wild grasses were edible and moved from collection to cultivation. Thanks to the work of British archaeologists such as Leonard Woolley, most people know that the earliest civilisation, generally dated around 6000 BC, was that of the Sumerians in Mesopotamia (now Iraq). Adrian Bailey, in a delightfully anecdotal book, *The Blessings of Bread*, which must be required reading for millers and bakers, claims that it was an early race of people called the Natufians, inhabiting the same region of Asia Minor about 6500 BC, who first began harvesting grain and sowing seed for cereal crops. This practice, of course, tended to settle a population in a given area, where they had led a nomadic existence before. Others place the date even earlier, around 15000–10000 BC.

The botanical name for wheat is *Triticum*. The earliest wild wheats, from which the modern grain is descended, were called *Triticum boeoticum* and *Triticum dicoccoides*. The first of these is believed to have grown on the sides of the Zagros Mountains in Asia Minor, and from it came a grain called einkorn, which was particularly suitable for dry, mountainous regions (though not much else). The second wild wheat grew in the fertile alluvial soils between the rivers Tigris and Euphrates, the "Fertile Crescent" of early history. Eventually, a wheat called emmer derived from this, and emmer is believed to be one of the progenitors of the present-day European and North American wheats. Botanically, all wheats are classified in three broad categories—diploid, tetraploid and hexaploid—according to the number of chromosomes they possess. The origin of wheat is however most complex and is still being argued about—at least one of the genomes (groups of genetic materials) came not from *Triticum* but from a related genus *Aegilops*.

At the same time a primitive kind of two-row barley, whose botanical name is *Hordeum spontaneum*, was grown in the same area. This appears to be the progenitor of modern barley, both two-row and six-row. In some ways this seems to have been more important to primitive man than wheat. Barley was the raw material for beer, and if mixed with millet would ferment and make yeast, which was used to leaven the first coarse and heavy barley bread. The barley now cultivated is *Hordeum vulgare*, *spontaneum* being reserved for a wild species.

The wheat grown in Egypt in the time of the Pharaohs seems to have been a kind of emmer. As well as being carried by travellers to Egypt and the North African Plain, emmer found its way into Eastern Europe, up the Danube and thence to Switzerland and Western Europe. From it developed the modern cultivated wheat, *Triticum aestivum*. (These botanical names are as important to traders as botanists since they are invariably used in the tariff codes used in international trade. Students may like to be aware that the convention for binomial names under the Linnaean system—Linnaeus being the celebrated Swedish botanist—is to write the genus with a capital initial and the specific epithet with lower case thus, *Triticum boeoticum*.)

Although barley is believed to have been first grown in Asia Minor, some authorities describe it as a native of the Ethiopian highlands, dating it around 5000 BC. Be that as it may, barley seems to have spread west to Europe by 3000 BC and east to the Indus valley by about the same time, since it is described there in Vedic literature; it was also known in China by 2800 BC. The Greeks and the Romans made their bread from barley, and this seems to have had some religious significance. But barley lost its place as a breadgrain in the late Middle Ages, when people discovered how to make leavened bread, for which barley is not especially suitable owing to its low gluten content. Now, it is mainly used as a feedgrain, and a very important one too, particularly in the United Kingdom, where the climate is especially suitable for barley production, whether of the feed or malting variety. Two or three decades ago, when cereals were relatively very cheap in the United Kingdom, barley-fed beef cattle were a profitable enterprise. Another important use for barley—some would say its most important use—is for making beer and malt whisky.

Oats (*Avenum spp*, i.e., there are several cultivated species) originated in Northern Europe according to most authorities, who cite in support historical evidence of their existence in Neolithic times notably in Thessaly. They are believed to have reached Britain in the Iron Age. Oats, of course, make splendid porridge, to be eaten in the correct way with salt in Scotland, and have been the traditional mainstay of the horse ration for as long as anyone can remember—hence the jokes about "food for men in Scotland and horses in England", and the rejoinder about the relative excellence of each. Dr Johnson, the celebrated lexicographer, is not the only one to have exercised his wit on the subject of oats. Sydney Smith, founder of the *Edinburgh Review*, took as the motto of his journal "*tenui musam meditamur avena*" (we cultivate literature on a little oatmeal), which is a fine enough text to be going on with. Apart from the Celtic predilection for oats as a food (the Bretons eat it, but their taste is not shared by many of their compatriots), in Germany and the more barren regions of Africa, where the crop thrives as wheat and barley do not, oats are mainly a fodder crop. This is also true of the United States. As work-horses decline so does the demand for oats, which do not yield highly and on which little recent research effort has been spent. Yet there are specialised markets which are growing—health foods, and feed for race horses and riding horses, where quality is all-important. The best quality oats are grown in Australia, and demand for them as feedstuff for European race horses has survived even the penal levy imposed by the EC Common Agricultural Policy. Australia has also developed a market in the growing racing sector in Japan.

Millet (*Panicum, Setaria, spp*) is another prehistoric grain, first found in Neolithic times. Familiar to Europeans as birdseed, millet is also a widely grown cereal: wheat occupies 32 per cent of the world's cereal acreage, rice 20 per cent, maize 20 per cent and millet 5 per cent. It is an important part of the diet for an estimated 500 million Indians, Africans and Chinese. It has the advantages of being high in protein and can be grown on poor soils. But it has no gluten, and millet flour will not make a loaf of bread. One French traveller, who ate it regularly in Ethiopia as a kind of flatbread, described it as resembling nothing so much as a towel soaked in mud. It is perhaps not surprising, therefore, that although more widely grown in Europe than wheat during the Middle Ages, it has now fallen into disfavour as food for humans in Europe.

Later arrivals include buckwheat, maize, sorghum and rye, while the latest of all is triticale. Of these the most important is maize (*Zea mays*), distinguished from the others by being native to the Western Hemisphere rather than Asia or Africa. Although the Americas were responsible for introducing both potatoes and tobacco to Europe, maize is remarkable for being the only cereal native to America.

Columbus relates in his journal how he was first introduced to maize in Cuba in 1492; Cortez in Mexico and Pizarro in Peru found that the empires of the Aztecs and the Incas were both nourished by maize. Maize and buffalo meat formed the main diet of Red Indians in North America—indeed, Captain John Smith and his Virginian settlers were saved from starvation during their first winter by the gift of 500 bushels of maize from friendly Indians. In Europe, maize was not highly esteemed as a human food and its value as animal feed, historically speaking, is of fairly recent origin. Maize found its way to Africa via the Portuguese in Brazil, and was subsequently grown there as the ubiquitous 'mealie'. In China it was represented pictorially in the sixteenth century, where it attracted the attention of Marco Polo.

In the United States Indian corn is a part of history. Cornfields were fought over in Virginia (resulting in the massacre of many white settlers in 1662) and were a cause of the nineteenth-century Blackhawk War in the Mississippi valley. George Washington milled corn at Mount Vernon; Harriet Martineau on a visit from England recorded that "a man who has corn may have everything". Exports of corn as well as wheat from the northern states during the American Civil War provided a counter-balance to exports of cotton from the southern states in influencing Britain against active intervention. There is only one species of maize (*Zea mays*), but it hybridises relatively easily and there are now over 200 different races of maize, sweet corn being the favourite for human consumption and yellow corn for animal feed.

Buckwheat (*Fagopyrum esculentum* and *Fagopyrum tataricum*) came originally from Central Asia, supposedly passed to Europe in the Middle Ages through the agency of the Saracens (the French word for buckwheat is "sarrasin", a derivation supported by Dauzat's *Dictionnaire Etymologique*), and though not a high yielder, is mainly grown on indifferent soils where other cereals will not produce a commercial crop. Buckwheat is of value for fattening livestock, and though not suitable for breadmaking, makes a nourishing porridge; "kasha" is familiar in Russian literature and was still a staple food of Russian peasants in the 1950s.

The origin of sorghum (*Sorgham bicolor*) is somewhat obscure. Most historians think it came from Ethiopia. It is certainly one of the major food crops, and may even be as widely grown as millet. Like maize it is grown for livestock feed, and is also a basic food—if not a particularly nutritious one—for some 300 million Africans, Indians and Chinese. In America sorghum was grown in the southern states in the nineteenth century as a sweetener, but in this capacity has since lost its place to sugar (and now perhaps to isoglucose), though now much used (as in Australia) as cattle feed. It is also grown in northern China (under the name of kaoliang), where it is a useful standby if the wheat crop fails.

Rye (*Secale cereale*) is the last of the widely grown cereals I shall mention here, but far from the least important. In terms of acreage sown, it is up among the leaders, but has a far lower yield. Variously accorded a Caucasian and a north east European origin, rye dates back to circa 1000 BC. Unlike wheat and barley, there is no mention of it in Egypt or India, but there is some evidence that it was eaten by the Greeks and Romans. Predominantly, however, it is an East European crop: 40 per cent of world production takes place in the CIS, where the damp and heavy round rye loaves are the universal (and wholesome) bread. In parts of Germany, Poland and other East European countries rye is the usual bread. It is the only cereal other than wheat to contain gluten (necessary to make bread rise). One of the modern uses of rye is to make crispbread: much of the continental crop ends up there, and virtually all the UK crop.

Rye, like wheat, originated as a grass, but endured almost as a weed. Difficult to get rid of in the fields, rye often grew together with wheat, and the resulting mixture of grain is known as maslin. Maslin flour was universal in Europe in the Middle Ages, and the description still occurs in EC terminology (*méteil* in French), so it is as well to know what it means.

Rye is also grown in America, having been particularly prominent in the first two centuries of European settlements when wheat was relatively more costly. Today its reputation endures most tenaciously as the base of American and Canadian (also Irish) whisky. Most people know that Bourbon whisky is made from rye: I suspect that fewer people could say with accuracy which cereal grain is the basis of Scotch Whisky.

One cannot leave rye without mentioning its catastrophic association with ergot, a small black fungus which contains 20 different poisons and in the Middle Ages was invested with supernatural attributes. Ergot poisoning was known as St Anthony's Fire, and is well documented in French and German history. The effects seem to have been not unlike localised outbreaks of the Black Death. As recently as the 1970s, an outbreak of ergot poisoning was reported in Turkey (though in this case the carrier grain was wheat). In miniscule quantity ergot is said to have some medicinal property, and perhaps this accounts for the fact that it is tolerated in EC cereals quality standards up to 0.05 per cent by content.

Nor can one pass over the newest addition to the family of cereals, triticale. This cross between rye and durum wheat evokes great enthusiasm among its supporters, who acclaim it as "the cereal crop with the big future". But, like Esperanto, its theoretical attractions have not yet been translated into widespread adoption. Dating back to an accidental cross in the nineteenth century, the first developmental programmes are of much more recent origin. The University of Manitoba became seriously interested in 1954; the Polish State Plant Breeding Institute in the 1960s. It was introduced into Mexico in 1965, and in Australia (New South Wales) in 1976. In recent years it has been increasingly grown in France, and seed became available on a commercial scale in the United Kingdom in 1983. In 1984 the European Commission included triticale in its rye support regulations. It is, however, in Russia and the Ukraine that the greatest area has been sown, mainly around the Black Sea. The advantages of the crop are its high yield (13.5 tonnes to the hectare has been claimed, though the Plant Breeding Institute at Cambridge obtained only two tons to the acre ($7\frac{1}{2}$ t/ha) on trial plots in the United Kingdom) and its high protein content, which makes it a valuable component in compound animal feed. However, it was the earlier varieties of triticale which impressed by their protein content—the latest, non-shrivelled, varieties have values only similar to that of wheat, although their lysine content is still better. Its main disadvantages—apart from the relatively few varieties available—seem to be length of straw and the relatively low market price, which so far it has commanded.

This bring me back to a fuller description of wheat. First in importance, wheat is in a class by itself to both the grain trader and the statistician. Wheat is a food grain (though much wheat is fed to animals in Europe); the other cereals are predominantly feed grains. One speaks of "wheat and coarse grains", meaning by the latter everything apart from wheat.

We left wheat at its point of introduction to Western Europe, as *Triticum aestivum*. This is the botanical description of soft wheat, from which is derived the present-day "common-wheat" used for breadmaking (*Triticum vulgare*). The other species of wheat grown on any scale today is durum wheat (*Triticum durum*), which is used mainly for pasta and semolina. (I hope these Latin terms have not confused the reader. If they have, then there is some consolation in the fact that even Linnaeus thought that winter-sown and spring-sown wheats were two different species, which they are not!)

This is a good moment to clear up any misunderstandings about the difference between hard and soft wheat, since in any international gathering in which both French and English are used they are invariably confused. Soft wheat, indeed all common wheat, is translated as *blé tendre*, which causes no problem, but one has only to mention hard wheat in the sense of United States and Canadian wheats, and the French interpreter will render it as *blé dur*, which means durum wheat and gets everyone at cross-purposes. Hardness and softness in wheat, as used in the milling trade, refer only to the milling quality, hardness denoting a certain desirable flintiness in the grain. Traders prefer to talk in terms of the strength of wheat, meaning its strength of gluten. This is what gives North American wheat its high protein content and makes it so desirable for North European breadmaking. Better, therefore to describe these North American wheats as "strong" rather than hard wheats. Then the

French interpreter will know to translate as *blé de force*, and rational discussion can continue.

Space does not permit a full history of wheat and its significance. But wheat travelled from the Egypt of the Pharaohs, where production on the fertile Nile delta became a fundamental factor in the Egyptian economy, to Greece and Rome. Wheat was naturally associated with deities: Demeter in Greek mythology and Ceres in the Roman pantheon. In ancient Greece, as quoted by Waverley Root in his voluminous work *Food*, "the first item on the agenda of the Assembly, held ten times a year, was to hear a report on the stocks of grain in the wheat hall at Piraeus, which was required always to contain enough wheat for the needs of the civilian population and the army should supplies from abroad be cut off by war". Such stock reporting must bring a wry smile to any member of the Cereals Management Committee of the present-day European Commission in Brussels, whose weekly meetings always contain a report on the stocks of grains held in intervention stores in the Community—though the anxiety is often more about finding ways of getting rid of them rather than preserving them. Greece did not produce enough wheat for its needs, hence it looked overseas to import wheat from Sicily and from the Black Sea area—this was the beginning of the grain trade. Some ascribe the fall of Greece to its failure to defend its overseas grain supplies. The Roman Empire was under similar pressure. The Punic Wars were fought and won by Scipio Africanus in order to secure the wheat production of Carthage (modern Tunisia), while the conquest of Egypt was inspired by a similar motive. Root's voluminous book contains fascinating snippets such as that the Romans distributed wheat from their conquered territories free to Roman citizens, thereby ruining their own agriculture (a warning of the danger of indiscriminate or inverted food aid), and that the conquest of Gaul by Julius Caesar was facilitated by the stocks of grain held in that country's warehouses which could not be destroyed before they were seized by the advancing legions. This may have been a lesson taken to heart 1,800 years later when Kutuzov's armies in Russia ensured that few supplies were left to the invading French, thus contributing to the defeat of Napoleon's *Grande Armée*.

Perhaps the ultimate, and certainly the most recent, example of the use of grain as a weapon of political and strategic importance is to be found in the embargo imposed on the Soviet Union following the latter's invasion of Afghanistan in 1979. Searching for a means to express condemnation of Soviet policy, President Carter cancelled all export contracts in excess of the maximum quantity provided for in the bilateral US/Soviet grain agreement, and invited the other major exporting nations to follow suit. The tactic met with varying degrees of success, but was ultimately frustrated by the ability of the Russians to find new sources of supply, in particular by replacing much American grain by grain from Argentina, which saw in the situation more an opportunity for expanding export markets than making a political point.

Wheat and coarse grains are almost unique in that the exportable surplus of the world's supplies is in the hands of five major exporting nations; in time of war it might by possible to agree, or to impose, control of supplies, but in time of peace nobody has yet succeeded in doing so.

No foodstuff is associated with so much folklore as wheat. Those in search of anecdotes can do no better than read the highly entertaining accounts which fill the pages of Adrian Bailey's *The Blessings of Bread*. Everything connected with wheat and bread, from the serious to the scatological, is here revealed, including the mythology and the legends and the symbolism—improving on J.G. Frazer's immortal *Golden Bough*—and exploring in impish detail even the sexual significance of breadmaking, of ovens and buns and banana flour.

Rice, mentioned as the first cereal at the beginning of this chapter, is of even greater antiquity than wheat. Persons not involved in the grain trade may even be surprised to learn that it is classified as a cereal, since its history and method of cultivation are strikingly different from those of the wheats and coarse grains described above, and its image is associated more with the Orient than the Occident.

Nobody knows for certain where it originated, though a legend has it that it first came to China through a fishergirl who held her net up to the sunbeams and, as the golden light fell through the meshes, it was changed to golden grains of rice. The *Cambridge Encyclopædia of Archæology* more prosaically points to the end of the Pleistocene and early Neolithic (Stone Age) periods as the time when rice was first brought into cultivation in south China and northern South East Asia. By the end of the Pleistocene period rice and millet provided reliable food supplies in East Asia, including Java and the Philippines.

In the fifth millennium BC rice stalks, both of the wild and domesticated (indica) varieties, were found at Ho-mu-tu (lower Yangtze), spread over 400 square metres, and in places 25–50 cm thick (giving the impression of a threshing floor). This was the richest find of early plant remains in China. In the fifth or sixth millennium BC the same source indicates that remains of rice "are said to have occurred" in Uttar Pradesh, India; rice chaff was found at Nok Nok Tha in Thailand around 4500 BC. In the Banyang Valley in north west Thailand the recovery of husks of rice (*oryza spp.*) and dating by radiocarbon showed a period lasting from 3000 BC to 700 AD. Rice was found at a Late Jomon site in South Hokkaido, Japan, but it is probable that the occupants depended on wild foods until the middle of the first millennium BC.

The *Cambridge Encyclopædia* cites evidence of rice in Bihar (middle Gangetic valley) as early as the third millennium BC, and in south-east

Rajasthan in 2000 BC. In the Near East rice and cotton were introduced in Mesopotamia during the first millennium BC, while the Greeks who accompanied Alexander the Great in the fourth century BC found rice to be growing in Bactria, Khuzistan, Babylonia and Syria. In the Red River delta in Vietnam and in Mali, West Africa, wet-rice cultivation was practised in 1000 BC. The elaboration of irrigation for wet-rice cultivation appears to date from about 500 BC.

Rice probably came to Europe as a result of Alexander's expeditions, and the European Crusaders are supposed to have acquired it from the Saracens. The Roman Empire imported rice, and the Italians—now the most important producers of rice in the EC—did not grow it until the Middle Ages, having received it either from the East or by a roundabout route from the Moors via Spain.

The Spaniards and Portuguese took rice with them to their conquests in South America, while Shelby Holder and Warrant Grant of the USDA in their book, *US Rice Industry*, state that early colonists experimented with rice in Virginia as early as 1609. Grist, in his book, *Rice*, points out that paddy cultivation (i.e. rice grown in water as opposed to dry land) first occurred in the United States in colonial times when Louisiana was still a French domain. Commercial cultivation in the United States began in South Carolina around 1686, and in North Carolina in 1730. Georgia and Florida followed suit in 1820 and 1840, but South Carolina remained predominant until 1890 when it was overtaken by Louisiana. Texas and Arkansas thereafter expanded production, the latter state currently being the leading producer in the United States.

Rice cultivation in Australia is of more recent date, the crop not having been established there until after World War I.

Rice is a grass, and its botanical name is *Oryza*. *Oryza fatua* and *Oryza sativa* are the Asian genetical sources, and most rice is grown in Asia. *Oryza stapfii* and *Oryza glaberrima* stem from West Africa, in all likelihood Nigeria, but very little rice stemming from these sources is now grown in the African continent, having been supplanted in modern times by *Oryza sativa*.

Wild rice, as known in America, is a grass rather than a cereal. Grown by the Chippewa Indians in Minnesota the grain is long and thin and is prized as a delicacy, not least in Europe where there is a small but significant import.

Historically, two chief methods of growing rice were recognised, either as a dry-land crop or planted in water. The varieties of seed required vary according to whether the rice is to be grown "dry" or in water, while a few will tolerate either method. The method of dry cultivation needs no special explanation—it is sown and harvested much as any other cereal crop. Water cultivation is a more complicated and varied process, requiring careful preparation of the land contours and control of irrigation. Both methods have their advantages and disadvantages, but cultivation in water is by far the most widespread method, the yield being generally higher.

With the development of growing "modern varieties" of rice (popularly known as the Green Revolution) it became apparent that the old-fashioned classification of "dry-land" and "wet-land" was no longer adequate to describe the complexities of the conditions under which different kinds of rice could be grown. It became necessary to develop an agreed classification and terminology to describe different rice growing environments, and after initial discussion at the International Rice Research Conference convened in 1982 by the International Rice Research Institute (IRRI) in the Philippines it was decided to establish a widely representative International Committee to develop an agreed terminology and classification system for rice. The results were summarised by Swaminathan in 1984 in his report, *Terminology for Rice Growing Environments*.

The terms now most generally used, including in the FAO, are "upland rice", "hydropomorphic rice" and "wetland rice". This, broadly speaking, corresponds to the extent the roots are above, touching or below the variable ground water level, and is best illustrated in Figure 1.1, developed by the West African Rice Development Association (WARDA) in co-operation with the FAO.

Figure 1.1 The upland–inland swamp continuum

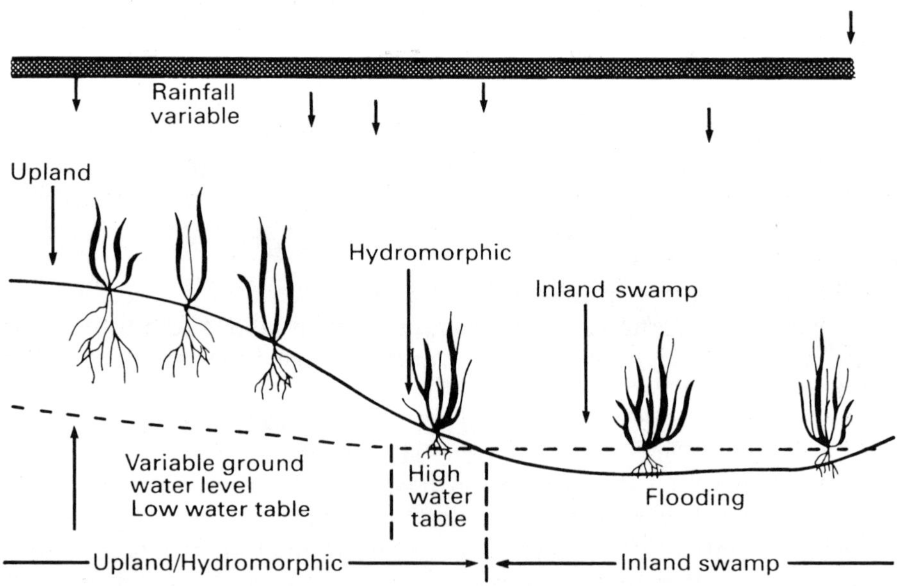

Source: WARDA, FAO.

One invariably hears the term "paddy" rice applied to rice before it has received any form of processing and some explanation is necessary. Strictly speaking the term "paddy" applies to the soil in which rice is grown—one can thus speak of "dry" paddy as well as "wet" paddy, although the mental picture of a paddy-field normally is of an expanse of sheet water being ploughed by a single man driving an ox or a buffalo before him. However, "paddy" is also applied to rice itself, after it has been threshed but before the husk has been removed. It is thus a standard term in which production statistics are calculated.

Although upland (or "dry-land") cultivation has been practised from primitive times, on the "slash and burn" system of clearing forest, the areas in which it can be successfully done are limited. There are a number of reasons for this. The majority of upland rice, about 80–90 per cent, is grown under conditions of shifting cultivation (as "slash and burn" is now more usually described) and only 10–20 per cent under fixed or permanent conditions. Not only does it require a fertile soil but, in spite of being "dry", it requires humidity and three or four months of rain during the growing season. Without such rain it would require equivalent irrigation, though less than is required for "wet" paddy. Cultivation for upland rice should be minimal if it is grown on dry-land conditions, to a depth of not more than 5 cm. The reason for this is that such cultivation usually occurs on sloping land and it is essential to avoid soil disturbance which could lead to deterioration of soil fertility or soil erosion.

Dry paddy is successfully grown in the following countries: India, Bangladesh, Myanmar, Thailand, Cambodia, Indonesia, Philippines and Vietnam as well as parts of tropical Africa and Latin America, particularly Brazil.

Approximately 90 per cent of rice is grown in the wet-paddy system. This is well suited to Asian climatic conditions. The Asian cultivator is essentially a peasant farmer, growing his crop on a few hectares of land, either on his own or with the help of family labour. He may co-operate with his neighbours in planting and harvesting, for rice-growing in the traditional way is a labour-intensive activity—but given the economic conditions in most of the Asian territories this is a positive advantage. The use of mechanisation in these processes, particularly harvesting, has of course been considered, but in the Philippines at least it is positively forbidden. If mechanisation led to displacement of workers from the land there was no other employment for them; the social costs of mechanisation would outweigh any economic benefits. Technical improvements are thus likely to continue to be simple and cautious.

With wet-land cultivation the rice seed is usually either grown in nurseries and transplanted when it has taken root, or drilled or broadcast direct in the field. An absolutely level growing area is required, bordered by small banks or "bunds" to hold the water—hence the elaborate terracing to be seen in hill country such as Myanmar, Thailand and the Philippines. Much of this terrace work was carried out hundreds of years ago and is an historical inheritance. If it did not already exist one wonders if it could possibly be constructed now.

Wet-land planting is carried out on land which is either flooded by monsoon rains or irrigated artificially; or even a combination of the second supplementing the first. The system of cultivation is still much as described by Grist. The land is first ploughed when the water level is down to a few inches, the soil—it might be more accurate to say "mud"—being turned over to bury the weeds. The land is rolled with a wooden roller and lightly harrowed; after a few weeks the process is repeated and a wooden plank dragged round to work the ground down into a smooth seed-bed lying under about an inch of water.

Since the typical field will be small, perhaps half a hectare or less, and if it is on a terraced hillside may be of any shape, the instruments are usually drawn by water-buffalo in Asia, where the soils are usually clay and therefore heavy; in other countries with more sandy soil oxen will be capable of the task. The operator usually stands on the ploughshare or harrow to force it into the ground as it moves along.

When the ground is ready, sowing or transplanting takes place. The latter operation is usually carried out by hand by the women and children of the family and done on a communal basis, again giving rise to the conventional picture of activity as the bundles of seedlings are transferred from one hand to the other and thrust into the soil.

In former times where traditional varieties were concerned the crop would be pruned half way through the growth stage, either by hand sickle or usually by grazing it. But for modern varieties this is not done since it reduces the leaf area for photosynthesis, and the plant is left undisturbed from planting to harvesting. During this time, however, frequent weeding is necessary.

Hand-harvesting is usually carried out with a sickle or small sharp knife. Just as with other cereals a rice harvest contains both straw and grain, and is stacked to dry out before being threshed. This is a critical period for the crop, since uneven drying can cause cracking, and hence breaking, during the milling process, so much skill and care is required.

Traditional methods of threshing include treading with the foot (not so primitive, really, if one compares it with treading the grapes to produce wine), or beating sheaves against a ladder inside a tub. Winnowing is performed on a plaited bamboo tray or sieve, the grain falling to the floor while the husk and chaff is blown on the wind. A refinement of the latter process may be to use a hand winnowing machine in which a draught is generated by a hand-turned fan.

Unlike the traditional crops of wheat, barley, oats, etc., grown in developed countries where one crop per year is usual, rice can often produce two crops a year. This is extensively done in China, Japan, India and parts of Java. Almost invariably it involves reliance on irrigation as well as natural rainfall, the soil must be right, and the timetable of planting and cultivation has to be very accurate.

Fertiliser use is now fairly similar for dry-land and non-irrigated wet-land, as far as nitrogen is concerned, 60 kg/ha being about the norm. For irrigated land the quantities recommended can be much higher, running from 120 kg/ha in Asia to a maximum of 150 kg/ha in the United States and as much as 150–300 kg/ha in North Korea. Approximately 60 kg/ha of phosphate and 40 kg/ha of potash are applied in both dry-land and wet-land cultivation.

Since rice is grown in so many different areas and under so many different systems it is impossible to generalise about yields. Anything from 5 cwt per acre (12.5 quintals per hectare) to 35 cwt per acre (85 quintals per hectare) seems to be acceptable.

Whereas production is generally reckoned in tons of paddy and much rice actually enters world trade in husked form, trade statistics are compiled in terms of milled-rice equivalent. Paddy rice has to pass through five stages of milling before it eventually reaches the consumer—cleaning, hulling or husking, pearling, polishing and grading. Each of the processes can be performed in a variety of ways, but the essential activity of passing the grain between two rotating surfaces, whether rollers, cones or discs, is very much the same.

Bran, a useful by-product of the milling process, is extracted either at the early stage of hulling or at the pearling stage. The first kind of bran is of low food value but the latter contains most of the vitamins and proteins of the grain and is of high food value, both for human consumption and as animal feed. Thereafter rice that passes beyond the stage of being husked or cargo rice is classified for trading purposes as being milled, semi-milled or brokens. The fractions normally accepted in international trade are as follows:

Paddy to husked	80 per cent
Paddy to semi-milled	66.7–80 per cent range
Paddy to milled	66.7 per cent (72 per cent in the United States)
Paddy to parboiled	70–75 per cent range
Brokens	Several grades are recognised in the trade

Apart from the above, paddy rice can be parboiled and sold as parboiled rice. Parboiling consists of soaking the paddy after cleaning, immersing it in hot water for 2 or 3 hours, and finally steam-heating and subsequently vacuum-drying it. After cooling it can then be milled. Parboiling has the advantages of better vitamin retention, better resistance to insect pests, less breaking in milling, less smell and better cooking quality. It is also said to give the rice better keeping qualities and is thus popular in India, Myanmar, the West Indies and parts of South America.

THE DIFFERENT FORMS OF RICE

An understanding of a certain amount of nomenclature is necessary when discussing rice, in order to appreciate the different forms in which it is commercialised.

Paddy rice	Rice as harvested, complete with husks.
Cargo rice	De-husked rice; this is the normal form in which rice is traded.
Milled rice	Cargo rice is polished by mechanical treatment, giving a white product.
Glazed rice	The final operations consist of polishing and glazing the rice to improve its appearance. The glazing may be done with a mixture of glucose and talc, whereas in the United States vaseline or paraffin oils are used.
Non-stick rice	Paddy rice is heat treated then dried and polished. The heat treatment gives the rice a yellow colour but strengthens it so that there is less breakage and more even cooking.
Brown rice	This receives the same heat treatment, but instead of being polished afterwards it is merely scratched to help in the cooking.

Naturally the mechanised treatments generate a certain amount of broken rice which is used in numerous industrial processes. The bulk of the good quality broken rice is either incorporated with whole rice, in countries that permit a high level of broken grains, or further milled to give semolina or rice flour.

CHAPTER 2

The techniques of cereal and rice husbandry and production methods, harvesting and storage. Cereals as livestock feed

INTRODUCTION

Everyone connected with the grain trade will probably be familiar with the basic technique of growing cereals. Two hundred years ago the majority of Europe's—let alone the world's—population were peasants, and if you want to know what it was like to be a farmer or cultivator at that time, the classics of each country's literature will tell you, so fundamental was the life of the countryside to the existence of all. Books written close to the soil are healthy antidotes for those condemned to spend much of their lives in capital cities.

Cereal-growing has always been a combination of art and science. Farmers must regret that the pursuit of efficiency has turned intensive cereal growing into much more of a science than an art. In this chapter I shall attempt to describe the main aspects of this science as it exists in the chief cereal-growing areas, starting with North America, the breadbasket of the world. The description will mainly concern wheat and corn (maize), the cereals which are most prominent in world trade. The science starts with the selection of the most suitable variety of seed, and thereafter it is a matter of growing that seed most efficiently to maturity.

ORIGINS AND REQUIREMENTS

Cereals are grasses with large edible grains. Cultivation began about 7,000 years ago in Egypt and adjacent countries. This was initially of barley, but wheat later became the staple bread grain both in the Near East and Europe. In the Americas corn, which derived from a wild grass called tesonite, played this role.

Both wheat and corn thrive in a variety of growing conditions. Wheat is grown from the southernmost parts of Australia and South America up to a latitude of about 60° north, and at heights from sea level to over 3,000 metres. Corn is grown in almost all temperate and tropical regions between latitudes of 58°N to 40°S and at heights from sea level to almost 4,000 metres. The annual rainfall of growing areas ranges from 20 cm in North Africa to 500 cm in parts of India. For wheat the range is from 25 to 180 cm per year.

Wheat grows best where moisture is plentiful after seeding, the daytime temperature is about 30°C, and days are long. It does not yield well in warm, humid conditions because of disease damage, lodging (falling flat before harvest) and loss in storage. On the other hand, wheat is subject to winterkill at temperatures of −15°C to −20°C if not covered by snow, or as high as 10°C if the ground is also frozen and winds strong. For corn, high yields are favoured by an abundance of sunshine and warm, but not hot, weather. The best temperature range is 20°C to 30°C. Most modern hybrid varieties of dent corn require a growing season of 110 to 140 days. Abundant moisture in July and August is needed and the crop is especially vulnerable to frost damage in the early autumn.

PHASES AND TIMING

For the purpose of agronomic advice and assessment of likely yields, the life-cycle of cereals can be divided into stages. Since it was first introduced in 1974 the Zadoks 100-point decimal scale is most widely used. In the United Kingdom the system devised by Tottman and Broad in 1987 (see the *Annual of Applied Biology*) is also current. The stages in the Zadoks scale are grouped into phases as follows:

- 0 Germination.
- 1 Seedling growth.
- 2 Tillering, i.e., the production of extra side shoots. The aim is not to maximise the number of tillers but rather to control density to achieve a maximum ear population. Tillering varies greatly between varieties and most corn cultivars produce few tillers.
- 3 Stem elongation.
- 4 Booting. A plant is in boot when the developing ear is swelling visibly inside the flag or top leaf.
- 5 Ear emergence.
- 6 Flowering.
- 7 Milk development: this is the critical phase of stowing away grain carbohydrate.
- 8 Dough development.
- 9 Ripening.

Figure 2.1 shows an application of the scale to spring wheat in Minnesota. The length and timing of the life-cycle varies between regions. Wheats are broadly divided into two types, winter or spring,

Figure 2.1 Spring wheat growth and development in Minnesota (approximate time to growth stages)

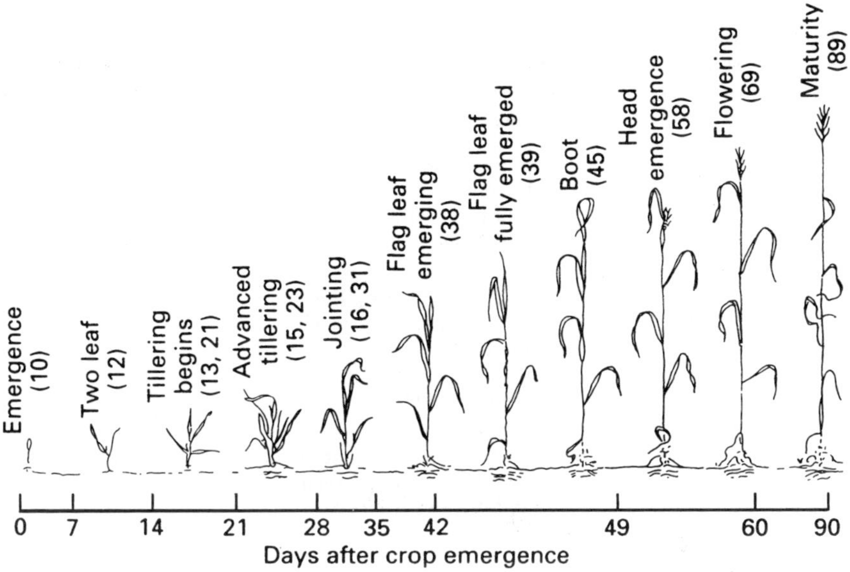

Note: Zadoks code for each stage in brackets.

Zadoks code			
Principal stage	Secondary stage	Description	Corresponding Feekes code
0		Germination	
	0	Dry kernel	
	1	Start of imbibition (water absorption)	
	6	Radicle emerged	
	7	Coleoptile emerged	
	9	Leaf just at coleoptile tip	
1		Seedling development	1
	0	First leaf through coleoptile	
	1	First leaf at least 50% emerged	
	2	Second leaf at least 50% emerged	
	3	Third leaf at least 50% emerged	
	4	Fourth leaf at least 50% emerged	
	5	Fifth leaf at least 50% emerged	
2		Tillering	2
	0	Main shoot only	
	1	Main shoot plus 1 tiller visible	
	2	Main shoot plus 2 tillers	
	3	Main shoot plus 3 tillers	
	4	Main shoot plus 4 tillers	
	5	Main shoot plus 5 tillers	3

Figure 2.1—*cont.*

Zadoks code			
Principal stage	Secondary stage	Description	Corresponding Feekes code
3		Stem elongation	
	1	First node detectable	6
	2	Second node detectable	7
	3	Third node detectable	
	7	Flag leaf just visible	8
	9	Flag leaf collar just visible	9
4		Boot	
	1	Flag leaf sheath extending	
	3	Boot just beginning to swell	
	5	Boot swollen	10
	7	Flag leaf sheath opening	
	9	First awns visible	
5		Head emergence	
	1	First spikelet of head just visible	10.1
	3	One-fourth of head emerged	10.2
	5	One-half of head emerged	10.3
	7	Three-fourths of head emerged	10.4
	9	Head emergence complete	10.5
6		Flowering (not readily visible in barley)	
	1	Beginning of flowering	10.5.1
	5	Half of florets have flowered	10.5.2
	9	Flowering complete	
7		Milk development in kernel	
	1	Kernel watery ripe	10.5.4
	3	Early milk	
	5	Medium milk	11.1
	7	Late milk	
8		Dough development in kernel	
	3	Early dough	
	5	Soft dough	11.2
	7	Hard dough, head losing green colour	
	9	Approximate physiological maturity	
9		Ripening	
	1	Kernel hard (difficult to divide with thumbnail)	11.3
	2	Kernel cannot be dented by thumbnail—harvest ripe	11.4

Source: University of Minnesota, Minnesota Extension Service.

depending on whether they are planted in autumn or spring. For all cereals the season in the Southern Hemisphere differs from that in the northern. Almost all wheat grown in Canada is spring wheat, being planted in April/May and harvested in July/September. About a third of production in the United States is spring wheat. In both countries the area of production is quite narrow. Canadian production is mainly in the three prairie provinces of Manitoba, Saskatchewan and Alberta. In the United States spring wheat comes mostly from North Dakota, Montana and Minnesota. Winter wheat is much more widely grown in the United States, and so both planting and harvesting dates are more variable (Figure 2.2).

Figure 2.2 Winter wheat, United States: (a) planting; (b) harvesting

(a)

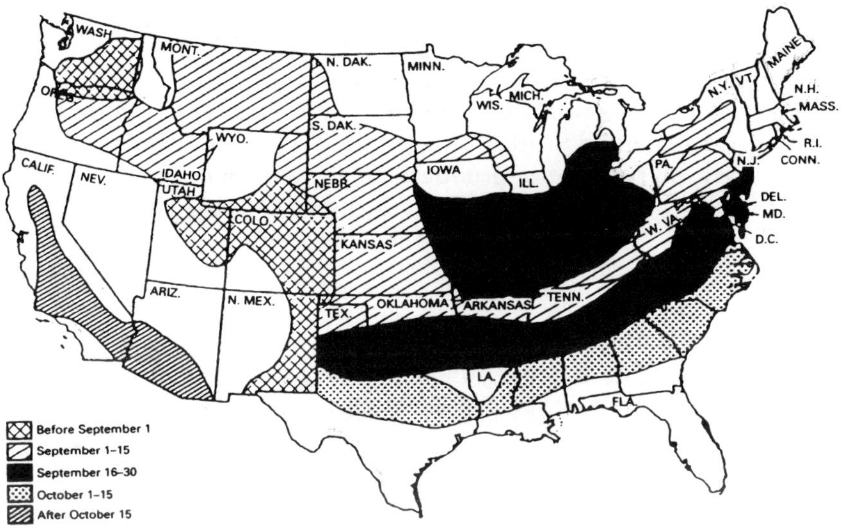

(b)

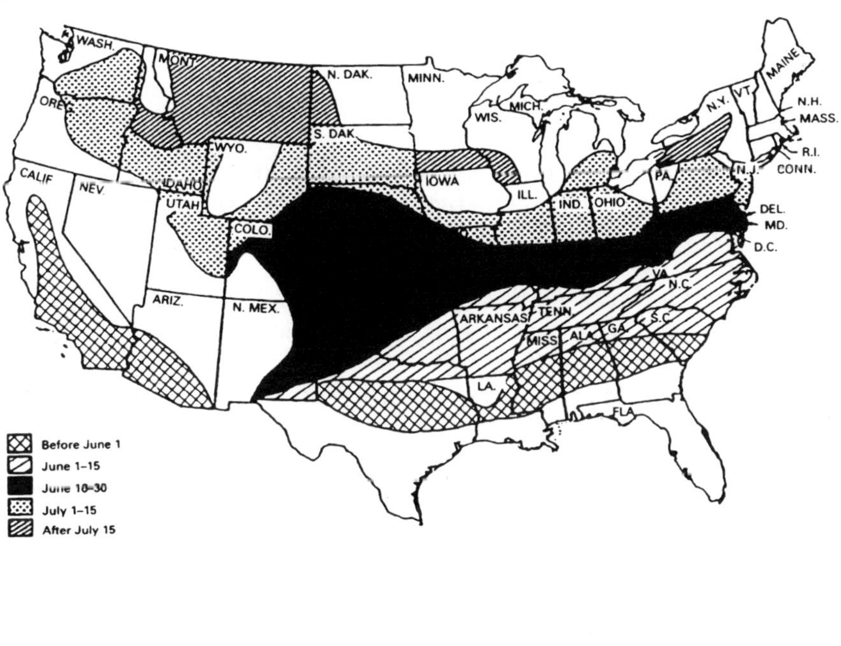

In both Western and Eastern Europe wheat is mainly of the red winter type, being planted in September/November and harvested in June/August. In the area of the former Soviet Union, for climatic reasons, about 50 per cent of production is spring wheat. This is grown in the regions north of the Caspian Sea and east of the Volga. Winter wheat is grown in the vicinity of the Black Sea, in the Ukraine, Moldavia, Volga and northern Caucasus.

In China wheat is mainly autumn-sown. Though it exceeds rice in area only in the northern provinces, wheat is grown throughout China.

Wheat grown in Australia and also in Argentina is white grained, some soft, some hard. Planting is in April/May, the Southern Hemisphere's autumn, and harvesting is in November/January.

For corn, half of the world production and over three-quarters of trade originates in the United States. Though widely grown in the eastern part of the country, 80 per cent of production comes from the Corn Belt. Here planting is typically in May and harvesting in October (Figure 2.3).

MANAGERIAL ELEMENTS

For the purposes of both management and technological development the main elements of production of cereals are:

Soil preparation.
Planting, including selection of variety.
Feeding.
Weed control.
Protection from pests.
Protection from diseases.
Harvesting.

Soil preparation

A primary element in management of cereal production is the selection of soils. Though much can be done by drainage, cultivation and fertilisation to modify soil characteristics, the natural features of soils are still critical in determining the success of cereal production.

Soils are crudely classed by their texture, i.e. the size of their particles, ranging from sand with particles of large diameter to clay with the finest particles. Another defining, though less readily measured, characteristic is tilth, i.e. the way in which particles are arranged. In soil of good tilth particles are clustered into granules which provide open irregular spaces through which air and water move to plant root hairs. A third important dimension is the degree of alkalinity or acidity, as measured by the pH.

Figure 2.3 Corn, United States: (a) planting; (b) harvesting

(a)

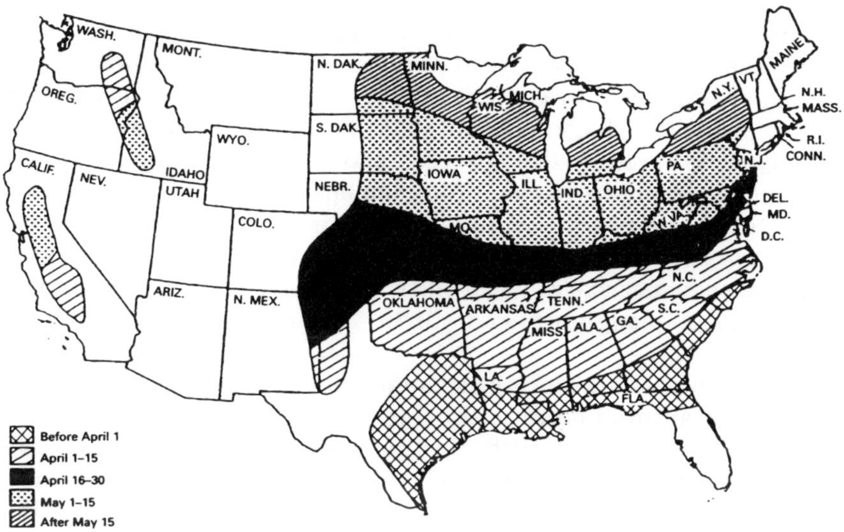

(b)

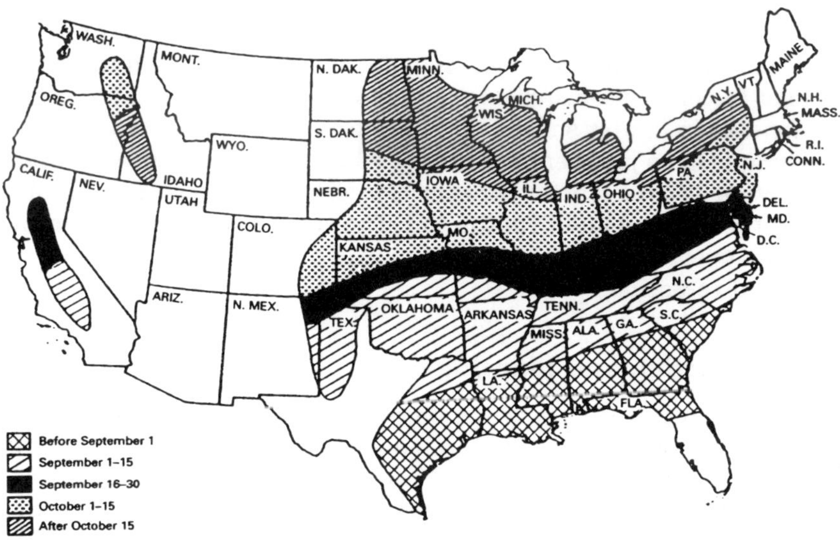

Wheat is best adapted to well-drained silt and clay loam soils which are not too acid (pH 7.0–8.5). Corn grows best on deep, medium textured soils with a pH range of 5.6–7.5. However, it will also thrive on other soils provided they hold water well and are well drained.

In many situations drainage has to be improved by laying pipes and making tunnels (moles). This encourages rooting, improves take-up of nutrients, reduces diseases and extends cultivation periods.

For each crop a seedbed must be prepared. The aims here are to provide the best possible conditions for germination, emergence and seedling growth, encourage absorption of water, control weeds and preserve soil tilth. The traditional and still common procedure involves inverting and bursting the topsoil, mixing and firming it, and then making it fine enough. The main implement types at each stage are the plough, the disc harrow and tine harrow or cultivator (sometimes also with rollers), though there are many varieties of each. Alternatives to the traditional sequence are reduced cultivation, involving in particular only light or chisel ploughing, and direct drilling, with no regular soil cultivation.

For spring wheat and corn it is usually desirable to plough the land in the preceding autumn because the later freezing and thawing breaks up clods and improves the tilth. In the semi-arid areas of the North American Great Plains and Australia, retention of moisture is the priority in seedbed preparation. A common practice, called mulch tillage, is to leave plant residue on the soil. In especially dry areas summer fallowing is also practised.

The general trend is to reduce the number of passes in preparing seedbeds. This is in part a response to higher energy costs, but also stems from a recognition that overworking of the soil may worsen its structure and lead to compaction. An example of a system of reduced cultivation used for corn in lighter soils in the United States is wheel-track planting. Ploughing is done just before planting without intervening operations. A combination of the tractor wheels and special wheels on the planter prepare the seedbed and firm the soil. The soil between the rows remains loose and open, and this discourages weed growth and favours water intake and retention.

Variety selection and planting

A key decision in cereal production and one that needs to be reviewed each year, given the pace of development, is the choice of varieties to grow. Let me say at the outset that one should not confuse "variety" with "class" of grain (or grade within a class). The variety of a cereal is its race and name (e.g. Hereward or Riband); its grade is the certified quality on the basis of which it is bought and traded (e.g. Canadian Western Red Spring No. 1). Many different varieties can qualify for inclusion in a traded grade, but the grade is indifferent to which specific varieties are offered for qualification, provided they can meet the requisite quality standards.

Varieties of cereal are produced by plant breeders, a dedicated and highly skilled band of geneticists. In some countries plant breeding is the prerogative of state institutions; in others it is in private hands. In the United States, which has the largest range of any country, plant breeding is a matter for private enterprise. The protection, or patenting, of the results of such enterprise is however a matter for the US Secretary of Agriculture, working through the Plant Varieties Protection Office, a service of the US Department of Agriculture. Applications are received from breeders, and certificates issued under the Plant Varieties Protection Act, information being published periodically in the PVPO Official Journal.

In Canada wheat was introduced by early settlers in Manitoba in 1812 and scientific breeding there dates from 1903. The famous Manitoba wheats all trace their origins back to Marquis and Red Fife, the original nineteenth-century strains.

British plant breeding is now largely in the hands of subsidiaries of multinational companies. The most spectacular breakthrough in yield performance in the United Kingdom—with extensive repercussions on the European continent—came in the 1970s with the development of Maris Huntsman, a high-yielding, hard-grained soft wheat, extremely prolific but at first regarded purely as a feed wheat totally unsuited to breadmaking. The advent of semi-dwarf wheats made an impact about the 1960s in the United States followed in the United Kingdom by the variety Hobbit around 1977 and a succession of numerous other varieties, most of which are now semi-dwarf. The advantage of semi-dwarf wheats is to improve harvest index and allow for a greater uptake of nitrogen. Grain which formerly took up 30 per cent of whole plant weight now accounts for about 55 per cent. Semi-dwarf varieties also possess extra standing power, which helps to preserve the quality of grain.

A selected list of recommended varieties of wheat, barley and oats, together with notes on available varieties of triticale, durum wheat and rye, is published annually by the National Institute of Agricultural Botany (NIAB) as a handbook. This is a short and readable document, intended primarily for the information of farmers; it also contains useful information on the geographical spread of diseases in England and Wales.

In corn breeding the great leap forward was the development of hybrid varieties, which first became widely grown in the 1940s. Commercial hybrids of wheat have yet to be produced, but a rapid rate of improvements has nevertheless been maintained. In the United Kingdom during the twentieth century half the increase in yield has been attributed to improved varieties.

The 1998 *Cereals Variety Handbook* contains the United Kingdom recommended list of cereals published by NIAB, whose variety trials are supported by the Home-Grown Cereals Authority. The recommended list of winter wheats for 1998 is shown as Table 2.1, while there is a further list of varieties to be considered for 1999. The recommended list of spring wheats for 1998 is shown as Table 2.2. Recommended lists of winter barleys and spring barleys are shown in Tables 2.3 and 2.4 respectively. The *Handbook* contains similar lists for oats and other cereals, and much useful information about yields.

The important features of seeds are their germinative capacity, purity (i.e., freedom from seeds of other crops and weeds, broken grains, dust and soil), health (absence of disease), vigour and boldness (i.e., size and plumpness as measured by the 1,000 grain weight). In choosing which varieties to grow, farmers will consider not only the potential yield under favourable conditions but also standing power, earliness of ripening, latest safe sowing date, resistance to sprouting in the ear, resistance to pests and diseases, and tolerance of chemical treatments. They will also take into account the intended end-use, e.g. milling or feed in the case of wheat, and the need to diversify plantings to reduce the risks of damage from disease or weather.

Seed is usually planted in rows by drills rather than broadcast. These combine devices for opening up small furrows, tubes for seed delivery and components for covering and then tamping down the furrow. Often the drill also applies fertilisers and herbicides. Seed rates usually range between 155 and 185 kg per hectare but the precise rate in any situation will depend on the target density of plant population, the 1,000 grain weight and the expected percentage establishment. The general trend has been towards more generous seed rates.

Feeding

To grow, cereal plants need oxygen and carbon from carbon dioxide in the air, oxygen and hydrogen from water and a range of elements from the soil. The major elements needed are nitrogen, phosphorous, potassium, magnesium, calcium and sulphur. Minor or trace elements are copper, manganese, iron, boron, sodium, chlorine, molybdenum and zinc. In most situations the natural nutrient cycles of the soil need to be supplemented by a programme of manuring and fertilisation. The aims are to provide all essential elements to start the crop off well, sustain supplies of nutrients till harvest, bind up soil nutrient reserves and stimulate beneficial biological activity. In selecting manures and fertilisers farmers further choose those that resist losses by leaching and breakdown, store well, spread easily and benefit soil structure.

First, acidity problems must be rectified by liming. Where available, nearby farmyard manure can provide all the requirements of high-yielding cereals except nitrogen, and also improve soil structure and the activity of beneficial organisms. On modern specialised farms, however, especially those using reduced cultivation, most feeding is by inorganic fertilisers. These are usually applied as solids in granular form or drilled, but may also be injected as liquids into the soil or sprayed on the leaves. For both corn and wheat in most situations the main nutrient added is nitrogen. This is applied either straight, such as ammonium nitrate or urea, or in a compound with other elements, most commonly potassium and phosphorus. In Australia exceptionally, mainly phosphatic fertilisers are applied.

On corn some of the fertiliser requirements are applied by broadcasting over the whole field area. In the cooler areas fertiliser is also applied as a "starter" at planting in a band along the side of the seed bed. Nitrogen also is often side-dressed into the soil in the middles of the rows at the earlier stages of growth up to knee high.

On winter wheat also split dressings of nitrogen are the rule. In Western Europe the optimal pattern is hotly debated, with applications being made from planting until June.

For other elements needs can be determined to some degree by soil tests. Those for calcium, magnesium and zinc are considered fairly reliable. However, requirements must largely be determined by observation of deficiency symptoms. Among the trace elements for cereal production deficiencies in magnesium and copper are most common.

Protection from weeds

Cereal weeds may be broadly classified into broad-leaved weeds, such as cleavers and poppies, and grass weeds, e.g. couch or wild oats. Weeds deprive cereal crops of food and water, shade them from light or smother them at the seedling stage. They also provide a home for plant pests and diseases, promote lodging and delay harvesting. Also, their seeds, when harvested, may reduce the value of the crop or cause expense in cleaning. The spread of weeds in cereals can be discouraged by seed cleaning, rotational husbandry, hand roguing or hoeing, straw burning (in countries where this is still permitted) and cultivation. For corn, cultivation can be done after, as well as before, planting using the rotary hoe, weeder and spike-toothed harrow.

On all cereals, however, weed control is now largely achieved by chemical measure. Herbicides for broad-leaved weeds were developed in the late nineteenth century but were not commonly used until the introduction of MCPA (methol-chloro-phenoxy-acetic acid) in 1942 and, more particularly, CMPP (mecoprop), in 1956, and dichlorpropin, in 1961.

In the past quarter of a century the pace of development has markedly increased, and in recent years effective controls on grass weeds have

Table 2.1 NIAB recommended list of winter wheat 1998

Based on trials from 1993–97. The control for yield comparisons is the mean of Brigadier, Hereward, Hussar, Rialto and Riband. Differences of less than 3% for the fully recommended varieties, and less than 4% for comparisons involving provisionally recommended varieties, should be treated with reserve.

	Fully Recommended									Provisionally Recommended						Becoming Outclassed			
Recommended categories: G General Use S Special Use R Regional Use P Provisional Use	**Reaper**	**Hussar**	**Rialto**	**Consort**	**Riband**	**Hereward**	**Spark**	**Buster**	**Soissons**	**Savannah**	**Harrier**	**Madrigal**	**Equinox**	**Charger**	**Abbot**	**Brigadier**	**Beaufort**	**Caxton**	**Cadenza**
O Becoming Outclassed	**G**	**G**	**G**	**G**	**G**	**G**	**G**	**S**	**RS**	**PG**	**PG**	**PG**	**PG**	**PG**	**PG**	**O**	**O**	**O**	**O**
Region of use	UK	UK	UK	UK	UK	UK	UK	UK	C/SE SW	UK	UK	UK	UK	UK	UK	UK	UK	UK	UK
UK yield as % treated control (9.73 t/ha)																			
With fungicide treatment	102	102	102	102	100	93	93	100	93	106	104	104	103	102	98	103	102	96	96
Without fungicide treatment	88	86	86	82	75	80	80	84	82	84	87	87	87	87	87	81	89	81	77
Standing power	6	6	7	8	8	8	7	9	7	8	6	8	9	5	7	7	8	6	6
Shortness of straw	7	7	6	8	7	7	5	8	7	7	8	8	9	8	8	8	7	8	4
Earliness of ripening	7	7	7	6	7	7	7	7	9	6	7	7	7	8	8	7	7	8	8
Resistance to shedding	6	8	5	6	6	7	6	7	5	–	7	8	6	5	8	7	5	5	8
Resistance to sprouting	(6)	6	6	6	6	6	7	7	7	–	(7)	(7)	(5)	(2)	(7)	6	5	(5)	8
Latest safe sowing date	End Jan	End Jan	End Jan	End Jan	Mid Feb	End Jan	Mid Mar	Mid Feb	Mid Feb	End Jan	End Jan	End Jan	End Jan	End Jan	End Jan	End Jan	End Jan	End Feb	Mid Apr
Resistance to disease																			
Mildew	7	7	7	6	7	6	7	5	8	8	7	6	6	8	7	6	8	6	7
Yellow rust	4	5	6	8	6	6	7	9	7	5	4	4	4	8	6	1	5	8	9
Brown rust	9	9	4	6	4	7	8	3	2	9	9	9	9	8	9	9	9	8	9
Septoria nodorum	7	6	5	6	5	6	7	7	4	5	7	7	6	7	6	4	7	5	4
Septoria tritici	6	5	5	4	3	6	7	5	6	4	6	5	5	5	6	4	4	4	5
Fusarium ear blight	5	6	5	7	6	6	7	6	5	(5)	(6)	(6)	(6)	4	(6)	6	4	5	6
Eyespot	5	5	6	5	5	5	5	6	4	6	6	5	6	5	6	5	6	5	5

Table 2.1—*cont.*

	Fully Recommended									Provisionally Recommended						Becoming Outclassed			
Recommended categories: G General Use S Special Use R Regional Use P Provisional Use O Becoming Outclassed	**Reaper**	**Hussar**	**Rialto**	**Consort**	**Riband**	**Hereward**	**Spark**	**Buster**	**Soissons**	**Savannah**	**Harrier**	**Madrigal**	**Equinox**	**Charger**	**Abbot**	**Brigadier**	**Beaufort**	**Caxton**	**Cadenza**
	G	**G**	**G**	**G**	**G**	**G**	**G**	**S**	**RS**	**PG**	**PG**	**PG**	**PG**	**PG**	**PG**	**O**	**O**	**O**	**O**
Grain quality																			
Bread-making quality	–	–	6	–	–	8	7	–	6	–	–	–	–	7	7	–	–	7	6
Biscuit-making quality	4	–	–	7	7	–	–	–	–	–	5	5	–	–	–	–	–	–	–
Endosperm texture	Hard	Hard	Hard	Soft	Soft	Hard	Hard	Hard	Hard	Hard	Soft	Soft	Hard	Hard	Hard	Hard	Hard	Hard	Hard
Protein content (% at 14% moisture)	10.5	10.1	10.9	10.3	10.1	11.4	11.4	10.9	11.4	9.7	10.3	10.3	10.4	10.4	11.1	10.1	10.5	10.8	11.2
Hagberg Falling Number	288	297	270	267	238	311	323	250	312	262	210	266	278	288	329	255	240	275	300
Zeleny volume	31.3	24.4	47.2	23.1	18.4	53.3	62.3	36.1	59.3	(23.7)	13.3	18.4	26.4	48.0	48.7	25.1	33.9	63.1	51.9
Specific weight (kg/hl)	76.8	79.0	78.8	77.3	75.8	80.0	79.3	76.7	80.4	77.0	77.3	78.2	76.1	77.7	78.0	77.1	78.5	77.2	77.6
1000 grain weight (g)	46.8	46.4	47.9	44.6	47.9	44.8	38.0	46.2	43.2	49.2	44.9	44.3	48.8	43.3	44.9	46.2	46.8	45.7	47.0
Year first listed	1996	1992	1995	1995	1989	1991	1993	1995	1995	1998	1997	1997	1997	1997	1997	1993	1995	1996	1994

The yield figures presented include data from the 1997 trials in the North-east region in which some varieties were affected by poor grain set. A high figure on the 1–9 scale indicates that the variety shows the character to a high degree.
( ) = limited data.

Source: NIAB.

Table 2.2 NIAB recommended list of spring wheat 1998

Based on trials from 1993–97. The control for yield comparisons is the mean of Axona, Chablis and Promessa. Differences of less than 3% for the fully recommended varieties, and less than 4% for comparisons involving provisionally recommended varieties, should be treated with reserve.

	Fully Recommended			**Prov. Rec.**	**Becoming Outclassed**	
Recommendation categories: G General Use S Special Use P Provisional O Becoming Outclassed	**Chablis**	**Shiraz**	**Axona**	**Imp**	**Baldus**	**Avans**
	G	**S**	**S**	**PG**	**O**	**O**
UK yield **spring sown** as % treated control (6.48 t/ha)						
With fungicide treatment	105	100	92	103	100	95
Without fungicide treatment	89	88	80	92	87	90
Standing power	6	6	7	6	6	8
Shortness of straw	7	7	5	6	7	7
Earliness of ripening	6	6	6	6	6	6
Resistance to shedding	7	6	7	7	7	7
Resistance to sprouting	8	8	8	(8)	8	7
Resistance to disease						
Mildew	6	5	6	8	5	9
Yellow rust	9	8	9	8	5	6
Brown rust	8	9	9	4	9	9
Septoria tritici	5	5	4	4	3	3
Quality						
Bread-making quality	6	7	7	7	6	8
Endosperm texture	Hard	Soft	Hard	Hard	Hard	Hard
Hagberg Falling Number	352	322	306	326	313	268
Protein content (% at 14%)	10.9	11.5	12.0	11.0	10.9	12.1
Specific weight (kg/hl)	76.2	76.9	78.1	77.0	78.9	77.5
1000 grain weight (g)	39.2	36.3	38.1	38.1	34.4	33.3
UK yield **late autumn sown** with fungicide treatment as % treated controls (8.06 t/ha)	106	98	91	103	98	93
Year first listed	1995	1995	1985	1997	1992	1994

A high figure on the 1–9 scale indicates that the variety shows the character to a high degree. ( ) = limited data.

Source: NIAB.

been developed. There are now a multiplicity of chemical brands available for weed control in cereals, and the best source of information for those is the *UK Pesticides Annual* (10th edition), published by the Commonwealth Agricultural Bureau at Wallingford in Oxfordshire. Apart from their chemical group, herbicides are commonly classified according to their application and mode of action and to the timing of treatment. Herbicides may be applied to the soil with a residual effect, or to foliage, as a contact or translocated action, i.e. killing parts beyond the point of entry. Main timing classes are pre-sowing, pre-emergence, post emergence and pre-harvest.

Correct timing of application is vital. This is determined by growth stage of the corn, weather and soil conditions, the stage of the weed growth and associated weed control. Control of weeds is obviously especially important in the early stages of crop growth. Nevertheless, on autumn sown crops spring treatments are also common in Western Europe, especially where cereals are grown continuously.

Protection from pests

The main animal pests causing economic loss in growing crops are insects. The spread of these is generally favoured by large areas of susceptible varieties, continuous cropping and absence of natural predators and particularly favoured by appropriate weather conditions.

Pest damage is especially severe when crops are very young, when the whole plant may be killed, and after ear emergence, when flowering may be impeded or the developing grains robbed. Pest problems can be greatly reduced by cultural means such as proper treatment of crop residues, rotational cropping, adjustment of planting time, good drainage and ploughing, selection of resistant varieties and feeding to promote crop vigour. In addition, against some pests chemical controls are effective, applied as seed dressings, baits, sprays or dust.

On corn, serious damage can be caused by various types of borers at the larval stage. These cause broken stunted plants, shrivelled ears and breaking of ears from the stalk. Some hybrid varieties are partly resistant, and ploughing under old stubble also markedly reduces their incidence. Chinch bugs, a flying pest, can be controlled by insecticides. In the southern growing regions of the United States corn is also vulnerable to the earworm, the most effective measure against which is late autumn ploughing. A more general pest, though one usually controllable by use of good rotation and proper cultural practices, is the corn root aphid.

In growing wheat in North America some insect pests—notably grasshoppers, greenbugs, wireworms and earworms—can be controlled by insecticides. Other pests, especially the wheat stem sawfly—a major problem in spring wheat areas—the joint-worm, the straw-worm and the hessian fly, can be controlled only by late planting, rotation or residue burying. In breeding resistance a major success has been achieved against the wheat stem sawfly. Under the more humid growing conditions of Western Europe there is a different range of insect pests. Aphids cause problems by sap sucking, robbing of photosynthesates and

Table 2.3 NIAB recommended list of winter barley 1998

Based on trials from 1993–97. The control for yield comparisons is the mean of Fanfare, Fighter, Halcyon, Manitou and Pastoral. Differences of less than 4% among fully recommended varieties, and less than 5% for comparisons involving provisionally recommended varieties, should be treated with reserve.

	Fully Recommended											Provisionally Rec.			Becoming Outclassed					
Recommended categories:	2 row varieties										6 row	2 row varieties								
G General Use S Special Use R Regional Use P Provisional	**Fanfare**	**Hanna**	**Intro**	**Pastoral**	**Regina**	**Gleam**	**Epic**	**Melanie**	**Halcyon**	**Muscat**	**Manitou**	**Vertige**	**Rifle**	**Jewel**	**Gaelic**	**Fighter**	**Linnet**	**Angora**	**Puffin**	**Pipkin**
O Becoming Outclassed	**G**	**G**	**G**	**G**	**S**	**S**	**S**	**S**	**S**	**G**	**RG**	**PG**	**PG**	**PS**	**O**	**O**	**O**	**O**	**O**	**O**
Region of use	UK	UK	UK	UK	UK	UK	UK	UK	UK	UK	NE NW	UK	UK	UK	UK	UK	UK	UK	UK	UK
UK Yield as % treated control (7.94 t/ha)																				
With fungicide treatment	102	102	101	101	105	100	98	97	93	108	105	104	101	102	101	99	99	98	94	93
Without fungicide treatment	85	85	84	80	86	84	83	80	74	87	87	87	84	86	82	83	82	80	79	71
Standing power	5	8	7	8	9	7	8	8	4	6	6	9	7	8	8	8	8	9	7	4
Shortness of straw	7	6	4	7	7	7	6	7	5	3	5	8	7	7	8	6	6	8	7	7
Earliness of ripening	5	5	5	6	5	6	6	7	5	7	7	6	5	6	4	4	6	7	7	5
Latest safe sowing date	End Jan	End Jan	End Jan	Mid Feb	End Feb	End Feb	End Feb	End Feb	End Feb	End Jan	End Feb	End Feb	Mid Feb	End Feb	End Feb	End Jan	End Feb	End Feb	End Feb	End Feb
Resistance to disease																				
Mildew	5	4	6	3	3	6	8	5	6	5	5	5	7	7	5	8	4	6	6	2
Yellow rust	7	6	5	8	2	8	8	2	7	4	5	(7)	8	(8)	6	7	5	2	8	7
Brown rust	7	7	8	6	6	7	7	4	7	6	5	6	8	8	8	6	7	3	8	6
Rhynchosporium	8	8	5	7	7	7	5	8	5	8	8	5	6	8	5	5	6	7	6	3
Net blotch	8	7	7	8	8	4	8	5	8	7	4	8	8	6	8	7	6	5	4	8
Barley yellow mosaic virus (BaYMV)	–	–	–	–	–	Res	Res	–	–	Res	–	–	–	Res	–	–	–	–	–	–

Table 2.3—*cont.*

Recommended categories:	Fully Recommended											Provisionally Rec.			Becoming Outclassed					
	2 row varieties									6 row		2 row varieties								
G General Use S Special Use R Regional Use P Provisional O Becoming Outclassed	**Fanfare**	**Hanna**	**Intro**	**Pastoral**	**Regina**	**Gleam**	**Epic**	**Melanie**	**Halcyon**	**Muscat**	**Manitou**	**Vertige**	**Rifle**	**Jewel**	**Gaelic**	**Fighter**	**Linnet**	**Angora**	**Puffin**	**Pipkin**
	G	**G**	**G**	**G**	**S**	**S**	**S**	**S**	**S**	**G**	**RG**	**PG**	**PG**	**PS**	**O**	**O**	**O**	**O**	**O**	**O**
Quality																				
Malting grade	9#	2	5	2	9#[++]	8#	1	8*	8*	4	1	–	9	–	3	6	3	8#	8	7#
Specific weight (kg/hl)	71.3	69.8	69.3	68.9	68.9	69.1	69.5	68.9	70.3	68.2	64.4	70.6	68.1	69.7	70.4	69.1	70.3	68.8	70.6	70.4
1000 grain weight (g)	42.2	50.4	53.1	46.1	48.6	40.4	47.8	48.3	38.6	38.9	44.5	47.4	41.7	45.8	48.2	44.9	42.0	48.7	42.8	36.7
Year first listed	1995	1995	1993	1989	1996	1996	1994	1995	1985	1996	1991	1998	1997	1998	1994	1991	1994	1996	1989	1986

Variety notes

Fanfare has shown more dormancy than other approved winter varieties – growers are advised to check with their maltster regarding movement after harvest. Gaelic is an early developing variety which should not be sown before October. Regina, Melanie and Angora – growers should pay careful attention to yellow rust control. A high figure on the 1–9 scale indicates that the variety shows the character to a high degree. ( ) = limited data.

* = Approved by the Institute of Brewing as a malting variety in the UK.
++ = Approved by the Institute of Brewing as a malting variety in the North-east and North-west regions.
\# = Approved by the Institute of Brewing as a malting variety in Central, South-east and South-west regions.
[] = Provisional approval by the Institute of Brewing as a malting variety.
BaYMV: Res = Resistant to BaMMV and the common strain of BaYMV.

Source: NIAB.

Table 2.4 NIAB recommended list of spring barley 1998

Based on trials from 1993–97. The control for yield comparisons is the mean of Alexis, Chariot, Cooper, Hart and Optic. Differences of less than 4% among fully recommended varieties, and less than 5% for comparisons involving provisionally recommended varieties, should be treated with reserve.

	Fully Recommended									Prov. Rec.		Becoming Outclassed		
Recommended categories: G General Use S Special Use R Regional Use P Provisional O Becoming Outclassed	**Optic** **G**	**Cooper** **G**	**Chariot** **G**	**Riviera** **RG**	**Delibes** **RG**	**Prisma** **RG**	**Hart** **RG**	**Dandy** **RG**	**Derkado** **RS**	**Landlord** **PG**	**Chalice** **RPG**	**Tankard** **O**	**Felicie** **O**	**Alexis** **O**
Region of use	UK	UK	UK	NW	NE NW	NE	NW SW	NW SW	NE	UK	NE	NE	NW SW	C/SE SW
UK yield as % treated control (6.70 t/ha)														
With fungicide treatment	105	102	98	105	103	(99)	98	(97)	95	100	103	100	98	96
Without fungicide treatment	93	91	92	97	93	(79)	92	(93)	87	93	96	93	92	87
Standing power	7	8	7	7	8	6	6	6	7	7	7	8	6	7
Shortness of straw	6	8	6	5	7	5	4	3	6	6	7	7	4	6
Earliness of ripening	4	5	6	6	6	6	6	6	5	6	6	6	6	5
Resistance to ear loss	6	8	7	6	7	5	7	9	7	7	8	7	8	7
Resistance to disease														
Mildew	7	7	9	9	6	3	9	9	9	9	9	9	7	9
Yellow rust	8	6	8	4	8	8	5	9	8	6	(8)	7	4	5
Brown rust	8	8	4	4	9	6	4	5	8	6	6	8	6	4
Rhynchosporium	5	6	3	5	7	6	6	7	3	6	5	3	7	4
Barley yellow dwarf virus (BYDV)	8	7	6	4	6	4	5	6	3	8	MR	4	4	5

Table 2.4—*cont.*

	Fully Recommended									Prov. Rec.		Becoming Outclassed		
Recommended categories: G General Use S Special Use R Regional Use P Provisional O Becoming Outclassed	**Optic** **G**	**Cooper** **G**	**Chariot** **G**	**Riviera** **RG**	**Delibes** **RG**	**Prisma** **RG**	**Hart** **RG**	**Dandy** **RG**	**Derkado** **RS**	**Landlord** **PG**	**Chalice** **RPG**	**Tankard** **O**	**Felicie** **O**	**Alexis** **O**
Quality														
Malting grade	9*	9#	9*	8	7++	8++	4	4	8++	9[++]	9	9	5	8#
Specific weight (kg/hl)	69.7	68.9	70.3	70.2	67.5	67.1	69.4	70.1	69.6	68.2	67.7	69.1	70.6	68.8
1000 grain weight (g)	45.9	43.0	42.0	48.3	45.6	49.0	49.6	49.1	45.1	45.5	44.7	46.2	45.0	45.5
Year first listed	1995	1994	1992	1995	1994	1989	1989	1988	1992	1997	1998	1996	1993	1990

A high figure on the 1–9 scale indicates that the variety shows the character to a high degree.
* = Approved by the Institute of Brewing as a malting variety in the UK.
++ = Approved by the Institute of Brewing as a malting variety in the North-east and North-west regions.
# = Approved by the Institute of Brewing as a malting variety in the Central, South-east and South-west regions.
[] = Provisional approval by the Institute of Brewing as a malting variety.

Source: NIAB.

spreading diseases. Spraying against these is effective but expensive. On winter wheat, slugs can have devastating effects on young crops but can be controlled by metaldehyde applied at, or close to, drilling. When winters are mild and wet, leather jackets, the larvae of the crane fly, become a problem which requires curative spraying and extra nitrogen application. Among flies the most serious pests to wheat growers are the frit fly and the wheat bulb fly. Both can be cured by spraying if detected early enough.

Protection against diseases

Diseases are often classified, according to the main part of the plant affected, into those of the root, leaf, ear and whole plant. Diseases of cereals mainly reduce yield but may also affect quality. Thus wheat grain from rusted plants is usually thin and low in bushel weight, with poor milling and baking quality. The most effective way to combat diseases is to breed varieties resistant to infection. This, however is laborious. Sources of genetic resistance in other plant material must be identified and this gene separated from undesirable features with which it may be linked. This characteristic must then be combined with the other desired features of yield, quality and agronomy. Furthermore, new strains of pathogen quickly develop to overcome the resistance so that the process is a never-ending battle.

Most cereal pathogens are fungi, though some are viruses. Microclimate strongly influences incidence. So also does the use of fungicides; as one pathogen is destroyed so plants become more vulnerable to others.

Farmers can reduce disease problems by selection of varieties, treating crop residues and controlling weed hosts and insect vectors. Managerial skills are extremely important, amongst which are early recognition of diseases and assessment of their severity. The recent drop in cereal prices (written in 1998) means more careful use needs to be made of the means of treatment. Further relevant managerial skills are the early recognition of diseases and the assessment of their severity.

In corn the most pervasive disease is smut. This is controlled mainly by rotation. There are also a range of rots which affect the plants at various stages of growth. Many of these have been effectively contained by plant breeding and seed treatments. This is to a degree true of leaf blights but, as was seen in 1970, new, virulent races can still appear with catastrophic effects.

In North America production of wheat was periodically blighted by smuts which cause kernels to be replaced by smut balls. This problem has been reduced to breeding and seed treatments. The potentially most destructive disease is black stem rust, but fortunately resistant cultivars are widely available. This is also true of powdery mildew. Less success has been achieved in control of wheat scab (mainly a problem in the Corn Belt and East Central regions) and septoria blotch.

In Western Europe economics has encouraged breeding for yield and greater reliance on fungicides for disease control. Some of the most serious diseases of wheat, causing losses of 10–30 per cent, are those which attack roots or stem bases at an early stage of the crop. Among these, take-all is distinguished by having neither chemical control nor resistant varieties. Control therefore depends on good early stubble cultivation and destruction of weed hosts. Eyespot, especially the common variety, and fusarium can be controlled by fungicides. The most common foliar diseases are powdery mildew, septoria and brown and yellow rusts. Of these, mildew, which is encouraged by warm humid weather, is the most regular and widespread problem, though yellow rust is potentially the most damaging of all the fungal diseases. All these diseases can be effectively controlled with chemicals. This is also true of ear diseases, with the important exception of ergot. The main whole plant disease encountered is the virus infection barley yellow dwarf virus. This is controlled by killing potentially infective aphids.

With reduced real prices for wheat in the European Community (EC), wheat growers have been inclined to choose a “fire engine” approach to disease control rather than a prophylactic spraying policy. This, of course, requires greater managerial input. There has also been some swing away from continuous cereal production and greater reliance of the use of break crops to control disease.

Harvesting

The final field operation in cereal production is the harvesting. The objectives here are to recover as much usable dry matter as possible, obtain the best quality for further use and leave as little behind as possible of material injurious to the following crop. In the developed world most grain is harvested by combine harvesters, which are self-propelled and have bulk tanks.

The combine harvester cuts standing crops with a cutter bar of reciprocating knives, then moves the cut crop by means of a reel, auger and elevator into a threshing drum. This is a cylinder of beater bars rotating within a concave, with a small clearance decreasing from the front, where the grain enters, to the rear. The straw then passes to walkers, which oscillate to separate remaining loose grains. The grain passes to sieves through which an air stream separates chaff and light fractions. Straw is discharged to the rear or into a chopper from the shakers, while grain is conveyed to a grain tank where it is transferred, to a trailer brought alongside, by an unloader auger. Cutting widths vary between three and eight metres.

In areas of Canada and the United States where shattering due to wind and hail is a problem, wheat may be cut and windrowed, then threshed with a combine equipped with a pick-up attachment.

Some corn is harvested with a picker sheller. Whatever machine is used, losses can be markedly reduced by proper adjustment and operation. On the combine harvester the main areas of adjustments are forward speed, concave clearance, drum speed, sieve setting and fan speed.

CEREAL GROWING WITHIN FARMING

Throughout the world cereals are the main use of arable land. Traditionally, when livestock manure was the main nutrient, production of wheat and corn was invariably associated with animal production. Such mixed farms are now much less common. A further degree of specialisation has also been permitted by the development of herbicides and more powerful machinery. The growing of cereals with rotational breaks of roots, legumes or temporary grass has been replaced to a degree by continuous cereal growing.

However, these patterns vary from one country to another. In Australia wheat farms typically still carry livestock, mainly sheep—indeed, less than a third of the area of wheat-growing farms is cropped.

In North America and Western Europe oilseeds are the main crops, grown rotationally with wheat and corn. In the United States corn-growing farms usually also grow soyabeans. In Canada and Western Europe rapeseed is the main break crop, though on lighter land in Western Europe sugar beet and potatoes are of great significance. The other main crop group grown in rotation with cereals is pulses. Peas and beans are grown either for human use or as a protein supplement in livestock feeding.

As incidental intelligence, US sources say that since the introduction of the "Freedom to Farm" legislation under the 1995 Act, farmers have made greater use of crop rotations. They no longer need to maintain an "acreage base" of particular crops to maximise their support payments.

CHAPTER 3

Value-added products of grain: flour, malt, starch, semolina and by-products. Industrial uses

FLOUR

Introduction

Flour is a very wide-ranging word used to describe a vast number of products, from the fine wheat flours produced in sophisticated modern mills to the hand-ground cereal products which are the staple diet of many African countries. Flour can be produced from any cereal and the object of the milling process is to produce a substance capable of being cooked more easily and made into more palatable forms than the unmilled cereal. This normally involves separation from the embryo and the husk, but wholemeal flours do blur the edges of this definition.

Other cereals such as rye, maize, sorghum, barley, etc., can all be milled into flour, but this chapter is principally concerned with wheat flour, which is by far the most common product.

Uses of flour

Apart from its use in bread, and other bread-type products like cakes or chapatis, wheat flour is used to make many other staple foods, such as pastries, different forms of dumplings, biscuits, piecrusts, etc. It is also used as a thickener in many dishes and sauces. These products all use more or less fine flours, while the coarser flours or semolinas are used to prepare another range of dishes from semolina puddings to couscous.

Types of flour

Flour is classified by its fineness, colour, protein content and the characteristics of the dough it produces. These characteristics are measured by properly defined tests. The fineness depends on the final sieving the flour receives in the flour mill, and the colour will depend on the amount of the fine particles of husk that are carried through. Thus, so-called low extraction flour gives a pure white colour but a poor yield to the miller. Protein content and dough characteristics are closely linked. The principal protein of wheat is gluten, which has very elastic properties. These are important in producing bread with an even bubble size and good keeping qualities. An elastic dough is also essential for pasta production. Hard wheats with high protein contents are sought after for English-type bread. The even harder durum wheats are used for pasta production. Flour from wheats of intermediate content are blended with hard wheat flours to give the bakers the required product. French-type bread is made from intermediate protein flours and the traditional product is only expected to stay fresh for a few hours. Soft wheats of low protein content are suitable for biscuits and most thickening and cooking applications.

Flour production methods

The traditional method of making flour was by grinding it between two large, flat, circular stones. This was typically a single passage operation giving a fairly crude separation of the ground starchy endosperm from the husk. Modern flour mills are highly sophisticated and automated, and the wheat will pass through several milling and sieving operations before emerging as flour.

Since the objective with conventional flour is to separate the starchy endosperm from the seed coat, it is important that the seed coat should be as flexible as possible and not break up in the process. Therefore, wheat is frequently conditioned with steam or moisture some hours before milling. The first milling operation is to break open the grain. This is done using a roller mill with fluted rolls. The large particles from this operation are passed to the next rolls which are more finely fluted. At each stage, more endosperm is removed from the seed coat until only the bran is left. Following each passage through a roller mill, the ground material is classified through multibed shaking sieves known as Plansifters. The fractions that are already fine enough for flour are separated off while the larger fragments for semolinas are passed to smooth roll mills for a further size reduction. If semolina is being made as a product, it can of course be taken off at whatever particle size is needed. The point at which the milling process of the bran containing particles is stopped determines the whiteness of the flour and thus the efficiency of the extraction or yield.

Flour analysis

The analysis of the flour is both physical and chemical, and the desired characteristics will vary greatly depending on the use for which the flour has been made. The physical tests are for particle size, colour and water absorption, while the chemical tests will be for protein content, enzyme levels, plus the tests for dough characteristics, fermentation behaviour, elasticity, machinability, etc. Perhaps the most important tests are those that measure the amylase content of the flour, as this is of great importance in dough character. The best-known tests for this are the Hagberg falling number test, a high number denoting low amylase activity, and the Brabender Amylograph test which measures the thickening of a flour paste with increasing temperature, again a high number shows low enzyme activity.

Other tests, such as the Brabender Extensograph test, measure the mechanical properties of the dough.

Flour additives

Various additives are commonly added to flour in order to improve its baking properties. For example, enzymes such as thermo-labile fungal amylases are used to improve dough fermentation, while proteolytic enzymes are used to modify dough quality for such products as crackers. Oxidising agents potassium bromate and azodicarbomamide are used to improve dough resistance. Lecithin is an emulsifier which improves mechanical handling properties and monocalcium phosphate may be added to improve rising. Other additives such as benzoyl dioxide and chlorine dioxide are used principally as bleaching agents, while L-ascorbic acid has long been employed to speed up dough development.

World flour production and trade

World flour statistics are very difficult to compile and the data used here were provided by the International Grains Council. The total production of wheat flour in the world is now around 310–330 million tons per year, and rising steadily. The figure for 1976 was 175.5 million. However, the IGC acknowledges that its figures are incomplete. The Indian estimate, for example, covers only flour production from large commercial mills and ignores the much greater quantity produced locally in rural areas. For these reasons the IGC has now dropped the 'total world' line from production tables. It may be added that world flour trade is highly competitive, and attracts huge export subsidies. EC export refunds in October 1991 on flour were running at over $160/ton, while the US EEP bonuses for flour were over $90. However, EU refunds for flour are now running at much lower levels—around $60/ton in August 1998—while the US has not used EEP for wheat or flour since July 1995. Production in Europe is more or less static at around 37 million tonnes, of which 20 million is made in the EC. Here France is the biggest producer with

5 million tons, followed by the United Kingdom with 4 million, and Germany 3.5 million. Figures for Russia and China are largely estimates and are thought to be around 37 million tons and 100 million tons respectively.

The United States has been increasing its flour production rapidly since 1980, and it is now running at well over 20 million tons, but Canada and Australia, despite their large wheat crops, produce only 1.8 and 1.4 million tons respectively. Production and exports of flour from both of these countries has been hard hit by the trend for importing countries to build their own mills and import wheat. Both Argentina and Brazil are now among the world's big flour producers.

As regards the rapid increase on flour consumption in the US (now 68 kg per person, having increased by 74% between 1970 and 1996), one of the world's leading authorities on flour milling, Morton Sosland, speaking at a conference in 1997 summarised this as due to four main influences—lifestyle, nutritional knowledge, demographic trends, and the impact of measures taken by producers. The rush for convenience foods meant that soon half the food consumed in America would be eaten or prepared outside the home. For flour this trend was typified by the "bun revolution"—fast food coming either on a bun or as finger food. What had happened in America could well happen in other countries too.

World trade in wheat flour is small, though the total has gone up sharply in recent seasons, to over 10 million tons in 1996–1997, of which 5.5 million come from the EU and 1 million from the US. The main importing regions are Near East Asia with 1.3 million tons and Africa with four million; included in this last figure is Egypt, which at between one and two million tons was until recently the world's biggest importing country, though its imports are now on a declining trend, reaching less than 200,000 tons in 1996–1997.

Semolina

Durum wheat, the hardest of all wheats, was specially bred for use in macaroni products. It is milled somewhat differently from other wheats, resulting in a coarse golden amber product called semolina and granulars. Semolina is mixed with water to form a dough, and then forced through dies, which shape it into spaghetti, macaroni and other pasta shapes. It is then dried and packaged. The granulars are ground into durum flour, which is combined with water and eggs to form a dough, then rolled and cut into noodles. Noodles, by legal definition in the United States, contain not less than 5.5 per cent egg solids or egg yolk. Trade in pasta has in the past been a subject of contention between the

EC and the United States, the argument centring on whether GATT rules allow subsidies (in the shape of export refunds) to be paid on processed products, or only on primary products. The GATT panel's opinion on the question was not clear-cut. The EC exports emanating from Italy, mainly to Algeria and North African destinations, are believed to amount to nearly 2 million tons per year, but figures are not published.

MALT

Introduction

The word "malting" means germination, and can thus be applied to any seed. However, it is normally associated with cereals and, in particular, barley. Modern malting requires the germination of the grain under controlled conditions. This germination is arrested at the required moment by drying or kilning to a low moisture content, typically around 4 per cent. Thus, at the end of the malting process, the appearance of the grain is little changed. The rootlets that grow during malting are removed after kilning. The density of the malt, however, is much lower than that of the original barley, around 56 kg/hl, as opposed to around 68 kg/hl, and malt grains have a somewhat shrivelled appearance. However, many important changes have occurred within the grain. Amylase enzymes, capable of turning the starch in the endosperm into sugar, have been produced. Proteolytic enzymes, to break down the protein reserves, have also been formed, and hydrolytic enzymes have acted on the endosperm cell wall structure breaking it down and making the grain friable.

Apart from barley, wheat is also malted, as is sorghum in some African countries. However, barley is by far the most popular cereal for malting, largely because of its husk. This gives it rigidity, protects it during the malting process, and also provides a filter bed in the subsequent brewing process.

Uses of malt

The principal use for malt is in the production of beer. Substantial quantities are also used for malt whisky production. Smaller quantities of wheat malt are used in the baking industry for the production of speciality breads. Malt is also used for malted milk drinks, malt vinegar production and confectionery. Malt extract, a thick syrup, is made by evaporating the sugary solution obtained from malt by mashing with hot water. This may be subsequently band-dried or spray-dried to give a powder. The early stages in the production of beer, whisky and malt extract are very similar. The malt is milled in a fluted roller mill. This may be either a wet or dry process and is then mashed with hot water. The mash may be a single temperature infusion mash at around 65°C or, more frequently, a temperature-programmed mash rising from 45°C to 70°C. During mashing, the enzymes formed in the malting process are activated and convert the starch to sugars and break down part of the protein into soluble protein and amino-acids. This liquid, known as wort, is then filtered off through the bed of barley husks.

When used for beer, this wort is boiled with hops, cooled and fermented with yeast. For whisky, there is no boiling with hops, and the wort is cooled and fermented directly with yeast, and subsequently distilled, whereas for malt extract, the wort is passed directly to an evaporator.

In the baking industry, wheat malt is preferred, as it has no true husk. The amylase enzymes act on the dough to produce sugar and this aids fermentation. Non-enzymic malt extracts are also used in baking to give flavour and texture.

Malt production methods

The malting process consists of three phases—steeping, germination and kilning. During steeping, the grain is immersed in water two or three times for periods of three to 12 hours, with air-rest periods of eight to 18 hours between the immersions. This raises the moisture content of the grain from 12–15 per cent to around 45 per cent and stimulates the beginning of germination. The steeped grain is then allowed to germinate for four to six days, being regularly turned to prevent the rootlets from matting together and to help control the temperature. Finally, the malted grain is loaded onto a kiln which has a perforated deck through which hot air is blown in order to dry and stabilise the malt without destroying the enzymes developed during germination.

The plant used to produce malt has evolved enormously since the turn of the century. For several hundred years before this, malt was produced by steeping barley in water continuously and then spreading it in a layer a few inches deep over the malting floors. A malthouse thus required a great floor area. The depth of the bed was limited by the necessity to keep the grain cool by regular turning with wooden shovels In modern malting, the grain is steeped in cylindro-conical or flat-bottomed steeping vessels which have perforated bases so that air can be drawn through the grain during the air-rest periods. After steeping, the grain is cast into germinating vessels with perforate floors. Grain depth is typically around one metre, and cool, humidified air is blown through the grain to maintain the required temperature. This is normally between 15°C and 20°C. The germination vessels are equipped with mechanical screw turners, which can move through the grain bed to prevent rootlet matting. Kilning is carried out in forced draft kilns equipped with heat recovery and recirculation systems for economic operation. The temperature programme ensures correct drying and minimises enzyme destruction.

The scale of maltings has developed as much as the methods used and batch sizes of 250–350 tons are typical for a modern plant, which will produce 50,000 to 60,000 tons *per annum*. In the old days, a floor maltings of 15-tons batch size and 5,000 tons *per annum* capacity was considered big.

Malt analysis

There are several analytical systems currently being used. The principal ones are:

1 The European Brewery Convention Method, or EBC.
2 The British Institute of Brewing Method, or IoB.
3 The American Society of Brewing Chemists Method, or ASBC.

The basic parameters being measured are the same: extract, moisture, total and soluble protein, colour, degree of modification, etc. Some, like moisture and extract, are basically economic factors, while others can have an influence on brewhouse performance or beer character.

World malt production and trade

The bulk of the world's malt is produced in areas of traditional barley growing and beer drinking. Thus the world market is dominated by Europe, particularly the EU. Eastern Europe also produces a lot of malt, but now exports relatively little. The United States is self-sufficient in malt but is not a major exporter. However, Canada and Australia are both major exporters.

The principal importing countries are Japan and the Philippines, Brazil, Venezuela and other South American countries. Africa also presents a large market, particularly in the Cameroons, Zaïre and South Africa. Nigeria has recently banned the import of malt for economic reasons.

Malt production is currently growing enormously in China. It is difficult to give a figure of the likely volumes there at this time.

Current total world usage excluding China and the USSR is around 12

12 million tons, of which 5 million tons are produced in the EU, 3 million in the United States, 1 million in Eastern Europe, and 600,000 each in Australia and Canada.

Starch

The wet-milling of grain for the production of starch and co-products is a capital intensive, highly industrialised activity, which bears little relation to primary production. It has great significance for agricultural producers and traders, however, since it provides an outlet for products with high added value. In a time of difficult economic conditions when farms are struggling to survive and politicians and farm leaders, constantly advocate addition of value, the importance of this industry is self-evident.

In the nineteenth century, starch was mainly manufactured from potatoes and wheat. The modern system of wet-milling using corn (maize) as the base was developed by Thomas Kingsford of New York; the United States was thus the early leader in establishing the industry, and remains paramount today. One billion bushels of corn are currently utilised by the American wet-milling industry, over 13 per cent of US corn consumption (for comparison, the related dry-milling industry uses some 165 million bushels). In the EU, on the other hand, wheat is used as well as maize as the basic grain, accounting for about one-third of the usage. The reason for this lies in the EU support system, which raises maize prices relative to wheat, and is also due to an increased demand for wheat gluten, mainly used as a protein supplement in bread grists. Rice is also used for the production of starch.

In the production process the entire corn kernel is used and, with the production of important by-products, yields are about 100 per cent. After weighing, sampling and cleaning, the shelled corn is then steeped in a solution of warm water and sulphur dioxide (producing steepwater, used in animal feed), the germ is then separated from the rest of the corn, heated and the oil extracted. About 50 per cent of the corn oil is used in edible oils, the rest used in soaps, paints and varnishes. The slurry is milled and the hulls separated from the starch and gluten and used in animal feed. The starch is then separated from the gluten by centrifuge, and dried and packed for sale or further treatment for specialised markets. A diagrammatic representation of these processes is shown in Figure 3.1.

In the EU, a system of production refunds, dating from 1975, was established to compensate producers of maize starch (and also of quellmehl used in breadmaking), as well as of wheat, potato and rice starch, maize grits and broken rice used for brewing, for the high costs of raw materials. A special provision was made in 1977 whereby exports of

Figure 3.1 Wet corn milling process

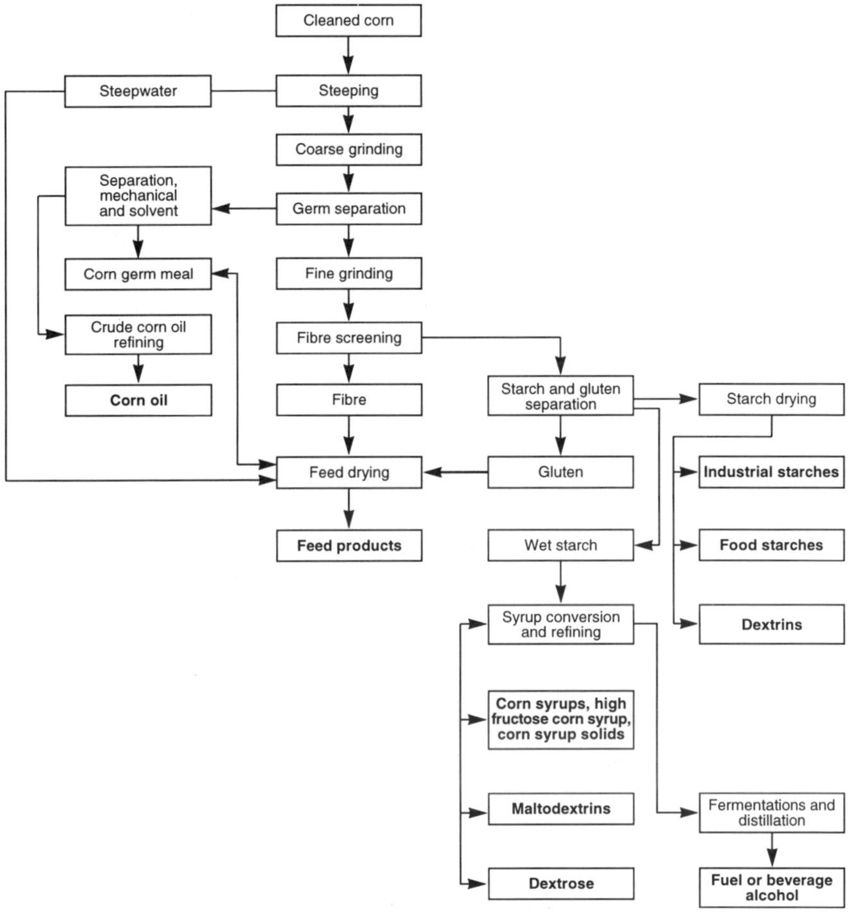

Source: Chicago Board of Trade.

the products were subject to a levy if the world prices of the raw materials rose above the EU threshold price (thus demonstrating the even-handedness of the CAP regime). One merit of this system was that it facilitated the collection of statistical information about the industry. However, production refunds for manufacturers under the 1975 arrangements were phased out by 1989/1990 (largely because starch products used in the food industry were already protected through the CAP), and refunds were henceforth confined to industrial users. A side-effect of this was that it became harder to record statistical information on the EU starch industry.

CEREAL BY-PRODUCTS

Introduction

All industrial processing of cereals results in by-products. These can often form a significant percentage of the weight of the original cereal. Some by-products have considerable value, usually as animal feed ingredients, while others are of little or no value. For ease of storage, handling and transport, by-products are frequently pelleted and thus require regrinding before incorporation into feed. Every industry that processes cereals produces one or more by-products, but there is only space here to consider the principal ones that are commercially available and regularly traded.

By-products from general cereal processing and handling

All processes involving the use of cereals require a cleaning and screening of the grain before use. Stones, straw, etc. are removed in the cleaning operation, while small corns and broken grains as well as a certain amount of husk are separated from the head corn by screening.

There are frequently two grades of screenings. The first consists of small-grained but otherwise sound samples of the starting cereal. This can be sold as bulk grain at a modest discount to the original material. However, the second fraction, consisting of broken corns, small grains, foreign seeds, etc., is normally pelleted and sold at substantial discounts to whole grain.

A typical analysis for pelleted grain screenings is:

Moisture	Oil	Protein	Fibre
10%	6%	12%	19%

The protein content is roughly the same as whole barley or wheat, while the oil content is far higher and the very high fibre level is indicative of the large amount of husk present. This is a low-grade component for ruminant feed rations.

By-products from wheat milling

Various by-product fractions occur during the many stages of flour production. Most are sieved off as bran, while some will be sucked off as dust. These days, the by-products are generally combined together, pelleted and sold as wheat feed.

Some of the bran fractions are collected separately and sold for human food, mainly to the baking industry for speciality breads or for incorporation into high fibre foods.

Wheat feed is used mainly in cattle rations and its value is very seasonal. Thus in the summer it will be discounted by about 20 per cent against cereals because of abundant pasture while in winter the discount may be only 10 per cent.

A typical analysis for wheat feed is:

Moisture	Oil	Protein	Fibre
14%	4%	16%	8.5%

The protein and oil contents are considerably higher than whole-wheat reflecting the amount of germ and aleurome layer present in the product.

By-products from maize

These fall into two main categories. First, the by-products derived from dry maize milling for the production of grits and maize flour and, secondly, those derived from the wet milling of maize to produce starch.

Maize by-product (maize germ meal)

The germ removed from the maize during dry milling will sometimes be crushed and extracted to give maize oil. The remnants of this process plus any husk fractions separated during the dry milling will be recombined and pelleted to give the so-called maize by-product (maize germ meal) with the following average analysis:

Oil	Protein	Fibre	Starch
4.5%	17%	7%	35%

There is an enormous variation in the analyses of this by-product. Oil content can vary from 1.5 per cent to 12 per cent and protein content from 11 per cent to 28 per cent. This obviously depends on the source of the product and the processes from which it has been derived.

The analysis will, of course, also determine the value of the product and the uses to which it can be put.

Maize gluten feed

The by-product from the wet milling of maize to produce starch is maize gluten feed. This again is normally pelleted though the pellets tend to break up easily during transport and handling. A typical analysis is:

Oil	Protein	Fibre	Starch
2%	20%	7%	33%

Considerable variations can occur in analysis of maize gluten feed, though they are normally less variable than those for maize by-products. However, colour can vary enormously, and this can give problems in animal feed rations, particularly when used for egg production. The principal sources of maize based by-products are the United States, and South American countries such as Brazil and Argentina.

By-products from rice

The milling of paddy rice gives rise to large quantities of husk and germ. Dependent on the types of rice being produced and the process used, the amount of oil in the by-product can vary enormously from the negligible to 20 per cent. Protein and fibre contents can also vary significantly, from between 10 and 15 per cent for protein and 7 and 15 per cent for fibre. The by-product is known as rice bran and is usually pelleted. The areas of production are principally those in which rice is produced, such as India, Indonesia, Myanmar, Pakistan and the United States.

A problem with rice bran is the large amount of sand or silica that may be present. This usually varies between 3 per cent and 7 per cent and can limit the level of incorporation in animal feeds.

Malting, brewing and distilling by-products

The main by-product from malting, apart from screenings, is the so-called malt culms. These are the dried rootlets that are removed from the germinated grain after kilning. They contain around 24 per cent protein and are usually pelleted together with other malt polishings.

After malt has been mashed in a brewery and the starch converted to sugar and filtered off, the husks of the grain remain. Most breweries sell these in the wet state as brewers' spent grains. They contain little carbohydrate, some protein and a lot of fibre. However they are still slightly sweet and highly palatable to cattle. They can also be used for making silage.

Spent grains are sometimes dried. This is particularly common in distilleries where they are blended during the drying process with an evaporated concentrate known as pot ale syrup. This is produced by concentrating the residues left after distilling which contain quite a lot of dextrin and also degraded yeast. This syrup greatly increases the feeding value of the spent grains, which are then known as distillers' solubles.

CHAPTER 4

The role of brokers and merchants, corn exchanges and futures markets

THE BROKER

The roles of the broker and merchant are quite different. The broker trades on behalf of a buyer or seller, and when the transactions are complete the names of each are passed with the contracts to both parties. The broker takes no financial risk, the commission is usually fixed before negotiations start and is paid by the seller. Although the production of cereals has greatly increased recently, a number of brokers have gone out of business due to the methods of trading having changed. Farmers have rarely made use of brokers as they prefer to sell to merchants. End-users or manufacturers, who are today much more concerned about quality, prefer to buy first-hand grain direct from a merchant rather than a string through brokers.

The broker still serves a useful purpose, particularly when a buyer or seller wants to enter the market and conceal his identity. For example, a shipper short of grain who urgently wants to fill a boat does not want to telephone all round the market which would raise the market prices—he would use a broker or maybe two brokers to buy the quantity for him. The broker ferrets all round the market to find out who are buyers and who are sellers, and if possible puts the two together.

THE MERCHANT

The role of the grain merchant in the United Kingdom is probably the most important in the whole marketing process from the farmer to ultimate user. Except where farmers form co-operatives, the merchant is the farmer's customer, and is also in many cases the adviser the farmer relies on not only for marketing, but for seed, fertilisers and agrochemicals. In spite of the record quantity of cereals grown throughout the world, the number of merchants has decreased. In countries where the co-operatives took over the merchant was driven out. In recent times the merchant who is prepared to give personal service to both the farmer and end-user is coming back. The small country merchant will not return, but the large multinational companies are buying their way into the merchant's business.

A number of the international shippers and merchants are specialising in the export trade. Some of the millers and compound food manufacturers bought up merchant firms in order to cut out one intermediary, but the firms operated by some of these millers and manufacturers still prefer to buy from independent specialist merchants who control the quality from the farm gate. Also many farmers support the independent merchant who gives them personal service. The difference between the broker and merchant is that the broker relies on a commission and the merchant trades as a principal and relies on the difference between the price he pays for the grain and the price at which he can sell. He takes over the responsibility for the grain as soon as it leaves the farmer's gate and pays the farmer promptly. The merchant often carries the grain from the time that the farmer wants to sell to the time the buyer wants the grain. A merchant whose word and deed cease to be trusted soon goes out of business.

The importance of the merchant in other European countries has been replaced by the co-operative system and the multinational companies play a bigger part and brokers are more widely used.

The role of the merchant in countries where grain business is in the control of statutory boards, or in North America, is slightly different. The following account of the role of a Canadian grain dealer is taken from a lecture given by Dave Champion at a course run by the Canadian International Grains Institute.

A grain dealer is probably as close to the old-fashioned merchant as you are going to find, the only assets he has being an office with the usual office equipment and, of course, one or more telephones. This type of merchant, although common elsewhere in the world, is not at all common to western Canadian agriculture. The type of Canadian merchant discussed here is usually a division of large agribusiness. An excellent example is XCAN, the merchandising arm of the three prairie pools. Although the bulk of their business is marketing the pools' non-board grains, they will also merchandise Canadian Wheat Board grains and even other companies' non-board grains.

The grain business is probably the most highly regulated of Canada's major primary industries. Consequently, a Canadian merchant who is not part of a larger agribusiness finds it difficult to operate in this regulatory atmosphere. Grain dealers, if they are content to deal only in non-board grains and confine the bulk of their activities to North America, can get by with only a grain dealer's licence obtained from the Canadian Grain Commission. If they do not buy directly from a producer they do not need a grain dealer's licence at all. About 80 per cent of the cereals grown in western Canada are wheat, barley and oats, and the import or export of these three grains requires approval by The Canadian Wheat Board.

In practice these three grains, along with other cereals and oilseeds produced outside the Wheat Board's designated area, can be exported with little difficulty, just as corn and soyabeans can be brought into Canada with virtually no problem. Cereals grown within the designated area are subject to strict supervision. Within this area, any wheat, barley or oats to be exported is originally purchased from the Wheat Board. Without an export permit from the Wheat Board an ocean vessel cannot be loaded and a truck or railcar cannot leave Canada.

The Canadian Wheat Board, under the provisions of the Wheat Board Act, is entitled to deal with companies holding an agency agreement. At present there are only 22 of these agreements. Obviously, not everyone can obtain one. Besides sound finances, the company seeking an agreement must have an investment in capital goods which will be a benefit to Canada such as handling facilities or modes of transportation. Infrequently, an agency agreement can be given to a foreign-based firm with a history of favouring Canada. Some foreign-based companies who buy a lot of Board grains have been refused an agency agreement simply because a Canadian company would not be granted the same privilege in their country. The agency agreements are renewed annually, the Board having the right to cancel an agreement at a moment's notice. This does not mean a Canadian merchant without an agency agreement cannot sell export Board grain, but he cannot deal directly with the Board. Instead, he must deal through one of the 22 accredited exporters. This is an example of how the Canadian merchant differs from a foreign merchant.

In the non-Board area, it is also difficult for a foreign merchant to come to Canada and trade Canadian canola (rapeseed), flax or rye. First, he cannot deal with producers without a grain dealer's licence. Secondly, he must obtain railcar transportation from the Grain Transportation Agency. Thirdly, he must have an export facility to handle non-Board commodities. At one time a foreign merchant could buy futures, take delivery of the flax and rye at Thunder Bay or rapeseed in Vancouver, and compete effectively, but with recent changes in transportation policies he now finds that Canadian companies are better equipped to handle a foreign customer's needs. This is another example of how regulations have created a unique Canadian merchant.

From this point, a Canadian merchant is no different from any other merchant in the world. To survive he must make a profit. To make a profit he must correctly assess the market, which involves a phenomenal amount of information. In today's grain business a buyer can seldom participate in back-to-back trades, a form of trading in which seller and buyer meet to make a deal with the merchant making a profit.

Today's grain merchant can do a number of things. He can sell a cargo of grain to a buyer without owning it, in the hope that he can buy at a lower price before he must deliver to the buyer. Another alternative for the merchant is to buy a cargo of grain from the producers or Wheat Board without having it sold because he believes the price will go higher.

When taking these decisions, the merchant looks at the size of production in competing areas such as America, the EC, Australia, Argentina or Brazil. He also tries to assess demand by estimating how much China, Russia, India, Algeria, Brazil, etc. are going to need. Two of the most difficult considerations are weather and government activities. Embargoes such as that on exports of soya imposed on 4 January 1980 by Washington distorted prices incredibly to the benefit of Canada, but not to the benefit of those in the American grain business. If the Canadian merchant does a lot of exporting, he must decide whether to go long or short freight. Because commodities such as coal and sugar compete with grain vessels, a merchant must be aware of world trade in these items. In 1984–1985 the American auto industry's enormous imports of steel into the lakes caught some merchants long-freight. The scramble to unload surplus tonnage resulted in the lowest lake freight rates in many years.

Because most world trade is done in US dollars, the Canadian merchant must decide whether to be long of US dollars or pre-sell them. He must also determine in which direction interest rates are going because the cost of financing inventory has a direct influence on demand.

This interplay can mean that a buyer will be able to buy grain cheaper than it appears on the real market because the seller has made the right decisions and is prepared to discount his price in order to sell and retain a customer. Another possibility is that the seller is left holding a cargo which is costing him money and he wants to get rid of it. On the other hand, a merchant may offer a premium over the market to buy a cargo because he has made a good sale and wants to ensure he fulfils it. By and large, grain merchants make every attempt to honour any commitment they make as either a seller or buyer. Sometimes business is done solely because a merchant is long a vessel and wants to avoid paying for the vessel while loading nothing. He will then load grain on the ship and hope to earn enough money to pay at least part of the freight.

The Canadian Wheat Board can deal directly with sovereign states. There are, however, many sovereign states that would like to deal directly with the Board but cannot. The merchant can because he is willing to take risks where the Board will not. The merchant is freer to accept terms of trade that a crown corporation like the Board cannot. Sometimes the problem may be nothing more than a document requirement. Some countries, for example, will only buy specifications which are better than the minimum standards established by the

Canadian Grain Commission. For example, a buyer asks for lower moisture than the Canadian maximum of 14.5 per cent on wheat. The buyer may want higher or lower protein levels. Test weight minima may not meet a buyer's contract terms. In many of these cases the Wheat Board will not take this risk, but a merchant will. Sometimes the Wheat Board cannot sell to their usual direct customers because they do not have any grain in the position required, but the merchant who assumed a position previously can make the sale.

Although the roles of brokers and merchants in the rice trade are not dissimilar in principle to those of their colleagues in the grain trade, some general points need to be established at the outset since the trades are in certain respects dissimilar.

First, wheat and coarse grains are most usually traded in the form in which they are harvested—i.e. without the need for processing. Rice, on the other hand, is harvested as paddy but is not traded as such, since it goes through some stage of a milling process before it is sold. Hence rice is always traded through millers in the country of origin. This fact, and the absence of adequate futures markets, means that the trader has little possibility of hedging.

A further point to bear in mind is that the degree of risk attached to rice trading is substantially higher than trading in other grains. Much rice comes from developing countries and in 1998 93 per cent (350 million tons) of the crop was consumed in the country of origin, only 7 per cent (24 million tons) of the world crop entering world trade. Much of this 7 per cent moreover is sold to other developing countries as bagged cargo: this entails smaller cargoes, usually carried in older ships than the bulk carriers employed in the grain trade. This in itself entails some risk, with the consequence that some buyers and sellers are perforce not too reliable. A well-known grain trader was once heard to remark that from the risk viewpoint 10,000 tons of rice were the equivalent of 100,000 tons of wheat.

The basic philosophy of a rice broker resembles that of his counterpart handling grain transactions, and differs from that of a merchant inasmuch as the broker acts as an intermediary agent for both buyer and seller and never as a principal. The broker takes his reward for good service in the form of a commission whereas the merchant or trader works to obtain a profit for himself or his firm.

Since much rice trading takes place in countries with a different cultural tradition and different concepts of law from those held in Europe or the Americas the broker sometimes comes up against circumstances in which I have referred previously to some of the differences between grain trading and rice trading. The former is often carried out by a team of experts—but the latter is much more a matter of individual judgement. The profit of a transaction in rice therefore often turns entirely on the skill of one person. Since the risk is that much higher a successful rice trader in a grain company will be more highly paid than the grain traders, since it is the individual rather than a team which produces results. It is no accident that rice traders are frequently strong, if not colourful, characters. (No reflection on grain traders is intended!)

Rice grading is not an exact science, and there is no universal agreement on definitions of length of grain. This leaves scope for a clever trader to switch qualities by buying on one specification and selling on another. It is also possible to play on the question of what is meant by a broken grain. Again, as mentioned in a preceding chapter, there is a large and growing market for brokers, not only for brewing (Anhauser Busch buy in the region of 500,000 tons a year for beer-making) but also for human consumption. Some countries, notably Senegal, Mali and the Gambia, find brokers best for the dishes they prefer.

London has always been regarded as the centre of rice broking, for historical reasons stemming from the former imperial connection. The London Rice Brokers Association owes its existence to the high volume of produce marketed through London. Rice trading, on the other hand, tends to be concentrated through Paris and Geneva. One reason for this is that a trader needs good communications, enormous lines of credit, sophisticated banking and low taxation on profits. This also indicates the attraction of tax havens such as Panama as the registered office of a rice trading company: in fact, it would not be unusual to find a grain company acting for its own subsidiary located in a tax haven.

In the 1920s and 1930s the biggest trading firms were Steel Brothers and the East Asiatic Company. The French firm of Louis Dreyfus was the first of the grain trading companies to become involved with rice. More recent history, especially the revolution in Egypt in the 1950s, brought big changes to the pattern of rice trading and to the mobility of the personalities involved. Many talented Jewish traders left Egypt at that time, establishing themselves elsewhere in positions of influence in commodity trading. This was the route by which such notable personalities as Rafael Totah established the rice trading arms of Continental Grain, and others in the French firm Riz Denrées, which for many years were a dominant factor in world rice markets.

Rice trading is nothing if not a situation of fluctuating fortunes, and in recent years it has been Thailand that has dominated the export market for rice. Thai traders by their nature seem more prepared than other nationalities to accept risk and to deal in the large quantities which the market requires. In their expansion they have been helped by the general economic prosperity of Thailand, by the increase in property values, and by diversification. Their nature allows them to be quick at establishing which qualities the market requires, at blending qualities, and at delivering on specification.

Many Thai traders are admired for these characteristics, and appreciated for their reputation for honouring their commitments, even when the market turns against them.

CORN EXCHANGES AND FUTURES MARKETS

I have visited many corn exchanges (usually known as Grain Exchanges in North America) and futures markets in my capacity either as a government official or as a trade consultant, starting with Mark Lane and the Baltic Exchange in London, Diss in East Anglia, also exchanges in Continental Europe and North America, including Canada, while holding a Visiting Fellowship at the University of Minnesota. I admired the fine buildings in Antwerp, Hamburg and Barcelona, some of which were no longer used for the purpose for which they were built. The most vigorous, of course, were the American establishments, where the tempo of business is frenetic and the walls fully tapestried with electronic screens recording each deal and price change as it takes place. In Chicago the noise and ordered confusion is legendary; in Kansas the exchange is a fine new building with the latest electronic equipment; in Minneapolis the atmosphere is more seigneurial and the trading desks convey something of the spirit of a university library.

The Chicago Board of Trade, which is the world's largest commodity futures exchange, deals mainly in grains, soyabean and soyabean products: the Kansas City Board of Trade deals in grains and soya; the MidAmerica Commodities Exchange deals in corn, oats, wheat and soyabeans, mainly in small units of 1,000 bushels; the Minneapolis Grain Exchange is the world's largest cash grain market, also handling futures trading in spring wheat. The New Orleans Commodity Exchange handles rice. The Winnipeg Commodity Exchange provides futures and cash trading facilities for rapeseed, rye, flaxseed, domestic feed wheat, oats and barley, as well as futures trading facilities for gold, silver, etc. and options trading for gold.

It is difficult for a non-member of an exchange to grasp the complexities of these organisations, and for much of the detailed information which follows I am indebted to James Mackie, until recently Director General of GAFTA, to Peter Donnelly, former Managing Director of the London office of the Chicago Board of Trade, and to Gordon Wood, doyen of UK merchants and one of the members of the original committee which set up the London Grain Futures Market. Material on the Winnipeg Commodity Exchange comes from the Canadian International Grains Institute.

It is important to distinguish between corn exchanges, which handle cash transactions in physical goods and forward contracts, and futures exchanges, which grew up to deal in futures contracts, defined as legally binding commitments to deliver or take delivery of a given quantity and quality of a commodity at a price agreed upon in the trading pit or ring of a commodity exchange at the time the contract is executed.

Until early in the twentieth century a very large proportion of Europe's domestic grain was traded on corn exchanges. Some, of course, was sold ex-farm direct to millers and other users, and some, certainly since the development of large-scale production in Russia and in North America, was imported by sea through European ports, but corn exchanges in agricultural towns had established their importance as business centres. Many of the older towns in Europe (including England and Scotland) have as one of their fine buildings a corn exchange, but very few of these nowadays operate in the role for which they were built.

Trading in the United Kingdom in the nineteenth century was a relatively uncomplicated matter, at any rate after the repeal of the Corn Laws in 1846. There were few government regulations. There was little need to buy large quantities as forward supplies. Farmers could take the grain they did not want to use themselves to the nearest market town. It would probably be carried in large sacks and wagons. One sack could be dropped off at the town centre so that merchants could take samples and examine them. The farmers and merchants would meet in the exchange and a bargain would be struck. Originally, such contracts were oral and the dealers' word on the exchange was as good as their bond. This is still the case of many exchanges, including the Baltic Exchange.

As time went on, trade became much more complex, the number of varieties increased and so did their different uses. Users' requirements became more stringent, so written contract forms were drawn up, and eventually these became standard. This meant that when two traders or merchants agreed on a deal they would confirm it with a written contract. A typical example of standard contracts are those produced by The Grain and Feed Trade Association (GAFTA).

The decline of exchanges must really have started with the development of the rapid post and telephone. Merchants could trade without even seeing each other and details could be confirmed in writing. This did not happen overnight. There was a long twilight period in which traders still met on exchanges, often to exchange information about crop progress, the availability of goods and likely requirements. They would also examine samples with a view to possible purchases. The development of grading also gave more confidence to trading on description.

Very few exchanges still function regularly for physical goods, and these are in agricultural areas such as East Anglia. The London Corn Exchange, which operated for well over a century in Mark Lane, moved to the Baltic Exchange (see p. 62). In many Continental cities the exchanges are closely linked with the Chambers of Commerce. A good example of this is Hamburg, where the Chamber houses the Commodity Exchange, as well as the Stock Exchange. There are variations of the arrangement in other German cities. In most EU countries, Chambers of Commerce have "public law status", which means that all businesses have to be registered with and pay a fee to the appropriate Chamber. The strength of the Chambers is therefore likely to be maintained or enhanced.

There is still a need for personal contacts and informal meetings of traders from time to time. This need is partly met by trade dinners, conferences or "contact days", etc.

The most striking demonstration of the need for personal contact is probably the European Commodities Exchange Association whose annual trading days have become more and more popular as the years go by, in spite of the contraction which has been taking place in the number of people engaged in the grain and feed trade.

Another important forum for the exchange of information and views on the state of the world grain situation is to be found in the International Grain Marketing Conferences held annually in Brussels. Sponsored by Sosland Publishing Company of Kansas and Agra Europe (London) Ltd., these bring together the grain industry's leaders over two days. They are business-like and informative, and trade is often done in the corridors. They are multilingual, with simultaneous interpretation into English, French and German. Another conference of this type is held each year by AgraEurope in London, though all proceedings take place in English. Apart from these events the major trade associations—COCERAL, FEFAC, etc.—hold annual congresses for their members, as do national associations in their own countries. Many of these combine social activities with business.

FUTURES TRADING

The history of modern futures trading began on the Midwestern frontier in the early 1800s. It was tied closely to the development of commerce in Chicago and grain trade in the Midwest. Chicago's strategic location at the base of the Great Lakes, close to the fertile farmlands of the Midwest, contributed to the city's rapid growth and development as a grain terminal. Problems of supply and demand, transportation and storage, however, led to a chaotic marketing situation, which resulted in the logical development of futures markets.

As grain trade expanded, a centralised market-place—the Chicago Board of Trade—was formed in 1848 by 82 merchants. Their purpose was to promote commerce in the city by providing a place where buyers and sellers could meet to exchange commodities. What made the CBOT increasingly popular as a centralised market-place was the growing use of contracts "to arrive". These contracts allowed buyers and sellers of agricultural commodities to specify delivery of a particular commodity at a predetermined price and date.

These early forward contracts in corn were first used by river merchants who received corn from farmers in late fall and early winter. But the merchants had to store the corn until it reached a low enough moisture content to ship, and the river and canal were free of ice.

Seeking to reduce the price risk of storing corn through the winter, these river merchants would travel to Chicago, where they would enter into contracts with processors for delivery of grain at an agreed price in the spring. In this way, they assured themselves a buyer and a price for grain. The earliest recorded forward contract in corn was made on 13 March 1851 for 3,000 bushels of corn to be delivered in June.

Cash forward contracts did have their drawbacks. They were not standardised according to quality or delivery time, and merchants and traders often did not fulfill their forward commitments. In 1865, the Chicago Board of Trade took a step to formalise grain trading by developing standardised agreements called futures contracts. Futures contracts, in contrast to forward contracts, were standardised as to quality, quantity, and time and location of delivery for the commodity being traded. The only variable was price, discovered through an auction-like process on the trading floor of an organised exchange.

The CBOT issues an excellent booklet about options on agricultural futures called *An Ag-Lenders Guide to Risk Management.*

In 1881 a grain exchange was established at Winnipeg to serve western Canada's growing grain industry. However, it did not survive the bad crops which plagued the prairies during the mid-1880s. A second attempt at organising an exchange in 1883 also failed. Finally, on 24 November 1887 the Winnipeg Grain and Produce Exchange was successfully organised to provide trading in cash grains. It was incorporated in 1891.

Having a place to carry out cash grain trading did not entirely solve the early Canadian grain industry's marketing problems. The primary elevator companies which bought grain from producers at country points owned the grain until it was resold to mills for export. They risked losses if the price dropped between the time they bought grain from the producer and the time they eventually sold it. In the early days of the Canadian grain industry, they tried to prevent losses by selling futures contracts in the Minneapolis or Chicago markets. Thus, when they bought grain from producers, they immediately sold grain for future delivery on these US exchanges. In response to this need for price protection, the Exchange established a wheat futures market in 1903, followed by a similar market for oats and flax seed in 1904, barley in

1913, rye in 1917, and for rapeseed at Vancouver in 1963 and at Thunder Bay in 1970.

In 1908, the Exchange was re-organised to form the Winnipeg Grain Exchange, a voluntary association, and moved to the Grain Exchange Building. In 1980 the Exchange moved to the Commodity Exchange Tower, a change that enabled its information-handling facilities to be computerised.

Although the Exchange remains today as a self-regulating organisation, not directly subject to government supervision, government action has influenced its history. During 1917–1918, the government of Canada suspended wheat futures trading and fixed the price of wheat to control distribution of Canadian grain crops and gather wheat supplies for Canada's allies. Fearing poor demand for wheat in 1919, the government appointed a Wheat Board to sell the crop and guarantee prices to producers. In 1920, the Canadian government allowed the open market for wheat to be re-established and, by 1925, the Winnipeg Grain Exchange was the largest cash wheat market in the world. But ten years later, the federal government once again appointed a Wheat Board to sell wheat and to guarantee minimum prices for producers.

At first, the Wheat Board operated side by side with the open market and producers were permitted to deliver their wheat to the Board or sell it privately through grain trade facilities. In 1943, the government again closed the wheat futures market as a war measure and, in 1947, the Canadian Wheat Board Act was passed to continue emergency powers given to the Canadian Wheat Board (CWB) during war conditions in 1943. These powers were extended in 1949 to include oats and barley marketing.

Therefore, although there is no regulatory body which now has direct authority over the Exchange, many government policies and activities have an impact on trading. These include the Wheat Board's complete control of all grain by delivery quotas, its position as sole buyer of export wheat, oats and barley, and its control over the grain transportation system. However, the CWB relinquished responsibility for oats marketing to the private trade in 1989, and some commentators believe that its monopoly position for other Canadian grains will not survive much longer, especially after the establishment of the North American Free Trade Area (NAFTA).

The Canadian Grain Commission also affects trading on the Exchange because it regulates grades and controls grain quality. Established grades assist trading on an exchange. In any transaction the quality of the commodity is an important part of the terms of the contract. In many markets grain is sold on the basis of samples. However, Winnipeg Commodity Exchange traders have a ready reference for quality terms in the grain grades established by the Canadian Grain Commission. A buyer can be confident that a cargo of grain will be as described in its shipping documents.

In 1971, GAFTA took over responsibility for the grain futures market from the London Corn Trade Association and with this transfer the trading floor moved from Mark Lane to the former site of the Baltic Exchange, St. Mary Axe (now being re-developed following the IRA bomb blast in 1991). Trading under the auspices of the Baltic Futures Exchange, the grain market was then joined by other new or recently formed futures markets in potatoes (1980), soyameal (1984, though the contract had started in 1975) and BIFFEX (shipping freight) (1985). Potatoes and BIFFEX are still intact today but soyameal went the way of other later and unsuccessful contracts for pigs and lamb and was discontinued in 1993. During its time at the Baltic Exchange, a traded options market was also opened for wheat and barley contracts (1998), providing an additional hedging instrument for the grain sector.

At the beginning of 1991, the Baltic Futures Exchange merged with the London Futures & Options Exchange (FOX), and the trading floor plus the necessary regulatory and administrative support staff were re-located at Commodity Quay, St. Katharine Docks, under the auspices of the FOX. In 1993, London Fox reverted to its original trading name of London Commodity Exchange (LCE) and in 1996 merged with the London International Financial Futures & Options Exchange (LIFFE). Although LIFFE has a much larger trading complex at Cannon Bridge for its financial markets, the commodity floor still remains at Commodity Quay although full integration with the Cannon Bridge site is expected soon.

Over the last five years, the London wheat market has witnessed significant growth with futures volumes doubling and options turnover increasing five-fold (though from a much lower base) between 1993 and 1997. Three main reasons for this expansion can be ascribed to:

(i) the abolition of the EU feed wheat intervention system and monetary compensatory amounts (mca) in 1993 (as part of CAP reform);
(ii) increased usage of wheat in animal feed rations (at the expense of barley);
(iii) exposure to currency fluctuations and grain market volatility in the 1990s.

The movement towards the freeing-up of the grain market over this period, begun by CAP reform and continued by the Uruguay Round of GATT, has tempted other forays into wheat futures elsewhere in Europe.

The *Marché à Terme International de France* (MATIF) SA, under the Presidency of Gérard Pfauwadel, is located in Paris at 115 rue Réaumur, and is similar to LIFFE in that it deals in financial futures and trades commodities such as rapeseed and milling wheat. It is also closely involved with the preparations for Economic and Monetary Union (EMU) in the EU and the introduction of the euro as currency in a majority of the Member States in 1999.

A Commodity Futures Exchange also opened in Hanover in April 1998, and many international banks are also involved in grain trade finance, a prominent example being the Rotterdam house of Mees Pierson, founded in 1720 as a cashier and maritime insurance company. Adam Smith dedicated the fourth edition of his famous book, *The Wealth of Nations*, to one of the founders of this bank.

CHAPTER 5

International agreements

GRAINS TRADE CONVENTION

International agreements in the grains sector are basically of two kinds: bilateral and multilateral. Bilateral agreements are merely supply arrangements, whereby the exporting country assures itself of a firm customer for its grain over a period and the importing country safeguards its source of supply. It is difficult to obtain full details of these, governments of both exporting and importing countries having withdrawn from that type of activity. As an example of past practice however, Tables 5.1 and 5.2 show the Grain Supply Agreements between the United States and the USSR concluded up to March 1990. Multilateral agreements have the much more ambitious aim of bringing order and stability into worldwide exchanges of grain.

The history of multilateral agreements is to all intents and purposes the history of wheat agreements (an attempt was made a few years ago to look at a possible separate Coarse Grains Agreement, but the project proved too ambitious for the circumstances of the time). These go back some 50 years, and are still very relevant today.

The Grains Trade Convention 1995 and the Food Aid Convention 1995 are the latest in the series, negotiations having finished at the end of 1994 and the Agreements having entered into force on 1 July 1995. They consist of two separate legal instruments—the Grains Trade Convention (which now includes coarse grains) and the Food Aid Convention, both followed by the date 1995 to distinguish them from their predecessors. These new accords replaced the expiring International Wheat Agreement 1986 and its Wheat Trade and Food Aid components. International co-operation in grain trade and food aid was therefore secured for another three years—indeed, probably into the twenty-first century since the life of the conventions may be extended for further periods. In June 1998 it was agreed to extend both Conventions for one year, until 30 June 1999.

Reflecting its wider responsibilities under the new Grains Trade Convention, the International Wheat Council was renamed as the International Grains Council.

Table 5.1 Grain supply agreements between the United States and the USSR (million tons)

Year Oct./Sept.	Agreement minimum	US offer to sell	Actual sales			Main conditions
			Wheat	Maize (corn)	Total	
1976/7	6.0	8.0	3.1	3.0	6.1	First LTA.
1977/8	6.0	15.0	3.5	11.1	14.6	Minimum purchases 6 m. tons, equal amounts
1978/9	6.0	17.0	4.0	11.5	15.5	of wheat and maize (corn).
1979/80	6.0	25.0[a]	2.2	5.8	8.0	Maximum 8 m. tons without prior consultation
1980/1	6.0	14.0	3.8	5.7	9.6	with US authorities.
1981/2	6.0	23.0	6.1	7.8	13.9	Each year an extension of terms and conditions
1982/3	6.0	23.0	3.0	3.2	6.2	of first LTA.
1983/4	9.0	22.0	7.6	6.5	14.1	Second LTA.
1984/5	9.0	22.0	2.9	15.7	18.6	Minimum purchases 9 m. tons, including 4 m.
1985/6	9.0	22.0	0.2	6.8	7.0	each of wheat and maize (corn). Remainder
1986/7	9.0	(12.0)[b]	4.1	4.1	8.2[c]	either grain, or 0.5 m. tons soyabeans or
1987/8	9.0	(12.0)[b]	9.0	5.2	14.2[d]	soyameal.
						Maximum 12 m. tons without prior consultation
						with US authorities.
1988/9	9.0	(12.0)[b]	5.4	16.3	21.7	Each year an extension of terms and conditions
1989/90[e]	[g]	(12.0)[b]	2.8[f]	11.0[f]	13.8[f]	of second LTA.[h]

a. Offer withdrawn; authorisation only for LTA maximum of 8 m. tons.
b. Not specified.
c. The USSR also purchased 68,000 tons of soyabeans.
d. Also purchased: 0.83 m. tons of soyabeans and 1.3 m. tons of soyameal.
e. October 1989–December 1990.
f. As at 8 March 1990.
g. 9 m. tons increased *pro rata* for the 15-month period October 1989–December 1990.
h. The maximum which could be supplied without prior consultation in 1989/90 has been progressively increased to 24 m. tons.

Source: IWC.

Table 5.2 USSR: other known long-term agreements for grain and oilseeds in force as at 23 March 1990

Exporter[a]	Signed/ Announced	Supply period	Quantity
Argentina[b]	18 October 1986	Jan. 1986–Dec. 1990	4.0 m. tons of grain and 0.5 m. tons of soyabeans annually
Australia	15 February 1990	1990–2	2.0 m. tons of wheat over three years
Canada	2 October 1986	Aug. 1986–July 1991	Minimum 25 m. tons of wheat and feed grains over five years
Turkey	12 march 1985	1986–90	100,000 tons of grain in 1986, rising to 1.5 m. tons by 1990

a. France and Hungary also have signed trade protocols with the USSR which may cover wheat and maize (corn). Details of these arrangements are not available.
b. New agreement under negotiation.

Source: IWC.

The point of having a Grains Trade Convention is explained in the objectives set out in Article 1, which speak for themselves.

ARTICLE 1: Objectives

The objectives of this Convention are:

(a) to further international co-operation in all aspects of trade in grains, especially insofar as these affect the food grain situation;
(b) to promote the expansion of the international trade in grains, and to secure the freest possible flow of this trade, including the elimination of trade barriers and unfair and discriminatory practices, in the interest of all members, in particular developing members.
(c) to contribute to the fullest extent possible to the stability of the international grain markets in the interests of all members, to enhance world food security, and to contribute to the development of countries whose economies are heavily dependent on commercial sales of grain.
(d) to provide a forum for exchange of information and discussion of members' concerns regarding trade in grains.

As one would expect of an international treaty negotiated by some 50 parties, these objectives are carefully balanced and contain something for everyone; they are extremely convincing if read quickly, and conceal more than they reveal. Revelation is made easier by knowing something about the long history of wheat negotiations, and the past triumphs, near-successes and disasters. With the melt-down some years ago of the tin buffer-stock arrangements international commodity agreements nowadays require justification to a somewhat sceptical public if they are to be adjudged worth all the time and money spent on their preparation.

Why have a Grains Agreement at all? To answer this question one must go back to the economic climate of the 1930s, when the world economy was in an even greater mess that it is today, and the international grain economy was not immune from successive problems which seemed to take it to the verge of breakdown. The only way of preventing breakdown seemed to be by inter-governmental co-operation. The problems, briefly, were lack of equilibrium between supply and demand, large surplus stocks overhanging the market, and an increasing resort by governments to special measures to stimulate exports, while importing countries took protectionist measures. If this scenario sounds familiar, it is.

Some 40 international commodity agreements have been negotiated since the 1930s, most of the post-war ones (except for the International Grains Agreement 1967 and the present 1995 Agreement, and possibly some others—coffee, for instance) under the auspices of the United Nations Conference on Trade and Development (UNCTAD). Most of the 40 relate to successive agreements on three commodities—tin, wheat and sugar. At the time I joined the International Wheat Council in 1972 the wheat agreements had reached a watershed in their existence, though this fact was not fully recognised at the time. All the conventions up to and including the 1967 Wheat Trade Convention had contained economic provisions—that is to say, they had clauses which operated pricing or quantitative mechanisms which governments undertook to respect. The 1971 Convention contained no such provisions—not for want of trying, but simply because the long-drawn-out negotiations which preceded its signature failed to reach agreement on what these might be. No Wheat Convention since the 1967 one has contained economic provisions. They have offered other attractions, otherwise nobody would have bothered to sign them, but regulatory mechanisms were not among them.

The first Wheat Agreement signed in 1933 established a system of export quotas and stockholding objectives, and also set up a Wheat Advisory Committee which served as a focus for discussions and consultation until it was superseded by the International Wheat Council, established, surprising as it may seem, in the middle of World War II, in 1942. This laid the foundation for what is generally regarded as the most successful of all the Wheat Conventions, that of 1949. In the spirit of post-war reconstruction and confidence, the first Article of this Agreement stated forthrightly: "the objectives of this Agreement are to assure supplies of wheat to importing countries and markets for wheat to exporting countries at equitable and stable prices". As a definition of the purpose of a commodity agreement this could hardly be improved upon, not even by the much longer-winded statement in the current Convention referred to at the beginning of this chapter. But then the 1949 Agreement was negotiated between 28 countries; the 1986 Agreement between 48. (The 1933 Agreement was signed by four exporting countries and 18 importing countries.)

The 1933 Agreement failed because bumper crops in Argentina put that country under too much pressure for it to remain able to respect its export quota. Learning from that experience, the 1949 Agreement did not attempt to limit production or exports, but took as its basic concept a sort of multilateral sale and purchase contract, that is to say, it established a maximum price and a minimum price at which exporting countries undertook to make available specific quantities of wheat each year and at which importing countries undertook to purchase specified amounts. Between these prices members were free to do what they wished. Of course, it was necessary to express these maximum and minimum prices in terms of a specified wheat, and to work out equivalent prices for other wheats traded on the international market, taking into account quality differences and transportation costs. This "working out" was not done in the text of the Agreement, but by the Secretariat each week using the latest freight rate information.

Establishing coefficients of equivalence for quality was a highly technical exercise which could not have been attempted without the advice of experienced members of the grain trade. That it was successfully accomplished, and that the same principles were retained in the succeeding Agreements of 1953 and 1956, says much for the expertise deployed in this work, particularly as the climate of grain trading changed from one of shortage and low stocks in 1945 to one of surplus and large stocks, at least in Canada and the United States, then the two principal exporting nations and the only ones to hold substantial stocks which could be carried over from the end of one season to the beginning of the next.

The 1949 Agreement turned out in practice to do very much what it said it would do—namely, stabilise world prices within a fairly narrow range. To a newly arrived trader on the present scene it must seem astonishing to reflect that between 1954–1955 and 1968–1969 the price of US No. 2 Hard Red Winter Wheat, fob Gulf ports, remained at prices between $58 and $66 a ton—that is to say, a range of $8 a ton over 14 years. This was accomplished under the successors to the 1949 Agreement, namely, those of 1953, 1956 and 1962. These arrangements only applied, of course, for the benefit of countries which were members of the Wheat Council and had undertaken to observe the terms of the Agreements. Two-thirds of world trade in wheat was covered by these arrangements. Non-member countries had to pay more for their wheat, at any rate up to the mid-1950s, after which there was no difference between IWA and non-IWA prices, but they could not always be certain of their supplies: the exporters, it is true, suffered the disadvantage of forgoing the higher prices they could have obtained on the open market for a proportion of their grain, but enjoyed the certainty of a given minimum return and were spared the fear of a sudden collapse in prices as had occurred in past history. One must here mention the willingness of the US and Canadian authorities to keep their stocks off the market in support of the price provisions of the IWA. Such behaviour, which shows a commendable sense of international solidarity, would now be seen by few in those governments as an acceptable price to pay for market stability.

Why then did the 1949 Agreement and its lineal descendants not survive until this day? Partly because the United Kingdom, then the largest single importer of wheat in the world, thought that the maximum price was pitched too high, and decided to withdraw. The United Kingdom left the Agreement in 1953 at the expiry of the 1949 Agreement and did not rejoin until 1959. As a consequence the proportion of world trade covered by the agreement declined, and with it its effectiveness. A perhaps greater reason was the complexity of the market, as developing countries became buyers and other exporters such as France started to take an increasing share of trade. Market priced became much less "visible", as deals were done by state-trading bodies. By the late 1960s it became apparent that the "1949-type" agreements could no longer cope with changed market conditions.

At this time it was customary to renew negotiations on the wheat agreement every three years, and when the time came to renegotiate in 1959 a rather more complicated but less rigid system was adopted. Instead of being committed to make guaranteed purchases from exporters, each importing member undertook to purchase from exporting members in each crop year (at prices within the price range) not less than a specified percentage of its total commercial purchases in that year. This made the agreement slightly more flexible from the importers' point of view. Exporting members undertook, for their part, to supply the commercial requirements of importing members at prices within the price range. If the maximum price level was reached, however, this obligation ceased to be absolute, and only applied to a certain "datum quantity" (based on average past purchases over a period). Thus in turn the exporters were given some flexibility.

About this time the Secretariat of the Council was given an additional new task, which was to prove immensely significant for the direction of its future activities. Hitherto mainly responsible for monitoring members' compliance with the terms of the agreements, the Council was now charged with the task of conducting an annual review of the world wheat situation, as a guide to governments in formulating their national agricultural policies. This was the start of the market analysis activity which is now the most valuable part of the Council's work.

Having been renewed again in 1962 the Agreement then had to stand up to the first price shock on a world scale, of the kind with which we have regrettably become all too familiar in recent years. I refer to the first significant Soviet harvest failure, in 1963–1964, when the absence of snow cover in the Ukraine resulted in substantial winter-kill of the Russian wheat crop. Khrushchev's government reluctantly embarked on large-scale purchases on the world market (this marked the transition of the Soviet Union from an exporting to an importing country), world trade in wheat increased to record levels and stocks dropped dramatically. However, stocks were at that time sufficiently large to take such developments in their stride, as did the Agreement itself.

It was at this time that the creation of the European Economic Community began to have far-reaching effects on world agricultural trade. The creation of the Common Agricultural Policy in the 1960s coincided with the GATT Kennedy Round of trade negotiations, and it became clear that a new wheat agreement must await conclusion of this. In fact, the Kennedy Round cereal negotiations were not concluded until May 1967, but when they did it was with the adoption of a Memorandum of Agreement laying down the basic elements of an international grains arrangement (which was for the first time to cover food aid as well as grain trade). The International Grains Agreement 1967 resulted, consisting of two separate instruments linked by a common Preamble—namely, a Wheat Trade Convention and a Food Aid Convention.

Apart from certain refinements, and the substitution of US Hard Red Winter Ordinary No. 2 fob Gulf ports in place of No. 1 Manitoba Northern in-store Fort William as the reference wheat, the 1967 Convention was not basically different from its predecessors. It tried to set out prices for different wheats, thus freezing quality differentials. Also, the price ranges were raised in the (misplaced) hope that markets, which had temporarily risen in the mid-1960s after monsoon failures in South Asia, were going to remain tight in the long term. Nonetheless, it did not survive long. Grain prices started to fall sharply as a result of abundant supplies coupled with a drop in demand, and export prices dropped below the prescribed minima. The exporting countries banded together in the first of many unsuccessful attempts to take concerted action, but without success, inhibited as they were by the circumstance that the Agreement sprang from the GATT negotiations and any modification to its terms could have an unpredictable chain reaction. Negotiations and any modification to its terms broke down for all practical purposes in 1969, when exporters found themselves unable to continue trading at minimum price levels and were obliged to abandon them. It is very difficult to establish which exporter broke the minimum first, as the calculations depend on estimated freight rates. Some US export prices started to fall before the end of July that year: Australian and Canadian ones followed suit in August, and by September practically all grades were below their respective IGA minima.

As mentioned earlier on in this account, the 1971 Conference failed in its attempt to establish a new convention with economic provisions and the Agreement eventually signed provided for little more than an exchange of information, together with a conviction among members that a forum must be preserved against the time when it might again be possible to undertake a successful negotiation. From this time dates the establishment of the Committee on Market Conditions, which meets twice a year. The IGC Secretariat publishes monthly Grain Market Reports, highly valued by governments and traders, and always well reported by Reuters. Shortly after this began that series of upheavals consequent on successive Soviet crop failures, which started with what became known in journalistic circles as the great American grain robbery of 1972. Wheat export prices, aided by speculative pressure, doubled in a matter of months and tripled in the course of two years. There were special factors—including an abundance of oil money after 1973 seeking profitable uses—and it has to be said that I cannot recall any other time during the last 25 years when speculation became a major factor in world grain markets. To describe the subsequent transformation of grain surplus into a grain shortage as creating near-panic among certain official circles would be an understatement. One only has to look back on the statements of that time issued by UN and FAO representatives to see how seriously the crisis was regarded. In the assessment of the world food situation prepared by the World Food Conference urgently convened in 1974 it was stated that "stocks declined abruptly to dangerously low levels. The wheat stocks of the main exporting countries fell by almost 20 million tons or 40 per cent in 1972/3, so that already by mid-1973 they were at the lowest level for 20 years, during which time the world's population had grown by about half".

In consequence a Preparatory Group of the International Wheat Council was instructed to examine "the feasibility of establishing grain resources to be located at strategic points". These discussions began to evolve recommendations for specific action, and soon became an integral part of a proposed negotiation for a new Wheat Agreement. A conference was convened in Geneva under UNCTAD auspices, and met amid high hopes of translating the recommendations into action. The idea was to have a system of nationally held reserve stocks, the accumulation and release of which would be internationally co-ordinated. The Conference Chairman was Arthur Dunkel of Switzerland (subsequently Director

General of GATT), who worked tirelessly to achieve the desired results: I led the UK delegation and was elected Chairman of the Administrative Committee of the Conference, charged with the task of drawing up an agreed text. In consequence I had a ring-side view of proceedings. We came very near to success. It eluded us on three issues: (1) the trigger price for activating stock measures; (2) the precise level of individual member states' stockpiles; and (3) certain special measures to help developing countries (which was as usual a wrangle over money). A breakthrough on any one of these points could have proved decisive. But it was not to be, and we had to disperse. A special committee was established to address these outstanding questions, but the momentum had been lost, and the committee was forced to look for alternative ways forward. Eventually, the idea of stockholding or any other economic measures was abandoned (at least temporarily—the objective of negotiating such provisions eventually was retained in the 1986 Convention), and it was decided that the Council should concentrate on what it was best at—namely, market analysis, long-term forecasting and, most important of all, serving as a centre of information and a meeting place where those leaders whose task it was to seek to influence grain policy could do so in knowledge of each other's views and in possession of comprehensive and up-to-date information, in the hope of avoiding calamities of the kind which had occurred in the past.

Thus was established the 1986 Convention, together with a new Food Aid Convention. An important new development was that the definition of "grain" in the Convention was extended to mean "wheat, wheat flour, rye, barley, oats, maize, millet and sorghum, and such other grains and products as the Council may decide". This integration had seemed to many of us long overdue, in view of the increasing "substitutability" of the different grains, and brought together in one place work hitherto performed somewhat intermittently by the InterGovernmental Grains Group of the FAO.

If I have seemed rather more positive about the work of the International Wheat Council than some, including even the UNCTAD Secretariat in its study of the progress of its Integrated Programme for Commodities prepared in June 1985, it is because I am a firm believer in the value of international discussion and co-operation as an alternative to confrontation and hasty action on the basis often of ill-informed advice. The Grains Council cannot achieve the impossible: it is not realistic to work for tightly defined economic provisions in an Agreement without the certainty of backing by the major exporters and importers, and the philosophy of recent US Administrations in particular had run in the direction of freedom from institutional control. But as Churchill is often quoted as remarking, "jaw-jaw" is preferable to "war-war". He was not thinking of commodity trading, but he might well have been. It is the mark of great men to enunciate general principles which turn out to be of universal validity even in unexpected particular cases.

It is interesting to look at the parties to the 1986 Agreement, together with the numbers of votes allocated to them on the basis of their then trade in wheat. Some parties are shown as both exporters and importers, as, for example, the EC, while the Soviet Union continued to maintain its status among the exporting members notwithstanding the fact that at that time it had become the world's largest importer.

The current Grains Trade Convention 1995 (GTC) is designed to further grain market stability and world food security by making available accurate, comprehensive and timely information to market participants, and by providing a forum where governments may discuss their concerns and engage in formal and informal consultations. The negotiators took account of the implications of the Uruguay Round negotiations in the GATT, completed at the end of 1993, while the text incorporates various improvements to the Council and Committee procedures.

The GTC gives scope for the further expansion and refinement of the Council's statistical and market information services. The role of the Market Conditions Committee—now open to all members of the council—has been enhanced. As well as its regular discussions of grain market conditions and prospects, ad hoc committee meetings will be held for in-depth consideration of particular issues. Through this, and other activities, notably the annual World Grain Conferences organised by the Council, contacts will be fostered between government officials, producers, traders and others concerned with the grain industry.

The initial membership of the Convention on signature in 1995 was as follows: Algeria, Argentina, Australia, Canada, Côte d'Ivoire, Cuba, Egypt (Arab Republic), European Community, Hungary, India, Iraq, Japan, Jordan, Korea (Republic of), Mauritius, Morocco, Norway, Pakistan, Panama, Russian Federation, South Africa, Switzerland, Tunisia, Turkey, United States of America and Vatican City.

Up to September 1997 a further seven countries had acceded, namely: Bolivia, Ecuador, Kazakhstan, Kenya, Malta, Saudi Arabia and Yemen (Republic of). In June 1998 Ukraine became a member.

FOOD AID CONVENTION

A word must be said here about the Food Aid Convention, though this is a book about trade, not aid. (Purists distinguish between the two, though in practice the frontier is a little blurred.) Food Aid Conventions had their origin in the Kennedy Round of the GATT negotiations, and the first one was concluded in 1967, coming into force in 1968, and ran for three years. It comprised 18 donor members, and their annual commitments totalled 4.5 million tons.

The United Kingdom was a founder member of the 1967 Convention with an annual obligation of 225,000 tons. It did not join the 1971 Food Aid Convention (nor did Denmark or Norway), the reason being that as it was a deficit country for wheat it seemed inappropriate, and also because the view was firmly held that the best form of aid to developing countries was to show them how to grow food for themselves—in other words, through extension services and technical assistance. However, the United Kingdom came back, with Denmark, on accession to the EC in 1973, while Norway rejoined in 1980. Membership of the Food Aid Convention was obligatory for those States acceding to the Treaty of Rome.

The 1986 Food Aid Convention included 12 donor members (the EC's 12 Member States being counted as one), with a total annual commitment of 7.5 million tons. The World Food Conference target was "at least 10 million tons", and in practice the FAC members not only donated more than their commitment from the outset of the 1986 Convention but even exceeded the World Food Conference target, reaching a peak figure of over 13 million tons in 1987–1988. Since then, however, shipments have halved.

The basic principles of the Food Aid Convention 1995 (FAC) are the same as those of its predecessor, namely to secure a guaranteed annual supply of grains suitable for human consumption for the benefit of developing countries, especially low-income countries. Financial pressures on donor governments obliged some to reduce their commitments: the combined total of their minimum annual contributions (in wheat equivalent) is now 5.35 million tons compared with 7.52 million previously. As before, however, it is expected that many donors will be able to ship more than the specified minima, and the objective—to supply 10 million tons of food aid to developing countries, through a joint effort by the international community—remains unchanged.

Contributions are to be supplied to the maximum extent possible as gifts of grains or grants of cash. Aid may be provided bilaterally, but members are urged to direct a greater proportion through multilateral channels, in particular the World Food Programme. Pulses (i.e., grain legumes) have been added to the admissible list of grains under the FAC. Cash contributions provided by some donors are to be used, as far as possible, to buy grain from developing countries, with first priority to developing members of the Convention. The new FAC states with greater clarity how contributions of grains, products and cash are to be evaluated in terms of their wheat equivalents. In the case of rice, a flexible formula has been introduced to take account of changing export price relationships between rice and wheat.

Precision has been given to the term "developing countries" by making specific reference to the categories of developing countries and territories recognised by the Development Assistance Committee of OECD. In supplying aid, donors are to give priority to countries and territories classified as least developed countries, other low-income countries, and lower-middle income countries.

To facilitate the accession to the FAC of new donors, the basic minimum annual food aid contribution of an acceding country (previously unspecified) has been set at 20,000 tons, and its contributions may be phased in over the first three years of membership.

The initial membership of the Convention and their respective minimum annual contributions in tons (wheat equivalent) are as follows: Argentina (35,000), Australia (300,000), Canada (400,000), European Community and its Member States (1,755,000), Japan (300,000), Norway (20,000), Switzerland (40,000), United States of America (2,500,000). A full list of the Membership of the Council and Food Aid Convention is shown in Table 5.3.

Table 5.3 Membership of the International Grains Council and Food Aid Convention

MEMBERSHIP, INTERNATIONAL GRAINS AGREEMENT, 1995

- **Grains Trade Convention, 1995 (GTC)**
- **Food Aid Convention, 1995 (FAC)**

All parties to the GTC are members of the International Grains Council (IGC) and of its Market Conditions Committee (MCC).

Membership of either Convention is provisional until the government has deposited its instrument of ratification or accession.

	Status* under GTC	IGC Executive Committee	FAC Food Aid Committee
Algeria	I	X	
Argentina	E	X	X
Australia	E	X	X
Bolivia	I		
Canada	E	X	X
Côte d'Ivoire	I		
Cuba	I	X	
Ecuador	I		
Egypt (Arab Rep)	I	X	
EC	E	X	X
15 Member States**			X
Hungary	E	X	
India	I		
Iraq	I		
Japan	I	X	X
Jordan	I		

Table 5.3 Membership of the International Grains Council and Food Aid Convention—*cont.*

	Status* under GTC	IGC Executive Committee	FAC Food Aid Committee
Kazakhstan	E		
Kenya	I		
Korea (Rep of)	I	X	
Malta	I		
Mauritius	I		
Morocco	I		
Norway	I		X
Pakistan	I		
Panama	I		
Russian Federation	I	X	
Saudi Arabia	E		
South Africa	I	X	
Switzerland	I	X	X
Tunisia	I		
Turkey	E		
USA	E	X	X
Vatican City	I		
Yemen (Rep of)	I		

* Under GTC Art. 12: E—exporting member; I—importing member
** Austria, Belgium, Denmark, Finland, France, Germany, Greece, Ireland, Italy, Luxembourg, Netherlands, Portugal, Spain, Sweden, United Kingdom

Source: IGC.

CHAPTER 6

The influence of the WTO on global grain trade

The World Trade Organisation (WTO) was born on 1 January 1995 as the successor organisation to the General Agreement on Tariffs and Trade (GATT), whose offices and establishment in Geneva it took over. The process was a metamorphosis, not a revolution. The same staff remained in place, including the GATT Director General who stayed as caretaker of WTO until a full-time successor, Renato Ruggiero, could be found. Until then GATT was to many people little more than a mystifying acronym—what did it mean?

A little history. The General Agreement was signed in Torquay in 1947 as part of the post-World War II rush to set up international bodies to regulate peace and war, finance and money supply, agriculture, labour, health, telecommunications, etc. Most of this was done as part of the United Nations Organisation. But GATT, which regulated international trade, was exceptionally and almost accidentally never a UN body, though it worked closely with the UN Conference on Trade and Development (UNCTAD).

GATT started with 23 members, the "Uruguay Round" (1987–1994) involved 120 countries, and in February 1996 the WTO had 119 members with another 39 countries as observers, of which 28 (including China and the Russian Federation) are currently negotiating accession.

The basic aims of GATT and its successor are to liberalise world trade and thus contribute to economic growth and development. It is the only international treaty which lays down rules for world trade.

It is probably best known for its successive rounds of multilateral trade negotiations (seven to date), designed to reduce tariffs and other trade barriers. The famous ones were the last four—the "Dillon Round" in 1960–1961, the "Kennedy Round" in 1964–1967, the "Tokyo Round" in 1973–1979, and the Uruguay Round recently finished. The Kennedy and Dillon Rounds each resulted in a cut of 34 per cent in duty collected by the world's customs authorities; in the Tokyo Round trade affected by tariff reductions and bindings was valued at US$155 billion.

The Tokyo Round, besides being plagued by bigger and better problems, such as the world's energy crisis, than any of its predecessors, took longer to conclude and was extremely ambitious. Its seven negotiating groups reached agreements on the following: differential treatment for developing countries; use of trade measures for balance-of-payment purposes; safeguard action for development purposes; understanding on dispute settlement and surveillance; subsidies and countervailing duties; technical barriers to trade; import licensing procedures; government procurement; customs valuation; revised anti-dumping code; also two important agricultural agreements—namely the Arrangement regarding Bovine Meat, and the International Dairy Arrangement.

When the EC was set up in 1957 the establishment of the common external tariff and the system of variable levies on agricultural commodities had to be paid for in the form of concessions in other directions to the trading partners of the original six.

These were successfully resolved in Article XXIV negotiations in GATT and the Dillon and Kennedy Rounds. The Americans and Canadians, like the rest of the world, accepted the EC system of import levies and export refunds on cereals, and as part of the *quid pro quo* for this the Community accepted a binding of the tariffs on imports of certain cereals products and raw materials, coming, for example, under tariff heading 07.06 (manioc, bound at 6 per cent); and headings 23.03, 23.06 and 23.07 (maize gluten feed, citrus pulp, etc. bound at zero). It should be noted, however, that tariffs on certain other cereals products were not bound in these negotiations, including tariff heading 23.02 which covers brans, sharps and other residues, and tariff heading I104 which covers manioc flour among other items.

Tariffs under headings such as these, therefore, can be (and in the case of brans already have been) changed without reference to GATT.

Article XIX of the General Agreement permits a member country to impose import restrictions or to suspend past tariff concessions on products which are being imported in such increased quantities and under such conditions that they cause or threaten to cause serious injury to competing domestic producers. Needless to say, the application of measures under this Article is a hotly debated issue. Revision of the safeguard system was one of the matters the Tokyo Round failed to resolve. It was left to a GATT Committee to continue to study the matter. Meanwhile, member countries can place a fairly wide interpretation on Article XIX, sometimes referred to as the safeguard clause.

On matters concerning the EC as a whole, the Commission has competence to negotiate on behalf of the Member States. The EC Delegation has in the past been led by a Director-General or a Commissioner, either for Agriculture or for External Affairs.

The Commission negotiating brief will have been cleared beforehand in discussion with representatives of Member States through the Article 113 Committee (so-called because it holds responsibility for matters covered by Article 113 of the Treaty of Rome) and the Committee of Permanent Representatives (COREPER), composed of the Ambassadors of the Member States to the European Communities. The negotiating brief receives final clearance from the Council of Ministers in Brussels. As may be imagined, preparation and clearance of the negotiating brief is a process almost as dramatic and important to the individual Member States as the actual GATT negotiations themselves.

The General Agreement has 38 Articles. They are briefly described below:

Part One

Article I is the key article guaranteeing most-favoured-nation treatment among all members.

Article II provides for the actual tariff reductions agreed to under GATT: they are listed in annexed Schedules and thus consolidated (i.e. form part of the Agreement itself).

Part Two

The General Agreement is applied "provisionally". Each member is required to apply the rules in Part Two "to the fullest extent not inconsistent with" its own legislation existing when it joined GATT. Article III prohibits internal taxes that discriminate against imports. Articles IV (cinematograph films), V (freedom of transit), VI (anti-dumping and countervailing duties), VII (customs valuation), VIII (fees and formalities), IX (marks of origin) and X (trade regulations) are the "technical Articles", designed to prevent or control possible substitutes for tariffs.

Articles XI–XIV deal with quantitative restrictions: XII specifies how they may be used for balance-of-payments reasons; XIII requires that they be used without discrimination, apart from exceptions specified in XIV (see also Article XVIII).

Article XV concerns GATT co-operation with the International Monetary Fund.

Article XVI calls for elimination of export subsidies.

Article XVII requires state-trading enterprises not to discriminate in their foreign trade.

Article XVIII recognises that developing countries may need tariff flexibility, and to be able to apply some quantitative restrictions to conserve foreign exchange.

Article XIX prescribes when emergency action can be taken against imports injuring domestic producers.

Articles XX and XXI specify respectively general and security exceptions to the Agreement (e.g. to protect public health).

Article XXII deals with consultations, and XXIII with the settlement of disputes.

Part Three

Article XXIV regulates how customs unions and free-trade areas may constitute exceptions to the most-favoured-nation rule.

Article XXV provides for action by the member governments: it is under this Article that waivers are granted.

Articles XXVI to XXXV are rules about the operation of GATT itself. They deal with its acceptance and entry into force (XXVI), withdrawal of tariff concessions from former members (XXVII), rules for tariff negotiations and changes in tariff schedules (XXVIII), the relationship between GATT and the stillborn Havana Charter (XXIX), amendment of the Agreement (XXX), withdrawal from GATT (XXXI), the definition of "contracting parties" (members) (XXXII), accession to GATT (XXXIII), the annexes to the Agreement (XXXIV), and non-application of the GATT rules between particular members (XXXV).

Part Four

Articles XXXVII and XXXVIII, added in 1965, concern the special needs of the developing countries. Article XXXVI sets out GATT's principles and objectives in meeting these needs. Article XXXVII states commitments which members undertake to this end, and Article XXXVIII provides for joint action by them.

THE URUGUAY ROUND

The latest round of GATT talks, called the Uruguay Round (since it was initiated at the GATT council meeting held in Punta del Este, Uruguay, from 15 to 20 September 1986), was the first in which agriculture had been accorded an equal status to the other main subjects.

While agriculture had a uniquely important role in the Uruguay Round, it did have a part to play in earlier GATT negotiations, particularly the Kennedy Round, when the GATT Memorandum of Agreement between the negotiating countries led directly to the International Grains Arrangement 1967. Agriculture had usually been sidestepped in the previous rounds because it was felt to be too contentious and too difficult, and might prejudice the success of the negotiations as a whole. This sober assessment appeared at times to be only too true as applied to the Uruguay Round.

The objectives of the negotiation relating to agriculture were laid down in the Ministerial Declaration broadly as follows: improved market access through the reduction of import barriers; increased discipline on the use of all direct and indirect subsidies; minimising the adverse effects of sanitary and phytosanitary regulations and barriers. The overall aim was stated as the achievement of greater liberalisation of trade in agriculture and bringing all measures affecting import access and export competition under strengthened and more operationally effective GATT rules and disciplines.

The opening US position was a demand for the ending of all subsidies on agriculture within 10 years. The EC response was to propose that existing policies should be adapted to reduce protectionist measures, and that there should be a long-term commitment to stabilising world agricultural markets and a "rebalancing" of trade, which would involve a review of all members' support measures. While reducing total protection, this could allow new protectionist policies for certain commodities (e.g. oilseeds, corn gluten feed, etc.) with the object of bringing the world trading environment into equilibrium. Other countries (e.g. Japan, Korea) put forward their proposals, and some 14 countries with substantial agricultural interests, who banded themselves into a body known as the Cairns Group (because the leading spirit was Australia), broadly backed the American position. The discussion was illuminated by illustrations of Producer Subsidy Equivalent (PSE) and Consumer Subsidy Equivalent (CSE), designed by each side to show who were the worst offenders in terms of protection. The United States subsequently suggested converting non-tariff import barriers (e.g. variable levies) into visible tariffs. These positions were sufficiently far apart to prevent any real progress from being made in the first years of negotiation.

In October 1990 the United States modified its stance to propose a 75 per cent reduction in internal support (from a base period 1986–1988), and a 90 per cent reduction in export refunds. The Cairns Group offered the same, but Canada submitted a separate proposal for a 50 per cent reduction (instead of 75 per cent) in internal support. To this the EC in November 1990 (after seven meetings of farm and trade ministers) proposed a 30 per cent reduction in internal support (over the period 1986–1995), coupled with tariffication of variable levies and a similar reduction of the tariffs to that on internal support—but maintained the requirement for "rebalancing" and offered no specific commitment to reduce export subsidies. An interesting encounter between the two main protagonists (affectionately known as the "elephants") took place at the Sixth International Grain Market Conference in October 1990. (See the next chapter for a description of the importance of these annual conferences.) This took the form of a teleconference held simultaneously in Brussels and Washington with a hook-up by satellite TV—the first time such an ambitious event had been staged. This enabled the leaders of the two sides to put their respective points of view in front of an informed and influential audience instead of arguing across the table in the privacy of a committee room. It was not expected to advance the progress of negotiations—open agreements openly arrived at is a self-defeating concept—but it did make clear where each side stood.

Ray MacSharry for the EC declared that he was not prepared to put at risk the livelihood of the average EC farmer, of whom there were 11 million, compared with only two million in the United States. To this Clayton Yeutter for the United States riposted that he had no desire to ruin 11 million farmers, and that the EC could support them in any way it liked so long as this support did not have trade-distorting effects. In political terms this is the nub of the argument. Jean-Marc Lucq, at that time Director of Agriculture for GATT in Geneva, said that agriculture accounted for 8 per cent of world trade and was a very important part of the Uruguay Round. Negotiations turned on three points: (1) domestic programmes; (2) export subsidies; (3) access to markets.

At present farmers were no better off after vast government expenditure: GATT wished to see less money spent on preserving the past and more on the present and future. They wanted a simplification of the obstacles to trade. The most difficult problem lay in the export subsidies, which were having a bad effect on many developing countries. On the question of what would constitute a successful negotiation, Lucq said that we had to end up with a substantial reduction in agricultural support. Dan Amstutz, for the United States, said that the negotiations could be counted successful if they marked the beginning of the end of agricultural subsidies.

The WTO is now four years old. According to a recent interview given by Ruggiero, it is "now working quite well". How has its creation influenced agricultural trade, particularly in grain? "Too early to say", is probably the answer of most traders. But to those at the sharp end of intergovernmental wrangling the distinction between WTO and GATT seems very marked, and to pose many problems which will impact on trade.

The agricultural provisions of the Uruguay Round are embodied in what is known as the Agreement on Agriculture. To quote a Commission official "the post-Uruguay Round trading environment is a whole new world and neither legislating for it nor operating in it is easy".

The fundamental difference as far as the EU protective system is concerned is the move from variable import levies to a regime of fixed tariffs. According to a Geneva source, "among the most important results of the Round is that trade in agriculture under the WTO is now subject to a tariffs-only regime and that legally binding commitments have been undertaken on market access which, taken together and given effective implementation, will substantially improve conditions of competition and opportunities for trade". Can merchants seize these opportunities?

A concomitant of the tariffs-only regime is a temptation by governments to turn to more use of non-tariff barriers (e.g. taking refuge behind sanitary and phyto-sanitary regulations), which were conditionally permitted under GATT Article XI:2(c) but are now forbidden under Article 21 of the Agreement on Agriculture.

Other well-publicised provisions of the GATT Uruguay Round include limitations on subsidised exports and limitations on the subsidisation of domestic support. The latter is based on the Aggregate Measurement of Support (AMS), and exemptions from limitation are available to such picturesquely named categories as Green Box, Blue Box and Amber Box. Into these boxes fall non-trade-distorting support payments, decoupled from production, and as such mainly of consequence to farmers rather than traders.

First, tariffication of imports. The EU variable levy has been replaced by the difference between the price of the product as landed in Europe and 155 per cent of the intervention price. In some cases, based on the carefully-chosen base period 1986–1988, this means some tariffs are over 100 per cent. Not surprisingly Australia and Canada have raised objections, and these cases will be looked at again. So much for the belief that the Uruguay Round would universally ease duties on imported goods.

However, besides tariffication of imports, the EU has had to face the implementation of a commitment to open import quotas at reduced or zero tariffs, to fulfil their current and minimum access engagements. Given the high level of protection which still exists these reduced or zero tariffs are worth a great deal of money.

In normal circumstances the limitation on subsidised exports which was agreed in the final months of the Round and embodied in the Blair House II Agreement might have been expected to attract most attention as it was the question on which negotiations almost broke down. But in the following 18 months market conditions were anything but normal. Far from granting export subsidies over this period the EU was engaged in levying taxes on cereal exports.

There are now signs that this period of exceptional market conditions has come to an end. The question of limitations on subsidised grain exports is thus again actual. In the Uruguay Round Agreement on Agriculture a ceiling quantity of subsidised exports was established which had to be reduced by 21 per cent over the six-year implementation period, with the financial outlay being similarly limited, in this case to fall by 36 per cent over the period. These reductions are by reference to the base period 1988 (but spread under Blair House). Since the EU has in many areas expanded exports since that base period—notably between 1990 and 1993—it was initially thought that the reductions would have to be greater. An unexpected quirk of the abnormal market conditions referred to above, whereby little exporting was done with subsidy in the past year, has modified this thought. A little-noticed Article 9(2) in the Blair House Agreement provided for "downstream flexibility". This means that unsubsidised exports can be carried forward to future years, and the same applies to financial outlays. However this flexibility runs out at the end of the fifth year.

In applying the Agriculture Agreement the bureaucrats have been faced with a number of practical problems. In the first place the commitments are by marketing year. So how should they monitor the quantities exported from, say, 1 July 1995 to 30 June 1996 when they actually do not know until a considerable time after the event that exports have physically taken place; how under those circumstances could they avoid the risk of exceeding the permitted quantity?

The Commission decided to take the date of export in WTO terms as the date on which the operator prefixes the exact refund he will have the right to claim when he exports a specified quantity of goods. The consequence of this for the trade is that prefixing has become *de facto* obligatory (in some sectors such as fruit and vegetables where prefixation of the refund was not normal practice this has had to be introduced).

Obligatory prefixation of the export refund has had the advantage of ensuring that trade is spread evenly over the whole of a normal marketing year rather than concentrated in the first few months. The regulations provide a five-day period in which the Commission can check whether the prefixed quantities are normal or excessive; and if the latter the Commission has the power either to cancel the refund and fix a lower one or to grant certificates for only given percentages of the quantities prefixed. This does not make life easier for traders!

This however is not all. As the restrictions on subsidised exports bite harder, as it seems they are bound to do now that the world price has declined, the incentives for speculation may increase. Speculation, though many think it necessary to oil the wheels of trade, is officially regarded as undesirable, since it tends to introduce distortion, and in such circumstances the Commission might feel obliged to make prefixed certificates non-transferable—a further limitation on traders' freedom to deal as they might wish. If faced with excessively large requests for prefixation the Commission may be obliged to fix refunds for grain exports by tender, as is done for olive oil.

Market access is the second area in which the trade will feel the impact of the WTO. Market access commitments in the form of tariff reductions and tariff quotas have been the stock in trade of the GATT multilateral trading system since its inception. These take effect through tariff bindings. "Binding" simply means that the tariff on a product cannot exceed the level specified in the legal schedule of a member. Before the Uruguay Round only about one third of agricultural tariffs were bound; under WTO virtually all now are. The situation in which unbound tariffs could be raised at will is thus now a thing of the past.

The Commission is anxious to open tariff quotas in the fairest possible way, and not to disrupt the market. But there are problems. At present wherever the quotas are not attributed to a specific country they are opened on a first-come-first-served basis. This however means that when, as frequently happens, the applications exceed the available quota they have to be scaled back. It has been known for applicants to receive as little as 1 per cent of their application—a frustrating experience, and one which can lead to importers asking for far more than they really require in the hope of obtaining approximately their real needs. There seems to be no satisfactory solution to this problem, though here again tendering is being considered.

A third area of difficulty in imports concerns price. The EU has a commitment to ensure that the duty-paid import price should not exceed the ceiling (155 per cent of the intervention price). An obvious method might be to take the invoice price and calculate the duty by reference to this. However, a multinational company acting as both exporter and importer might see advantage in invoicing the goods at or near the ceiling so as to minimise duty payable. In order to compete, other traders might be obliged to disturb the market and the GATT-bound level of protection of the Community would be undermined. To avoid this the Commission has developed a system of fixing representative prices believed to represent the realities of the market.

Finally, dispute settlement by the WTO has been significantly strengthened, and a detailed timetable laid down for action by the Dispute Settlement Body (DSB), starting with consultations, mediation by the Director-General, establishment of a panel, appeals, implementation of recommendations, arbitration, compensation, and as a last resort retaliation. The final time limit for urgent cases is 516 days, and for non-urgent cases 646 days. As at end-July 1996, 50 disputes had been presented, ranging from gasoline to textiles and dessicated coconut, and 10 had been settled out of court.

The US is the main user of the DSB, having initiated 18 of the 50 cases. Main disputes concerning agricultural trade include EU, Canada and US complaints against Japanese taxes on alcoholic beverages; several countries against the EU regime for importation, sale and distribution of bananas; and Thailand and Uruguay against EU duties on rice.

A major case, which was settled in 1995, concerned the question of compensation to be made by the EU to the US, Canada and Australia in order to avert threatened retaliatory action over EU enlargement compensation and over the WTO dispute proceedings in connection with the EU's cereals and rice import regimes.

The main provisions, which took effect from 1 January 1996, gave Canada concessions on high-quality wheat and on durum wheat, canary seed and oats; gave the US concessions on rice and petfood, and agreement to review the "reference price" system for cereals and rice;

and Australia concessions on oats and rice, as well as agreement to review the functioning of the "reference price" system for cereals. These results were of considerable importance to traders, welcomed by some, less so by others.

There is considerable political will for the Disputes Settlement Body to show results. Director-General Ruggiero describes the DSB as the WTO's "finest achievement" and as "the heart of the multilateral trading system". An unusual aspect of it is the notable recourse to the DSB being taken by developing countries, who were involved in 50 per cent of the disputes initiated in 1995. Their participation in the multilateral trading system is in marked contrast to the old GATT, where disputes principally concerned the industrialised countries.

During 1997 problems arising from the two-tier system of customs duty rates known as tariff quotas, which are applied to imports of a number of agricultural products, were the subject of extensive questioning in the Agriculture Committee.

The questioning came during a regular review of notifications—that is to say, countries' reports to the WTO on how they are implementing their commitments on market access, domestic support and export subsidies under the Agriculture Agreement—and in discussions of specific implementation issues that some countries raised.

Overall, about 250 questions were raised by some eight countries. They dealt with almost 40 notifications out of a total of about 70 that were up for review. The Agriculture Agreement, like other WTO agreements, requires members to report on how they are complying with their commitments so that the actions taken can be seen by all.

Questions were asked both about the way the tariff quotas were being allocated among importers or exporters, and about cases where the volumes imported did not reach the quota limits. Thirty-five WTO members have tariff quota commitments on various agricultural products.

In one or two cases, the notifying country reported that some imports were categorised as "out-of-quota" and charged the higher rate even though the quantity inside the quota fell short of the quota limit. This indicates that in some cases tariff quota import licences are not being fully used, despite prices in import markets often being significantly higher than world market prices. In many cases, the countries being questioned attributed the shortfall to demand and supply conditions.

Questioning countries expressed concern about the various methods of implementing tariff quota commitments—how the quotas are shared out and other related questions. They said these might be too burdensome for the trade, preventing imports from filling the quotas.

A number of countries also wanted to know whether some of the figures for imports within the lower-duty quotas included imports under regional arrangements such as free trade agreements. They suggested that to include preferential trade within the lower-duty quotas could be a violation of GATT. One exporting country put forward the view at the end of the discussions on tariff quotas, that if shortfalls persist over several years, importing countries should scrap the quotas. Only the lower in-quota tariff rates should be used if demand really was the reason for imports failing to fill the quotas.

On a separate but related agenda item, some exporting countries criticised some importing countries' use of special safeguard measures even when domestic producers were not suffering. Under the Agriculture Agreement, special safeguard restrictions on imports can be used if low import prices or surges in import quantities meet certain criteria. However, the right to use the special safeguard is restricted to 37 members and to designated products, and the additional duties which might be imposed cannot be applied to imports under tariff quotas.

Under regular GATT safeguards rules for goods in general, governments have to show that the lower import prices or increases in imports are hurting domestic producers. Under the Agriculture Agreement they do not. One exporting country said that the way some importing countries are applying the special agricultural safeguard provisions almost automatically, instead of when they were really needed, is a misuse of the provisions. This argument was countered by the assertion that the actions taken were fully justified.

In its third 1997 meeting the WTO's Agriculture Committee considered more than 100 questions on the way the Agriculture Agreement is being put into practice. Many of the questions dealt with the latest information that individual members had supplied to the WTO on the measures they had implemented under the Agreement. Twelve members asked almost 90 questions about information notified by about 25 members on their export subsidies, domestic support programmes, and market access policies—particularly tariff quotas.

An issue that aroused a considerable amount of discussion was the interpretation of Article 9, paragraph 2(b), of the Agriculture Agreement. This Article allows governments some flexibility in fulfilling their commitments to reduce agricultural export subsidies gradually over the Agreement's six-year implementation period ("downstream flexibility"). The central question was this: if a country's agricultural export subsidies in one year fall short of the limit in its WTO commitment, can it transfer the shortfall for later use—in any of the second to fifth years of the implementation period? Some countries argued that the Agriculture Agreement allows them to do just that.

Other countries said the interpretation conflicted with the letter or the spirit of the Agreement, or both. These countries maintained that interpreting the Agreement to allow unused export subsidy commitments to be rolled over in full (rather than within the narrower margins specified in the Article) could destabilise world markets, increase market uncertainty, and could even revive subsidy wars.

To this the reply was given that the narrower view was not supported by the text of the Article as a whole, and that it was the text itself which was paramount. They added that their rights under these provisions would be exercised responsibly.

One point was not contested: the Agreement says that whatever happens in an individual year, over the full implementation period export subsidies cannot exceed the total committed for the whole of the period.

The debate has arisen because, in 1995 and 1996, agricultural prices on world markets were relatively high, especially for cereals. Many countries with export subsidy reduction commitments were therefore able to export without using the full amount of export subsidies that were available to them.

Two issues which the Committee had previously discussed were raised again at this September meeting: one concerning exported milk products, and one about the "inward processing" arrangements for cheese exports that exceed export commitments. The question of "inward processing" could arise again in connection with cereals, since some processed cereal products can be subject to this.

All in all, Renato Ruggiero's remarks about the value of the Disputes Settlement Body seem to be justified by the increasing use being made of it.

CHAPTER 7

Soya and oilseed

In the 1998–1999 season global oilseed production is forecast to reach a record 288.5 million tons, nearly 5 million tons above the previous year. Most of this increase comes from rapeseed and sunflowerseed, while soya will remain unchanged and cottonseed decline. The large Latin American production will further influence the figures by the autumn of 1998, while consumption is not expected to keep pace with the increased production, leading to a rise in end-stocks and a fall in some prices to the lowest level for ten years. But within these figures there is some variety, for oilseed is a comprehensive description. USDA's projections for global supply and distribution are shown in Table 7.1.

Oilseed is grown primarily for its vegetable oil, which is used both in human consumption directly and/or, depending on the crop, for industrial use. Very broadly, around half the original bulk of oilseed remains after the oil has been extracted. For soya the figure is two-thirds.

The protein-rich residue after crushing or processing has a direct impact on cereal supply and demand due to its growth as a raw material in animal feed. Moreover, a major contributory factor in the growth in demand and subsequently production of oilseed has been among the health-conscious in developed countries, where consumption of unsaturated and polyunsaturated fatty acids present in such crops is perceived as healthier in terms of reducing heart-related diseases than those in animal fats.

The main oilseed crops are copra, cottonseed, linseed, palm, rapeseed and sunflower seed. Strictly speaking, soya is a pulse crop, but the scale of production of its oil and meal inextricably links it with oilseeds, especially in terms of price.

Soya also has a major impact on maize and maize oil, fishmeal and even industrial single cell protein production and values. Its versatility has also had an influence on supermarket food. Developments in food technology, textured vegetable protein and other meat extenders, for example, commonly use soya as a base.

Oilseed and soya meals have grown in importance for animal feed

Table 7.1 Major oilseeds: world supply and distribution (million metric tons)

	1993/94	1994/95	1995/96	Prelim. 1996/97	April 1997/98	May 1997/98
Production						
Soyabean	117.83	137.72	124.96	131.65	152.21	152.60
Cottonseed	29.49	32.90	35.93	34.37	34.47	34.22
Peanut	25.23	28.32	28.40	28.98	27.74	28.60
Sunflowerseed	20.83	23.48	25.89	24.13	23.66	23.44
Rapeseed	26.80	30.38	34.52	31.44	33.67	33.75
Copra	4.97	5.48	5.03	5.81	5.67	5.66
Palm kernel	4.25	4.61	4.98	5.30	5.38	5.38
Total	229.40	262.90	259.71	261.69	282.79	283.65
Exports						
Soyabean	28.18	32.16	31.95	36.94	39.05	39.03
Cottonseed	0.91	1.03	0.94	0.80	1.05	1.03
Peanut	1.49	1.60	1.66	1.52	1.75	1.78
Sunflowerseed	2.57	3.19	3.67	3.94	2.85	2.85
Rapeseed	5.28	5.85	5.86	5.53	5.81	5.82
Copra	0.24	0.21	0.21	0.20	0.19	0.19
Palm kernel	0.06	0.06	0.06	0.06	0.06	0.06
Total	38.73	44.11	44.34	49.00	50.76	50.76
Imports						
Soyabean	28.40	32.76	32.27	36.81	39.08	39.01
Cottonseed	0.89	1.04	0.89	0.88	0.97	0.97
Peanut	1.44	1.53	1.53	1.48	1.70	1.73
Sunflowerseed	2.51	3.14	3.68	3.86	2.90	2.90
Rapeseed	5.20	5.91	5.64	5.50	5.83	5.83
Copra	0.26	0.24	0.22	0.24	0.24	0.24
Palm kernel	0.04	0.05	0.05	0.06	0.05	0.05
Total	38.73	44.67	44.28	48.83	50.78	50.74
Crush						
Soyabean	102.07	110.24	112.02	116.00	123.57	123.82
Cottonseed	22.98	25.26	28.18	26.44	26.36	26.16
Peanut	13.45	15.21	14.63	14.97	13.81	14.36
Sunflowerseed	18.01	20.61	22.56	21.78	21.55	21.43
Rapeseed	24.42	27.24	30.54	28.99	30.80	30.87
Copra	4.95	5.50	4.97	5.81	5.69	5.67
Palm kernel	4.26	4.51	4.94	5.26	5.33	5.33
Total	190.14	208.56	217.83	219.25	227.11	227.65
Ending stocks						
Soyabean	17.35	23.70	17.58	12.91	19.62	19.68
Cottonseed	0.53	0.63	0.59	0.58	0.56	0.56
Peanut	0.61	0.75	0.55	0.49	0.47	0.47
Sunflowerseed	0.79	0.94	1.64	1.32	0.90	0.89
Rapeseed	0.80	0.97	1.59	1.38	1.13	1.13
Copra	0.11	0.08	0.11	0.11	0.11	0.11
Palm kernel	0.12	0.18	0.17	0.16	0.16	0.16
Total	20.31	27.24	22.24	16.95	22.94	23.00

Note: Totals may not add due to rounding. For notes and description of areas designated.

Source: Official statistics, USDA estimates (date: May 1998).

consumption since soya can deliver up to five times more crude protein than cereals. Its range of available amino acids—increasingly important for intensive livestock production, pigs and poultry—is reasonably good, although methionine frequently needs to be added to provide a better balance.

Fishmeal and other marine derivatives provide a more complete protein mix since they contain an excess of methionine and, at the same time, can utilize the excess tryptophane in oilseed. In addition, fishmeal can compensate for mineral shortages and overcome phytic acid problems in oilseeds.

Environmental and health factors have also more recently assisted the growth of oilseeds as a world protein resource. There have been moratoria on fishing anchovy off the north-west coast of South America, the major source of fishmeal for feed compounding, due to stock depletion. In addition, the greater awareness and steps taken to improve public hygiene has produced a higher incidence of salmonellosis in South American fishmeal exports. At one time a number of major European feed compounders struck South American fishmeal off their list of protein sources.

These factors have also contributed to a wide price differential between fishmeal and the most commonly used oilseed meal, soya. The former was up to $300 a ton more than soyameal by early 1990, by 1996–1997 had more than doubled the soya price, and in April 1998 fishmeal was quoted at US$684 per ton to soya's US$168.

But it is political decisions that have had the greatest impact on the growth of oilseed production and subsequently its price and availability. The EC took a decision to encourage Community oilseed output—mainly of rape and sunflower and, to a lesser extent, soya—to reduce dependence on imports.

With a structure of support prices for farmers and crushing subsidies to encourage processors to use the crop, production during the latter part of the 1980s rose by almost a third. By 1989–1990, EC Commission figures showed output of rape, soya and sunflower at 10,268 million tons for the 10 Member States. In 1997–1998 the forecast for the 15 States is 14,472 million tons.

The cost of supporting production from the Community budget also ballooned to about $3 billion by the end of the 1980s. This was in addition to the $1.4 billion annual EC expenditure in supporting olive oil production in the Mediterranean countries of the Community. The olive oil sector of the CAP has been much plagued by complaints of fraud, from which Commission officials have not themselves been free, and indeed a well-publicised case of suicide occurred a few years back. Forged ship's papers, transport documents and loading and unloading manifests, soya oil described as olive oil in order to attract a higher rate of refund, are examples of fraud which have involved the EU in millions of ecus of losses. Recently the Commission have attempted to cut back on the expenditure in this sector, and the draft Budget of the European Communities for 1999 shows anticipated appropriations for olive oil falling by 3.1 per cent, from 2.25 billion ecus to 2.18 billion.

As a result of CAP support, EU prices for oils and fats are generally in line with world market levels for most products, with the notable exception of butter and olive oil. EC olive oil output usually ranges between one million and 1.4 million tons annually, approximately equivalent to consumption. For 1997–1998 EU consumption of olive oil is forecast at 1.5 million tons. Since olive trees are perennials, the crop is not demand-led but almost entirely dependent on the weather.

Despite the level of support from the EU budget, it is ironic that less than 40 per cent of the Community's oilseed crush is based on production from the fifteen Member States. This was a key factor in the EC's decision to attempt to limit further expansion and thus expenditure by introducing its stabiliser mechanism which automatically reduces farm support prices if total rape and sunflower production exceeds 3.5 million and 1.7 million tons respectively.

At the same time, the European Community remains the largest single market for vegetable oil and oil cake. Oilseed imports are at 14 million tons, oil cake at over 21 million and oil at almost 700,000 tons. With EC agricultural budgetary expenditure only slowly coming under control, oilseeds is one of the current and future battlegrounds in the long-running soap opera that is characteristic of EC/US trade disputes.

THE PRODUCTS

Both edible vegetable oil and high protein cake for animal feed emerge from crushing and processing factories, which are usually sited at or near the world's major ports. Typically, edible oil factories receive raw material in seed and crude oil form. The seed or bean is crushed to extract the oil before further processing, while the crude oil is refined to meet various market specifications.

Each seed requires a different treatment before extraction. For example, rape is mechanically expelled (oil is squeezed out under pressure), while palm kernels are steam-conditioned and flaked by rolling. Edible vegetable oil is consumed directly or, especially in the European Union, blended and then sold through supermarkets. Further processed edible oil is also retailed in the form of prepared fats, such as margarine.

The other largest users of vegetable oils and fats are the baking and catering sectors for products ranging from cake and confectionery, pastry and bread. Ice cream fats, produced from palm kernel oil, allows the product to retain its structure in warm weather, yet melt in the mouth. Soap, based on blends of palm kernel or coconut oils with tallow, and/or increasingly palm oil, is the main industrial use for oilseed.

Within the European Union basic oilseed products are interchangeable, but their end-uses vary between Member States. While fats are mainly consumed in the form of butter and margarine in the northern countries, in France, Italy, Greece, Spain and Portugal vegetable oils account for the majority of consumption.

THE PRODUCERS

The average acreage of oilseeds worldwide in the early 1990s was 153 million has., rising to a forcast of 168 million has. in 1997–1998. Average yields during the same period have risen from 1.51 t/ha. to 1.62 t/ha. Forecasts for 1997–1998 (see Table 7.2) show that soya accounts for over half global oilseed production, and out of this US production of soya at 74 million tonnes will account for one quarter of total oilseed production. Next in importance as producers of soya are Brazil, Argentina and China.

Oilseed production is not restricted to any particular geographical area, China and the US being the leaders in cottonseed, India and China in peanuts, Eastern Europe including the former Soviet Union, in sunflowerseed, and China, the EU and Canada for rapeseed.

THE CONSUMERS

Global consumption of cakes and meals is forecast to increase in 1997–1998 over the previous year, reaching about 68 million tonnes in protein equivalent in 1997–1998. The bulk of the increase is expected to occur in China and the United States, while in the abovementioned Asian countries reduced economic growth is expected to slow down the expansion in the consumption of meat (as a more income-sensitive, high-value-added product), which in turn may result in lower demand for oilmeals.

In the EC, where consumption of cakes and meals has been affected by the substantial increase in international prices over the last two seasons, consumption is anticipated to stagnate in 1997–1998, while in Eastern European countries only moderate increases are foreseen, because of problems still encountered in their livestock sectors. As to the different meals, a strong rise in soyabean meal consumption is considered likely, while global consumption of vegetable cakes and meals other than

Table 7.2. Major oilseeds—area, yield and production by main producers

	Average 1991/92–1995/96			Preliminary 1996/97			Forecast 1997/98		
	Area (1)	Yield (2)	Prod (3)	Area (1)	Yield (2)	Prod (3)	Area (1)	Yield (2)	Prod (3)
Soyabean									
United States	23.96	2.44	58.47	25.66	2.53	64.84	28.28	2.62	74.22
Brazil	10.88	2.14	23.31	11.80	2.27	26.80	13.00	2.36	30.70
China	8.21	1.58	12.96	7.47	1.77	13.22	8.25	1.67	13.80
Argentina	5.36	2.23	11.97	6.20	1.81	11.20	6.80	2.35	16.00
European Union (4)	0.38	2.95	1.12	0.34	3.44	1.15	0.42	3.38	1.43
Paraguay	1.03	1.84	1.89	1.20	2.31	2.77	1.30	2.08	2.70
Other	9.72	1.17	11.34	10.51	1.11	11.67	11.33	1.21	13.75
Total	59.54	2.03	121.06	63.18	2.08	131.65	69.39	2.20	152.60
Cottonseed									
China	5.87	1.37	8.05	4.72	1.60	7.56	4.50	1.72	7.72
United States	5.36	1.15	6.16	5.21	1.24	6.48	5.38	1.23	6.60
FSU-12	2.82	1.31	3.69	2.52	1.10	2.77	2.58	1.22	3.16
India	7.92	0.58	4.57	9.17	0.64	5.88	9.00	0.53	4.80
Pakistan	2.84	1.16	3.29	3.20	0.99	3.18	2.90	1.05	3.05
Brazil	1.32	0.65	0.86	0.70	0.71	0.49	0.92	0.71	0.65
Other	7.05	0.95	6.67	8.27	0.97	8.01	8.25	1.00	8.25
Total	33.16	1.00	33.30	33.78	1.02	34.37	33.53	1.02	34.22
Peanut									
India	8.22	0.96	7.87	8.20	1.00	8.20	8.10	0.99	8.00
China	3.37	2.41	8.11	3.62	2.80	10.14	3.74	2.58	9.62
United States	0.69	2.67	1.84	0.56	2.98	1.66	0.57	2.81	1.60
Senegal	0.88	0.80	0.70	0.92	0.70	0.65	0.79	0.70	0.55
Sudan	0.55	0.71	0.39	0.55	0.67	0.37	0.55	0.67	0.37
Brazil	0.09	1.72	0.15	0.09	1.55	0.14	0.09	1.67	0.15
Argentina	0.16	1.72	0.27	0.28	1.09	0.30	0.41	1.83	0.75
South Africa	0.14	1.08	0.15	0.10	1.47	0.14	0.06	1.45	0.08
Other	6.72	0.96	6.41	7.82	0.94	7.39	8.05	0.93	7.48
Total	20.81	1.25	25.91	22.12	1.31	28.98	22.35	1.28	28.60

Table 7.2—*cont.*

	Average 1991/92–1995/96			Preliminary 1996/97			Forecast 1997/98		
	Area (1)	Yield (2)	Prod (3)	Area (1)	Yield (2)	Prod (3)	Area (1)	Yield (2)	Prod (3)
Sunflowerseed									
FSU-12	5.26	1.08	5.66	6.59	0.79	5.21	6.17	0.88	5.43
Argentina	2.63	1.69	4.45	2.90	1.86	5.40	3.10	1.61	5.00
Eastern Europe	1.70	1.47	2.48	2.14	1.42	3.04	1.91	1.35	2.58
United States	1.13	1.41	1.60	1.01	1.61	1.63	1.15	1.48	1.71
China	0.79	1.73	1.36	0.69	1.92	1.33	0.67	1.79	1.20
European Union (4)	2.64	1.43	3.77	2.35	1.65	3.89	2.28	1.64	3.73
Other	4.42	0.76	3.36	4.44	0.82	3.64	4.46	0.85	3.80
Total	18.57	1.22	22.68	20.11	1.20	24.13	19.74	1.19	23.44
Rapeseed									
China	6.02	1.31	7.86	6.73	1.37	9.20	6.35	1.48	9.37
European Union (4)	2.66	2.73	7.27	2.65	2.70	7.14	2.71	3.16	8.55
Canada	4.26	1.28	5.45	3.45	1.47	5.06	4.80	1.29	6.20
India	6.39	0.88	5.60	6.86	1.01	6.94	6.40	0.92	5.90
Eastern Europe	0.71	2.13	1.52	0.69	1.83	1.27	0.74	2.04	1.52
Other	1.50	0.91	1.36	1.78	1.02	1.82	2.22	1.00	2.21
Total	21.54	1.35	29.06	22.16	1.42	31.44	23.22	1.45	33.75
Total Oilseeds	153.62	1.51	232.00	161.35	1.55	250.57	168.24	1.62	272.62

(1) In million hectares.
(2) In tons per hectare.
(3) In million metric tons.
(4) Includes the statistics from the former German Democratic Republic.

Source: Official statistics, USDA estimates (date: May 1998).

soyabean meal is anticipated to change little and ultilisation of fishmeal is expected to decline due to a shortfall in production.

STOCKS

Based on the supply and demand forecasts for the 1997–1998 season, stocks of oils and fats at the end of the season should recover slightly from the previous season's below-average level, while the stock-to-utilisation ratio is, nevertheless, anticipated to fall further by the end of 1997–1998. As a result, prices for oils and fats apart from soya are expected to remain at relatively high levels in 1997–1998.

TRADE

Figures for exports and imports of oils and fats are shown in Tables 7.3 and 7.4. As in 1996–1997, further expansion in global demand for oilseed products is expected to lead to an increase in world trade in oilseed products in 1997–1998. With regard to imports, a sharp rise in purchases of oilseed-based products is expected in China. From a net exporter in 1993–1994, this country has become one of the largest importers of oilseed products. A further widening in the domestic supply/demand gap for oilseeds, oils and meals, mainly due to production difficulties, is expected to bring the country's net imports of oils and fats as well as cakes and meals from 4.4 and 3.9 million tonnes respectively in 1996–1997 to 5.6 and 5.2 million tonnes respectively in 1997–1998. The timing and magnitude of Chinese purchases of oilseed based products will be a major factor influencing international price developments for these products (see Table 7.5). Net imports of oils and fats are expectd to rise further also in other major importing countries, i.e. India, Pakistan, Mexico, Japan, the EC and the Republic of Korea. As to imports of cakes and meals, the anticipated slowdown in oilmeal consumption in parts of South-East Asia should translate into some reduction in imports, but it is not expected to have a significant impact on global import demand.

Net exports of oils and fats are estimated to reach 36 million tonnes in 1997–1998, rising some 3 per cent above the previous season's level. Following the usual pattern, the main suppliers of oils will be Argentina, Brazil and the United States for soyabeans, sunflowerseeds and their oils; Indonesia and Malaysia for palm and palmkernel oil; the Philippines for copra and coconut oil; and Canada for rapeseed and its oil. The shares of soyabean oil and palm oil in total shipments of oils and fats are estimated at 32 and 28 per cent respectively—basically the reverse of 1996–1997—followed by sunflowerseed oil (9 per cent), rapeseed oil (7 per

Table 7.3 Exports of oils and fats[1]

	1991/92 1993/94 Average	1994/95	1995/96	1996/97 Prel.
		Million tonnes		
WORLD TOTALS				
All fats and oils	**27.78**	**33.49**	**32.35**	**34.92**
Edible/soap fats and oils	**27.25**	**32.77**	**31.66**	**34.23**
Edible fats	**0.72**	**0.67**	**0.62**	**0.88**
Butter (fat content)	0.56	0.51	0.42	0.67
Lard	0.16	0.16	0.20	0.30
Soft oils[2]	**13.94**	**17.77**	**16.76**	**17.53**
Soyabean	7.88	9.97	8.83	9.60
Sunflowerseed	1.93	2.94	3.19	3.05
Groundnut	0.67	0.69	0.74	0.68
Cottonseed	0.30	0.37	0.31	0.33
Rapeseed	2.26	2.91	2.68	2.19
Olive	0.26	0.18	0.18	0.83
Lauric acid oils	**2.27**	**2.54**	**2.31**	**2.55**
Coconut	1.43	1.73	1.40	1.64
Palm kernel[3]	0.84	0.81	0.91	0.91
Others[4]	**10.32**	**11.80**	**13.27**	**13.43**
Tallow and greases	1.95	2.28	1.95	2.10
Palm	7.89	8.89	9.43	10.62
Marine	0.46	0.60	0.58	0.53
Technical oils[5]	**0.47**	**0.65**	**0.61**	**0.56**
Linseed	0.25	0.33	0.32	0.28
Castorseed	0.18	0.28	0.26	0.25
Tung	0.03	0.02	0.02	0.02
Miscellaneous oils[6]	**0.06**	**0.06**	**0.08**	**0.04**
REGIONAL TOTALS				
Developing countries	**16.84**	**19.87**	**19.61**	**21.60**
Latin America	5.60	7.26	6.78	6.72
Argentina	3.21	4.13	4.00	3.67
Africa	0.69	0.56	0.60	0.84
Near East	0.13	0.19	0.22	0.23
Far East	10.09	11.54	11.69	13.48
Indonesia	2.09	2.05	2.38	3.31
Malaysia	6.43	7.34	7.73	8.10
Developed countries	**10.94**	**13.62**	**12.74**	**13.32**
North America	8.14	11.13	9.21	9.56
Canada	1.74	2.67	2.28	2.09
United States	6.40	8.45	6.93	7.48
Europe	1.51	1.14	1.21	1.71
EC	0.83	0.49	0.49	0.83
Eastern Europe	0.49	0.53	0.61	0.76
Oceania	0.76	0.79	0.89	1.00

[1] Including oil equivalent of oilseeds; excluding main re-exports of oil from imported oilseeds.
[2] In addition to the oils listed, includes maize, mustard, rice bran, safflower and sesameseed oils.
[3] Including babassu oil.
[4] In addition to the fats and oils listed, includes peanut butter.
[5] In addition to the oils listed, includes poppyseed, hempseed oils.
[6] Mainly seed oils not specified elsewhere.

Source: FAO.

Table 7.4 Imports of oils and fats[1,2]

	1991/92 1993/94 Average	1994/95	1995/96	1996/97 Prel.
		Million tonnes		
World total	**26.77**	**32.53**	**31.96**	**34.84**
Developing countries	**14.56**	**19.64**	**19.14**	**21.45**
Latin America	3.30	3.48	3.61	4.31
Mexico	1.51	1.50	1.71	1.99
Africa	2.85	3.09	3.33	3.78
Near East	3.40	4.29	3.55	4.29
Egypt	0.81	0.92	1.01	1.13
Far East	5.95	9.82	9.79	10.32
China	1.99	4.39	4.10	4.43
Pakistan	1.26	1.47	1.37	1.64
Developed countries	**12.21**	**12.89**	**12.82**	**13.40**
North America	1.53	1.49	1.55	1.68
United States	1.39	1.33	1.39	1.51
Europe	6.91	7.43	7.48	7.94
EC	5.98	6.50	6.65	7.06
Eastern Europe	0.42	0.47	0.51	0.56
Oceania	0.26	0.26	0.25	0.23
Other developed countries	3.51	3.71	3.54	3.32
Japan	2.19	2.60	2.62	2.64

[1] Excluding quantities subsequently re-exported.
[2] Including the oil equivalent of oilseeds.

Source: FAO.

cent), tallow (6 per cent) and coconut oil (5 per cent). Net exports of cakes and meals are likely to increase around 5 per cent, possibly exceeding 3.3 million tonnes of protein equivalent in 1997–1998. The share of soyabean meal in world export trade is estimated to rise to 80 per cent, while the share of fishmeal will decrease because of the reduction in output. No significant expansion in shipments of oils and cakes from exporting Asian countries (in particular Malaysia, Indonesia and the Philippines) is likely. While their exports have become more competitive due to strong devaluations in local currencies, adverse weather (El Niño) has negatively affected production prospects in those countries thus limiting export availabilities in 1998.

Table 7.5 Prices of oils and fats

	1991/92 1993/94 Average	1994/95	1995/96	1996/97 Prel.
	FAO price index 1984–87 = 100[1]			
All fats and oils	**97**	**130**	**120**	**114**
Edible/soap	97	131	120	115
Soft[2]	100	131	117	110
Lauric acid[3]	88	109	123	114
Others[4]	93	139	124	125
Technical[5]	87	115	106	102
	$/tonne			
Soyabean oil[6]	491	641	574	537
Sunflowerseed oil[7]	525	691	617	543
Groundnut oil[8]	762	1008	933	967
Rapeseed oil[6]	479	635	566	540
Palm oil[9]	407	645	544	545
Coconut oil[10]	541	666	768	708

[1] Fats and oils index excludes butter and lard.
[2] Cottonseed, groundnut, rapeseed, soyabean and sunflowerseed oils.
[3] Coconut and palm kernel oils.
[4] Fish and palm oils and tallow.
[5] Castor and linseed oils.
[6] Dutch, fob ex-mill.
[7] Any origin ex tank, Rotterdam.
[8] Any origin cif, Rotterdam.
[9] Generally Indonesian origin, cif NW Europe.
[10] Philippines, Indonesia, cif Rotterdam/Hamburg.

Source: FAO.

NOTE ON STATISTICAL SOURCES

The three main sources of statistical information on soya and oilseeds are the FAO, USDA and Internationale Statistische Informationen Mielke GmbH of Hamburg (ISTA). There are minor differences in presentation, viz. FAO and USDA present groundnuts on an unshelled basis, ISTA on a shelled basis. On a crop year basis ISTA data refer uniformly to October/September for all countries, while USDA adds up different national crop years to a world total, and FAO issues no crop year data. There are slightly greater differences where crushing and consequently oil and meal data are concerned. Apart from adding up different national crop years, all FAO data and part of the USDA data represent potential crushings rather than actual crushings.

Thus, the data from these two sources represent the conversion of the crops to oil and meal after deducting estimated amounts for seed, food and feed and assuming certain oil and meal conversion rates. This has the result that in years of increases in the soya and oilseeds stocks the crushing as well as the oil and meal production data of the FAO and USDA can be above the actual data, and vice versa. ISTA, on the other hand, publishes, through its magazine *Oil World*, actual data on crushings and hence also on oil and meal production in a uniform period for all countries of the world.

PART 2

World production, consumption and trade

CHAPTER 8

World production

World production of wheat and coarse grains has risen progressively, if sometimes erratically, since the second world war, reflecting not only improvements in yield and the techniques of growing but also government policy. Of course, the rising trend of production fluctuates from year to year, mainly influenced by the weather. Despite the fact that the world needs to produce about an extra 12 million tonnes of wheat each year compared with the preceding year in order to feed the extra mouths born in the interval, production tends to outrun consumption (i.e. effective demand), leading to burdensome stocks, and has to be brought under control by governments. Stocks peaked in 1987, reaching a point of crisis, where much of the stored grain was virtually unsaleable for one reason or another.

In any analysis of world grain production and trade the student must start with an examination of statistical data. Here he or she is at once confronted with the problem of where to seek such information. In fact, there is no shortage of sources. Some are international bodies, others national. The choice will often depend on accessibility. Thus, of the international organisations the United Nations concentrates its agricultural expertise in the Food and Agricultural Organisation (FAO), which is based in Rome. The Organisation for Economic Co-operation and Development (OECD) has its headquarters in Paris. The international Grains Council (IGC) is centred in London. The European Union (EU), which is still at the time of writing as assemblage of nation-states and thus has international attributes, has a statistical service in Luxembourg, known as Eurostat.

Of the national bodies, the United States Department of Agriculture (USDA) operates on such a world-wide scale that it is virtually equivalent to an international organisation. The Foreign Agricultural Service of USDA has representation in all major countries and many minor ones. Each country also runs its own statistical service, typically a branch of the Agricultural Ministry or a semi-statal body, usually confining its activities to producing information on domestic agriculture. Thus, in the United Kingdom the service provided by the Ministry of

Agriculture Fisheries and Food (MAFF), and by equivalent Departments in Scotland and Northern Ireland, complemented by information and analysis from the Home-Grown Cereals Authority (HGCA), is mainly devoted to domestic topics. The HGCA does not duplicate the MAFF statistical service, but produces price information and valuable analyses covering agriculture throughout the European Community where this has relevance for UK producers and traders. In France there is something of the same division of activity between the French Ministry of Agriculture and *Office National Inter-Professionnel des Céréales* (ONIC), though ONIC also has responsibility for intervention and tendering, which HGCA does not. Other Member States of the Community have their own ministries and intervention boards. In Canada and Australia there are boards for wheat and other grains which combine functions of information and marketing. Additionally, many trade associations provide their own figures, as do some of the larger firms.

Some people regard the international bodies as more objective than national bodies: on the other hand, the information provided by international bodies is often only as reliable as the information supplied to them by the national bodies. Unless there are technical reasons for preferring one source to another the analyst is well-advised to make use of that which is most conveniently situated for him or her.

When considering production on a national basis, it is now customary to divide the world's countries into economic classes and regions, according to a system generally used by the United Nations in its reports and statistical surveys. In order to understand what people mean when they talk about "developed" and "developing" countries, for example—expressions familiar to everyone working in international commodity organisations but perhaps not so well understood by those outside—it is as well to be aware of this classification.

In the Commodity Divisions of the FAO it is usual to speak of developed and developing counties and geographical regions. They also refer to economies in transition (the former Soviet Union and the countries of central eastern Europe). Countries formerly labelled Asian centrally planned economies are now merged with the developing countries. The International Grains Council has refined and simplified these classes by also dropping the concept of "centrally planned economies" and recognising four main groupings without regional distinction: (1) developed market economies; (2) socialist countries of Eastern Europe; (3) socialist countries of Asia; and (4) developing countries and territories, and, most recently, by dropping references to socialist countries altogether. IGC analyses are not based only on geographical regions, listing countries according to the continents in which they are situated. Thus the world production of wheat, including durum wheat, from 1995–1996 to 1998–1999, is shown in the periodical IGC Grain Market Report (Table 8.1). (It should be noted that IGC estimates are updated regularly.) World production of coarse grains is shown in Table 8.2.

Coarse grain statistics are often further broken down into maize (corn), barley, sorghum, oats, rye, millet, triticale and mixed grain, but to show these in this book would occupy too much space. Only maize (corn) with a world production ranging between 380 million and 490 million tons, barley around 170 million to 180 million tons, and sorghum around 50 to 75 million tons, enter world trade to any considerable extent (though rye is domestically significant in Germany and Poland). Every decade has its share of good and bad seasons, and if one takes wheat the steady rise in production is masked by the exceptional conditions of 1984, which produced record figures in all the major exporting countries except Australia, and by the drought of 1988, which sharply reduced the spring-sown wheat crop in the Northern Hemisphere. They are put in perspective by looking at 10-year averages. Thus, in the 1960s world wheat production averaged 277 million tons, in the 1970s 381 million tons, and in the 1980s 500 million tons. In fact, the 1990 wheat crop very nearly reached 600 million tons, and the 1997–1998 harvest exceeded this figure. It might be reasonable to consider the "normal" level of production now as 600 million tons.

Of equal importance in the world context are the figures for end-season stocks. Total closing stocks of wheat peaked at the end of 1986–1987 at 167 million tons. This was long after the "great American grain robbery" of 1972–1973 mentioned earlier; in 1964–1965 they were 46 million tons. Back in 1958 they rose as high as 61 million tons, which in those days caused the same sort of crisis of oversupply as we have been seeing in recent years. A word of caution, however, about these figures. Because of the great uncertainty about the size of stocks in China and the FSU world totals should not be used for analysis. A better indicator is the combined stocks in the major exporting countries. A couple of years ago when the exporters' combined closing stocks of wheat amounted to 29 million tons this was regarded as very tight. In 1998 their carryover is 41 million tons, regarded as more than adequate. A major reason for the current weakness of markets is the prospects of exporters' stocks reaching 50 million tons in 1999.

I have already described briefly the main physical characteristics of grain production in the various major exporters. It is now time to turn to government support policies and consider how these compare with each other.

One has to start from the premise that all governments in developed countries support their agriculture in one way or another and to a greater or lesser degree: they cannot afford not to do so as the political

Table 8.1 Production: all wheat

COUNTRY	1995	1996	1997 (est.)	1998 29.04.98	Million tons (f'cast) 03.06.98
EUROPE	**123.7**	**126.8**	**130.0**	**132.3**	**132.6** <
Bulgaria	3.2	1.7	3.1	3.4	3.4
Czech Rep.	3.8	3.7	3.5	3.3	3.3
EC	87.5	99.8	94.9	99.9	99.7 <
Denmark	*4.5*	*4.8*	*5.0*	*5.1*	*5.1*
France	*30.9*	*35.9*	*33.8*	*35.2*	*35.0* <
Germany	*17.8*	*18.9*	*19.8*	*20.0*	*20.0*
Greece	*2.3*	*1.8*	*2.0*	*2.2*	*2.2*
Italy	*7.7*	*8.0*	*6.9*	*8.3*	*8.3*
Spain	*3.1*	*6.2*	*4.5*	*5.2*	*5.2*
Sweden	*1.6*	*2.0*	*2.2*	*2.1*	*2.1*
United Kingdom	*14.3*	*16.1*	*15.1*	*16.2*	*16.2*
Other EC	*5.3*	*6.1*	*5.8*	*5.6*	*5.6*
Hungary	4.9	3.9	5.3	4.8	4.8
Poland	8.7	8.5	8.2	8.0	8.5 <
Romania	7.7	3.1	7.2	5.0	5.0
Slovakia	1.9	1.7	1.9	2.0	2.0
Yugoslavia (Fed. R.)	3.0	1.5	2.9	3.0	3.0
Others	3.1	2.7	3.0	3.0	3.0
CIS & BALTICS	**60.4**	**64.9**	**80.0**	**74.7**	**73.5** <
Baltic States	1.0	1.4	1.1	1.3	1.3
CIS	59.5	63.5	78.8	73.4	72.2 <
Kazakhstan	*6.5*	*8.0*	*8.7*	*8.3*	*8.1* <
Russia	*30.1*	*34.9*	*44.2*	*41.0*	*40.0* <
Ukraine	*16.3*	*13.5*	*18.4*	*16.0*	*16.0*
Other CIS	*6.6*	*7.1*	*7.5*	*8.1*	*8.1*
N & C AMERICA	**88.0**	**95.3**	**96.6**	**90.1**	**92.1** <
Canada	25.0	29.8	24.3	24.5	24.5
Mexico	3.5	3.4	3.6	3.6	3.6
USA	59.5	62.1	68.8	62.0	64.0 <
Others	T	T	T	T	T
SOUTH AMERICA	**13.0**	**22.1**	**20.1**	**18.8**	**18.0** <
Argentina	9.4	15.9	14.7	13.0	13.0
Brazil	1.5	3.2	2.8	3.0	2.2 <
Chile	1.1	1.5	1.4	1.4	1.4
Uruguay	0.4	0.6	0.6	0.5	0.5
Others	0.6	0.8	0.7	0.8	0.8
NEAR EAST ASIA	**34.8**	**32.0**	**33.5**	**33.8**	**33.8**
Iran	11.3	8.8	10.2	10.5	10.5
Saudi Arabia	2.0	1.2	1.8	1.5	1.5
Syria	4.2	4.1	3.5	4.0	4.0
Turkey	15.5	16.2	16.5	16.2	16.2
Others	1.8	1.7	1.5	1.6	1.6
FAR EAST ASIA	**189.9**	**195.1**	**215.5**	**204.1**	**205.1** <
Pacific Asia	*103.1*	*111.5*	*125.1*	*116.0*	*117.0* <
China	102.2	110.6	124.0	115.0	116.0 <
Others	0.9	0.9	1.1	1.0	1.0
South Asia	*86.8*	*83.6*	*90.4*	*88.1*	*88.1*
Afghanistan	1.7	1.7	2.7	2.2	2.2
India	65.8	62.6	68.7	66.0	66.0
Pakistan	17.0	16.9	16.7	17.5	17.5
Others	2.3	2.4	2.4	2.4	2.4

Table 8.1—*cont.*

COUNTRY	1995	1996	1997 (est.)	1998 29.04.98	Million tons (f'cast) 03.06.98
AFRICA	**13.8**	**22.2**	**15.0**	**19.9**	**18.7** <
North Africa	*9.1*	*16.6*	*9.6*	*14.5*	*13.3* <
Algeria	1.6	2.8	0.8	2.0	2.0
Egypt	5.7	5.7	5.6	5.8	5.8
Libya	0.2	0.2	0.2	0.2	0.2
Morocco	1.1	5.9	2.3	5.2	4.0 <
Tunisia	0.5	2.0	0.7	1.3	1.3
Sub-Sahara	*4.7*	*5.6*	*5.4*	*5.4*	*5.4*
Ethiopia	1.4	1.6	1.6	1.5	1.5
South Africa	2.0	2.6	2.3	2.5	2.5
Others	1.4	1.4	1.4	1.5	1.5
OCEANIA	**17.2**	**23.9**	**19.2**	**18.2**	**18.2**
Australia	17.0	23.7	19.0	18.0	18.0
WORLD TOTAL	**540.7**	**582.2**	**609.9**	**591.9**	**592.0** <

Source: IGC.

Table 8.2 Production: coarse grains

COUNTRY	1995	1996	1997 (est.)	1998 29.04.98	Million tons (f'cast) 03.06.98 <
EUROPE	**142.7**	**156.1**	**169.5**	**158.8**	**160.6** <
Czech Rep.	2.8	2.9	2.8	2.9	2.9
EC	89.2	105.0	109.7	103.6	105.4 <
Denmark	*4.5*	*4.5*	*4.8*	*4.5*	*4.5*
Finland	*3.0*	*3.2*	*3.4*	*3.3*	*3.3*
France	*22.0*	*26.0*	*28.9*	*26.7*	*28.0* <
Germany	*21.6*	*23.2*	*25.6*	*23.9*	*23.9*
Italy	*10.5*	*11.5*	*11.7*	*10.9*	*10.9*
Spain	*8.1*	*15.1*	*13.6*	*13.4*	*13.9* <
Sweden	*3.3*	*4.0*	*4.0*	*3.9*	*3.9*
United Kingdom	*7.5*	*8.5*	*8.5*	*8.0*	*8.0*
Other EC	*8.6*	*9.1*	*9.5*	*9.1*	*9.1*
Hungary	6.4	7.1	7.8	6.9	6.9
Poland	17.2	16.5	17.1	16.3	16.3
Romania	12.2	11.0	15.0	12.1	12.1
Yugoslavia (Fed. R.)	5.5	5.2	8.0	8.1	8.1
Others	9.4	8.3	9.0	9.0	9.0
CIS & BALTICS	**62.7**	**57.6**	**74.3**	**67.3**	**67.3**
Baltic States	2.2	2.8	3.0	2.8	2.8
CIS	60.5	54.7	71.4	64.5	64.5
Belarus	*5.3*	*5.7*	*5.7*	*6.0*	*6.0*
Kazakhstan	*2.8*	*3.6*	*3.7*	*2.9*	*2.9*
Russia	*33.0*	*32.5*	*42.8*	*38.5*	*38.5*
Ukraine	*16.1*	*10.1*	*16.1*	*13.4*	*13.4*
Other CIS	*3.4*	*2.8*	*3.1*	*3.7*	*3.7*

Table 8.2—*cont.*

COUNTRY	1995	1996	1997 (est.)	1998 29.04.98	Million tons (f'cast) 03.06.98 <
N & C AMERICA	**260.7**	**326.0**	**318.6**	**323.0**	**324.1** <
Canada	24.1	28.2	24.8	26.2	26.2
Mexico	23.3	26.5	24.3	23.4	24.1
USA	209.4	267.6	265.4	269.4	269.8 <
Others	3.9	3.8	4.0	3.9	3.9
SOUTH AMERICA	**54.2**	**64.1**	**65.6**	**64.0**	**65.0**
Argentina	13.4	19.0	24.2	21.1	22.1 <
Brazil	33.0	36.9	33.3	34.7	34.7
Others	7.9	8.3	8.0	8.2	8.2
NEAR EAST ASIA	**18.0**	**17.6**	**18.3**	**18.4**	**18.4**
Iran	3.7	3.7	3.8	4.0	4.0
Turkey	9.2	9.7	10.1	9.7	9.7
Others	5.2	4.2	4.4	4.7	4.7
FAR EAST ASIA	**179.3**	**199.8**	**176.5**	**178.7**	**183.7** <
Pacific Asia	*145.4*	*161.6*	*141.3*	*143.8*	*148.8* <
China	126.0	141.6	123.2	124.7	129.7 <
Indonesia	6.0	6.0	5.7	5.8	5.8
Korea (N)	2.0	2.1	1.2	1.3	1.3
Philippines	4.3	4.2	4.3	4.0	4.0
Thailand	4.4	4.8	4.0	5.2	5.2
Others	2.7	2.9	2.8	2.8	2.8
South Asia	*33.8*	*38.2*	*35.2*	*34.9*	*34.9*
India	29.7	34.0	31.0	30.5	30.5
Others	4.2	4.2	4.2	4.4	4.4
AFRICA	**72.3**	**79.2**	**75.3**	**77.1**	**76.9** <
North Africa	*8.1*	*13.8*	*9.4*	*12.3*	*11.6* <
Egypt	6.5	6.7	6.9	6.8	6.8
Morocco	0.7	4.1	1.6	3.1	2.8 <
Others	1.0	3.0	1.0	2.5	2.1 <
Sub-Sahara	*64.2*	*65.4*	*65.9*	*64.7*	*65.2* <
Ethiopia	5.5	6.6	5.0	5.6	5.6
Kenya	2.9	2.3	2.9	2.4	2.4
Nigeria	13.6	14.4	17.0	17.2	17.2
South Africa	11.0	9.5	8.5	8.2	8.7 <
Sudan	2.9	4.5	4.6	4.1	4.1
Tanzania	3.5	3.6	2.8	2.8	2.8
Zimbabwe	2.8	2.3	2.2	1.7	1.7
Others	22.1	22.3	22.8	22.7	22.7
OCEANIA	**10.3**	**11.5**	**9.9**	**9.1**	**9.1**
Australia	9.7	10.9	9.3	8.5	8.5
New Zealand	0.6	0.7	0.6	0.7	0.7
WORLD TOTAL	**800.3**	**911.9**	**908.0**	**896.3**	**905.0** <

Source: IGC.

price for a derelict domestic agricultural sector is too high for survival, as the Greeks and Romans found. The essential distinction is the price level at which support is aimed. The support always has to be paid for, either by the consumer or the taxpayer. Traditionally, the most economic producers have gone for low prices and minimum support, coupled with insistence on free trade, trusting that this will bring them the greatest benefit. High cost producers have gone, as did most continental countries and as did the Common Agricultural Policy of the European Community until budgetary pressures became intolerable, for high prices—that is to say, prices which stimulate production beyond that of a free market—coupled with protection at the frontier to prevent these prices being undercut by cheap imports.

UNITED KINGDOM

The United Kingdom, as befitted the state which was the first to experience the Industrial Revolution, was something of an exception, being a relatively high-cost producer with what is now a century-old preference for cheap food. In the Agriculture Act 1947 an ingenious way was found of subsidising relatively expensive production and yet keeping prices down—namely, the deficiency payments system as applied to cereals, which was in essence a simple concept. Imports were allowed in at world prices which set the internal domestic market price. The home producer, through his farm organisation, negotiated with the government to agree a price sufficient to give the producer a reasonable return: the guaranteed price. The producer then sold his grain on the market at the best price he could get. Records were kept of the average market price throughout the marketing year, and at the end of the year the producer was paid the difference between the guaranteed price and the average market price to make up the deficiency in his income. This did not remove the incentive to good marketing since the seller suffered no disadvantage if he sold his grain for more than the average market price. The UK deficiency payments system was phased out over a transitional period of five years once the country became a member of the European Community, after which the price support system enshrined in the Common Agricultural Policy applied. Nonetheless many support systems, including the current American one until the introduction of the FAIR Act in 1995, contain elements of these principles. A difficulty is that as domestic production rises relative to imports a deficiency payments scheme can be expensive for the taxpayer. Even before the United Kingdom joined the EC it had been found necessary to introduce a scale of minimum import prices to contain expenditure.

UNITED STATES

Until the FAIR Act the US support system for grain was based on the Agriculture Act 1949, as amended (better known as the Farm Act, or Food Security Act, or under its style as the US Farm Bill, which is what it was called until passed into law by Congress and the President). New Farm Acts are passed every five years. Basically, this set two prices—a target price and a loan rate. The target price is guaranteed for a portion of the producer's crop; the loan rate, which is lower that the target price, is the figure at which he can lend (effectively, sell) his grain to the government. The producer had to undertake to participate in voluntary "set-aside" or "acreage reduction" schemes (i.e. take some of his land out of production—15 per cent in 1991) in order to benefit from government support. A later provision allowed increased flexibility by enabling farmers to respond more readily to market signals by switching their set-asides between grains—this was regarded by the Administration as an important improvement. Of similar importance is the conservation reserve, which keeps large areas out of production until the end of the 1990s.

The practical consequence of these provisions was that if, in the course of the season, the market prices rose above loan rate, it paid the producer to sell the grain in the market. If it did not, the government assumed responsibility for it. In either case the participating producer's return was topped up by payment from the government of the difference between target price and loan rate (i.e. a deficiency payment). Of course, it was more complicated than that, but those are the bones of the system. As part of the policy to make US agriculture more responsive to market signals, there was a considerable reduction in loan rates over successive seasons, and also a small drop in target prices.

The US Support Programme for 1991 wheat crops was as follows:

Target price	\$4.00 per bushel
Loan rate	\$2.04 per bushel (the basic, i.e. statutory, loan of \$2.52 was reduced to \$2.04 to maintain the competitiveness of US exports: this reduction also served to reduce the stockholding liability of the US Government)
Deficiency payment	\$1.40 per bushel, of which \$0.56 per bushel was cash advance payment.

There was a separate programme for feed grains, on the same principles, covering corn (maize), grain sorghum, barley and oats. Rice and two kinds of cotton is also provided for. Details of all the programmes were issued annually by the Agricultural Stabilisation and Conservation Service of the USDA.

CANADA

Canada's vast size (some 7,400 km across) and high proportion of exports to production led to the establishment of a complicated structure of grain movement and grain support institutions, both governmental and non-governmental. The basis of support for grain growers lay until recently in the Western Grain Stabilisation Act, established in 1976, and the Agriculture Stabilisation Act, both of which were administered through the Farm Income Services Branch of Agriculture Canada (as the Federal Department of Agriculture is known). The former Act protected farmers in the Canadian Wheat Board (CWB) area from severe price fluctuations: the latter Act provided the support prices for nine "named" commodities including soyabeans, oats and barley grown outside the CWB area.

The Western Grain Stabilisation Programme was operated on the basis that when the net cash revenue from grain sales in a given year fell below the average for the preceding five-year period, a stabilisation payment equal to the shortfall was made to farmers participating in the programme.

The payments made varied considerably from year to year. Thus, in 1987–1988 the initial payment for the widely-grown No 1 CWRS wheat was only Can$110 (subsequently revised to $120), while in 1988–1989, a year of widespread drought on the prairies, the initial payment was set at Can$150. In order to encourage production of the higher protein wheat a special premium for 14.5 per cent protein and higher was authorised. The Federal Government also announced the allocation of Can$12 million for drought assistance measures to prairie producers, to be used for drilling new wells and for the construction of water storage facilities.

A new gross revenue insurance programme was introduced in 1991 and effectively replaced the Western Grain Stabilisation Act and other *ad hoc* measures (three-quarters of eligible producers signed up in 1991). The aim was to protect participating farmers (who had to contribute to the cost) against low yields or low prices, and some commentators believed that this assurance of reasonable income would induce farmers to maintain their wheat plantings at higher levels than they might otherwise have done.

In 1995 it was announced that as part of its overall deficit reduction programme, the government would reduce the budget for Agriculture and Agri-Food Canada by 19 per cent over the next three years from C$2.1 billion to C$1.7 billion. One of the most important changes affecting cereals would be a comprehensive reform of grain transportation. The reform package and related transition measures included:

1. Elimination of the annual railway subsidy under the Western Grain Transportation Act (WGTA) resulting in annual savings

to the government of Can$540.6 million starting in August 1995;
2. An ex-gratia capital payment of Can$1.6 billion to owners of prairie farmland in recognition of the impact on land values that might result from the termination of long-standing freight rate subsidies;
3. A multi-year Western Grain Transportation Reform Adjustment Fund of Can$300 million to assist with the transition, and help maximise the opportunities from WGTA reform. This fund would be used to address specific issues such as local transportation alternatives to branch lines, the impact of pooling changes on producers in Manitoba and eastern Saskatchewan and the impact of reform on the alfalfa dehydration industry;
4. Applying the shipper-oriented provisions of the National Transportation Act to the transportation of prairie grains;
5. An efficiencies package to help reduce overall system costs and provide shippers with the opportunity to benefit from lower freight rates; a maximum freight rate would be established to protect the interests of farmers shipping grains and oilseeds;
6. Changes to the freight pooling system for CWB wheat and barley, to better reflect current market conditions and the costs of shipping; and in recognition of the continued importance of grain exports to the economy, credit guarantees worth up to Can$1 billion for exports of grains and other agri-food products to offshore private sector buyers to help Canadian producers continue to compete effectively in export markets.

These reforms would result in more higher-value crops and more value-added activities in western grain-producing regions. Overall returns from the market-place were expected to increase in the prairie provinces as a result of new exports, increases in further processing and the addition of new commodities.

In order to comply with agreements under the World Trade Organisation (WTO), the Food Freight Assistance (FFA) transportation subsidy was discontinued. Compensation payments totalling Can$72 million, disbursed over five years, would be made to eligible producers to offset this loss. The fund would be divided among affected provinces and territories in proportion to their use of the FFA between 1990 and 1995.

Net Income Stabilisation Account

The Net Income Stabilisation Account (NISA) is funded by producers and the federal and provincial governments. Before 1994, producers could contribute up to 2 per cent of the value of their eligible net sales, while the federal and provincial governments contributed 1 per cent each, raised in 1994 to 2.55 and 1.5 per cent, and in 1995 to 3 per cent and 2 per cent.

Western Grain Marketing Panel

A panel representing various sectors of the industry was at the same time set up to review grain marketing in western Canada, including the role of the Canadian Wheat Board, and covering oilseeds and special crops as well. Against the trend in other exporting nations outright privatisation has little appeal for Canadian farmers and the CWB will remain in place as the marketing agency for Western Grains, but the Board structure has been changed to make it more accountable.

ARGENTINA

Of other major grain producers, Argentina began a new system in 1987–1988 whereby farmers could obtain production inputs such as seed, fuel and fertilisers in exchange for wheat to be handed over after harvest. No subsidies were involved, though the interest was set at an advantageous rate of 1 per cent per month. This, together with the withdrawal of export taxes, improved the position of wheat growers, but this was more than offset by lower market prices, and more and more farmers started to turn to other crops.

New grading standards for wheat

With effect from the crop harvested at the beginning of 1997, new quality standards were introduced for wheat. For "trigo plata", a new grade, the following specifications apply: moisture 13 per cent maximum; specific weight 81 kgs/hl minimum; protein 13 per cent minimum (at 13.5 per cent moisture); wet gluten 32 per cent minimum; falling number 350 seconds minimum; ash 1.7 per cent maximum. "Soft white wheat" must have a protein content below 10 per cent (at 13.5 per cent moisture) and be white in colour to distinguish it from high protein samples.

It was subsequently indicated that the wheat quality improvement programme promoted by the Ministry of Agriculture had proved successful and, by enabling wheat to be differentiated by protein content, had helped to open up export markets. Average protein content had risen from 11.5 per cent at the beginning of the programme to 12.5 per cent in mid-1997.

World Bank loan

The World Bank granted the Government of Argentina a loan of $75 million to provide assistance to small and medium-sized agricultural businesses. The loan, supplemented by $25 million from government funds, will be used to improve the financial viability of some 40,000 small farms. Part may be allocated to rural infrastructure projects.

AUSTRALIA

In Australia, like Canada, grains are sold through marketing boards—the Australian Wheat Board and the Australian Barley Board. Returns to producers are assured through guaranteed minimum prices, reflecting world price movements.

In May 1988 the Australian Government announced a major packet of policy changes, consistent with Australia's commitment to the Punta del Este declaration of the Uruguay Round of GATT negotiations. It was stated that the effective rate of assistance to rural industries would be reduced from 16 per cent in 1986–1987 to an estimated 11 per cent in 1992–1993, though this would be offset by a general benefit through reductions in the general tariff rates. Australia and Argentina both frequently emphasise that they are the only large non-subsidising grain exporting countries.

WHEAT: NATIONAL POOL PRICES

The current Australian Wheat Marketing Act empowers the Australian Wheat Board to make advance payments for pool wheat and decide the size and timing of those payments. Harvest and post-harvest payments may also be made, according to the returns from domestic and export sales. In the past, pools for a particular crop were sometimes not closed for several years after its harvest, but the target is now that all pools should be finalised within approximately 18 months of the respective crop. Starting with the 1997 pools, growers may opt to deliver their grain to a pool offering 40 per cent of the expected pool return within 21 days and a further 50 per cent in August. This allows the AWB to save on interest charges on borrowings, the benefit being passed on to producers choosing this option. The AWB is to be privatised in July 1999.

EUROPEAN UNION

In the European Union, last of the big five producers in the economically developed western world, agricultural support is provided through the Common Agricultural Policy (see Chapter 23), probably the most controversial support system in the world. Denounced by its critics as an absurdity and hailed by its supporters as a miracle, a more balanced judgement would probably place it on par with the fabled curate's egg—good in parts.

CHAPTER 9

The pattern of world trade

An analysis of world trade in grain must start from an examination of the supply/demand equation. Supply—that is to say, production, minus net exports—should equal consumption plus stock increase. Such an equation can be established statistically where grain crosses frontiers and is recorded in customs documents: even here it is very rare to find that one country's version of imports equals exactly another country's record of exports. Statistics are peculiarly vulnerable where questions of transhipment arise: this was extremely evident whenever an attempt was made to reconcile trade passing through Rotterdam, the European *entrepôt* of world trade. Cargoes from the United States arrive in enormous bulk carriers, too large for most European ports: the bulk is broken in Rotterdam, and small parcels are carried in merchantmen and coastal vessels, across the North Sea to UK ports or to other ports on the continental mainland. Other cargoes continue by rail or barge to inland destinations in Germany or beyond. Are these cargoes all to be considered as exports to the Netherlands, or is none to be so designated? Logically, one would assume that only those parcels that remain in the Netherlands are to be counted as Dutch imports. Yet it is very difficult to ensure that this is what actually happens: how do you count items which are off-loaded and allowed to pass through Dutch customs and are then re-exported? Sometimes there may be financial advantage in such double handling.

But if there are difficulties in identifying precisely exports and imports that is as nothing compared to attempting to track the movement of grain which does not cross frontiers, and whose only record is contained in invoices. For grain there is no system of movement control as is applied to livestock movement: grain is the commodity which is quickest to lose its identity.

Nonetheless, in an examination of trading patterns it is instructive to look at the domestic patterns first. It is a truism to say that grain moves from areas of surplus to areas of deficit. In a perfect world economy this is, of course, to be expected, but natural channels can be blocked or diverted by government policy and action; by severe weather conditions or natural disasters; by industrial action; or by what the insurance documents describe as riots and civil commotion, even local wars.

Within a country, where there are no tariff barriers between regions, the natural flows prevail. For example, in Great Britain grain flows naturally from the East Midlands—the area with the largest net surplus—to the predominantly livestock areas of western and south-western England and Wales. East Anglia, though a large producer of cereals, is deficit in feedgrain because of its great production of malting barley and milling wheat. The South-East is only marginally in deficit: the counties of Surrey and Sussex are "importers", but Oxfordshire, Buckinghamshire, Berkshire and Kent are substantial surplus areas. Hence a substantial export trade has developed through the port of Southampton in Hampshire. For a time, the pattern tended to change as grain prices reached peaks at the end of the transitional period of UK accession to the EC: it became profitable to turn grazing land in the west and south over to cereal production and to export abroad more of the grain produced in the east, but as EC prices are being cut back the marginal producers tend to drop out and the traditional pattern to reassert itself. In quite a few countries (e.g. China, Russia), however, transport costs or rail car shortages are a significant factor inhibiting natural flows.

UNITED STATES

Figures 9.1 to 9.4 show the main areas of production in the United States as being broadly in the central states. Grain flows from the central plains area to the industrial east and west coasts, much of it moving south by barge down the Mississippi to Gulf ports, much by rail across the continent. Western White quality wheat grown in the western part of the country is also shipped from Pacific ports to mainly Pacific destinations. These figures were drawn up by USDA in 1985 but are broadly applicable in 1998. No later diagrams are available. In a detailed study of grain production and trade flows in the United States a French writer, Jean-Paul Charvet, has identified what he designates "poles of production" from which the grain flows outward, placing the principal such pole in central Illinois, 1,330 km from New York, 2,600 km from Los Angeles and 1,040 km from New Orleans.

Continuing this theme, Charvet establishes the cereal pole for France in the Beauce area, between the Loire and the Seine south of Paris, where the main areas of production of soft wheat, durum wheat and barley all overlap one another. Thus these grains flow from the Paris Basin to the areas of consumption and exportation, while there is a different pole of production for maize, south of the Loire. In the European

Figure 9.1 US wheat movements to points of export, 1985

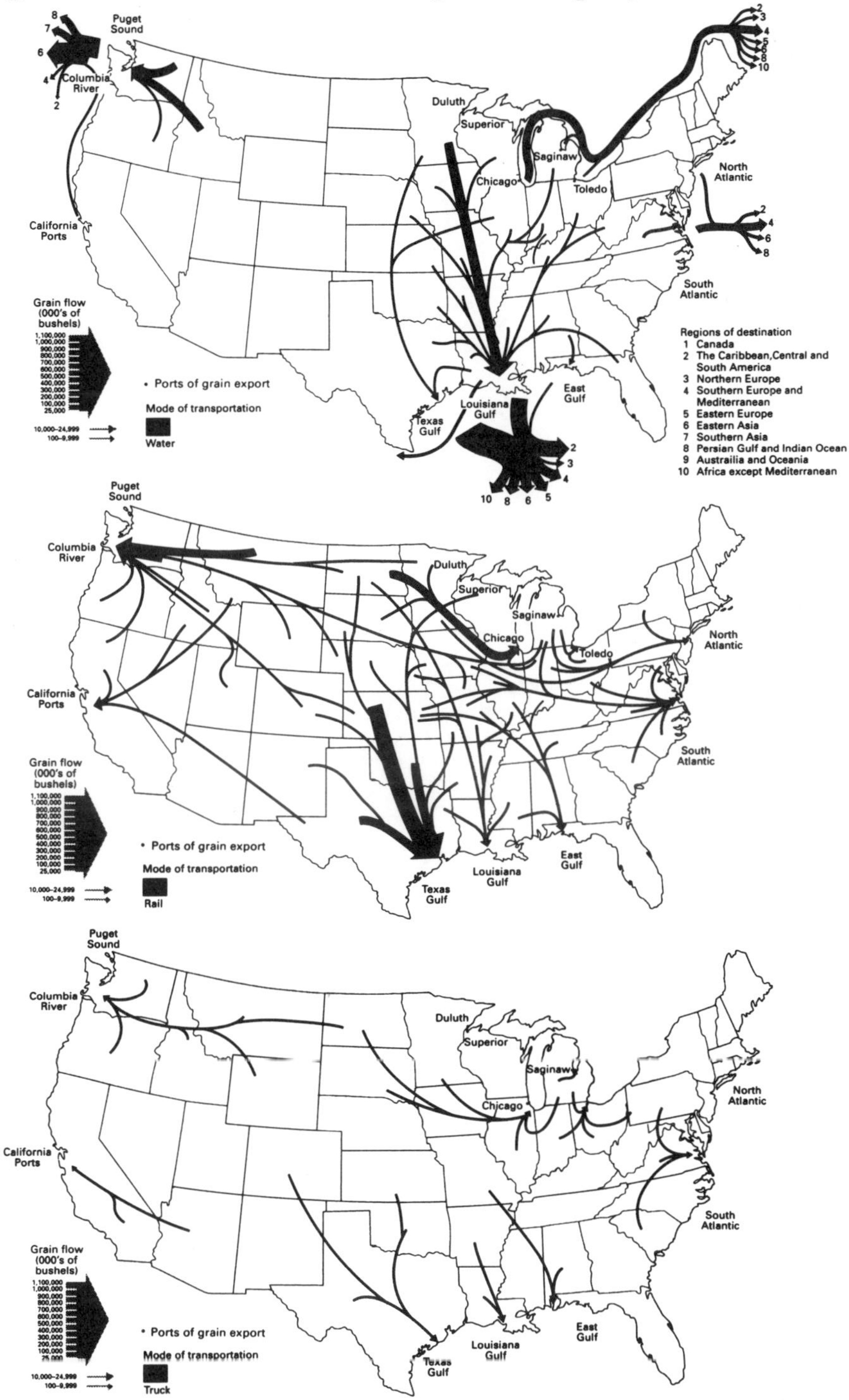

Source: USDA.

Figure 9.2 US corn movements to points of export, 1985

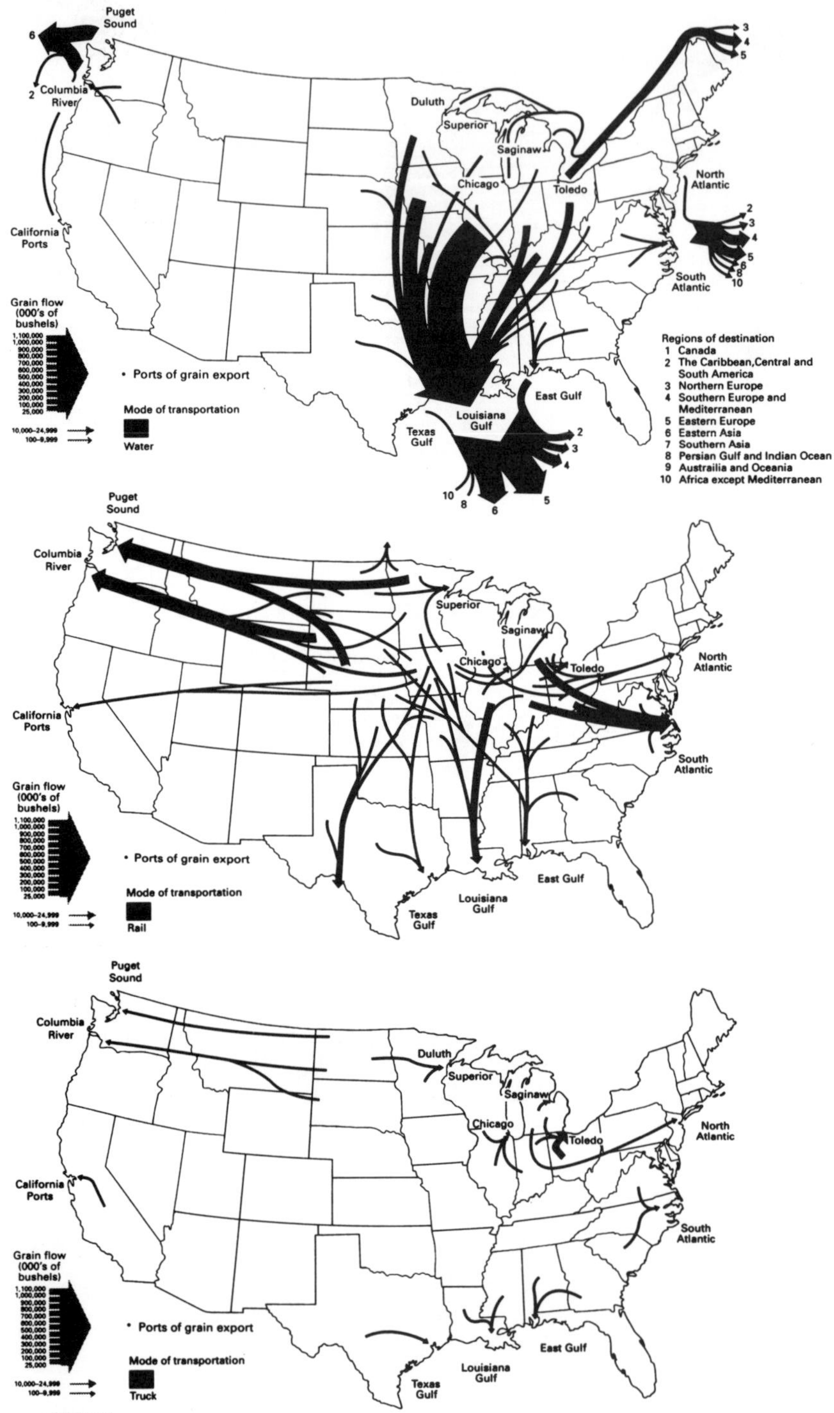

Source: USDA.

Figure 9.3 US soyabean movements to points of export, 1985

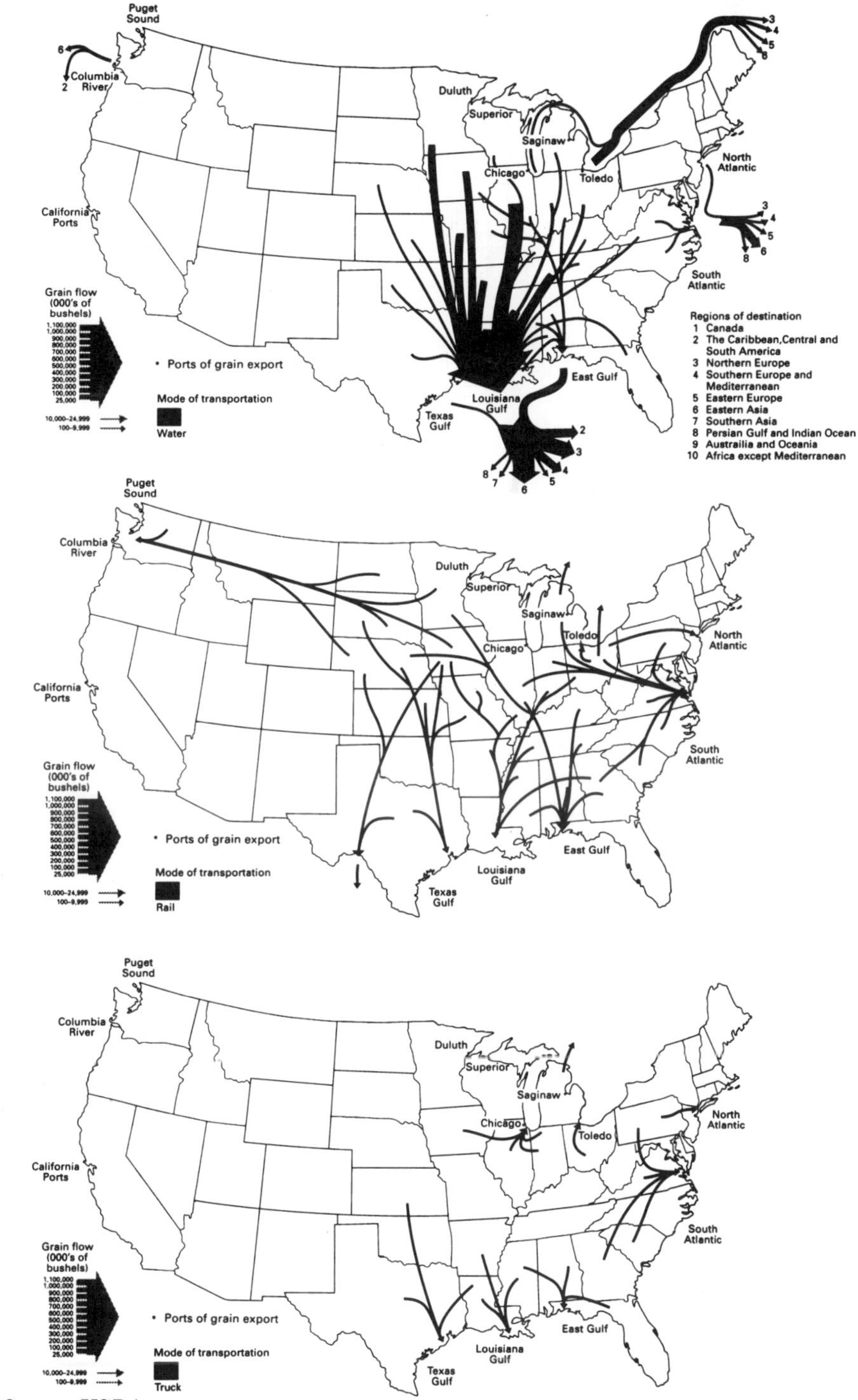

Source: USDA.

Figure 9.4 Corn, soyabeans and wheat: production and origin of movements to points of export, 1985

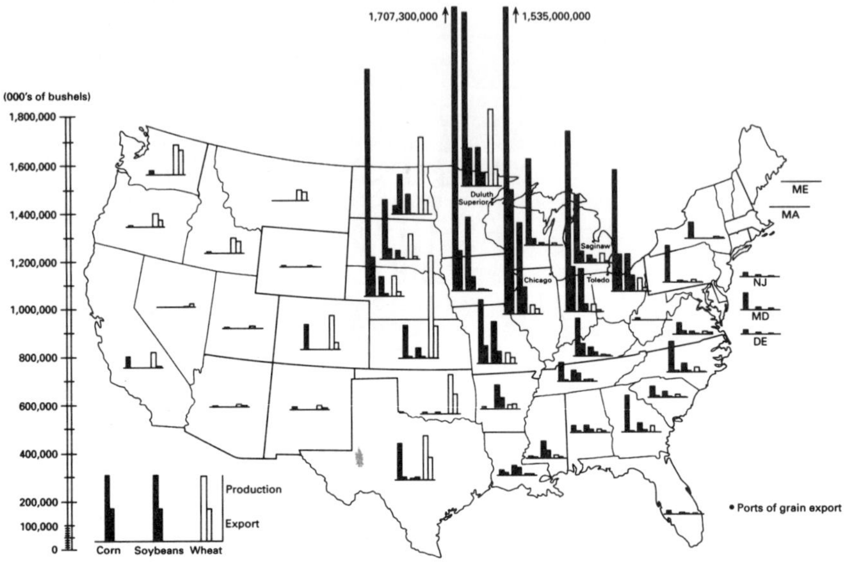

Source: USDA.

Community area the whole internal price policy since the abandonment of regional prices in the mid-1970s is based on the difference between the price in the area of greatest surplus (Ormes in France) to the area of greatest deficit (Duisburg in Germany).

In all countries grain flows from the rural producing countryside to the urban consuming cities, acquiring added value as it is processed at various stages in the chain. In developing countries this flow is accentuated by government policy, which insists for political reasons on giving priority to cheap food for the mass of voting consumers in the towns over the economic return to less politically important producers on the farms.

FRANCE

France is the most important cereal-producing country in the European Union, and is a good subject for closer analysis. Wheat and barley production is concentrated mainly in four regions, headed by the Paris Basin mentioned above, and followed by the Centre (round Orléans), the Champagne Region (round Chalons-sur-Marne and Rheims), and Picardy (round Amiens). These four regions in 1997–1998 accounted for 14.4 million tons out of a total of 32.9 million tons in total wheat production, and 4.4 million tons out of a total of 10.2 million tons in barley production.

French maize production is more diverse. Again, there are four main producing areas, but these are located, as one would expect for climatic reasons, predominantly in the southern part of France. These regions are Aquitaine (round Bordeaux), Poitou Charente, the Centre, and the Midi-Pyrénées (round Toulouse). These four regions account for 6.07 million tons out of a total maize production of 16.8 million tons.

The pattern of internal trade follows the general principles described above. The Paris region is the centre of wheat consumption, processing into flour taking place in the great flour mills owned by major firms, Grands Moulins de Paris, Soufflet and Champagne Céréales. Similarly, there are important flour mills in the consuming areas of Bordeaux, Toulouse, etc.

Starch is produced from both wheat and maize, the main processing area being the Nord region, where Roquette and Cerestar have important mills. There are maltings in the north and north-east, the

Figure 9.5 Maize export flows from France by maritime routes

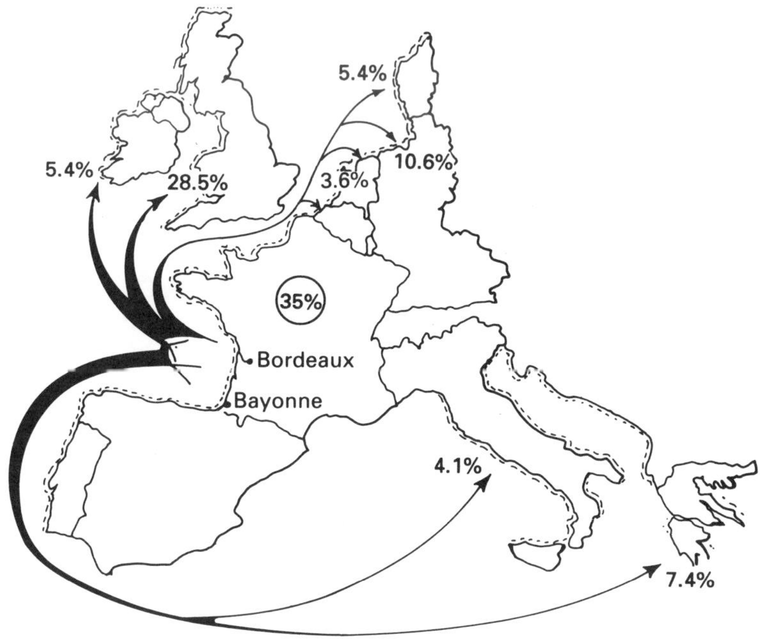

Source: Maisica.

most important being the Marne region (Champagne Céréales), the Aube Region (Soufflet) and at Strasbourg.

Figure 9.5 is a flow chart showing French maize exports by percentage and destination; total domestic consumption is 35 per cent of production and exports comprise 65 per cent of production.

CANADA

The second great cereals producer in North America is Canada, where agriculture is more significant than in the US in terms of a percentage of the gross national product. Production is largely concentrated in the prairie provinces of Alberta, Saskatchewan and Manitoba. Here the principal crop is spring-sown wheat, the variety known as Canadian Western Red Spring (CWRS) being among the finest breadmaking quality hard wheats in the world. About 75 per cent of the Canadian wheat crop is exported to over 60 countries in the world. The balance is evenly split between seed, feed and food consumption in Canada.

Barley is produced in all three prairie provinces, with Alberta the most important. Two-thirds of barley production is consumed domestically. Not much maize (corn) is grown in the prairie provinces, but canola (rapeseed) is a very important oilseed crop, producing a high-quality edible oil.

Corn is grown in Ontario and Quebec, mainly destined for local feedlots. Alberta also possesses a substantial feed industry, the meat being consumed domestically or exported to the United States and Japan. Although the border is officially open with the US, States and Provinces are liable to introduce their own restrictions. I am told that US farmers are more inclined to complain about Canadian grain coming south than the reverse.

Grain for export leaves Canada via the west coast ports of Vancouver and Prince Rupert, which together account for about 60 per cent of export shipping, and eastward from Thunder Bay at the head of the Great Lakes, thence via the St Lawrence and across the Atlantic mainly to the Soviet Union (St Petersburg), Europe (United Kingdom), South America and the Middle East. The export flow of wheat has gradually shifted from the east coast to the west coast. Some grain has been exported to Europe through west coast ports via the Panama Canal, though this is not common.

Internally, the grain makes great use of both rail and ship (relatively little moves by road)—by rail westwards from the prairies across the Rocky Mountains along the two rail systems, the Canadian National and the Canadian Pacific, to west coast ports, as well as to Thunder Bay in the east. Few deep-water vessels, or "salties", as they are called, use

Thunder Bay. Rather, the grain is moved by large lake vessels to export ports in the St Lawrence such as Sorel, Trois Rivières and Montreal.

AUSTRALIA

Australia's main grain crops are wheat, barley, sorghum and oats. Of these wheat is by far the most important, production averaging around 17 million tons *per annum* (rising in 1996 to 23.7 million). The breakdown by states shows Western Australia as largest producer, followed by New South Wales, South Australia, and Victoria and Queensland. Varieties of cereal are developed at state level, 70 per cent of Australian wheat being of Australian Standard White (ASW) variety, which is a sought-after filler wheat for bread grists and produces a natural white flour with an extraction rate 2 per cent better than average wheats. ASW can give an extraction rate of 90 per cent for atta, the coarse flour produced for export to India and the Middle East where it is used for the baking of unleavened bread.

Australia used to sell large amounts of grain to the USSR and China, but this trade has largely disappeared in recent years. Currently the largest markets are Iran (2.5 million tons in 1996–1970), Indonesia (1.8 million tons in 1996–1997 and 1.9 million tons in 1997–1998), India (1.2 million tons in 1996–1997 and 1.0 million tons in 1997–1998), and Pakistan (1.2 million tons in 1997–1998). Trade with Europe has virtually disappeared (a mere 174,000 tons to the EU in 1997–1998). However, regional markets for Australian wheat also included Muscat and Oman and Yemen, as well as Japan, South Korea and Thailand. The Middle East and Far East Asia areas increased in importance as an outlet as the market in the United Kingdom and Western Europe diminished with the rise in EC production and external protection, following UK entry into the Community.

The domestic market uses up to 2.5 million tons of wheat, about 1.5 million in the form of flour for human consumption, one million for animal feed and about 400,000 tons for industrial use. The balance goes for export. The main export ports are Perth (Kwinana), which has been developed into a very large terminal handling three million tons in a year and able to accommodate bulk carriers up to 70,000 tons; Port Lincoln in South Australia; Geelong in Victoria; Port Kembla and Newcastle in New South Wales; and Fisherman Island in Queensland.

Barley is the second most important cereal crop, averaging around five or six million tons *per annum*. Here South Australia is the predominant producer, followed by Western Australia, Queensland and Victoria. Domestic consumption is around one million tons a year, basically used for the pig industry, mainly located on the Victoria/New South Wales border. Export of the remaining three million tons is distributed among Saudi Arabia (where 75 per cent of the cargoes go for camel feed), China (much of it as malting barley, to meet the increasing beer consumption), Japan and Europe. The feed market in Japan accounts for about 400,000 tons a year. Australian barley in processed form as malt is also exported to Europe.

Sorghum and oats production amount to 1.3 million tons each *per annum*. The sorghum is mainly grown in Queensland and northern New South Wales, and mostly goes to the livestock industry, either as compound feed or in direct despatch to feedlots. Little sorghum is exported.

Australian oats are renowned for high quality. Production is centred in Western Australia and Victoria, and the bulk of production is consumed domestically, going for breakfast foods, sheep and horses, in that order. Graziers use the high nutritional value of the oats to supplement sheep feed in the autumn prior to lambing. There is a limited export of oats to Europe: among other uses Australian oats are valued by the bloodstock industry as racehorse feed. But because oats are bulky for their weight they take up a lot of shipping space relative to their value. Australian oats therefore suffer a considerable freight disadvantage in Europe compared with nearer supplies.

Australian wheat exports are in the hands of the Australian Wheat Board, based in Melbourne; and until recently the Australian Barley Board (comprising two separate state boards, of which the most important are in Victoria and South Australia, with smaller boards in New South Wales and Queensland); and the Grain Pool in Western Australia. The statutes of these boards are contained in state Statutory Marketing Acts, currently under revision.

ARGENTINA

Argentina is the fifth of the world's great cereals exporting nations. Production of wheat fluctuates, from figures as low as 2.1 million tons in 1951 to 15.9 million tons in 1996. Recent harvests have been around 10 million to 14 million tons. Argentina produces a larger quantity of coarse grains (24.2 million tons in 1997), three-quarters of which is corn (maize) and one-quarter sorghum.

Exports of wheat and wheat flour ranged around 2–3 million tons in the 1960s and early 1970s, more or less doubling after the shortages induced by Soviet grain purchases, peaking at 9.7 million tons in 1983–1984. The forecast for 1997–1998 is 9 million tons, while coarse grain exports have declined in recent years.

Argentina is unlike the other four major exporters in being a developing country, whereas the other four are classified as developed economies. Yet it is a developing country which produces agricultural goods in a temperate climate, competing with produce which tends to be more subsidised than tropical production.

An interesting analysis prepared by Guillermo Nielsen for the Fifth International Grain Market Conference in 1989 showed the evolution of exports of cereals, oilseeds, oilseeds products and beef in terms of volume indices. These (Table 9.1) showed the decline in beef exports, in favour of an expansion in cereals and oilseeds and oilseed products—in other words, a switch of exports from animal protein to vegetable protein and oils. The strongest characteristic of Argentine agriculture is its capacity to adapt in this fashion, to seek out new markets through discounting prices, and to trade with partners (e.g. Iran, Cuba) which were not targeted by competing exporters for political reasons. Argentina also aims at expanding trade with the newly industrialised countries.

For the student seeking to keep track of world grain trade in terms of who is supplying whom at any given time, there are a number of sources. The supply/demand data, to which reference was made at the beginning of this chapter, are probably best found in the USDA Foreign Agricultural Service monthly bulletin World Grain Situation and Outlook. This contains supply/demand tables for world wheat and wheat flour, for coarse grains, and for each individual grain (including rice).

A concise survey of international trade showing shipments of wheat and coarse grains by the five major exporting countries for various periods of the year is contained in the International Grains Council periodic documents (see Table 9.2). A detailed analysis by destination and source is also regularly reported by the IGC. An example from the latter's June 1998 Grain Market Report contains the figures of shipments for wheat and flour (with a separate table for durum and semolina); and also the shipments of the major coarse grains (maize and barley) and malt. These are shown in Tables 9.3 and 9.4.

Table 9.1 Argentine exports of selected agricultural products—volume indices 1976/80 = 100

	1961–65	*1966–70*	*1971–75*	*1976–80*	*1981–85*	*1986*	*1987*	*1988*
Cereals	56	67	69	100	146	106	74	82
Wheat	84	74	42	100	181	105	116	107
Maize	55	83	94	100	139	154	84	94
Others	29	41	65	100	121	50	24	44
Oilseeds	1	0	0	100	141	181	81	118
Sunflower seed	0	0	0	100	282	1287	125	135
Soya	0	0	0	100	139	159	79	125
Peanut	0	0	5	100	158	261	252	0
By-products	62	58	36	100	192	287	344	327
Oils	55	55	38	100	184	309	335	306
Cakes	65	60	35	100	195	277	348	336
Beef[a]	91	111	76	100	64	42	43	48

[a] Bone in equivalent.

Source: Paper presented at Fifth International Grain Market Conference, Brussels, 1989.

Table 9.2 Shipments: wheat and coarse grains (major exporters)

'000 tons

EXPORTS	MONTHLY					PROVISIONAL			
	NOVEMBER		DECEMBER		JANUARY		FEB	MAR	APR
	1996	1997	1996	1997	1997	1998	1998	1998	1998
Argentina									
All Wheat	433	403	1,914	765	2,565	1,768	1,235	1,374	908
Coarse grains	267	347	280	427	171	213	271	1821	2,552
Maize	261	338	280	427	130	209	247	1,661	2,180
Sorghum	6	10	–	–	17	4	20	138	354
Total	**700**	**750**	**2,194**	**1,192**	**2,736**	**1,981**	**1,506**	**3,195**	**3,460**
Australia									
All Wheat	981	1,273	1,660	1,671	2,147	1,678	1,122	1,108	1,422
Coarse grains	280	231	606	276	596	115	332	183	n/a
Barley	254	220	593	268	590	101	191	183	n/a
Sorghum	3	6	2	1	2	1	125	–	n/a
Total	**1,261**	**1,504**	**2,266**	**1,947**	**2,743**	**1,793**	**1,454**	**1,291**	**n/a**
Canada									
All Wheat	1,853	2,126	1,227	1,883	1,121	1,587	1,619	1,512	1,565
Coarse grains	687	460	554	297	346	172	159	234	251
Barley	443	286	365	181	229	107	83	188	225
Oats	181	154	149	105	88	58	66	35	27
Total	**2,540**	**2,586**	**1,781**	**2,180**	**1,467**	**1,759**	**1,778**	**1,746**	**1,816**
EC (c)									
All Wheat	1,827	1,283	2,067	1,302	1,163	830	206	490	416
Coarse grains (a)	889	269	932	70	514	88	129	200	149
Barley	883	253	919	69	500	63	129	186	126
Maize	6	16	14	1	14	25	–	24	23
Total	**2,716**	**1,552**	**2,999**	**1,372**	**1,677**	**918**	**335**	**690**	**565**
									(b) 4 wks
USA									
All Wheat	2,105	2,152	1,402	2,278	1,697	2,674	1,949	1,754	1,631
Coarse grains	6,737	3,640	5,325	4,218	5,250	3,632	3,985	4,000	4,346
Barley	49	163	53	62	29	31	42	73	44
Maize	6,128	3,050	4,770	3,567	4,635	2,991	3,044	3,324	3,778
Sorghum	558	422	500	587	584	609	896	559	524
Total	**8,842**	**5,792**	**6,727**	**6,496**	**6,947**	**6,306**	**5,934**	**5,754**	**5,977**

Table 9.2—*cont.*

'000 tons

EXPORTS	QUARTERLY APR/JUN 1996	APR/JUN 1997	JUL/SEP 1996	JUL/SEP 1997	OCT/DEC 1996	OCT/DEC 1997	CALENDAR YEAR 1996 JAN/DEC	CALENDAR YEAR 1997 JAN/DEC	IGC CROP YEAR 1996/97 JUL/JAN	IGC CROP YEAR 1997/98 JUL/JAN
Argentina										
All Wheat	976	1,551	755	1,068	2,701	1,492	6,332	9,402	6,021	4,328
Coarse grains	3,597	6,056	2,498	2,315	776	1,375	7,744	11,795	3,446	3,903
Maize	3,079	5,650	2,401	2,176	758	1,359	7,044	10,921	3,289	3,744
Sorghum	518	321	98	132	18	17	634	642	133	153
Total	**4,573**	**7,607**	**3,253**	**3,383**	**3,477**	**2,867**	**14,075**	**21,197**	**9,466**	**8,231**
Australia										
All Wheat	3,794	4,931	2,554	3,288	3,600	4,017	14,463	19,053	8,301	8,984
Coarse grains	1,413	771	736	719	1,156	674	4,652	3,867	2,488	1,508
Barley	949	698	496	576	1,073	626	3,752	3,562	2,159	1,302
Sorghum	321	46	198	98	34	13	596	170	234	112
Total	**5,207**	**5,703**	**3,290**	**4,007**	**4,756**	**4,691**	**19,116**	**22,920**	**10,790**	**10,492**
Canada										
All Wheat	4,196	5,564	3,366	6,382	4,957	5,875	16,414	21,844	9,444	13,844
Coarse grains	1,170	1,250	955	1,179	2,003	1,367	5,060	4,850	3,304	2,717
Barley	816	802	533	544	1,256	857	3,110	2,843	2,019	1,508
Oats	168	317	298	475	594	463	1,276	1,548	980	996
Total	**5,366**	**6,814**	**4,321**	**7,561**	**6,960**	**7,241**	**21,474**	**26,694**	**12,748**	**16,561**
EC (c)										
All Wheat	2,228	4,438	2,541	2,190	5,644	3,595	13,807	14,604	9,348	6,615
Coarse grains (a)	522	1,771	1,142	489	2,406	703	4,559	4,632	4,062	1,280
Barley	441	1,719	1,114	448	2,371	645	4,320	4,386	3,985	1,157
Maize	82	53	29	41	36	58	242	247	79	124
Total	**2,750**	**6,209**	**3,683**	**2,679**	**8,050**	**4,298**	**18,366**	**19,237**	**13,410**	**7,895**
USA										
All Wheat	6,759	4,979	10,489	9,187	6,188	6,922	31,550	25,955	18,374	18,783
Coarse grains	14,462	10,889	10,528	11,392	16,290	11,598	58,071	48,334	32,068	26,621
Barley	220	219	228	672	190	603	1,048	1,628	447	1,306
Maize	13,522	9,602	9,090	9,694	14,571	9,595	52,178	41,603	28,296	22,280
Sorghum	705	1,066	1,201	1,018	1,519	1,389	4,807	5,077	3,304	3,016
Total	**21,221**	**15,868**	**21,017**	**20,579**	**22,478**	**18,520**	**89,621**	**74,290**	**50,442**	**45,405**

(a) EC coarse grains includes barley and maize only.
(b) Based on weekly shipment reports, covering 4 or 5 weeks (as stated).
(c) Wheat and Coarse Grains based on following unofficial Member State data: Jan '98: France, Germany and UK; Feb '98: France and UK only; Mar '98: France and UK only; Apr '98: France only.

Source: IGC

Table 9.3 Shipments by destination: all wheat (incl. durum) (major exporters)

'000 tons

IMPORTERS	ARGENTINA (b)		AUSTRALIA (a)		CANADA		EC		USA	
	Jul/Apr		Jul/Apr		Jul/Apr		Jul/Dec		Jul/Mar	
	1996/97	1997/98	1996/97	1997/98	1996/97	1997/98	1996/97	1997/98	1996/97	1997/98
Europe	**415**	**179**	**256**	**199**	**833**	**1,264**	**1,591**	**408**	**1,043**	**1,101**
Albania										
EC	164	108	194	199	750	1,174	0	0	631	882
Norway	–	–	–	–	6	20	36	110	62	33
Poland	122	–	–	–	66	23	1,024	13	81	10
Romania	–	–	–	–	–	–	3	3	–	–
Switzerland	–	–	T	–	2	30	9	18	2	24
Others	293	179	256	–	767	1,241	564	392	961	1,091
CIS & Baltics	**120**	**20**	**0**	**1**	**0**	**44**	**676**	**335**	**425**	**468**
Baltic States	52	0	0	0	0	0	72	33	0	0
CIS	67	20	0	1	T	44	603	302	425	468
Russia	*25*	–	*T*	*1*	*T*	*44*	*128*	*92*	*58*	*77*
Other CIS	*42*	*20*	*0*	–	*T*	–	*475*	*210*	*367*	*391*
N & C America	**204**	**3**	**0**	**3**	**2,139**	**2,695**	**327**	**326**	**2,530**	**2,117**
Cuba	200	–	–	–	36	110	268	307	–	–
Mexico	–	–	–	–	347	721	–	–	1,295	891
USA	–	T	–	–	1,529	1,535	1	1	–	–
Others/unspec.	5	3	0	3	227	329	58	19	1,234	1,226
South America	**4,279**	**3,518**	**222**	**16**	**1,762**	**2,663**	**73**	**31**	**2,201**	**1,307**
Bolivia	149	85	–	–	30	50	–	10	125	100
Brazil	3,495	3,199	–	–	483	647	T	3	759	T
Chile	70	37	66	–	256	311	27	14	T	52
Colombia	94	–	74	–	298	490	–	–	272	312
Ecuador	37	3	82	16	85	117	T	2	181	210
Peru	339	176	–	–	150	520	41	T	377	184
Venezuela	40	5	–	–	458	527	T	T	434	403
Others/unspec.	55	13	–	–	0	–	5	2	53	45

Table 9.3—*cont.*

'000 tons

IMPORTERS	ARGENTINA (b)		AUSTRALIA (a)		CANADA		EC		USA	
	Jul/Apr		Jul/Apr		Jul/Apr		Jul/Dec		Jul/Mar	
	1996/97	1997/98	1996/97	1997/98	1996/97	1997/98	1996/97	1997/98	1996/97	1997/98
Near East Asia	**1,769**	**1,324**	**4,946**	**3,386**	**2,073**	**2,649**	**1,068**	**672**	**1,531**	**2,454**
Iran	504	885	2,855	486	2,014	2,143	41	–	–	–
Iraq	99	–	308	1,239	–	–	98	67	16	665
Israel	58	–	–	–	15	–	22	2	491	703
Jordan	222	142	98	–	–	T	25	5	107	229
Kuwait	–	26	167	105	8	–	27	T	–	T
Muscat & Oman	–	–	214	329	–	–	T	T	–	–
Syria	–	–	1	–	–	–	6	10	–	–
Turkey	812	137	296	248	28	216	284	66	226	272
Yemen	–	75	411	545	–	–	505	488	486	383
Others/unspec.	74	58	596	434	8	290	60	34	205	201
Far East Asia	**886**	**423**	**7,212**	**7,675**	**5,608**	**5,683**	**318**	**165**	**8,623**	**8,075**
Pacific Asia	*628*	*165*	*4,887*	*4,921*	*5,123*	*5,227*	*209*	*78*	*6,421*	*5,619*
China	43	–	121	133	1,552	1,391	15	T	787	242
Chinese Taipei	–	–	36	28	36	–	–	2	721	660
Indonesia	297	110	2,045	2,122	1,149	1,127	53	T	86	T
Japan	–	–	1,049	1,003	1,380	1,292	T	T	2,167	2,311
Korea (N)	–	–	–	–	–	10	1	T	–	–
Korea (S)	148	55	572	544	658	570	T	T	1,195	1,081
Malaysia	118	–	597	535	123	340	–	–	33	8
Philippines	–	–	102	21	85	359	–	T	1,194	1,049
Singapore	–	–	43	86	12	6	T	T	46	24
Thailand	21	–	211	237	121	88	–	T	178	212
Vietnam	–	–	79	183	–	39	129	69	–	10
Others	109	0	2,100	2,703	378	410	120	94	2,068	2,259
South Asia	*258*	*258*	*2,326*	*2,754*	*485*	*456*	*110*	*87*	*2,203*	*2,456*
Bangladesh	14	–	167	130	82	161	95	72	226	150
India	95	–	1,394	1,264	266	–	T	–	22	37
Pakistan	–	–	507	1,250	–	244	–	13	1,805	2,023
Sri Lanka	149	258	258	80	114	51	T	T	150	218
Others	149	258	258	110	138	51	15	2	150	247

Table 9.3—*cont.*

'000 tons

IMPORTERS	ARGENTINA (b)		AUSTRALIA (a)		CANADA		EC		USA	
	Jul/Apr		Jul/Apr		Jul/Apr		Jul/Dec		Jul/Mar	
	1996/97	1997/98	1996/97	1997/98	1996/97	1997/98	1996/97	1997/98	1996/97	1997/98
Africa	**1,884**	**1,472**	**1,981**	**1,073**	**1,607**	**3,463**	**4,121**	**3,831**	**4,524**	**6,795**
North Africa	*1,314*	*1,072*	*1,269*	*468*	*1,291*	*2,554*	*2,690*	*2,447*	*3,104*	*5,491*
Algeria	142	102	–	–	906	1,918	701	882	207	173
Egypt	742	455	1,269	449	14	7	984	486	2,327	4,400
Libya	–	145	–	–	137	206	416	281	–	–
Morocco	191	252	–	19	211	374	462	583	418	449
Tunisia	239	117	–	–	23	49	128	215	152	469
Sub Sahara	*570*	*401*	*712*	*605*	*316*	*909*	*1,431*	*1,384*	*1,420*	*1,305*
Cameroon	14	–	–	–	–	20	73	63	24	36
Congo Dem. Rep.	8	–	–	–	–	–	77	56	71	60
Ethiopia	–	–	6	28	–	54	60	190	120	50
Somalia	–	–	–	–	–	–	5	9	–	–
South Africa	95	23	279	T	86	224	T	1	345	123
Sudan	32	–	68	93	–	100	240	106	33	–
Others/unspec.	421	377	359	484	230	510	976	960	828	1,036
Oceania	**0**	**0**	**323**	**284**	**68**	**77**	**9**	**12**	**14**	**9**
New Zealand	–	–	160	90	60	63	T	T	–	6
Others/unspec.	–	–	163	193	8	14	9	12	14	3
Unspecified	**–**	**908**	**28**	**–**	**–**	**T**	**1**	**5**	**652**	**162**
WORLD TOTAL	**9,557**	**7,847**	**14,969**	**12,636**	**14,090**	**18,539**	**8,185**	**5,786**	**21,543**	**22,487**

(a) Including wheat flour for July/February.
(b) Including wheat flour for July/November.
T = Trace (less than half the unit in which the table is expressed).

Source: IGC.

Table 9.4 Shipments by destination: durum wheat (inc. semolina) (major exporters)

'000 tons

IMPORTERS	CANADA 1996/97	CANADA Jul/Apr 1997/98	EC 1996/97	EC Jul/Dec 1997/98	USA 1996/97	USA Jul/Mar 1997/98
Europe	**333**	**655**	**20**	**30**	**273**	**352**
EC	308	603	–	–	272	322
Poland	19	23	6	6	–	10
Others	6	29	14	23	1	20
CIS & Baltics	**–**	**T**	**5**	**T**	**2**	**27**
Baltic States	0	0	0	0	0	0
CIS	–	T	5	T	2	27
Russia	–	*T*	*T*	*T*	–	*14*
Other CIS	–	–	*5*	*T*	*2*	*13*
N & C America	**339**	**410**	**1**	**1**	**73**	**85**
Cuba	6	5	–	–	–	–
USA	294	388	T	1	–	–
South America	**357**	**379**	**0**	**0**	**114**	**70**
Brazil	T	15	T	T	–	–
Chile	40	73	–	–	–	–
Peru	90	120	–	–	15	5
Venezuela	214	168	–	–	62	53
Near East	**638**	**0**	**37**	**22**	**25**	**36**
Turkey	–	–	14	3	19	–
Far East	**201**	**177**	**0**	**0**	**24**	**96**
Pacific Asia	*201*	*177*	–	*T*	*24*	*67*
Indonesia	26	11	T	T	–	–
Japan	175	166	–	T	21	63

Table 9.4—*cont.*

'000 tons

	CANADA		EC		USA	
IMPORTERS	**1996/97**	**Jul/Apr 1997/98**	**1996/97**	**Jul/Dec 1997/98**	**1996/97**	**Jul/Mar 1997/98**
South Asia	–	–	–	–	–	*30*
India	–	–	–	–	–	–
Africa	**1,205**	**1,961**	**98**	**87**	**260**	**560**
North Africa	*1,205*	*1.961*	–	*69*	*243*	*502*
Algeria	906	1,456	61	25	179	70
Libya	65	173	11	4	–	–
Morocco	211	308	T	20	40	74
Tunisia	23	25	3	13	24	286
Sub Sahara	–	–	–	*18*	*17*	*58*
Oceania	**0**	**0**	**0**	**0**	**0**	**0**
Unspecified	**-**	**-**	**1**	**T**	**-**	**83**
World Total	**3,072**	**3,583**	**163**	**141**	**770**	**1,310**

T = Trace (less than half the unit in which the table is expressed).

Source: IGC.

Table 9.5 Shipments by destination: maize (corn) (major exporters)

'000 tons

	ARGENTINA		CHINA		USA	
IMPORTERS	Jul/Apr		Jul/Apr		Jul/Mar	
	1996/97	1997/98	1996/97	1997/98	1996/97	1997/98
Europe	**699**	**885**	**–**	**–**	**1,674**	**197**
EC	551	836	–	–	1,231	155
Poland	50	28	–	–	322	–
Others	97	21	–	–	120	42
CIS & Baltics	**0**	**0**	**9**	**10**	**112**	**66**
Baltic States	–	–	–	–	69	18
CIS	–	–	9	10	42	48
Russia	–	–	*9*	*10*	*36*	*41*
Other CIS	–	–	–	–	*6*	*8*
N & C America	**202**	**176**	**–**	**–**	**5,257**	**4,719**
Canada	–	T	–	–	806	852
Costa Rica	T	T	–	–	233	256
Dominican Rep	9	T	–	–	527	516
El Salvador	22	55	–	–	191	98
Guatemala	17	18	–	–	227	135
Jamaica	–	T	–	–	136	145
Mexico	1	T	–	–	2,823	2,385
Panama	–	–	–	–	131	157
Others	154	102	–	–	182	175
South America	**1,236**	**1,977**	**–**	**–**	**2,247**	**1,853**
Brazil	227	421	–	–	11	5
Chile	166	480	–	–	395	104
Colombia	243	163	–	–	1,073	954
Ecuador	1	30	–	–	114	56
Peru	327	637	–	–	191	173
Venezuela	254	225	–	–	548	548
Others	19	22	–	–	14	13
N E Asia	**1,444**	**1,032**	**–**	**–**	**2,325**	**1,599**
Iran	591	509	–	–	–	–
Israel	115	17	–	–	422	147
Jordan	41	198	–	–	251	78
Saudi Arabia	156	131	–	–	737	771
Turkey	140	7	–	–	330	136
Others	402	171	–	–	586	466
F E Asia	**2,010**	**664**	**664**	**6,311**	**21,774**	**17,015**
Pacific Asia	*2,010*	*664*	*648*	*6,275*	*21,752*	*17,015*
China	–	–	–	–	53	53
Chinese Taipai	125	45	–	–	4,316	3,616
Japan	239	101	15	119	11,089	11,200
Korea (S)	722	23	143	3,963	5,205	1,927
Malaysia	487	388	195	1,124	790	54
Philippines	–	T	119	107	166	2
Others	437	107	148	962	132	164

Table 9.5—*cont.*

						'000 tons
	ARGENTINA		**CHINA**		**USA**	
IMPORTERS	**Jul/Apr**		**Jul/Apr**		**Jul/Mar**	
	1996/97	**1997/98**	**1996/97**	**1997/98**	**1996/97**	**1997/98**
South Asia	–	*T*	*16*	*36*	*22*	–
Africa	**1,689**	**917**	**–**	**–**	**2,668**	**3,013**
North Africa	*1,465*	*719*	–	–	*2,478*	*2,788*
Algeria	126	T	–	–	467	725
Egypt	846	497	–	–	1,645	1,570
Morocco	251	56	–	–	252	331
Tunisia	176	94	–	–	114	162
Sub Sahara	*224*	*197*	–	–	*190*	*224*
South Africa	–	–	9	10	36	41
Oceania	**0**	**0**	**0**	**0**	**7**	**0**
Unspecified	**–**	**2,181**	**–**	**13**	**211**	**187**
World Total	**7,281**	**7,833**	**673**	**6,334**	**36,374**	**28,649**

T = Trace (less than half the unit in which the table is expressed).

Source: IGC.

Table 9.6 Shipments by destination: barley (major exporters)

'000 tons

IMPORTERS	CANADA Jul/Apr 1996/97	CANADA Jul/Apr 1997/98	EC Jul/Dec 1996/97	EC Jul/Dec 1997/98	USA Jul/Mar 1996/97	USA Jul/Mar 1997/98
Europe	**–**	**–**	**651**	**48**	**31**	**26**
Norway	–	–	112	T	–	–
Poland	–	–	35	23	–	–
CIS & Baltics	**0**	**0**	**10**	**26**	**0**	**0**
CIS	–	–	3	17	T	T
Russia	–	–	*3*	*17*	*T*	*T*
N & C America	**472**	**589**	**T**	**T**	**166**	**106**
Mexico	29	19	–	–	142	92
USA	443	570	T	T	–	–
South America	**28**	**14**	**23**	**27**	**18**	**T**
Colombia	20	–	23	27	–	T
N E Asia	**1,093**	**623**	**2,595**	**533**	**160**	**610**
Iran	158	106	105	105	–	–
Israel	34	–	30	–	21	–
Jordan	–	–	–	–	50	53
Saudi Arabia	886	486	2,320	386	88	507
F E Asia	**1,029**	**763**	**59**	**28**	**169**	**377**
Pacific Asia	*1,029*	*763*	*59*	*28*	*169*	*377*
China	485	571	59	28	–	–
Chinese Taipai	–	–	–	–	35	86
Japan	493	173	–	–	134	290
Korea (S)	51	19	–	–	–	–
South Asia	–	–	–	–	–	–
Africa	**8**	**15**	**147**	**431**	**8**	**25**
North Africa	*8*	*15*	*130*	*363*	*2*	–
Algeria	–	–	T	47	–	–
Libya	8	–	109	206	–	–
Morocco	–	–	10	27	–	–
Tunisia	–	15	3	83	–	–
Sub Sahara	–	–	*16*	*68*	*6*	*25*
South Africa	–	–	3	17	T	T
Oceania/Unsp.	**–**	**–**	**–**	**–**	**–**	**276**
World Total	**2,631**	**2,003**	**3,484**	**1,093**	**552**	**1,420**

T = Trace (less than half the unit in which the table is expressed).

Source: IGC.

Table 9.7 Shipments by destination: malt (major exporters)

'000 tons (grain equivalent)

	ARGENTINA		AUSTRALIA		EC	
IMPORTERS	**Jul/Apr**		**Jul/Feb**		**Jul/Dec**	
	1996/97	**1997/98**	**1996/97**	**1997/98**	**1996/97**	**1997/98**
Poland	–	–	–	–	23	45
Russia	–	–	–	–	109	134
Mexico	–	–	–	–	–	T
Brazil	126	167	14	13	171	224
Venezuela	–	–	–	–	117	157
Japan	–	–	103	97	178	170
Malaysia	–	21	16	9	7	15
Philippines	–	–	81	71	33	49
Thailand	–	–	11	30	80	59
South Africa	–	–	–	8	52	71
Others	–	–	78	102	460	484
World Total	**126**	**187**	**303**	**331**	**1,229**	**1,407**

T = Trace (less than half the unit in which the table is expressed).

Source: IGC.

CHAPTER 10

Northern hemisphere grains: production, consumption, trade and prices

Cereals differ from other commodities in that the world exports are largely in the hands of five major exporting nations—United States, Canada, European Union, Australia and Argentina. All but the last-named are industrialised communities, with Western-democracy styles of governments. Argentina is classified as a Third World country, but under its present government has many of the attributes of an industrialised democracy.

World exports of grain are thus divided, though not equally, between the three Northern Hemisphere countries and the two Southern Hemisphere countries. Apart from the difference in quantities exported, there is a sharp distinction between the seasonal harvests, those of the Northern Hemisphere taking place in the northern summer and autumn, from July to October, and those in the Southern Hemisphere in the southern summer and autumn, from January to April.

It is useful to take a snapshot of the production, trade and prices just after each harvest, so that it can be seen how the annual programme dovetails in. The present chapter gives an overview of grain production, trade and prices in the Northern Hemisphere, based on the autumn of 1997.

Weather, currency fluctuations, politics and tight stocks—in that order—have been the dominant influences in the grain market situation in the northern hemisphere, as the 1997 harvests were gathered in. It is usually possible to make a reasonable forecast as far as wheat and most coarse grains are concerned by the end of September, though the maize (corn) harvests are generally not finished until mid- to end-October.

In the USA about two-thirds of the wheat production is planted in the autumn, usually completed by the end of September, and harvested before 1 June in the southern states. The combines move northwards with the warmer weather and reach Montana and North Dakota after 15 July. Almost all Canadian wheat is spring sown and harvested from July to September (though efforts are being made to encourage winter sowing into stubble, which has the advantage of fewer disease problems and serves to spread the labour load).

The important corn crop in the USA is planted during April as far north as Kansas and Missouri, and completed in Minnesota and Wisconsin after mid-May. It is grown almost entirely in the eastern half of the country. Harvesting gets under way in September, not usually being completed until after mid-October. Again the harvest starts in the south and proceeds northwards. Early frosts can be critical and affect yields and prices.

In 1997–1998 the world estimates of wheat production (588 million tons) as compiled by the International Grains Council (IGC) were similar to 1996–1997 while coarse grains were forecast to be down by 20 million tons on the previous year, at 877 million tons (see Table 10.1).

USDA figures appeared to be somewhat higher since they are measured in metric tonnes while IGC figures are in tons.

Wheat production has increased in the last two years while coarse grains production has fluctuated depending on whether or not there has been a drought affecting the US corn crop (which accounts for about one-third of the total world production of coarse grains, including barley, sorghum, etc.).

The quality of the 1997–1998 harvest was generally good, though indifferent weather conditions in Europe meant that more than usual would be sold for feed, leading to slightly increased demand for US hard wheats for the bread grist and downward pressure on coarse grain prices. In the US prairies there was every indication of a record wheat harvest. Russian production was also much higher than the previous year.

Stock levels for wheat remained steady, except for durum, which requires a special mention as being down by a quarter on 1996–1997;

Table 10.1 World estimates (million tons)

		1994/95	*1995/96*	*1996/97*	*1997/98*
Total	Production	1,400	1,339	1,485	1,465
	Trade	183	182	182	185
	Consumption	1,412	1,383	1,450	1,479
	Stocks	229	184	218	204
Wheat	Production	526	540	583	588
	Trade	92	90	92	93
	Consumption	554	555	579	584
	Stocks	110	95	98	102
Coarse grains	Production	874	799	902	877
	Trade	91	92	90	92
	Consumption	858	828	871	895
	Stocks	119	89	120	102

Source: International Grains Council (IGC).

coarse grain stocks were also down, though not to the calamitous levels of two years before. The figures are a far cry from the record stocks of the 1980s.

WHEAT

North America was shown to be heading for approximately the same production in 1997 as in the previous year, but this masked a substantial variation in the contributions from Canada and the USA. The USA was forecast to be heading for a high figure of 68 million tons, while Canadian production was expected to be down by 7 million tons on the previous year, giving an outturn of about 23 million tons. These changes are not entirely due to the weather, though it had been exceptionally favourable in the southern states of the Union (but not so good in the northern states). The Canadian reduction was mainly due to a shift into other more profitable crops, such as flax and canola, though the weather also contributed by being too dry to produce high yields.

Statistics Canada projections put the reduction in sown area of all wheats in Canada at nearly 1 million hectares, down from the 1996–1997 record area of 12.3 million hectares. Canola area was up 1.4 million hectares and flax up 260,000 hectares, contributing to a total oilseeds area of 6.7 million hectares—approximately the same as 1995–1996. The yields in 1996–1997 were exceptionally high for all crops, and total supplies of grains were higher than in 1997–1998 while oilseeds supplies were lower. What we were seeing therefore may not be a permanent trend so much as a return to normal.

In the European Union the IGC forecast wheat harvest at 95.3 million tons was somewhat lower than production in 1996–1997, placed at 99.3 million tons. Trade estimates usually tend to be slightly lower than government figures, and COCERAL, the European Association of Grain Traders, put the harvest at 86.6 million tons for soft wheat and 6.3 million tons for durum, making a total of 93 million tons. Nonetheless there is a generally rising trend since 1994, when figures for the last enlargement of the European Union started to take effect and when the total was only 85.5 million tons. This is accounted for by the reduction in set-aside coupled—in normal weather conditions—with increased yields.

The main influence was to be seen in France, always the largest producer and the most important exporter. Its forecast harvest at 34.4 million tons (COCERAL 34 million tons) was equal to the sum of the harvests in the two next most important producers—namely, Germany with 19.7 million tons and the UK with 14.8 million tons. Italy and Spain normally produce about 7 million tons and 4 million tons respectively, but the position in the Iberian peninsula has in recent years been abnormally influenced by rainfall or lack of it. The bumper 1996–1997 EU harvest was partially due to Spain producing 2 million tons more than usual, but this did not happen again this year.

Russia confounded the pessimists by having an exceptionally good harvest in 1997 (by post-independence standards). President Yeltsin claimed in mid-September that the harvest would be 80 million tons. It was not entirely clear how he arrived at this figure. However since the IGC was at that time putting the Russian wheat crop at 38.5 million tons and coarse grains at 35.5 million tons, Yeltsin's figure would only be some 8 per cent above international estimates and may have been influential in keeping down expectations of Russian imports.

Outside North America and Europe the most important wheat producers are China and India. China's harvest was put at 115 million tons—well up on previous years when it seldom exceeded 100 million tons—and India's at 66.5 million tons, about 10 per cent above the average of less than a decade ago.

The stock position is also relevant to the market situation. The historically high stocks of a decade ago, when wheat reached the record of 175 million tons in 1985–1986, have given place to a global figure of 102 million tons. Most of the reduction has taken place in the five major exporting countries, most of all in Canada. Here stocks are down to 5.9 million tons compared with the previous season's 9.1 million tons. The special feature is the durum stock position in Canada, now only 0.9 million tons, against the previous year's 1.5 million tons. This is because exports are forecast to keep up despite the lower production. The tight stock position impacts on prices, maintaining the incentive to export. The combined carryover stocks of durum in Canada the US and the EU are now, in 1998 according to the IGC, the lowest for 24 years.

Wheat stocks in the EU seemed also likely to fall, the reason being the high level of domestic use. Intervention stocks were expected to remain around half a million tonnes, and a return to the grain mountains of yesteryear was considered unlikely.

However the recently prepared Agenda 2000 policy paper of the European Commission, which is to set the discussion at the foreseeable Summit Meetings, makes dire predictions about increases in production, set-aside and intervention stocks if the CAP is not reformed. This paper sees set-aside returning to the reference level of 17.5 per cent, supplies remaining tight up until 2001, followed by a vertiginous increase in intervention stocks to a level of 58 million tons by 2005. This estimate is based on the supposition that cereal yields will continue to increase, while GATT constraints will operate to restrain subsidised exports.

The purpose of giving publicity to these alarming figures was to concentrate the minds of Member States on the need for further CAP reform in the direction of reduced support prices. The figures were meant to be taken seriously. They also sound the alarm that the CAP in its present form could not possibly be extended to a group of new Member States in Central and Eastern Europe with their much higher agricultural populations.

Trade and prices

The balance of wheat available for export in the five major exporting countries in the 1997–1998 trading year was 84.5 million tons, some 8 million tons lower than the corresponding figure for 1996–1997. The main reason for the decrease was the lower availability in the Southern Hemisphere (Australia and Argentina), while export availability in the three Northern Hemisphere regions of Canada, EU and the USA remained similar to the previous trading year. The main difference was that the USA availability (with an export availability of 29.9 million tons) was some 2.7 million tons higher than last year owing to the large harvest.

The major importers of wheat at the present time are the EU (which has greatly increased imports from Canada and the USA and reduced those from Australia); Latin American countries, especially Peru, Venezuela and Brazil (the last-named having switched its source of supply from the USA to Canada); Japan (which has doubled imports from Canada); and Pakistan, which has taken nearly 400,000 tons from Australia compared with only 29,000 tons in 1996–1997.

Egypt, as usual, was a substantial importer of wheat and flour, having already doubled imports from the USA to 871,000 tons. Egypt bought 50,000 tonnes from France in early September, enough to stimulate US exporters to lower their prices. Feed wheat prices were thought also likely to decline under the influence of availability in Central and Eastern Europe.

Developing countries with rising populations continue to increase their requirements for wheat, the largest importers in this group being Indonesia, South Korea, Yemen and the Philippines. South Korea re-entered the market for feed wheat, while Iraq made some purchases under the UN food-for-oil agreement, mainly from Australia and the USA.

Export prices for wheat since mid-summer remained between US$170–190 per ton for the Canadian and US strong wheats, US$160–180 for Australian Standard White and US$140–160 for Argentine Trigo Pan, for US Western White (fob Pacific) and for Hard Red Winters (fob Gulf). Having maintained the export refund at zero throughout the summer, the EU reintroduced small refunds in mid-September, influenced by the decline in the value of the dollar in relation to the Ecu.

COARSE GRAINS

World coarse grain production and trade are shown in Table 10.1 (see page 144).

Within these figures the US maize (corn) crop dominates markets and prices. Corn is always harvested up to two or three months later than the majority of feedgrain crops and, as the weather develops and leads to variations in the forecasts, this creates fluctuations in markets and prices. The estimate by the IGC on 25 September 1997 was for a crop of 237 million tons, which was the same as the previous year. This compares with a total world crop forecast at 567.5 million tons—i.e. nearly half the global production.

Canada does not produce significant quantities of maize, being too far North, so the total for North America, including Mexico, was 266.1 million tons.

China is the next largest producer and the estimate here was for 104 million tons, over 95 per cent of which is consumed domestically. Third is Brazil with 34 million tons. Net importer Argentina was forecast to produce 12.5 million tons, 7 million tons of which was expected to go for export. France, India, South Africa and Romania are also producers worthy of mention, though none of them is a significant exporter on the world market (France exports to other Member States of the EU, but this counts as intra-trade and does not show in global statistics).

Barley is next to maize in the coarse grains league and in 1997–1998 had a forecast world production of 147.6 million tons (previous year 153.4 million tons), half of which comes from Europe. The greater part of this is produced in the EU where France is a major producer with a forecast crop in 1997–1998 of 13.4 million tons, followed by Germany (9.8 million tons), UK (7.7 million tons) and Spain (7.6 million tons). In Eastern Europe and the Confederation of Independent States (CIS) Russia is the major producer with a forecast crop in 1997–1998 of 17.5 million tons and Ukraine with 7 million tons. In North America, Canada is a big producer with 13.6 millions tons (last year 15.6 million tons), of which over 3 million tons is likely to be exported.

The USA is important as a producer with 8.3 million tons forecast for this year, some 75 per cent, of which is exported. Turkey with 7.5 million tons, Ukraine with 7 million tons and Australia and China with 4 million tons apiece are noteworthy. Of the last four only Australia has a significant export.

Sorghum, oats and rye complete the coarse grains crops, with minor production of triticale, mixed grains, milo, etc. Of these sorghum is the most important, with a production of 64.8 million tons this year. Oats production was 31.1 million tons and rye production 23.9 million tons. All these forecasts show little change on the previous year.

The USA and India dominate sorghum production. Russia is the leading producer of oats and rye (though Australia deserves a mention because of the high quality of its oat crop). Germany also produces half a million tonnes of rye, much of it for bread.

Trade and prices

World trade in coarse grains, as shown in Table 10.1, should be some 2 million tons above last year, mainly because of higher forecast maize (corn) shipments. US exports of corn are forecast to increase to 50.5 million tons, up from 45.8 million tons the preceding year. Demand is expected to increase in Indonesia, Thailand and the Philippines, where the feed industry continues to expand and production has not kept pace.

Japan is the largest purchaser and a consistent buyer of maize, its annual average of imports running at 16 million tons. It imported as much as 16.8 million tons in 1994–1995 and 16.4 million tons in 1992–1993, and this year is forecast to import 15.8 million tons. It is noticeable, however, that early forecasts of imports into Japan often prove to be on the low side when the final year figures are available, sometimes by as much as 1 million tons.

Other large importers of maize are South Korea at 8.5 million tons and Chinese Taipei at 4.9 million tons. The Taipei forecast of imports is noticeably down on last year, because of the effect of foot and mouth disease on its pig industry. Egypt regularly imports about 3 million tons every year. The EU imports 2.2 million tons despite the substantial French production which, as mentioned above, is mainly absorbed by intra-trade among the other Members of the Union. Spain, owing to this year's poor harvest, has already shipped 109,000 tonnes from the USA, twice as much as the entire import last year.

Apart from these, Mexico is forecast to take 3.5 million tons from the US, Egypt 3.1 million tons and Malaysia 2.6 million tons. Iran and Saudi Arabia are smaller importers, forecast to take just over 1 million tons apiece in the current trading year. Colombia, not usually recorded as a large importer, had already shipped 160,000 tons from the USA by end-August this year.

US exports have already been highlighted and, apart from these, only Argentina is a substantial regular supplier to the world market. This year Argentinian exports of maize are forecast to be 7 million tons, down from the previous year's 10.5 million tons (which coincided with reduced US availabilities). Main customers are other Latin American countries, notably Peru and Venezuela, and Iran (which does not take maize from the USA) had already taken 168,320 tons from Argentina by the end of August.

Barley importers include Saudi Arabia (the largest, with a forecast figure of 5 million tons, approximately one-third of the world total), China and Japan. Most exports come from the EU (forecast 6.2 million tons, about the same as last year), Canada (3.3 million tons, same as last year) and Australia (2.2 million tons, half that of last year). Up to end-August this year, Saudi Arabia had already imported 216,900 tons from Canada, and the USA had taken over 100,000 tons from Canada. EU exports do not develop until later in the season, and none had been reported up to the end of August.

Importers of sorghum follow much the same pattern as barley, though the quantities are naturally smaller since total trade is not as great. The main exporter is the USA and the main importers Japan and Mexico. Oat trade mainly takes place between Canada and the USA, the former being the exporter and the latter the importer. US imports are forecast to reach 1,600 million tons, while Canada exports 1,350 million tons and the EU 350 million tons.

Reference has already been made to the likelihood of substantial substitution of feed wheat for other feed grains—a trend difficult to establish statistically since customs returns do not usually specify the end use. But it is a fair indication that, if wheat is priced at US$100 per ton for Black Sea ports, it is not going to be of breadmaking quality. This is the price at which Ukrainian and Russian wheat was offered at in mid-October 1997. For comparison, Black Sea barley is quoted at about US$120 per ton, and European milling wheat at US$145. Given the nutritional advantages of wheat who is going to feed barley at those prices?

OUTLOOK

Global trade in grain has been static for the past three years at around 182–186 million tons per annum. The prospects for an increase in either the wheat or coarse grain trade are not bright, with larger crops in China and Russia, formerly the two main importers. Hopes continue to be pinned on the non-producing developing countries, but the full effects of the currency collapse in the tiger economies of South East Asia has not yet been evaluated. In North Africa only Egypt and Morocco have the potential to expand trade in wheat and possess the financial strength to absorb additional imports. Saudi Arabia in the Middle East has the resources but does not import wheat. Political questions impede trade with Iran and Iraq, where demand exists. For coarse grains the Middle East, especially Saudi Arabia, continues to offer a stable market.

An important factor is the determination of the USA to seek a greater market share following the liberating effect of the 1995 US Farm Act (FAIR) on farmers' planting decisions, while Europe will shortly be preoccupied by questions of expansion to the East, which are due to come up following the Amsterdam Treaty of 1997, together with difficult decisions on a common currency. Will this be introduced in 1999 as projected by Maastricht and Amsterdam and, if so, will it stick? Over all looms the prospect of a renewal of World Trade Organisation negotiations on agriculture in 1999 and greater pressure for liberalisation and the total abolition of subsidised exports. The consequence may be lower prices but not necessarily greater trade.

The term "former Soviet Union" is now less used than it was, as the Commonwealth of Independent States (CIS) has superseded it. The CIS comprises most of the republics loosely linked after the collapse of Communism, except Chechnya, Moldavia, Georgia and Azerbaijan. Of these republics, Russia, Ukraine and Kazakhstan are the most important from the point of view of grains production and trade.

Agriculture in the Soviet Union was collectivised in the 1920s, often with the help of machine guns. The change to democratic institutions, coupled with transition from a command economy to a market economy has posed drastic problems of administration. In 1991 the economy was on the verge of collapse. With it went a large percentage of agricultural production including about 50 per cent of the livestock herd. Now at last there are signs of consistent recovery; though the problem of land tenure has not yet been solved. Until it is, there will continue to be constraints on production.

The signs of recovery in the grain sector have become clear this season, with the harvest figures at last returning to the average of 1991–1995 (see Table 10.1, on p. 144).

The harvest has gone well this year. By mid-September 76 per cent of the sown area had been cut and brought in, and the summer losses which had so affected the two previous years have been avoided.

The total harvest will be about 20 per cent up on last year, and in the important Povolzhsk and Central Black Earth regions the improvement is even greater. In Eastern Siberia the weather continues fair.

RUSSIA

The total wheat production in Russia in 1998 was 40–42 million tons, equivalent to an increase of 20 per cent on 1996–1997, though the quality of the wheat is lower. As much as 55 per cent of the wheat crop is regarded as unsuitable for milling (36 per cent in 1996–1997). Since domestic demand is still weak, there should be scope for increased exports, mainly of feed quality for livestock consumption. Russian barley production is forecast at 17.5 million tons out of a total CIS production of 30.2 million tons.

Table 10.2 Total grain output by main producing regions (million tons)

Region	*Av. 1991–95*	*1995*	*1996*	*1997* (forecast)	*97 as* % of 96
Russia total	87.9	63.4	69.3	82.0–84.0	118–121
Central	8.7	6.1	6.7	7.2– 7.4	108–111
Volgo-Vyatsk	5.0	3.1	4.7	5.1– 5.3	109–113
Central-Chernozem	9.9	5.5	6.8	8.9– 9.1	130–133
Povolzhsk	15.6	8.7	13.5	18.6–19.2	138–142
N Caucasus	19.3	14.6	12.1	13.4–14.0	111–116
Urals	12.3	8.9	11.9	14.0–14.5	118–122
W Siberia	10.7	11.2	9.1	8.2– 9.0	90– 98
E Siberia	4.6	4.0	3.7	3.5– 4.0	110–125
Far East	0.9	0.5	0.6	0.55– 0.6	96–105

Source: SovEcon.

The situation as regards external trade is shown in Table 10.3. Barley exports have risen to a record monthly level in August, nearly 100,000 tons. SovEcon expects that total feed grain exports in 1997–1998 may amount to as much as 3 million tons.

UKRAINE

The 1998 grain harvest in the Ukraine was reported to be nearly complete by mid-September, with an output of 28.35 million tons (excluding grain maize), 7.1 million tons greater than the previous year. Total output including maize is forecast by the Ukrainian ministry figures as 37.2 million tons (33.4–35.7 million tons by SovEcon, the difference due to variations in forecasts of the grain maize results). The ministry expects the maize crop to be 4.8 million tons, but wet weather has hindered harvesting, hence SovEcon's lower estimate, nearer 3.1 million tons.

Wheat is forecast at 19.3 million tons (13.55 million tons in 1996–1997) and barley at 8.1 million tons (5.7 million tons in 1996–1997). Lower wheat prices, together with some increase in *per capita* incomes, may result in higher consumption of cereal and livestock products. The livestock decline is thought to have bottomed out, and numbers may now be increasing. Wheat for alcohol production is expected to increase to 0.88 million tons owing to special budget allocations for the benefit of distilleries.

Wheat exports from the Ukraine are expected to increase to 1 million tons (0.5 million tons in 1996–1997). However, this increase, together with domestic demand, will not meet availabilities, leading to a rise in end-stocks to 3.4 million tons from 940,000 tons at the end of 1996–1997.

Table 10.3 Russia—External trade (thousand tons)

	Apr 97	*May 97*	*June 97*	*Total 96/97*	*July 97*	*Aug 97*
			Wheat			
Imports						
Total	228.8	179.4	216.1	1,609.0	208.5	195.9
Third countries	44.9	6.5	11.6	268.6	25.7	14.0
CIS	183.9	172.9	204.5	1,340.4	182.7	181.9
Exports						
Total	64.4	81.7	34.5	593.8	19.6	43.5
Third countries	21.5	16.2	10.2	336.7	10.1	27.7
CIS	42.8	65.5	24.4	257.2	9.5	15.8
			Barley			
Imports						
Total	67.2	61.3	70.1	538.6	68.7	68.2
Third countries	12.3	4.3	12.1	43.2	8.8	10.0
CIS	50.0	37.0	58.1	495.5	59.9	9.9
Exports						
Total	0.6	2.9	2.2	149.2	13.3	92.5
Third countries	–	2.9	2.1	142.6	13.3	92.4
CIS	0.6	0.0	0.1	6.6	0.0	0.1

Source: SovEcon.

Similar trends are expected in the barley balance sheet, though barley exports are likely to rise faster than wheat exports due to demand on third-country markets.

KAZAKHSTAN

Grain production in Kazakhstan is a relatively new phenomenon dating from Khrushchev's grandiose "virgin lands" programme of the 1960s, inspired by the Soviet crop failure and resulting famine in 1963. Both praised and derided at the time, the experiment got off to a bad start and was partly responsible for Khrushchev's subsequent downfall in 1964. However, spring wheat cultivation on what was previously steppe land is now an established factor in the world grain balance, though the vagaries of the weather account for considerable fluctuations in output. Thus, Kazakhstan's wheat harvest reached 9.1 million tons in 1994, 6.5 million tons in 1995, 8 million tons in 1996 and is forecast by the IGC at 9.6 million tons this year. The State Food Contract Corporation (SFCC) in Almaty (Alma Ata) put it slightly lower, as Table 10.3 shows.

Coarse grain production is even more volatile, having reached 12.8 million tons in 1992, sunk to 2.8 million tons in 1995 and is forecast by the IGC at 2.9 million tons this year. SFCC forecasts are marginally more optimistic (see Table 10.3).

Table 10.4 Kazakhstan wheat, feed barley and rice production—harvest 1997: Total

Area			*Yield*			*Production*		
wheat	*barley*	*rice*	*wheat*	*barley*	*rice*	*wheat*	*barley*	*rice*
10,841	3,168	85.2	7–10	8–12	24–28	8,131	3,000	272.7

(area given in 1,000 ha, yield in centners/ha, production in 1,000 tons)

Source: SFCC.

CHAPTER 11

Southern hemisphere grains: production, consumption, trade and prices

The production of grain in the Southern Hemisphere—predominantly Australia, Argentina, Brazil and South Africa—is strongly influenced by weather conditions, perhaps more so than in the Northern Hemisphere where intensive cultivation is more prevalent than in the south. Seldom has this been more evident than in the 1997–1998 season when the influence of the El Niño phenomenon was strongly pronounced.

Readers need no reminding of the dependence of agricultural production on weather conditions. 1997–1998 was dominated—especially in the Southern Hemisphere where agriculture is extensive rather than intensive—by fear of and realisation of the effects of the El Niño phenomenon.

What is El Niño? Literally "the Christ Child" because it first appeared one Christmas, by contrast with the long-familiar Humboldt Current. It, like the Humboldt, is an inhabitant of the Pacific Ocean. While the Humboldt is a cool current flowing up the Western littoral of the South American continent, profoundly affecting the climate and the fishing industries (especially the *anchovetas* fishmeal feed industry) of Chile and Peru, El Niño is a warm current flowing from West to East in mid-Pacific. When pronounced, as this year, it leads to dramatic rainfall variations in the rest of the world. Its influence brought welcome rain in Argentina and South Africa, while its less than expected presence in Australia distorted the normal pattern of planting.

World grain production in 1997–1998 as forecast by the International Grains Council (IGC), and compared with the previous three years, is shown in Table 11.1.

WHEAT

World wheat production (including durum) in 1997–1998 is forecast to be 16 million tons above the previous year, at 610 million tons. This is a record figure, easily surpassing the 1990–1991 record of 592 million tons. In South America the Argentine harvest, helped by timely rains, at 14.5

million tons is close to the previous year's record of 15.9 million tons and well above the poor year of 1995–1996 when the output was only 9.4 million tons. Brazil, Chile and Uruguay, the only other statistically significant wheat producers in South America, have all had average-sized crops, the forecast figures for production being 2.8 million tons, 1.4 million tons, and 0.6 million tons respectively. These were slightly less than the previous year but above those of 1995.

Dry conditions at the start of the season in Australia, when rain was expected as a consequence of El Niño (and many growers had switched to shorter-strawed varieties, not expecting drought) together with a 4.4 per cent reduction in planted area, led to a harvest of only 18.5 million tons (in 1996, 23.7 million tons). Nonetheless this was still a good figure, the average of recent years being around 12–16 million tons (and even descending as low as 9 million tons in the catastrophic year of 1994). Elsewhere in the region Papua New Guinea and Indonesia were badly affected by El Niño. South Africa experienced a drop in yields and produced a wheat harvest of only 2.3 million tons, about the recent average, though lower than the pre-1988 years when it regularly exceeded 3 million tons. The country experienced little effect from the Pacific currents, early apprehensions being unfounded.

On a global basis, wheat consumption at 591 million tons is forecast to be up by 7 million tons on the previous year, rather less than the increase in production, and thereby boosting world stocks, though not to the level of five years previously. Now that most countries have opted out of government holdings of stocks, this figure is liable to fluctuation; moreover it can never be completely accurate since neither Russia nor China cares to reveal its stock holdings for reasons of security. The publication of US quarterly stocks statistics at the end of March 1998 led to selling on the market, since these appeared to confirm the downturn in US feed consumption and to confirm the upward trend in closing stocks.

As regards consumption trends, it would appear that the downturn in consumption noted after the upheavals in the former Soviet Union and Eastern Europe is now beginning to reverse. 71 per cent of global wheat consumption is reckoned to be for food use, 17 per cent for animal feed, and the remainder for seed, industrial use and wastage.

In Australia the deregulation of the domestic grain market and the establishment of a tender system have given growers more options for the sale of their crops. Expansion of the livestock industry, including chicken meat, has led to increased consumption of feed wheat, helped by the increased availability of weather-damaged grain. Quality problems have led to increased blending by the Australian Wheat Board. During the 1997–1998 crop year the growth in wheat consumption in some Latin American countries was inhibited by subsidies on maize- (corn-)based foods, while in others such as Brazil the poor maize crops appeared likely

Table 11.1 World grain production estimates (1997–1998): million tons

	95/96	96/97	97/98	98/99 (forecast) As at 29.04.98	98/99 (forecast) As at 04.06.98
Wheat					
Production	541	582	610	592	592
Trade	90	95	97	98	96
Consumption	553	580	587	599	599
Stocks	110	112	134	124	127
Coarse grains					
Production	800	912	908	896	905
Trade	92	93	88	93	90
Consumption	832	881	900	908	901
Stocks	93	124	132	116	135
Total					
Production	1,341	1,494	1,518	1,488	1,497
Trade	182	188	185	191	186
Consumption	1,385	1,461	1,487	1,507	1,500
Stocks	203	236	266	240	262

Source: IGC.

to stimulate wheat use. Only in Brazil, at 8.6 million tons, does wheat consumption appear to be on a rising trend.

COARSE GRAINS

World coarse grains production in 1997–1998 is forecast to be down on the previous year by some 4 million tons, but substantially up to the extent of 108 million tons—on two years previously. Maize (corn) is the major coarse grain crop grown in the Southern Hemisphere, the bulk of it in Argentina and Brazil. Though no other country approaches the United States in volume of maize (corn) production, where the harvest regularly exceeds 200 million tons, Brazil and Argentina have made substantial progress, much of it with US technical assistance. Thus, Brazil has increased production from 25 million tons to 35 million tons in the last 10 years, while in the same period the equivalent figures for Argentina are 9 million tons and 17 million tons—almost doubling.

The size of the Argentine maize crop was helped by record yields, due to the excellent growing conditions and timely rainfall (thanks to El

Niño), and this factor outweighed the drop of 10 per cent in the planted area (due to producers switching to oilseed production). Producers are reported to be moving away from the production of flint maize to semi-flint or semi-dent varieties.

Australian sorghum production is estimated by the International Grains Council (IGC) at 1.3 million tons—about the average for the past two years, though the Australian Bureau of Agricultural and Resource Economics (ABARE) puts it up by 30 per cent due to the high yields and large crops planted in New South Wales and Queensland.

Argentina produces much maize but little barley: Australia on the other hand produces little maize but a substantial amount of barley and oats. The Australian barley crop for 1997–1998 is forecast at 5.9 million tons, and would have been higher but for a decline in yield compared with the previous two years, due to unfavourable weather in many states. The yield for this crop appears to be on a progressively declining trend even allowing for a return to normal seasonal conditions. An important proportion of the crop, estimated at 37 per cent in 1998 (slightly below the average of the last five years) is of malting quality (see below, regarding exports). Australian oat production, despite its high quality, is also decreasing, dropping from 1.9 million tons in 1995 to 1.3 million tons in the current year.

South Africa is the next most important producer of maize in the Southern Hemisphere, after Brazil and Argentina, with a current production in 1997–1998 officially estimated by the National Crops Estimates Committee (NEC) at 7.3 million tons. This may perhaps be considered a disappointing figure, despite the good rains which fell in the area during February. The corresponding figure for 1996–1997 was nine million tons, while back in 1988–1989 it was as high as 12.4 million tons. Two reasons are adduced to account for the decline—first, that the area planted was smaller than usual because producers were frightened by reports of the havoc likely to be caused by the El Niño effect, and secondly because of the end of the controlled marketing system with the abolition of the Maize Board.

Australia is also a producer of rice, mainly in the fertile areas of the Murray and Murrumbidgee Valleys. Rice growing in Queensland ceased in 1992–1993, but a small area was opened up in Victoria in 1996. Total production of milled rice in 1996–1997 (the latest year for which preliminary estimates are available) was 1.4 million tons. The 1997–1998 crop, grown on 14 per cent lower area due to decreased availability of irrigation water, is forecast to have a 2 per cent higher yield, which will compensate to some extent. Rice is grown both for export and for import substitution, domestic consumption having increased due to the rise in the immigrant population.

World consumption of coarse grains in the 1997–1998 season is forecast at 900 million tons, a figure which, after remaining constant at around 830 million tons between 1992 and 1996, has in the past two years been on a rising trend, increasing by 5 per cent *per annum*. The split in this figure between the Northern and Southern Hemispheres is not readily available, though the greater proportion is undoubtedly consumed north of the Equator. The use of coarse grains (mainly maize) in Argentina for cattle feed is expected to increase by around 1 million tons this year.

TRADE AND PRICES

Argentina and Australia are ranked among the five major exporting countries for wheat. In the 1997–1998 season export availabilities after allowing for stock change are put at 10 million tons and 14.0 million tons respectively. Shipments of wheat and flour reported by Argentina up to April 1998 (approximately half way through the season) amounted to just over 4 million tons; and by Australia (for the first seven months of the season) to just over 10 million tons. About half the Argentine shipments went within the South American Continent, mainly to her neighbour Brazil, with lesser amounts to more distant destinations including Iran, Turkey, Indonesia, Sri Lanka, Egypt, and Morocco. Jordan recently took 100,000 tons, mainly from Argentina, at a price of US$ 142 per ton (c & f), on deferred payment terms. Australian shipments have mainly gone to China, Indonesia, Iraq, India and Egypt.

The Australian Wheat Board announced in March that it had committed virtually the whole of the 1998 export surplus (i.e., a further 4 million tons on deals already reported). A large purchase of 1.5 million tons by India, also at a price of US $142 per ton was reported at the end of February, with delivery April to June. Controversy continues over the future of the Australian Wheat Board, currently the sole Australian exporter. A section of the industry composed of large growers and large exporting companies has argued in favour of terminating this power, but is vigorously opposed by the Board and by the Grains Council of Australia. This dispute has had the effect of stimulating the AWB into expanding its overseas marketing activities, including the setting up of a hot bread shop in Moscow, the installation of grain storage in Egypt, a Training Bakery and a flour and feed mill in China, bunker storage in Iran and further enterprises in Vietnam and Japan.

The weekly export prices for wheat and maize (corn) between December 1997 and the end of March 1998 compiled by the IGC (see Figure 11.1) show stability for high protein bread wheats, a slight decline in the US Hard Red Winters (fob Gulf)—usually taken as the world price of wheat—and US Western White (fob Pacific), prices broadly ranging

Fig. 11.1 Weekly export price quotations: wheat and maize (corn) since 27 February 1998

US$ per ton

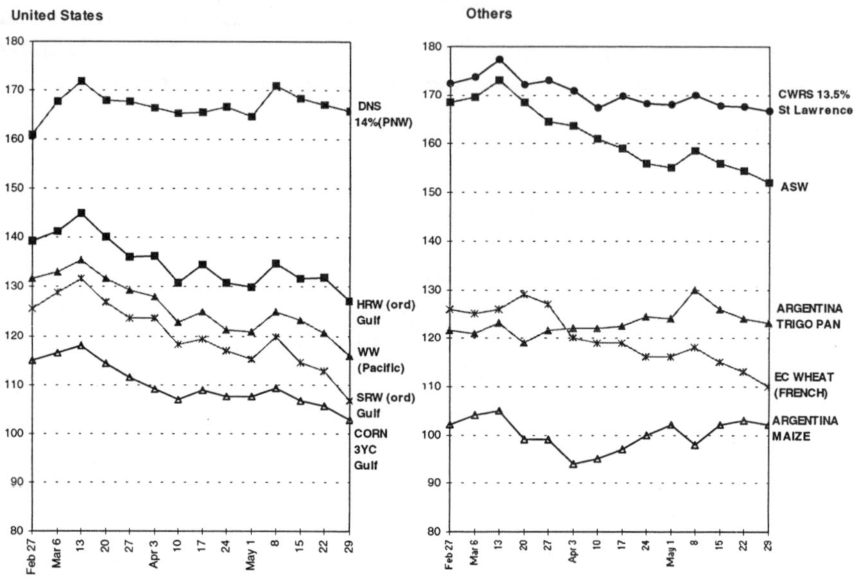

Source: IGC.

within a 10-dollar/ton bracket. A brief rise in prices in the second half of February and early March was caused by the Australian Wheat Board announcement referred to above, and by reports of winter freeze damage which later turned out to have been exaggerated. By the end of March prices were back to December levels, receiving no encouragement from sluggish export demand. By the beginning of April export quotations for both US Soft Red Winters (fob Gulf) and European Union (EU) export prices were similar at about US$ 122. Argentine prices for Trigo Pan (breadwheat) followed suit, finishing just over US$ 120 towards the end of March.

Currency movements over the past eight months have given a marked benefit to Australian exporters through the weakness of the Australian dollar, which has moved since July last year's value of 1.336 to the US dollar to 1.4818 by the end of March 1998, a fall of 10.9 per cent. During the same period the value of the Argentine peso has remained constant *vis-à-vis* the US dollar. Exporters, including those of the Southern Hemisphere, have been handicapped in trading with Japan, however, by the fall in value of the yen, which has depreciated by 14 per cent against the US dollar over the same period, thus to some extent negating the weakness of the Australian currency in this market.

South America produces little durum wheat (the Argentine crop is estimated at only 100,000 tons *per annum*) and imports small amounts, mainly from Canada but also from the USA. Venezuela is the most important market in this region for Canadian durum, regularly taking over 100,000 tons *per annum*, followed by Chile and Peru. The latter country's imports were already as great as those of Venezuela by the middle of the 1997–1998 season. Venezuela has accounted for 42,000 tons of durum imports from the USA over the same period, while her forecast imports from all sources for the 1997–1998 year exceed 370,000 tons. Peru and Chile are forecast to take 170,000 and 120,000 tons respectively from all sources in 1997–1998. Durum is used extensively for the production of semolina and pasta, and the price premium over soft wheats has remained strong, partly because of the relative decline in the prices of the latter and partly buoyed by the significant drawdown of stocks (world stocks of durum are forecast to reduce to 1.9 million tons in 1997–1998, down from 3.1 million tons in 1994–1995). This is likely to have consequences for production and trade next year (see below).

The world trade in coarse grains is scarcely less varied than that in wheat and flour. The major exporters are again the big five, joined by South Africa and China. The main Southern Hemisphere exporter is Argentina, with a forecast total export in 1997–1998 of 12.2 million tons of coarse grains of which no less than 11 million tons is maize. Export sales of Argentine maize had already reached 6.2 million tons by the end of March, compared with 5.6 million tons at the same period a year ago.

Australian exports of coarse grains in 1997–1998 are forecast at 3.1 million tons, of which 2.7 million tons is barley, divided between feed and malting quality as 1.5 million tons and 1.2 million tons respectively. The Australian Barley Marketing Act is under revision and the Barley Board is currently under fire from a recent report by consultants, who have recommended that its powers on exports and in the internal market be phased out and that both markets be deregulated. The Australian malting barley industry was also studied by a report issued in January 1995 which recommended steps to maintain the high-growth market in China and seeking new opportunities in the emerging markets.

South African exports of coarse grains are put at 1.3 million tons, mainly maize. Prices of both white and yellow corn dropped markedly in March due to late rains: prices for white corn expressed in US dollars at the end of February 1998 were $160 per ton compared with $182 three weeks previously, yellow corn having dropped from $132 per ton to $123 in the same period.

As for sorghum, Argentine exports are likely to rise to 1.1 million tons, destinations being as varied as Japan (the major buyer, having already taken 1.2 million tons up to the end of March, or 10 times as much as in the previous year) and Mexico. The latter was quick to make purchases at a price of US $80 per ton, being US $30 cheaper than US sorghum. This represents a great increase on previous years, while forecast Australian exports at 250,000 tons are little more than half the previous average. These figures compare with a global export of 7 million tons. Australian exports of high quality oats are also worth a mention, forecast at 160,000 tons out of a world total of 2 million tons, a market dominated by the USA and Canada.

Thus, Southern Hemisphere countries are forecast to export approximately 16 million tons of coarse grains this season, out of a world total of 89 million tons. However, current big oilseeds harvests in Latin America may mean that non-cereal feed ingredients become more competitive as the season wears on.

FREIGHT

Stagnant trade has depressed the freight market. For large size vessels from the Gulf to Bordeaux/Hamburg rates fell from US$7.90 per ton to US$6.75 per ton over the past month, while rates from Argentina and Canadian/US Atlantic ports to Antwerp/Rotterdam remained constant between US$7.25 per ton for shipment ex-St Lawrence and US$9.50/9.75 from Argentina and the USA. From Australia to Egypt the rate for Panamax vessels declined from US$14 per ton in February to US$11.25 per ton at the end of March, US Gulf rates having shown an even greater decline over the same period from US$13 per ton to US$8.50. One effect of this decline has been to help Argentina to sell to North Africa and the Middle East.

OUTLOOK

Although the seed is not at time of writing in the ground in the Southern Hemisphere for the 1998–1999 grain harvests, analysts are already at work on the prospects. In the Northern Hemisphere the sown areas are known, the grain is already well-established, and the outturn given normal weather has already been assessed by producers and traders. As is well known, the weather is seldom normal, but that does not deter prediction. Sown areas are slightly down in the USA (switching to oilseeds) and Canada (due to a switch to barley and canola, likely to be more profitable) and slightly up in Europe where they may reach record levels again. This has its implications for Southern Hemisphere producers, where Argentinian and Brazilian planting intentions are slightly higher, and in Australia where they are down by 3 per cent. Australian farmers are attracted by the better prospects for wool production (rather than cattle), one of the key factors in which is the likely pattern of Chinese imports.

In consequence world wheat production in 1998–1999 is forecast at 592 million tons compared with the present season's record figure of 609 million tons. Farmers in Europe and the USA are planting 25 per cent more durum in the hope of higher prices, while Canadian producers have planted 10 per cent more.

Consumption patterns are likely to be affected by currency depreciations of 50 per cent or more in Pacific Asia, where consumer incomes are falling. Unless the higher costs of wheat products are offset by higher subsidies wheat for food use is likely to fall. The switch from rice to cereals as food is unlikely to be maintained, despite the fact that high-quality rice prices have remained firm, since rice of inferior quality (including brokens) is readily available at a discount. Far East Asia accounts for one-third of global grain trade.

Coarse grain predictions for 1998–1999 are tentative, the principal crop—maize (corn)—being sown later than most other cereals, but show that production is likely to rise to 905 million tons (previous year 896 million tons). In South Africa, local reports indicate that production of white and yellow corn will be down by 1.7 million tons in total. Some white corn may be available for export next year but a substantial amount of yellow corn is likely to have to be imported. Futures prices for December 1998 put white corn at the equivalent of US$162 per ton *ex* Randfontein and yellow corn at the equivalent of US$147. The extra costs for inland transport make comparisons with US prices difficult: however at the current US price fob Gulf of US$106 per ton the addition of shipping, offloading and wharfage costs, plus inland transport, would entail a parity price of about US$156 per ton.

However, national ministries and trade organisations may be less influential on the 1998–1999 outlook than the National Oceanic and Atmospheric Administration in Washington, DC. As El Niño fades away, as it is thought it will by summer 1998, it may be replaced by the colder reverse flow of La Niña ("little girl"). A climatic prediction scientist with the Meteorological Office in the UK is on record as comparing the process to water sloshing about in the bath. If he is right next winter could just be colder than normal.

CHAPTER 12

The importance of the developing countries

In the world grain economy the importance of the developing countries lies mainly in their capacity as importers. This is not to say that there is not significant production in the developing countries—far from it. China (including Taiwan) is by far the world's largest cereal producer, while Indian production exceeds that of the European Community and follows that of the United States and the former USSR. Thereafter there is a big gap, until we come to Brazil, with production one quarter that of the EC. Table 12.1 shows that the production of the developing countries has now overtaken that of the developed countries.

Taking trade in cereals as a whole, it is also evident that while the developed world exports over five times as much as the developing countries, the latter now import nearly half as much again as the developed countries. Were it not for the fact that a developed country (Japan) is the world's biggest importer, the equation would be less balanced. The evolution of the developing countries' imports over the past decade, and the way in which they have overtaken the developed countries' imports, is also shown in Table 12.2.

It is perhaps ironic that as stocks of grain began to decline from their peak of 1986–1987 the problem of disposing of the industrial world's accumulation of grain appeared to be receiving increasing attention. If the overhanging stocks could be further reduced, so the reasoning went, the competition in subsidising exports would become less acute, to the relief of governments in the industrialised world and to the improvement of US/European trade relations, and to the eventual improvement in farmers' returns. Hence the importance of finding new markets. As grain surpluses appear to be increasing again with the collapse of world prices (including those of the EU, helped by reform beginning to bite) this problem is present again.

In 1988 an interesting initiative was taken—a round-table discussion on the market potential of the developing countries launched by the IGC (then still named the International Wheat Council) in London. Participants in the round table included representatives of the US Wheat Associates, the Canadian Wheat Board and the Australian Wheat

Table 12.1 Cereal production (developing countries)

	1985	1986	1987	1988	1989	1990	1991	1992	1993	1994	1995
					(million tons)						
ASIA	**754.3**	**775.4**	**766.8**	**803.9**	**830.7**	**872.9**	**863.4**	**889.5**	**905.7**	**896.5**	**935.4**
Bangladesh	24.1	24.3	24.3	24.4	27.9	27.7	28.5	28.7	28.3	26.5	27.9
China[1]	339.8	352.6	359.6	352.2	368.0	404.8	395.4	400.2	405.7	393.2	418.6
India	165.7	165.0	156.1	183.9	199.4	193.9	191.6	202.1	208.9	211.8	215.7
Indonesia	43.4	45.6	45.2	48.3	50.9	51.9	50.9	56.2	54.6	53.5	56.7
Iran, Islamic Rep. of	10.7	11.9	12.2	12.1	10.8	13.7	14.4	15.8	16.3	16.7	17.3
Japan	15.9	15.7	14.4	13.8	14.3	14.4	13.1	14.3	10.7	15.8	14.1
Korea, D.P.R.	6.3	8.8	8.1	7.5	7.0	6.6	6.1	6.0	7.0	5.9	5.1
Korea, Rep. of	8.8	8.6	8.5	9.3	8.9	8.4	7.9	7.8	6.9	7.3	6.8
Myanmar	15.1	14.9	14.2	13.6	14.3	14.4	13.6	15.3	17.3	18.7	20.1
Pakistan	17.7	21.0	17.9	19.2	21.0	21.0	21.1	22.1	23.9	22.3	24.8
Philippines	12.7	13.0	13.0	13.6	13.5	14.7	13.8	14.0	14.9	14.9	15.3
Saudi Arabia	2.2	2.5	2.9	3.7	3.9	4.1	4.6	4.7	5.0	5.1	4.5
Thailand	25.6	23.4	21.4	26.2	25.2	21.2	24.1	23.9	22.0	25.3	25.8
Turkey	26.5	29.4	29.3	30.9	23.5	30.2	31.1	29.2	31.7	27.0	28.2
Vietnam	16.5	15.5	18.0	19.1	20.2	19.5	22.9	23.4	25.1	25.8	26.4
AFRICA	**83.4**	**89.6**	**83.5**	**94.9**	**97.8**	**92.0**	**104.6**	**91.3**	**100.4**	**112.8**	**100.1**
North Africa	**19.1**	**19.9**	**18.0**	**19.3**	**21.5**	**22.8**	**29.2**	**23.4**	**21.5**	**27.0**	**22.0**
Egypt	8.6	8.8	9.4	9.8	11.1	13.0	13.8	14.6	14.9	15.4	17.1
Morocco	5.3	7.8	4.3	8.0	7.4	6.3	8.7	3.0	2.8	9.6	1.8
Sub-Saharan Africa	**64.3**	**69.8**	**65.5**	**75.6**	**76.3**	**69.2**	**75.4**	**67.9**	**78.9**	**85.8**	**78.1**
Western Africa	**23.8**	**26.5**	**27.1**	**30.4**	**29.8**	**28.9**	**33.3**	**33.9**	**33.3**	**35.8**	**37.1**
Nigeria	11.9	14.6	15.8	16.6	16.7	17.7	18.6	20.0	18.5	20.3	22.4
Central Africa	**2.1**	**2.6**	**2.2**	**2.4**	**2.5**	**2.5**	**2.6**	**2.7**	**2.7**	**2.7**	**3.1**
Eastern Africa	**17.7**	**19.8**	**17.2**	**21.1**	**19.1**	**17.5**	**19.9**	**21.5**	**19.1**	**22.7**	**22.7**
Ethiopia	4.8	6.5	6.2	6.4	6.4	6.5	6.3	7.1	7.0	7.6	8.6
Sudan	4.0	3.8	1.7	5.1	2.0	1.7	4.6	5.4	3.1	5.1	3.3
Southern Africa	**20.7**	**20.9**	**19.0**	**21.7**	**24.9**	**20.3**	**19.6**	**9.8**	**23.8**	**24.6**	**15.1**
Madagascar	2.3	2.3	2.3	2.3	2.5	2.6	2.5	2.6	2.7	2.5	2.6
South Africa	10.9	11.4	11.5	11.3	14.9	11.0	10.8	4.6	12.7	16.0	7.2
Zimbabwe	3.4	3.1	1.5	3.1	2.6	2.6	2.1	0.5	3.0	2.2	1.0

Table 12.1—*cont.*

	1985	1986	1987	1988	1989	1990	1991	1992	1993	1994	1995
					(million tons)						
CENTRAL AMERICA	**32.9**	**28.9**	**28.9**	**26.5**	**27.2**	**31.0**	**29.0**	**32.6**	**32.2**	**31.7**	**29.8**
Mexico	27.4	23.5	23.6	21.1	21.5	25.5	23.7	26.9	26.7	26.8	24.7
SOUTH AMERICA	**77.2**	**76.7**	**82.3**	**81.2**	**78.4**	**68.9**	**74.4**	**85.2**	**85.1**	**89.0**	**90.6**
Argentina	28.1	26.1	22.9	22.3	18.1	20.1	21.6	25.5	25.1	25.3	24.0
Brazil	36.0	36.8	44.3	42.9	44.0	33.0	37.2	44.2	42.8	45.8	49.3
Colombia	3.1	3.1	3.2	3.6	3.8	4.5	3.9	3.6	3.7	3.8	3.5
NORTH AMERICA	**395.3**	**372.2**	**332.1**	**242.2**	**332.4**	**369.1**	**333.7**	**402.6**	**310.4**	**404.2**	**326.3**
Canada	48.2	57.0	51.7	35.8	48.4	56.8	53.9	49.6	51.4	46.8	49.3
United States	347.1	315.3	280.4	206.5	284.0	312.3	279.8	353.0	259.0	357.4	276.9
EUROPE[3]	**283.3**	**282.2**	**275.1**	**285.9**	**292.7**	**284.9**	**309.1**	**258.4**	**263.5**	**264.8**	**273.2**
Bulgaria	5.4	8.5	7.3	7.8	9.5	8.1	9.0	6.6	5.7	6.4	6.5
EC[2]	162.4	156.2	157.0	166.3	165.5	172.5	183.7	170.7	167.8	163.6	180.2
Hungary	14.8	14.3	14.2	15.0	15.4	12.6	15.8	10.0	8.5	11.7	11.0
Poland	23.7	25.0	26.1	24.5	27.0	28.0	27.8	20.0	23.4	21.8	25.9
Romania	19.5	19.7	17.0	19.3	18.4	17.2	19.3	12.3	15.5	18.2	19.6
CIS[4]	**169.7**	**187.0**	**185.0**	**172.2**	**188.0**	**209.1**	**149.6**	**183.4**	**177.7**	**141.8**	**125.6**
OCEANIA	**26.2**	**25.3**	**21.0**	**22.7**	**23.1**	**23.9**	**19.6**	**26.0**	**27.9**	**15.9**	**28.6**
Australia	24.9	24.0	20.0	21.9	22.4	23.0	18.7	25.3	27.1	15.0	27.7
WORLD	**1,822.2**	**1,836.7**	**1,774.7**	**1,729.4**	**1,870.7**	**1,951.9**	**1,885.4**	**1,969.0**	**1,902.8**	**1,956.6**	**1,909.4**
Developing countries	920.9	943.4	935.3	981.3	1,004.8	1,039.1	1,047.3	1,079.4	1,099.7	1,098.1	1,134.4
Developed countries	901.3	893.2	839.4	748.1	865.9	912.8	838.1	889.6	803.1	858.5	775.0

[1]Including Taiwan Province.
[2]Up to 1994, 12 member countries (from 1990 includes New Länder of Germany); 1995, 15 member countries.
[3]From 1991 including Estonia, Latvia and Lithuania.
[4]In cleaned weight; up to 1990, former USSR; thereafter, Commonwealth of Independent States.
[5]Including rice as paddy.

Source: FAO—Food Outlook Statistical Supplement, January 1997.

Table 12.2 World imports of cereals (developing countries)

	1985 /86	1986 /87	1987 /88	1988 /89	1989 /90	1990 /91	1991 /92	1992 /93	1993 /94	1994 /95	1995 /96
						(million tons)					
ASIA	**82.1**	**90.0**	**98.6**	**100.1**	**104.0**	**92.8**	**104.5**	**98.1**	**98.4**	**110.3**	**114.2**
Bangladesh	1.9	2.3	2.5	2.4	1.2	1.6	1.6	1.1	1.3	3.1	2.2
China[1]	12.2	14.7	21.4	23.0	21.2	17.8	22.5	13.9	14.8	19.5	26.7
Hong Kong	0.8	0.9	0.9	0.9	0.8	0.8	1.0	1.0	0.9	1.0	1.0
India	0.3	0.2	1.2	2.8	0.5	0.3	0.4	3.4	0.4	0.3	0.3
Indonesia	1.7	1.9	2.1	2.3	2.0	2.1	3.1	2.7	3.6	7.4	5.9
Iran, Islamic Rep. of	3.9	4.4	6.0	5.1	7.6	5.9	5.9	5.4	5.2	6.0	6.0
Japan	27.3	27.7	27.5	27.2	27.4	26.9	27.5	27.6	29.2	26.9	26.2
Korea, Rep. of	6.9	8.3	9.3	8.8	8.7	9.9	10.6	10.8	11.9	13.2	13.1
Malaysia	1.9	2.1	2.3	1.9	2.4	2.9	3.0	3.0	3.3	3.8	3.7
Pakistan	1.8	0.4	0.6	2.2	2.1	0.9	2.1	2.9	1.9	2.6	2.1
Philippines	0.9	1.3	1.4	1.4	2.3	1.8	1.8	2.2	2.3	2.6	4.0
Saudi Arabia	7.9	10.3	6.6	5.7	5.2	6.5	8.1	7.1	6.7	6.9	5.6
Singapore	1.0	0.9	1.0	0.9	0.8	0.8	0.8	0.8	0.8	0.8	0.7
Sri Lanka	0.9	0.8	0.8	1.1	0.9	0.9	0.9	1.0	0.9	0.9	1.3
Syria	1.2	0.8	1.4	1.1	1.8	2.1	1.4	1.0	1.0	0.7	0.6
Yemen	1.0	1.2	1.3	0.9	1.5	1.8	2.0	1.7	2.0	2.3	1.7
AFRICA	**27.7**	**27.0**	**28.4**	**26.7**	**26.3**	**29.2**	**30.5**	**36.6**	**34.3**	**33.2**	**33.6**
North Africa	**16.7**	**16.4**	**19.1**	**18.2**	**17.6**	**17.6**	**17.5**	**18.3**	**20.6**	**20.9**	**20.2**
Algeria	3.5	3.6	4.9	4.7	4.5	4.6	4.4	3.9	6.3	6.2	4.2
Egypt	8.6	8.3	9.0	8.5	8.5	7.3	8.0	7.9	8.1	9.2	8.8
Morocco	1.5	1.5	1.6	1.6	1.7	2.2	2.1	1.7	2.0	1.6	1.7
Tunisia	2.1	1.6	2.4	1.4	1.1	2.3	2.0	3.8	3.1	1.7	3.9
Sub-Saharan Africa	**11.0**	**10.5**	**9.3**	**8.5**	**8.7**	**11.6**	**13.0**	**18.3**	**13.7**	**12.3**	**13.4**
Côte d'Ivoire	0.6	0.7	0.6	0.6	0.6	0.6	0.5	0.6	0.5	0.7	0.6
Ethiopia	1.3	0.9	0.8	0.7	0.5	0.7	0.8	0.9	0.9	0.8	0.3
Kenya	0.3	0.2	0.2	0.3	0.2	0.4	0.5	0.7	1.7	0.5	0.7
Madagascar	0.2	0.2	0.1	0.1	0.1	0.1	0.1	0.1	0.1	0.1	0.1
Senegal	0.6	0.5	0.5	0.6	0.6	0.7	0.6	0.6	0.6	0.7	0.7
Sudan	1.1	0.9	0.7	0.5	0.4	1.1	0.7	0.5	0.8	0.5	0.6

Table 12.2—*cont.*

	1985/86	1986/87	1987/88	1988/89	1989/90	1990/91	1991/92	1992/93	1993/94	1994/95	1995/96
						(million tons)					
CENTRAL AMERICA	**7.2**	**9.1**	**9.6**	**12.0**	**14.8**	**11.3**	**12.7**	**12.1**	**12.4**	**13.4**	**15.6**
Mexico	2.5	4.1	4.4	6.6	8.9	6.0	7.2	6.6	6.4	7.1	9.2
SOUTH AMERICA	**11.3**	**10.8**	**9.0**	**7.0**	**6.8**	**10.2**	**13.2**	**15.4**	**17.7**	**18.5**	**17.3**
Brazil	5.2	4.9	2.3	1.2	2.4	4.9	6.6	7.6	8.2	9.5	7.2
Colombia	0.9	0.9	0.9	0.8	0.7	0.8	1.1	1.6	2.2	2.0	2.4
Peru	1.4	1.8	1.8	1.3	1.4	1.6	2.2	2.1	2.5	2.4	2.6
Venezuela	2.2	1.8	2.7	2.5	1.3	1.6	1.5	2.2	2.3	2.2	2.4
NORTH AMERICA	**1.8**	**2.0**	**1.9**	**3.3**	**2.7**	**3.4**	**4.2**	**4.9**	**8.4**	**6.8**	**6.1**
EUROPE[3]	**21.3**	**16.8**	**18.8**	**18.0**	**14.5**	**13.0**	**11.0**	**13.5**	**12.8**	**11.8**	**12.9**
EC[8]	10.7	6.6	8.3	6.9	6.2	6.2	5.3	3.7	4.9	6.1	7.6
CIS[4]	**29.5**	**28.6**	**30.3**	**37.6**	**38.0**	**26.9**	**39.1**	**28.9**	**11.0**	**5.9**	**4.8**
OCEANIA	**0.5**	**0.5**	**0.6**	**0.6**	**0.8**	**0.8**	**0.7**	**0.8**	**0.9**	**1.2**	**1.0**
WORLD	**181.3**	**184.8**	**197.3**	**205.4**	**207.9**	**187.5**	**215.9**	**210.4**	**196.0**	**201.0**	**205.5**
Developing countries	99.0	106.7	116.2	117.1	122.7	113.8	129.7	128.0	130.3	145.3	150.8
Developed countries	82.2	78.1	81.1	88.3	85.2	73.7	86.2	82.4	65.7	55.8	54.7

[1]Including Taiwan Province.
[3]From 1991/92 including Estonia, Latvia and Lithuania.
[4]Up to 1990/91, former USSR; thereafter, Commonwealth of Independent States.
[7]Wheat (including wheat flour in grain equivalent but excluding semolina) and coarse grains: July/June; rice, calendar year of second year shown.
[8]Excluding trade between member countries; from 1990/91 including New Länder of Germany, 1995/96, 15 member countries.

Source: FAO—Food Outlook Statistical Supplement, January 1997.

Board. The significance of the developing countries, including China and other centrally-planned economies in Asia, as an expanding market for grain exports had not until then been fully explored. But facts and projections presented by the International Wheat Council in a study of trends up to the year 2000 made their significance clear.

Both production and consumption—especially the latter—in the developing countries are growing much faster than in industrialised countries. Imports have risen rapidly in recent years from 40 per cent of the world market 20 years ago to over 50 per cent now. To some extent these figures are affected by the decline in British imports due to membership of the European Community. Also, French exports to Britain now count as intra-trade and do not figure separately in world statistics.

The latest figures of trade (Table 12.3) shown in the IGC's Market Reports show that the trends referred to above are continuing. The increasing demand in developing countries for grain, especially wheat, is the most dynamic element in the world grain situation. A number of causes are responsible for this—among them, population and income growth, accelerating urbanisation, and dietary improvements flowing from economic growth. Despite the parlous state of the economies of many developing countries, consumers in a number of them have incomes high enough to diversify their diets into meat. There has been considerable growth in poultry industries in particular, with a consequent increase in demand for feeds, especially maize, but also wheat when it is available at competitive prices. Demand for feed is now significant in a number of markets in the Far East (e.g. Republic of Korea and Taiwan) and is starting to emerge in many others including the Middle East (e.g. Egypt, Algeria). Though there has been some slackening in the increase in demand in the 1980s compared with the 1970s it is still significant.

Current estimates of population growth in the developing countries put the increase between 1985 and the year 2000 at about one-third. This would produce a figure of 6.1 billion, of whom over two-thirds will be in Asia. Moreover, urbanisation has been proceeding at a rate of over 5 per cent per year, with no signs of slowing down, and this process leads to an increase in the consumption of wheat at the expense of coarse grains and non-grain staple foods.

The reverse side of the coin is the relative inability to finance increased imports. This is a matter which must be obvious to anyone who reads about the astronomical figures of total indebtedness incurred by the developing countries, which by 1990 had reached a total of US$1,300 billion. The FAO, along with UNCTAD, is customarily the international organisation which devotes most attention to the fortunes of the developing countries, and in his annual *Commodity Review and Outlook*

Table 12.3 Grain imports and exports (developing countries). Trade: all wheat (July/June)

Million tons

IMPORTS	**95/96**	**96/97**	**97/98 (est.)**	**98/99 (f'cast) 03.06.98**
EUROPE	**5.4**	**7.6**	**5.4**	**5.0**
Albania	0.2	0.5	0.4	0.4
Bulgaria	0.2	0.6	0.2	0.1
EC	2.8	2.6	3.0	2.6
Norway	0.2	0.2	0.2	0.2
Poland	0.9	1.9	0.4	0.5
Switzerland	0.2	0.1	0.2	0.2
Others	0.9	1.7	1.0	1.1
CIS & BALTICS	**3.8**	**2.7**	**2.4**	**2.7**
Baltic States	0.1	0.2	0.1	0.1
CIS	3.7	2.5	2.3	2.5
Georgia	*0.5*	*0.6*	*0.5*	*0.5*
Russia	*1.3*	*0.6*	*0.5*	*0.5*
Uzbekistan	*0.8*	*0.5*	*0.3*	*0.5*
Other CIS	*1.1*	*0.7*	*1.1*	*1.0*
N & C AMERICA	**5.2**	**7.1**	**6.9**	**6.8**
Cuba	0.7	1.0	0.9	1.0
Mexico	1.6	2.1	1.8	1.9
USA	1.1	2.0	2.0	1.7
Others	1.8	2.1	2.2	2.2
SOUTH AMERICA	**10.4**	**10.9**	**11.1**	**11.5**
Bolivia	0.3	0.4	0.4	0.4
Brazil	5.6	5.9	5.8	6.0
Chile	0.8	0.5	0.7	0.8
Colombia	1.0	1.0	1.1	1.1
Ecuador	0.4	0.5	0.5	0.5
Peru	0.9	1.3	1.2	1.3
Venezuela	1.1	1.2	1.2	1.3
Others	0.2	0.2	0.2	0.3
NEAR EAST ASIA	**10.7**	**16.3**	**15.0**	**15.5**
Iran	2.8	7.1	4.7	4.5
Iraq	0.5	1.2	2.6	3.2
Israel	0.9	0.9	1.3	1.1
Jordan	0.8	0.6	0.7	0.7
Lebanon	0.6	0.5	0.5	0.5
Syria	0.1	0.1	T	0.1
Turkey	2.3	2.4	1.4	1.7
Yemen	1.9	2.3	2.4	2.5
Others	0.9	1.4	1.5	1.4

Table 12.3—*cont.*

IMPORTS	95/96	96/97	97/98 (est.)	Million tons 98/99 (f'cast) 03.06.98
FAR EAST ASIA	**34.2**	**29.2**	**30.8**	**31.0**
Pacific Asia	*30.0*	*22.4*	*22.5*	*23.8*
China	12.5	2.7	2.2	3.0
Chinese Taipei	1.0	1.0	1.1	1.1
Indonesia	3.5	4.2	4.2	4.3
Japan	5.7	6.0	6.1	6.2
Korea (N)	0.2	0.2	0.3	0.2
Korea (S)	2.4	3.4	3.5	3.7
Malaysia	0.9	1.2	1.2	1.2
Philippines	2.0	2.1	2.1	2.2
Singapore	0.3	0.3	0.3	0.3
Thailand	0.8	0.7	0.8	0.8
Vietnam	0.3	0.4	0.5	0.5
Others	0.5	0.4	0.4	0.4
South Asia	*4.1*	*6.8*	*8.3*	*7.2*
Bangladesh	1.2	0.9	1.1	1.1
India	T	1.8	2.1	1.5
Pakistan	1.9	3.1	4.1	3.5
Sri Lanka	0.9	0.9	0.9	0.9
Others	0.1	0.1	0.2	0.2
AFRICA	**19.9**	**21.4**	**23.7**	**22.1**
North Africa	*14.4*	*14.6*	*17.0*	*15.4*
Algeria	3.9	3.6	4.5	4.0
Egypt	6.3	6.9	7.1	7.2
Libya	1.0	1.4	1.3	1.3
Morocco	2.3	1.7	2.7	1.9
Tunisia	0.9	1.0	1.4	1.0
Sub-Sahara	*5.5*	*6.8*	*6.7*	*6.7*
Côte d'Ivoire	0.1	0.3	0.3	0.3
Ethiopia	0.5	0.3	0.5	0.5
Kenya	0.2	0.4	0.4	0.3
Nigeria	0.8	1.0	1.0	1.1
South Africa	0.6	0.9	0.6	0.5
Sudan	0.4	0.6	0.5	0.4
Others	2.9	3.4	3.6	3.6
OCEANIA	**0.5**	**0.5**	**0.5**	**0.5**
New Zealand	0.2	0.2	0.2	0.2
Others	0.3	0.3	0.3	0.3
UNSPECIFIED	**1.6**	**0.8**	**1.6**	**2.0**
SUB-TOTAL	**91.5**	**96.5**	**97.5**	**97.1**
Less:				
Processed secondary trade (PST)	1.1	1.1	1.0	1.0
WORLD TOTAL	**90.4**	**95.4**	**96.5**	**96.1**

Table 12.3—*cont.*

EXPORTS	**95/96**	**96/97**	**97/98 (est.)**	Million tons **98/99 (f'cast) 03.06.98**
Argentina	4.4	10.3	9.0	8.5
Australia	12.1	17.9	14.8	13.5
Canada	16.9	17.9	21.0	16.5
EC	12.2	17.0	15.0	18.0
USA	33.4	26.5	28.5	32.0
5 EXPORTERS	**79.0**	**89.6**	**88.3**	**88.5**
Hungary	2.4	0.8	1.4	1.0
India	1.5	0.6	–	–
Romania	1.7	0.1	1.2	0.2
Saudi Arabia	0.3	–	–	–
Syria	0.6	0.8	0.6	0.9
Turkey	0.9	0.9	1.0	0.9
Others	4.1	2.6	4.0	4.6
WORLD TOTAL	**90.5**	**95.4**	**96.5**	**96.1**

Source: IGC.

for 1990 the Director-General drew special attention to this factor. In the past year, 1997–1998, the financial plight of Asian countries has become acute.

Much of the blame for the deteriorating financial situation is due to the fact that the general level of world prices for agricultural commodities, even in nominal dollars, is less than it was 10 years earlier. In real terms the decrease is one-third on the 1980 level, intensified by a fall in the coffee price. Apart from the primary products on which so many developing countries depend, their overall merchandise trade has lost market share not only to the developed countries but also to the newly-industrialising countries of Asia. Despite the help provided through the Generalized System of Trade Preferences (GSP) in promoting intra-trade among the developing countries such commerce has failed to take off. The Director-General concluded his survey with the warning that more needed to be done to expand debt-reduction measures.

Another important factor in the financial situation of developing countries is debt repayment. Figures for 1989 (contained in the World Bank's *World Development Report 1991*) suggest that annual interest payments by developing countries were on average 10 per cent of the value of their exports of goods and services, but that in many cases the ratio was over 15 per cent. Much of this debt was, perhaps rashly, incurred in the 1970s and early 1980s when petro-dollars were being recycled and interest rates comparatively low.

A viewpoint expressed by an UNCTAD speaker (World Food Conference, Brussels, 1988) might suggest that, contrary to expectation, low world food prices are not to the benefit of developing countries, since they discourage domestic agriculture and depress returns to local farmers. It is clear that developing countries that try to export surplus grain (e.g. India) lose out when world prices are low, but other analysts point out that high transport costs and the relative insulation of farmers in many developing countries from world market conditions mean that their prices are rarely undermined by, say, US export prices. Further examination of this argument might be useful. Food aid which may be delivered free to the recipient country is, of course, another matter. Since producers in many developing countries benefit from certain subsidies—for example, on seeds, fertiliser and fuel—their production costs ought to be relatively low. The lack of proper market organisation is most usually to blame for their plight.

It was estimated in the IWC survey that grain demand in developing countries would continue to grow at a rate of 2.5 per cent *per annum* up to the year 2000, and that there could be a considerable increase in grain requirements for animal feed in a number of countries, particularly China. This could mirror the expansion which took place in the former Soviet Union two or three decades previously, when livestock production started to increase.

Since the collapse of Communism and the Russian transition to a market economy this trend has reversed, as is well known. Some commentators fear that a similar effect may arise following democratic reforms in the Asian countries, but this reasoning overlooks the very different basis from which reforms started. Although production in developing countries is still on an increasing trend—though increasing much more slowly than a decade previously—much of this is due to the effect of the introduction of new high-yielding varieties of cereals (particularly rice) and to much increased fertiliser use, but both of these factors are exposed to constraints, whether administrative or financial.

Tables 12.4 to 12.6 give projections up to the year 2000, covering estimated world population growth, world grain consumption and world grain trade.

The conclusion is that developing countries' import requirements for wheat could double between 1985 and 2000, while requirements for feed grains could quadruple. If this were to be fulfilled, it would mean that imports by developing countries would dominate world grain trade markets by the year 2000, accounting for over 80 per cent of world trade instead of 55 per cent as previously.

The IWC, which prepared these forecasts on the basis of information available at the time, has cautioned that the projections of feed requirements in China must be treated with reserve. Official Chinese forecasts pointed to a great expansion in compound feed output, from a few million tons in the 1980s to over 100 million tons by the year 2000.

Table 12.4 Grain imports and exports (developing countries). Trade: coarse grains (July/June)

IMPORTS	**95/96**	**96/97**	**97/98 (est.)**	Million tons **98/99 (f'cast) 03.06.98**
EUROPE	**7.0**	**6.4**	**4.5**	**4.5**
EC	5.2	3.2	2.6	2.7
Norway	0.2	0.3	0.3	0.3
Poland	0.7	1.0	0.5	0.5
Others	0.9	1.9	1.2	1.0
CIS & BALTICS	**0.4**	**0.5**	**0.5**	**0.5**
Baltic States	0.2	0.2	0.1	0.1
CIS	0.3	0.3	0.4	0.4
Russia	*0.2*	*0.2*	*0.2*	*0.1*
Other CIS	*0.1*	*0.1*	*0.3*	*0.3*
N & C AMERICA	**13.7**	**13.2**	**12.7**	**13.3**
Mexico	8.1	6.4	6.1	6.7
USA	2.4	2.9	2.7	2.6
Others	3.1	3.9	3.8	4.1
SOUTH AMERICA	**5.1**	**5.8**	**6.0**	**6.7**
Brazil	0.6	0.7	0.8	1.5
Chile	0.6	1.0	0.8	0.9
Colombia	1.3	1.7	1.8	1.8
Venezuela	1.3	1.3	1.2	1.3
Others	1.3	1.2	1.4	1.2
NEAR EAST ASIA	**10.0**	**13.8**	**12.0**	**12.7**
Iran	1.7	2.0	2.0	2.0
Israel	1.2	1.5	1.0	1.1
Saudi Arabia	3.8	6.5	5.5	5.9
Others	3.3	3.8	3.5	3.7
FAR EAST ASIA	**45.5**	**43.0**	**40.2**	**40.8**
Pacific Asia	*45.5*	*42.9*	*40.1*	*40.8*
China	4.7	2.1	1.9	2.7
Chinese Taipei	6.3	6.0	5.2	5.5
Japan	19.8	20.8	20.8	20.7
Korea (S)	10.4	9.0	7.6	7.8
Malaysia	2.3	2.6	2.1	2.2
Others	1.8	2.5	2.6	1.9
South Asia	*0.1*	*0.1*	*0.1*	*0.1*
AFRICA	**6.8**	**8.6**	**9.3**	**8.4**
North Africa	*4.9*	*6.1*	*6.7*	*6.7*
Algeria	0.7	0.9	1.2	1.2
Egypt	2.4	3.1	3.3	3.3
Morocco	0.9	0.7	0.9	0.8
Tunisia	0.6	0.6	0.8	0.9
Others	0.3	0.8	0.6	0.6

Table 12.4—*cont.*

IMPORTS	**95/96**	**96/97**	**97/98 (est.)**	Million tons **98/99 (f'cast) 03.06.98**
Sub-Sahara	*1.9*	*2.5*	*2.7*	*1.7*
South Africa	0.5	0.3	0.4	0.2
Others	1.5	2.1	2.3	1.6
OTHERS & UNSP.	**3.1**	**1.8**	**2.9**	**3.4**
WORLD TOTAL	**91.6**	**93.1**	**88.2**	**90.2**
EXPORTS				
Argentina	6.2	11.4	13.2	13.0
Australia	3.7	4.4	3.1	2.9
Canada	4.3	5.3	4.2	4.4
China	T	2.4	7.1	3.1
EC	3.8	8.6	4.8	6.8
South Africa	0.5	2.9	1.6	1.6
USA	66.4	52.2	45.0	50.1
Others	6.6	6.0	9.2	8.4
WORLD TOTAL	**91.6**	**93.1**	**88.2**	**90.2**
Maize (corn)	69.8	66.1	63.2	64.2
Barley	11.7	16.0	14.3	15.1
Sorghum	6.2	6.9	7.0	6.9
Oats	1.6	2.2	2.2	2.0
Rye	2.1	1.7	0.9	1.4

Source: IGC.

This could not have been met from domestic production, and would have led to a major expansion in the world feed grain trade. However, these targets have not been mentioned recently, and it is possible that China has modified or abandoned them. Nevertheless, the forecast of developing countries' share of world grain imports increasing to around 80 per cent by the year 2000 still has validity, because of the decline in imports by Eastern Europe and the former USSR.

The round-table conference discussed above addressed the questions of what more could be done by the developed countries to assist in the fulfillment of these projections. Contributions to the debate from the exporting countries concentrated on the facilities available to help buyers assess the quantity and quality of their needs, on the provision of credit either through government or non-government sources, on the provision of food aid either in kind or in the form of technical assistance, and on the facilities for construction of infrastructure and storage.

The training facilities offered were of particular interest. The Canadian International Grains Institute runs courses on grain handling,

Table 12.5 World population growth, 1965–2000

	Population (million)				Annual increase (%)		
	1965	1975	1985 (est.)	2000 (proj.)	1965–75	1975–85 (est.)	1985–2000 (proj.)
Developing countries of which:	2,329	2,974	3,649	4,861	+2.5	+2.1	+1.9
Latin America	249	321	405	538	+2.6	+2.4	+1.9
Northern Africa	61	78	101	147	+2.5	+2.6	+2.5
Sub-Saharan Africa	236	310	421	667	+2.8	+3.1	+3.1
Total Africa	296	388	522	814	+2.7	+3.0	+3.0
China	729	927	1,060	1,274	+2.4	+1.3	+1.2
India	495	621	759	996	+2.3	+2.0	+1.8
Near East Asia	83	115	153	232	+3.3	+2.9	+2.8
Other Asia	453	576	721	974	+2.4	+2.3	+2.0
Total Asia	1,760	2,239	2,693	3,476	+2.4	+1.9	+1.7
Industrialized countries	1,006	1,103	1,187	1,285	+0.9	+0.7	+0.5
World total	3,335	4,077	4,836	6,146	+2.0	+1.7	+1.6

Source: FAO and the World Bcnk.

Table 12.6 Projected changes in grain consumption, 1985–2000

	1985[a]								2000 (projected)							
	Consumption (million tons)				Annual change 1975–85 (%)				Annual change 1985–2000 (%)				Consumption (million tons)			
	Wheat	Coarse grains	Rice[b]	Total grains	Wheat	Coarse grains	Rice[b]	Total grains	Wheat	Coarse grains	Rice[b]	Total grains	Wheat	Coarse grains	Rice[b]	Total grains
Developing countries	272	299	305	876	+5.5	+3.1	+3.6	+4.0	+3.0	+2.6	+2.0	+2.5	422	438	413	1,272
of which:																
Latin America	25	69	12	106	+2.6	+3.8	+3.2	+3.4	+2.5	+2.6	+2.1	+2.5	37	101	16	154
Northern Africa	20	13	2	35	+4.4	+4.4	+0.6	+4.2	+2.0	+3.3	+1.6	+2.5	27	21	2	50
Sub-Saharan Africa	7	39	8	54	+6.9	+2.0	+5.8	+3.0	+5.4	+3.1	+3.3	+3.4	15	62	12	89
Total Africa	27	52	9	88	+4.9	+2.5	+4.7	+3.4	+3.0	+3.1	+3.5	+3.1	42	82	15	139
China	99	89	124	313	+8.2	+2.9	+4.2	+4.9	+3.0	+2.0	+1.6	+2.2	156	120	159	435
India	46	29	61	135	+6.0	+0.3	+3.4	+3.4	+3.4	+1.2	+2.4	+2.5	76	34	87	197
Near East Asia	36	23	4	62	+7.8	+6.2	+4.9	+4.7	−0.5	+1.4	+1.1	+0.1	51	42	6	99
Other Asia	34	26	95	155	+5.1	+4.9	+2.9	+3.7	+3.1	+3.5	+2.1	+2.6	54	44	131	229
Total Asia	215	166	284	665	+6.2	+3.1	+3.6	+4.2	+3.0	+2.5	+2.0	+2.5	337	241	383	960
Industrialised countries	241	492	18	750	+1.6	+1.3	+0.2	+1.4	−0.8	+0.3	−0.1	0	216	517	18	750
World total	513	791	323	1.626	+3.5	+1.9	+3.4	+2.7	+1.5	+1.3	+1.9	+1.5	637	955	431	2,022

[a] Three-year average.
[b] Milled basis.

Source: IGC.

Table 12.7 Projected world grains trade in 2000 (million tons)

	1985[a]								2000 (projected)							
	Imports				Exports				Imports				Exports			
	Wheat	Coarse grains	Rice[b]	Total grains	Wheat	Coarse grains	Rice[b]	Total grains	Wheat	Coarse grains	Rice[b]	Total grains	Wheat	Coarse grains	Rice[b]	Total grains
Developing countries of which:	57	35	9	101	7	21	9	37	82	72	14	168	9	14	9	32
Latin America	10	9	1	21	6	10	1	17	12	9	2	23	8	8	T	17
Northern Africa	13	4	T	17	–	T	T	T	16	7	T	23	–	–	T	T
Sub-Saharan Africa	5	2	3	10	–	1	T	1	12	5	5	22	–	1	1	2
Total Africa	18	6	3	27	–	1	T	1	28	12	5	45	–	1	1	2
China	9	4	T	13	–	5	1	6	6	20	2	28	–	–	–	–
India	T	–	T	T	T	T	T	1	–	T	–	T	–	–	–	–
Near East Asia	9	9	2	21	1	T	T	1	11	18	4	33	1	1	T	1
Other Asia	11	7	2	20	T	3	6	10	25	12	2	40	–	2	8	10
Total Asia	28	20	5	54	1	9	8	18	42	51	8	101	1	3	8	11
Industrialised countries	34	66	3	103	84	82	4	170	12	33	2	47	85	92	7	184
World total	91	101	12	204	91	103	12	207	94	105	16	215	94	105	16	215

[a] Three-year average.
[b] Milled basis.
T Less than 0.5 million tons.

Source: IGC.

marketing and technology, including specific milling, baking and quality control, tailored to the customers' requirements. The Australian Wheat Board sponsors training seminars on subjects ranging from flour milling, baking, laboratory techniques, grain storage/hygiene and international marketing. Australia is particularly active in China and Egypt. The US Wheat Associates place their major emphasis on trade servicing and technical assistance, including the highly-regarded milling training carried out at Kansas and North Dakota State Universities. This organisation is also active overseas, paying much attention to China. Particularly valued by recipient countries is the help in establishing grain storage and improving port facilities.

PART 3

The carriage of grain by sea

CHAPTER 13

Ship types and sizes employed to carry grain

Much has been written on dry bulk shipping since World War II, most notably by Birger Nossum in Oslo, who has made a study of the period from 1945 to 1990, and more recent analyses have been produced by Agriculture and Agri-Food Canada based in Winnipeg.

The ocean shipping industry can be divided into two major sectors: bulk shipping and general cargo shipping. There are two types of bulk shipping services. Dry carriers provide bulk full-load services for commodities such as grain, coal and iron ore. With the exception of some shipments to the USA, most of the grain exported from Canada is transported in ocean bulk vessels. Wet carriers or tankers provide services for petroleum and other liquid commodities. In addition, vessels operate either as part of a liner service or as tramp vessels.

The liner shipping market is composed of carriers that provide service over fixed time and route schedules. Liner service vessels are designed to carry containerised cargo such as meat and horticultural products, grain products such as flour, planting seed, rice, high-value speciality grains and non-agricultural products. Liner service shipments account for only a very small portion of total world grain and feed trade.

Tramp vessels operate in the charter market with no regular scheduled routes and are contracted to shippers on an as-needed basis. Vessels operate like a rental car service where a ship, like a car, is hired or chartered for a single voyage or period of time.

There is a wide range of sizes and configurations of tramp vessels in the world fleet, and many are designed to carry dry bulk cargo such as grain, coal, ore or fertilisers. There are also combination vessels designed to carry either dry bulk cargo or liquid bulk cargo, such as petroleum. Grain exporters and importers charter vessels from shipowners, frequently through agents or brokers in New York or at the Baltic Exchange in London.

The dry carrier shipping sector consists mainly of five major bulk commodities including iron ore, coal, phosphates, bauxite and grain. Although grain is grouped with iron ore and coal as one of the five major bulk commodities, it is fundamentally a different business in both economic and shipping terms. Iron ore and coal form part of a carefully scheduled industrial operation, whereas grain is an agricultural commodity, seasonal in its trade and irregular in both volume and route. Consequently, it is extremely difficult to optimise, or even plan, grain shipments. As a result, the grain trade depends heavily on general-purpose vessels drawn from the charter market.

Many different ship types are used for bulk transport but the main ones fall into four groups: tankers, general-purpose dry bulk carriers, combined carriers and specialist bulk vessels. There are over 5,400 bulk vessels in the world fleet. Capesize vessels are the largest and carry 120,000 dead weight tonnage (dwt) or more. Capesize vessels are too large to cross the Panama Canal or the Suez Canal and are used for transporting coal, iron ore, phosphate and bauxite. Panamax vessels, the largest ships that can negotiate the Panama Canal, are commonly used for grain shipment across the Atlantic and Pacific Oceans. These ships typically carry a range of 55,000 to 65,000 dwt. The smaller vessels are known as Handysize and are used in shallow waters and in other lower-volume trade routes around the world. Handysize vessels range between 20,000 to 40,000 dwt.

In Canada, laker freight vessels, which fall into the Handysize vessel category, move most of the grain from Thunder Bay through the Great Lakes and St Lawrence Seaway to ports on the St Lawrence River. These vessels are limited to about 25,000 to 29,000 tons of grain due to the size of the St Lawrence Seaway. The bulk of these vessels are a captive fleet, relying almost completely on grain as a main haul and iron ore as a backhaul.

The importance of the grain trade in the overall seaborne dry bulk market has declined considerably in recent years, simply because grain tonnage has not grown as quickly as many other trades—certainly not as quickly as coal and iron ore, the other two of the traditionally considered three major dry bulks. Grain traffic used to account for just over 13 per cent of all dry cargoes moved as recently as 1980, but this percentage share had fallen to just about 11 per cent by 1990 and still lower to less than 10 per cent today (1997 figures). By the turn of the new century, the proportion of grain trade in total dry cargo traffic moving internationally by sea is expected to fall yet lower to around 9 per cent, but nevertheless, at a volume of around 190 million tons a year, it will still be substantial.

Grain is a comparatively light and easily free-flowing commodity to handle, so virtually any commercial ship type can be used and has been used to move it by sea. Typical handling and physical characteristics of different grain types, including average weights, stowage factors and angles of repose during carriage and storage, are shown in Table 13.1.

Stowage factors illustrated are largely approximations, since carriage

Table 13.1 Physical characteristics of main grain types

Grain Products	Weight (Kg/Cbm)	Stowage Factor (Cbm/tonne)	Angle of Repose
Barley	643	1.36–1.50	46 degrees
Maize	708	1.25–1.41	21 degrees
Oats	514	1.81–2.06	21 degrees
Millet	733	1.37–1.53	22 degrees
Wheat	780	1.18–1.34	23 degrees
Rye	746	1.34–1.69	32 degrees
Sorghum	733	1.35–1.38	31 degrees
Rice	772	1.28–1.32	20 degrees
Soyabeans	720	1.35–1.39	22 degrees
Soyameal	520	1.67–1.72	40 degrees

Source: BulkShip consultants.

varies a great deal depending often upon the season and the port of loading; varying considerably even between, for example, US Atlantic Coast and US Gulf Coast loading ports. Illustrating a case in point, an old US Coast Guard listing of typical soyabean meal characteristics loaded at selected ports shows that one product loaded at Baltimore, Maryland, was described as a cracked bean to fine material; yellow colour; odourless; with variable moisture: having a stowage factor measured at between 1.53 to 1.81 m^3/tonne (equivalent to 55 to 60 ft^3/ton) with an angle of repose approximating 24–26 degrees. At the same time, another soyabean meal product loaded at Duluth, Minnesota, was described as a ground meal in coarse powder form; 10.5 per cent moisture, odourless; yellow colour: with a stowage factor measured at 1.68 m^3/tonne (60 ft^3/ton) and an approximate 40 degree angle of repose. Yet another soyabean meal product loaded at New Orleans, Louisiana, was described as 100 per cent powder; yellow colour; slight odour; 8 per cent moisture: with a stowage factor measured at 1.67 m^3/tonne (60 ft^3/ton) and with an approximate 43 degree angle of repose.

The list continues with further different descriptions for soyabean meals loaded at Chicago, Illinois; Galveston and Houston in Texas; and two products described alternatively as coarse and fine loaded at Toledo, Ohio. Often, too, grains are bagged, and in such case the cargo will occupy an extra 8–10 per cent of hold space in a bulk carrier. While annual shipment of bagged grains, especially re-exports from some of the major Belgian and Dutch ports, has fallen considerably in recent years, it is a practice which continues to be employed for deliveries to countries in the developing world where bulk-handling facilities remain few and far between.

Meanwhile, as illustrated in Table 13.1, the lightest of the grain types is oats (averaging about 40 lbs/bushel, or roughly 514 kg/m^3), while heaviest is wheat (at between 59 and 62 lbs/bushel, or roughly

780 kg/m^3). Oats has a stowage factor of some 1.81–2.06 m^3/tonne, while wheat averages around 1.18–1.34 m^3/tonne. Most grains have a fairly low angle of repose (the natural angle of rest if poured into a storage hold) at between 20 and 23 degrees, but sorghum with 31 degrees, rye with 32 degrees, and barley with highest of all at 46 degrees have comparatively high angles of repose.

Throughout the two decades prior to the start of the 1970s, grain was very commonly transported in tankers (especially old T2-type tankers), combined carriers (ore/oil and ore/bulk/oil carriers), and—most especially of all—in the ubiquitous tweendecker or general dry cargo carrier. Most commonly utilised today, however, is the standard, relatively unsophisticated, straightforward bulk carrier. These latter typically comprise three-, four- or five-hold single deck vessels, generally lacking any deck gear.

Factors of note in considering transportation needs, and specifically the selection of types and sizes of ships utilised for the carriage of grain, include:

- the predominantly sporadic and short-term nature of the grain trades;
- physical limitations at port facilities for handling the largest bulk carrier sizes;
- the generally longer average shipping distances involved in the transport of grain compared with other major dry bulk commodities;
- and the highly scattered dispersion of import markets for grain.

Concerning the first point above, due to the high degree of seasonality attached to the grain trades and, because of the rapidly fluctuating nature of the trades as result of vagaries of the weather on world grains production and import demand patterns, grain shipping patterns tend to be highly variable. Major trading emphasis can periodically switch between a number of principal sea routes, generating considerable requirement among traders and shippers for highly flexible vessel selection policies.

The second point is best illustrated by reference to the physical limitations of grain loading and (especially) grain discharging facilities, as listed in Annexes 1 and 2. As illustrated, the vast majority of grain export loading and import/discharge facilities are limited to bulk vessels below 60,000 dwt, while load/discharge facilities for vessels above Panamax size are extremely few and far between.

Regarding the third point above, average annual grain transport distances have been of the order of 5,600–5,900 nm (nautical miles) compared with around 5,400 nm for coal, only 5,200 nm for iron ore, and yet far shorter distances in other principal dry bulk commodity trades.

Recent grain transport distance trends are illustrated in Table 13.2, and according to the latest Fernresearch figures, the trend in very recent years has been markedly upwards. At the start of the 1990s, annual grain shipping distances averaged around 5,300–5,600 nm, but by 1995–1996, the average had increased substantially to around 5,800–5,900 nm.

On the fourth point in particular, it is worth commenting that the grain trade is dominated by just four major exporting countries—the United States, Canada, Australia and Argentina accounted for as much as 82 per cent of all exports in the early 1980s and still provide above three-quarters of the total shipped overseas more recently. On the imports side, however, the six consistently largest importers (Japan, China, the former Soviet Union, South Korea, Egypt and Taiwan) have together accounted for something considerably below the 50 per cent level of overall import traffic, even during the peak middle to late 1980s, while today their share of total imports is closer to 30 per cent of total trade.

Taking all these and some other factors into consideration provides an insight into the seaborne transport of grain in very brief overview. Perhaps one singularly interesting area for expanded comment concerns the trend towards increasing ship sizes utilised in the grain trades.

Traditionally, the mainstay of the grain transport fleet of ships was the tweendecker—an older vintage general dry cargo carrier with a second deck providing a separation between an upper and a lower hold, and in which the upper deck is the main deck. However, the advent of larger, single deck, straightforward bulk carriers throughout the later 1970s, 1980s and 1990s has virtually eliminated the tweendecker from the grain trades in recent years. These newer dry bulk carriers designed to carry grain featured sloping bulkheads aimed at cutting out the dead space at the tops of cargo holds, while also easing the need for trimming and cutting the size of cargo gangs during both loading and discharging.

Table 13.2 Average grain trade shipping distances 1990–1996

Year	*Trade**	*Tonne / Miles***	*Average Distance****
1990	191.53	1,073	5,600
1991	200.20	1,069	5,340
1992	208.34	1,091	5,240
1993	193.74	1,038	5,360
1994	184.35	992	5,380
1995	196.16	1,160	5,910
1996	192.63	1,126	5,850

*Million Tonnes.
**Billion Tonne/Miles.
***Thousand Nautical Miles.

Source: Fearnleys, Fernresearch, Norway.

Often they were built as a series type by many of the major shipbuilding yards, such as the IHI "F Series" including the 35,000–37,000 dwt Future 32 and Future 32–A vessels; the Burmeister & Wain BC 60 Series; and the Hitachi Panamax Series of 65,000 dwt ships.

Nevertheless, even to the present day, tweendeckers continue to play a small, albeit rapidly decreasing, role in the carriage of short-haul, low-volume grain business, particularly within the less developed countries of the world. The role of tankers and combined carriers in the grain trades has meanwhile almost disappeared, mainly due to requirements of increasingly stringent cleaning of ships' holds between alternate movement of liquid and/or different mineral dry bulk cargoes.

Small coastal bulkers and dry cargo freighters of 2,000–10,000 dwt are generally employed in the short sea North European trades and for local distribution by sea and navigable river or for transhipment traffics of grain. However, the vast bulk of the international grain trade is now moved in bulk carriers of above 20,000 dwt, with only very small continuing contribution from combined carriers. Significant change in the average size of vessel transporting grain has been seen over the last couple of decades. For example, in 1970 around 10 per cent of total grain trade was carried in vessels between 40,000 and 60,000 dwt while only a mere 1 per cent was carried in vessels above 60,000 dwt, the rest (or 89 per cent) of the total went in ships below 40,000 dwt as a maximum. By the mid-1980s the situation was that 40 per cent plus of total grain trade was carried in ships over 60,000 dwt (Panamax and above size), while less than 40 per cent was carried in vessels of below 40,000 dwt, the residual 20 per cent and more being accounted for by the so-called Handysizes of 40,000–60,000 dwt. These estimates have been calculated annually by the Fernresearch Division of Fearnleys A/S of Norway.

More recently, Fernresearch figures have suggested that in 1996, bulk vessels above 60,000 dwt carried approximately 52 per cent of all grain cargoes, another 6 per cent was carried in ships of between 50,000 and 60,000 dwt, but only 42 per cent was transported in vessels below 50,000 dwt. The annual size distribution of vessels carrying grain during the 1990s is shown in Table 13.3.

Table 13.3 Grain shipments vessel size distribution 1990–1996 (per cent)

Size Range (Dwt)	*1990*	*1991*	*1992*	*1993*	*1994*	*1995*	*1996*
Below 50,000	49	50	48	47	51	43	42
50–60,000	13	10	8	7	7	7	6
60–80,000	34	36	37	35	33	38	41
80–100,000	1	1	2	2	2	2	1
Above 100,000	3	3	5	9	7	10	10
Total	100	100	100	100	100	100	100

Source: Fearnleys, Fernresearch, Norway.

The increase in average ship sizes transporting grain world-wide would undoubtedly have been larger in recent years but for the fact that port and terminal constraints, especially in the receiving ports, have had a major impact on the underlying trend.

CHAPTER 14

Problems associated with the carriage of grain by sea

Prior to accepting a consignment of grain, the vessel must first pass charter party surveys, which necessitate that all cargo space must be properly cleansed in order to eliminate any possibility of cargo contamination. It is essential that all cargo spaces intended for grain transport are thoroughly clean, free of odour, and free of loose rust and/or paint scale, and must in every respect be fit to receive the loaded grain. This can mean that cargo holds will require to be swept and washed, if necessary, as well as dried thereafter. Particular care must be taken to ensure that overhead beams and ledges are cleaned; bilges and/or drain wells must be cleaned and then sealed with burlap or similar modern synthetic material which is grain-tight but not watertight. Bilge suctions and sounding pipes must be clear, and any tweendeck scuppers must be made grain-tight.

Bulkheads adjacent to the engineroom compartment and subject to temperatures of 110 degrees Fahrenheit (43.3 degrees Centigrade) and above must be sheathed to avoid cargo heating in the hold.

After clean loading is completed, relatively little is required by way of on-board cargo maintenance for the carriage of grain by sea, with perhaps the exception under special circumstances, or at shipper's specific request, for in-hold fumigation against insect pests, such as beetles and weevils etc., and/or against mould infestations.

Other on-board requirements will certainly ensure watertight hatch covering on deck hatches, for obvious reasons with carriage of a product which can be contaminated by moisture (especially sea water), while adequate venting of cargo holds is also preferred to prevent internal sweating of the cargo and related moisture and mould problems. Precautions must be taken to prevent leakage of water into grain cargoes through the joints of metal weatherdeck hatch covers which may be caused by the working of the vessel in heavy weather. Sealing of these joints by special tape and/or available proprietary hatch seals made of rubberised compounds is recommended.

Cargoes of oats and maize, in particular, can be liable to problems associated with heating and sweating during transit, which causes souring of the product. Adequate measures to ensure that the cargo is in fit state to be loaded are the responsibility of the exporter/loading terminal operator, but thereafter become the responsibility of the shipper/charterer.

Special care and attention need to be taken also with the loading and transport of soyabeans, and especially soyabean meals and cake. These products again can be subject to problems with heating, sweating and fermentation. The handling of soyabean meal/cake is subject to IMO guidelines concerning the handling of Dangerous Goods (IMDG) which stipulates that all due care and attention is given to ensure adequate ventilation is provided.

Cargoes of soyabean meal always contain a small percentage of vegetable oil in which there is an element of danger arising from cargo heating and potential for self combustion. In a recently highlighted case, the London Protection & Indemnity Club drew attention to a number of claims arising from the carriage of soyabean meal from the port of Mumbai in India. According to the P&I Club, problems of overheating in cargoes may have been caused by freak monsoon conditions affecting the country, while it added that most shippers had stopped moving the product from the affected area temporarily. The London P&I Club recommended that basic checks should be made on suspect cargoes, including product condition checks and necessary segregation of a suspect product before loading on board ships. Cargo temperatures should be checked accurately, with readings greater than 5 per cent over ambient temperatures considered highly suspect. The colour of the cargo should also be checked to ensure there are no dark spots, which would indicate problems, and moisture content should also be closely monitored for any excesses.

Trimming of the grain cargoes during loading to ensure even distribution of grain throughout the holds is necessary to prevent the product (which mostly has a low angle of repose) from shifting during ocean transit. Consequently, in most single voyage charter contracts for grain transport, fiot (free in and out and trimmed) is always stated in the terms, which means the cargo is loaded on board and discharged from the vessel at the cost of the charterer or shipper, and not for the account of the shipowner.

All grain cargoes settle during transit by as much as 5 per cent, so adequate trimming is essential. US grain regulations are predicated on cargo spaces being as full as possible and well trimmed. Constant supervision and inspection by ships' officers and agents is required to ensure that this is done. When loading dusty cargoes, it may be necessary to interrupt loading periodically to allow the dust to settle sufficiently properly to inspect the trimming of holds. During mechanical trimming with loading spouts, throwing distances should be kept to a minimum.

CHAPTER 15

Grain loading and unloading, major ports and terminals

Much of the following describing "grain loading and unloading operations" at major bulk ports and terminals around the globe summarises the detailed information contained within Appendices 1 and 2 of this book. Further examination of these Appendices will provide the reader with more extensive information than can be included here.

Grain loading facilities world-wide are concentrated within just a few main areas of the world, especially within the USA, Canada, Argentina and Australia. Grain export shipments have increased from the European Community since the early 1980s, generating developments especially at UK and French ports, while Brazil's potential for vastly increased grains and oilseeds exports in particular has yet to be fully exploited.

The major US grain export facilities are located around the Gulf Coast, and especially the Lower Mississippi ports; the North Pacific ports and Great Lakes ports; and to a lesser extent, also the Atlantic Coast ports. Principal amongst these are the ten major export facilities within the Baton Rouge–South Louisiana–New Orleans–Plaquemines Parish, Lower Mississippi corridor, which can handle between them as much as 20 million tonnes or more of grain exports annually. The only limitation, if it is, for loading facilities in this area is the dredged depth of the Mississippi River at 13.7 m from the mouth of the river to Mile Post 150 north of New Orleans, and at 12.2 m from there up-stream to Baton Rouge.

The next biggest US grain export loading centre is the North Pacific Coast/Colombia River area, where the ports of Portland, Kalama, Longview and Vancouver feature prominently. Elsewhere, the US East Coast offers major grain loading facilities at the ports of Norfolk, Baltimore and Charleston. The Great Lakes and St Lawrence ports on both the US and Canadian sides can generally be placed together as a major loading centre, if only for their common exit limitations imposed by the St Lawrence River Seaway and the restrictions of the Seaway Locks. The Great Lakes shipping season is also a common limiting factor, transportation having to close for most of the four winter months between December and March. Overall Great Lakes grain export tonnages have declined considerably since the late 1980s, however, especially following repeal of the Crow Rail Rates Legislation, and with the expansion of export loading terminals capacity in the North Pacific Coast ports of Vancouver and Prince Rupert in particular.

Argentina grain loading facilities can broadly be categorised as "Upper" and "Lower River" locations, or as "Coastal" in general location.

Export of grain from the ports of the Parana River fall under the conditions imposed within the terms of the Centrocon charter party agreement. Vessels cannot load at a port higher than San Lorenzo and must load at subsequent ports in proper rotation, thus port congestion cannot be avoided by moving down to the next port. While both Santa Fe and Diamante provide grain berths with good loading facilities up-river from San Lorenzo, under the terms of the Centrocon conditions, grain loading must comply with the options clause of the contract which limits the number of downstream calls possible.

Most of the Argentine river ports suffer from the draught limitations imposed by restrictions of the Mitre Channel and Martin Garcia Bar on the Uruguay and Parana Rivers. The maximum draught of the Mitre Channel is 8.8 m, with a channel width of 130 m, while the Martin Garcia Bar is restricted to a maximum draught of 7.92 m.

Coastal facilities at the Argentine ports of Bahia Blanca and Quequen/Necochea provide for deeper draught loading operations, however. Consequently, almost two-thirds of Argentinian grain exports have left from these ports in recent years.

The situation at Australian grain export loading facilities has improved considerably with the adoption of more sensible manning and work practice regulations, including the acceptance of two shift/continuous loading operating procedures. Consequently, typical vessel loading times have been reduced by anything between 50 and 60 per cent, down from an average of four to five days per vessel during the late 1980s to just two days and less at present.

This means that Australia's grain exports can take full advantage of the well-developed export facilities in existence at the major ports of Geelong and Portland in Victoria; Port Kembla, Sydney and Newcastle in New South Wales; Brisbane, Gladstone and Mackay in Queensland; and Geraldton, Fremantle and Albany in Western Australia.

As a way and means of improving the effective transport of grains to imports markets and in availing capture of scale economies to reduce as far as possible the final delivered cost of products, transhipment has been practised widely within the grain trades for many years. The result has been the establishment of notable transhipment centres at strategic port locations within the imports sector of West Europe especially, these intended to accommodate the largest vessel sizes possible in the long-haul ocean transport of grain, adjacent to or close by the eventual end-destination markets.

Principal among these centres is the port of Rotterdam in the Netherlands, which serves the wide-ranging north-west European area. Competing against Rotterdam in the same region is the other major Dutch port of Amsterdam, the Belgian ports of Antwerp and Ghent, and the West German ports of Bremen and Hamburg.

In addition, too, the German port of Rostock has a relatively newly constructed high capacity grain import elevator which in recent years has taken a large grain transhipment tonnage (as much as 10 million tons annually in the 1980s) away from Hamburg. This latter traffic has been handled on behalf of the Soviet Union for transhipment in smaller vessel sizes to the draught-restricted Baltic Sea ports. However, with commissioning of the high capacity imports facility at Tallinn even more recently, grain import cargoes are planned to go directly into Russia via this Estonian port in the larger bulk vessel sizes. However, independence of the Baltic States and vastly reduced FSU grain purchasing has impeded progress, and until proper arrangements can be finalised between Estonia and Russia, little grain has been or will be handled by this facility.

Development of Rotterdam as the principal transhipment base for grains moving into western and eastern Europe had provided substantial impetus to the employment of 100,000 dwt plus bulk carriers in the transatlantic trades, especially during the early 1980s.

In Rotterdam, the EBS (European Bulk Stevedores) deepwater facilities in the Europoort area in particular have handled the bulk of the transhipment cargoes. While overall agri-bulks (grains plus grain by-products or derivatives) receipts have declined considerably from about the 22 million tons annual level during the early 1980s down to less than 12 million tons lately, such tonnage is still far ahead of the other competing ports in the region.

Table 15.1 shows the volume of agri-bulk arrivals in the ports of the so-called Antwerp–Hamburg range of northern Europe during the 17-year period from 1981 to 1997. In the early years of the last decade, the volume of imports fluctuated around a level of 45–46 million tons, declining rapidly since 1988–1989 to not much more than 31 million tons today. Rotterdam continues to pick up most of this flow, however.

Over time the composition of the incoming flow of agri-bulks into the port of Rotterdam has changed. Table 15.2 clearly illlustrates this changing composition, and shows that the importance of non-grain animal feed ingredients has increased tremendously.

Products such as corn gluten feed, tapioca, soyabean meal, soyabean pellets, copra and palm kernel pellets belong to this category. It is within this group of commodities that the position of Rotterdam is particularly

Table 15.1 Main Agribulk discharge ports in northern Europe 1981–1997 (million tons)

Years / Ports	*Rotter-dam*	*Amster-dam*	*Antwerp*	*Ghent*	*Bremen*	*Hamburg*	*Total*
1981	22.0	4.1	3.9	3.9	2.9	8.3	45.1
1982	21.0	4.3	4.7	5.8	2.4	8.0	46.2
1983	22.0	4.3	4.2	5.3	2.3	NA	38.1
1984	18.4	5.4	3.0	4.7	2.0	NA	33.5
1985	19.2	5.1	3.0	4.7	2.3	NA	34.3
1986	19.5	3.9	2.4	4.1	2.5	NA	32.4
1987	18.8	4.1	2.1	4.4	2.0	NA	31.4
1988	20.0	3.5	1.8	4.1	2.2	NA	31.6
1989	18.0	4.0	0.8	4.2	1.8	NA	28.8
1990	17.1	3.8	1.1	4.7	1.8	3.3	31.8
1994	13.9	7.1	2.8	4.6	3.2	2.9	34.5
1995	13.2	6.5	2.1	4.5	3.1	3.2	32.6
1996	13.2	7.7	1.9	3.8	2.6	3.4	32.6
1997	11.9	8.4	1.5	4.0	2.1	3.2	31.1

NB. Totals for the years 1983–1989 exclude tonnages imported through the Port of Hamburg.

Source: Individual Port Authorities and EBS Rotterdam.

strong. Quite literally, the port of Rotterdam is at the crossroads of the agri-bulk trade into northern Europe, and it is especially at this point that buyers and sellers congregate.

Elsewhere in Europe, the IGMA terminal at the port of Amsterdam handles between 10 and 20 per cent of its annual 3.0–3.5 million ton traffic as transhipped cargo for third-party interests, and has extended its operations into the outer harbour of Ijmuiden for the accommodation of Capesize (120,000 dwt plus) tonnage. In Bremen, the Feedstuffs/Grain Terminals River Weser Co-operative can accept inbound vessels part

Table 15.2. Composition of Agribulk handling at the port of Rotterdam (per cent of total unloaded)

Year	*Grains*	*Oilseeds*	*Other*	*Total*
1970	37	25	38	100
1975	39	24	37	100
1980	14	33	53	100
1985	12	22	66	100
1990	6	25	69	100
1994	8	39	53	100
1995	10	39	51	100
1996	10	44	46	100
1997	9	51	40	100

EBS handled tonnage only.

Source: EBS Rotterdam.

laden up to 125,000 dwt and over half of the total 2.5–3.0 million tons handled annually, not all grains and consisting mostly of feedstuffs, is transhipped on to markets outside Germany.

Grain transhipment facilities in the Belgian ports consist essentially of the GGT (Ghent Grain Terminal) and Eurosilo facilities at Ghent, and in Antwerp it is largely the Samga and Sobelgra grain terminals which handle transit cargoes via its respective 120,000 ton and 166,000 ton storage capacity facilities. Antwerp in particular did, until very recent years, have an especially strong role in the reception of bulk grains for later transhipment in bags to many of the African and Middle Eastern countries, but changing domestic supply patterns and provision of new bulk handling facilities within the latter area has meant reduction of this former business.

Grain transhipment is very much part of the market extension philosophies of three other European import terminals in recent years, the Tagol and Silopor facilities at Lisbon, and the Kordin Grain Terminal in Malta. The latter was constructed on the basis of an expectation that it could serve a potential 45 million ton annual eastern Mediterranean market, with as much as a third of this tonnage being transhipped through Malta. However, the Malta grain terminal (and other transhipment proposals in various developing countries) has never really fulfilled its hopes because:

- the decline in the number of destinations which need to take their grain or flour in the form of bags at the port of discharge;
- improved port facilities in some major developing countries (e.g. Egypt, and also Algeria) which mean that they can receive large modern bulk carriers and discharge them at high rates;
- the development of cheap and efficient vacuvators/baggers which mean that grain vessels can discharge their grain directly into barges or lorries at any port where the water is deep enough to receive them.

These terminals have all commenced high capacity operations during the early to mid-1980s, but to date the volumes of transhipped cargoes have been negligible. For the future, however, they are ideally placed to serve the wider market areas of North Africa and the whole of the Mediterranean basin, as well as West Africa, the Middle East and much of north-west Europe. The main grain transhipment terminal within the Middle East at present is the Jebel Ali facility of the Gulf Import and Export Company in the United Arab Emirates state of Dubai. This terminal provides for the reception of bulk carriers of between Panamax and Capesize 60,000–120,000 dwt in the handling of foodgrains for the whole of the region. Already committed to the facility is the Australian Wheat Board, which has arranged for the reception and storage of considerable volumes of its wheat here to provide immediately accessible stocks to the local countries either as a bulk or bagged onward cargo.

In other ports of the Middle East there has been a tendency to employ floating transhipment facilities, which have largely comprised converted tankers and/or bulk carriers. These can be provided on site where required much more quickly and at very substantially reduced cost compared with permanent land-based facilities. Examples in the past have included an 80,000 dwt converted vessel at Fujaira in the United Arab Emirates where cargoes have been off-loaded at rates up to 1,000 tph into small feeder ships for distribution, plus other similar floating installations at Aqaba in Jordan, Alexandria and Port Said in Egypt, and Jubail in Saudi Arabia.

In the Far East, Japanese import facilities dominate the scene, with no fewer than 30 large scale, high capacity, receiving terminals currently available to discharge grains, feedstuffs and oilseeds. Together they handle around 18–20 million tons of grain imports—mostly maize, wheat, soyabeans, and soyabean meals and pellets—every year.

Japanese grain imports are frequently shipped in under combination discharge ports basis, to take advantage of maximum ship size abilities of several of the port of Yokohama's larger grain import terminals, the Kokusai Futo berths especially which can accept Capesize vessels with draughts up to 17.3 m. Most of the other major Japanese ports can accommodate ships of around Panamax size at maximum.

Latest among the new grain receiving terminals in the Far East Asian growth markets is the Mariveles Asia Terminals facility in the Philippines. Having begun operations towards the end of 1996, this terminal is now fully operational with four 750 tph Siwertell screw-type ship unloaders and adequate quay length to accommodate reception and discharge of two fully laden 80,000 dwt vessels simultaneously.

CHAPTER 16

Freight rates, charter markets and charterparties

The main authority on freight rates on a regular basis is the International Grains Council (IGC) in London, whose senior economist charts their progress on a regular basis through the *Monthly Grain Market Report* issued by the Council. Information on freight rates in a more condensed form is also issued from time to time by Agriculture Canada in its bi-weekly bulletin.

As for chartering in all its aspects, the most prestigious and longest-established authority is the Baltic Exchange in London. This organisation traces its origins back to a club established in 1823 at the Baltic Coffee House, and this in turn—as transatlantic students may like to know—started as a coffee house called the Virginia and Maryland until 1744, when it became the Virginia and Baltic, before assuming its subsequent identity.

Members of the Baltic, which is a limited company owned by its shareholders, both corporations and individuals, are brokers acting in the various markets as intermediaries. The largest activity is the international freight market, with chartering of vessels of all flags by charterers of all trading nations. Commodity trading is the other main function of the Exchange. Several futures markets operate under the auspices of the Baltic Futures Exchange (BIFFEX), which started in 1985, trading in agricultural commodities, specifically wheat, barley, potatoes, soya and meat, and in freight futures.

Volatility in the charter market presents the shipper with a degree of uncertainty over future freight costs, and the function of BIFFEX is to enable shippers, owners and charterers to hedge against sudden changes in freight rates.

Other shipping organisations with which the student should be familiar include BIMCO Copenhagen, GCBS, Lloyd's, the Institute of Chartered Shipbrokers and FONASBA. A brief description of their functions follows.

The Baltic and International Maritime Council was founded in 1905 by a group of shipowners engaged principally in the Baltic and White Sea trades. Its membership is now international and consists of owners, shipbrokers and agents, and P & I Clubs. It aims to unite shipowners and others connected with the shipping industry and to take action on behalf of shipowners' interests and to communicate to members instances of unfair charges throughout the world and other useful information which may come to the knowledge of BIMCO. For many years it has issued approved documents, e.g. charterparties and bills of lading, sometimes in collaboration with other bodies such as the GCBS and FONASBA, and sometimes after agreement with organisations of charterers or shippers.

The General Council of British Shipping (GCBS) is the representative body of the British shipping industry nationally and internationally. It consults with government departments on policies affecting the interests of its members; negotiates with seafarers' unions on industrial relations and manpower questions; is active in the provision of services to members in the recruitment of seafarers and their training and the provision of crews. Its members are shipowners in the UK, both liner and tramp.

LLOYD'S OF LONDON

Lloyd's is the most famous insurance market in the world. It is made up of syndicates or groups of underwriters ("Names") who have become specialists in various types of risks, marine and non-marine. There is competition between groups, but the importance of the market as a cohesive whole is recognised. Edward Lloyd opened his coffee house in the 1680s; today the Corporation occupies sites on each side of Lime Street in the City of London. The market is the "Room" and insurance may only be placed through brokers who make up roughly half of the 4,000 or so people likely to be engaged in the daily business at any one time.

LLOYD'S REGISTER OF SHIPPING

Lloyd's Register developed from the same coffee house source as Lloyd's of London, but since 1834 has been separate. It produces a register of ships and it has been acting as a classification society for ships for over 200 years, setting standards for design, construction and maintenance.

There are other ship classification societies throughout the world centred in the traditional maritime countries; Lloyd's Register is among the largest.

INSTITUTE OF CHARTERED SHIPBROKERS

The Institute is a professional body whose membership is open to individuals who are engaged or employed in a firm or company operating in shipbroking. Its main objects are to test the qualifications of candidates for admission to the Institute by examination in theory and in practice; to hold or to take part in conferences and meetings for the discussion of professional affairs, the reading of papers and the delivery of lectures; to ascertain and notify the law and practice relating to shipbrokers.

The Institute's examination syllabus is designed to equip the member for employment in any of the branches of the shipbroking profession, for example Chartering/Port Agency/Liner Agency/Sale and Purchase/Shipowning or Ship Management. It has formed a library for the use of members of the Institute which is available to members of the Baltic Exchange and which aims to provide a student interest and a shipping law reference. Fellows (FICS) ("Chartered Shipbrokers"), Members (MICS) and Honorary Members are the three categories of individual membership. Membership is also available to eligible companies.

FONASBA

The Federation of National Associations of Ship Brokers and Agents was formed in 1969 from national European shipbroker and agent associations to encompass the interests of the Liner Agent, the Tramp Port Agent, and the Shipbroker engaged in the chartering of ships. Some 22 countries worldwide are now represented through their national member associations. The Secretariat is located in the same offices as the Institute of Chartered Shipbrokers in London. FONASBA has consultative status with UNCTAD and attends the meetings in Geneva when shipping documentation is discussed and it speaks there as the voice of shipbrokers and agents internationally.

FACTORS DETERMINING FREIGHT RATES

The major determinants of freight rates paid under charter agreements include supply and demand, loading and unloading time, shipment size, trade route, manufacturing activity and other factors.

Supply and demand

A change in the balance of supply and demand affects the level of freight rates. When there is a shortage of transport capacity freight rates rise, and this has two effects. First, the older and less efficient vessels become profitable to operate and are progressively brought back into service until all the physically operational fleet is at sea. Secondly, shipowners operate their ships at full speed and minimise avoidable time out of service for routine maintenance.

On the other hand, if there is an oversupply of vessels, freight rates fall. The least efficient vessels in the fleet—or those that cannot find employment—are unable to cover their operating costs and move into lay-up. Gradually the operational fleet falls toward the level of demand.

Loading and unloading

The time that it takes to load and unload a ship impacts on vessel operating and fleet capital costs. Ships incur labour, insurance, interest and other costs while at port, as well as opportunity costs. Port congestion, both at the origin and destination, as well as inadequate grain handling facilities increase the discharge time leading to higher freight costs. For example, freight rates for shipments to countries with smaller ports can be significantly higher than those to more efficient ports of comparable distance.

Shipment size

There are economies of scale associated with grain shipments. Larger ships usually have lower per-unit at-sea operating costs. However, not all ports are accessible to large bulk cargo ships. As a result, there are limits to ship-size economies of scale on freight rates.

Route

Busier routes tend to have more favourable rates because of backhaul cargo opportunities. This is particularly true for very large vessels not suited for lower-volume trade routes. There also tends to be more seasonality of demand in some shipping lanes due to trade patterns or prevailing conditions in bulk commodity markets. Two of the world's most important routes are the transpacific, linking the orient to the West Coast of North America, and the transatlantic, connecting Western Europe to the east coast of North America.

Manufacturing activity

Freight rates in the dry cargo sector are influenced by the pace of manufacturing activity, particularly in OECD countries. OECD countries account for the greatest proportion of world demand for coal and iron ore. Both commodities compete with grain for freight vessels, often for Panamax-size vessels. Japan and the EU each account for almost one-third of seaborne coal trade. Major supplying countries are Australia, Canada and the USA.

Other factors

Canal tolls also affect freight rates. Shipments moving through the St Lawrence Seaway, Panama Canal or Suez Canal incur toll charges. Other factors that impact on freight rates include distance travelled, nationality of vessel registry, fuel costs, economic conditions, excess capacity regulations, weather conditions, port conditions and government subsidies. There are also typically seasonal rate fluctuations. Grain rates generally decline during June and July due to a lower level of trade as suppliers wait for new crop supplies.

GENERAL TRENDS

In general, ocean freight rates have been volatile during the 1990s because of factors such as a recession in Japan, reduced imports from the former Soviet Union due to a sharp decline in livestock numbers and a lack of foreign exchange and fluctuating Chinese grain imports and exports. In early 1993, freight rates dropped sharply due to weak coal and grain trade to Europe and Japan and a steadily expanding fleet of Panamax vessels. By the second half of 1994, many rates were once more on an upward trend due to a large increase in coal and ore movement in response to rising steel production and industrial activity in Russia. The firm trend of freight rates continued into the first quarter of 1995, supported by ore shipments from South America to Western Europe and Far East Asia, although tempered by a growing number of new Capesize and Handysize vessels.

In addition, there were some unusual influences at work in the grain sector. Korea switched from importing Chinese corn to US corn. Although US free on board (fob) corn prices were significantly above those of suppliers in the Southern Hemisphere, lower freight costs resulted in more attractive landed prices (including cost and freight).

The freight market started to weaken around May 1995, due to lower coal and iron ore deliveries and the normal summer slowdown resulting from holidays in major trading countries. A build-up of excess vessels and weaker demand in the mineral sector reduced freight rates during much of the remainder of 1995.

In 1996, reduced export activity in major exporting countries continued to lower freight rates. Freight rates on major grain trading routes strengthened during the final quarter of 1996 as cold weather in many parts of the Northern Hemisphere supported shipments of coal and oil. Manufacturing activity was also stronger in the Far East, increasing requirements for iron ore. Since most of this activity was concentrated in the Capesize sector, there were occasional shortages of suitable vessels. The supply of Panamax vessels was adequate as the world demand for grain remained limited. Subsequently, however, there was a sharp acceleration in grain transactions, as new crop supplies from Argentina and Australia became available. Both countries harvested bumper crops of wheat and were seeking new export outlets.

There were also events in subsequent months that distorted trading patterns. Canada experienced delays throughout its grain handling system, due mostly to severe winter conditions. Ice formation along the Mississippi River obstructed the movement of US grain to Gulf ports. Stormy weather extended voyage time on Atlantic routes. Strikes by dockers delayed unloading vessels at Buena Ventura, the principal Pacific port in Colombia. Several ports in China were saturated with large imports restricting elevator space for other imports.

ROUTE COMPARISONS

The Canadian economy is directly tied to its ability to trade in a constantly expanding global economy. Therefore, commercial shipping continues to be the mainstay for the exchange of goods internationally. Canada exports up to 80 per cent of its agricultural production. The bulk of these products moves by water to China, Japan, the USA, Brazil, Algeria and other major importing nations. The bulk of Canadian grains and oilseeds are exported out of Pacific ports. In 1995–1996, about 65 per cent of total grains and oilseeds exports went out of the Canadian west coast.

Japan is the world's largest importer of grains and oilseeds. Canada exports about 4 million tons of grain to Japan every year through the west coast ports. Japanese corn imports have averaged over 16 million tons over the last five years, and have been primarily sourced from the USA through the Gulf ports. Japan also imports wheat and barley, sourced largely from Canada, the USA and Australia. Canadian and US barley exports to Japan go through Pacific North West (PNW) and Canadian west coast ports and compete with US corn.

A comparison of freight rates from the PNW and the US Gulf to Japan shows that Canadian and US barley exports had about a US$10 a ton advantage over US corn shipments during 1991–1992 to 1995–1996.

China is also one of the world's largest importers of grains and oilseeds. About 20 to 25 per cent of Canadian grains and oilseeds are exported to China annually. On average, freight rates from the PNW had a $11 a ton advantage over those originating from the US Gulf during 1991–1992 to 1995–1996. Australia paid about US$2 a ton more than North Pacific rates for grain shipments to China over the same period.

Wheat is the major grain imported by Iran, with Canada and Australia the dominant suppliers. Canadian wheat exports to Iran are primarily through the St Lawrence Seaway. As volumes have increased through the 1990s, freight costs have declined from about US$38 a ton in 1991–1992 and 1992–1993 to around US$25 a ton in 1993–1994, 1994–1995 and 1995–1996 for small vessels. This makes large vessel rates from the St Lawrence comparable to small vessel rates from Australia to Iran.

Algeria is Canada's major export destination for durum wheat. Canada competes with the USA and the EU in this market. US and Canadian durum wheat are primarily shipped from the St Lawrence Seaway. Freight rates from the St Lawrence Seaway to Algeria averaged US$22.90 a tonne from 1991–1992 to 1995–1996 for small vessels compared to about US$5.60 a ton less from the EU for large vessels.

Although the EU is a major competitor of Canadian grains and oilseeds exports, the EU also imports significant volumes of Canadian and US grains and oilseeds through the St Lawrence and US Gulf ports. North American grain exports through the St Lawrence ports to the EU had a small advantage of about US$1.50 a ton compared to exports through the US Gulf ports from 1991–1992 to 1995–1996.

Brazil is generally self-sufficient in food with the major exception of wheat. Brazil relies heavily on Argentina for the majority of its wheat imports. Argentina, as part of the MERCOSUR trade agreement, the Southern Zone Common Market made up of Brazil, Argentina, Paraguay and Uruguay, has a large competitive advantage in the Brazilian market because of lower transportation costs to Brazil, shorter delivery times and a zero duty on wheat. Canada is the largest non-MERCOSUR supplier of wheat to Brazil and competes with the USA, and to a smaller extent the EU. Canada exported 1.4 million tons of wheat on average to Brazil during 1991–1992 to 1995–1996.

Bulk carrier freight rates generally reflect the comparative balance between the supply of and the demand for shipping at a single point in time, or as it is anticipated by market participants within the grains shipping market as it develops over time in the future.

Vessel hire contracts are defined largely according to the length of time (short or long) a ship remains on charter, either short term for single voyage fixtures or longer term on a variety of alternative time charter arrangements. Time charter contracts enable the charterer to move a variety of cargoes on different routes with the same vessel, whereas the single voyage fixture stipulates the exact cargo to be carried from loading port to discharge port. Charter payments (freight rates) likewise vary accordingly, both in terms of the method of payment calculation—which can be based on a US dollar rate per ton of cargo moved or on a US dollar rate per day of charter hire—and as a result of changes in market strength. The latter can show particularly large variations in payment terms, the current quoted freight rate at any time being dependent on the highly volatile nature of the immediate market for spot single voyage or trip time charter contracts versus the less volatile but nevertheless still quite changeable time charter market.

Rates are most often reported to the shipping community on a day-to-day basis by shipbrokers, which act as agents on behalf of shipowners as their principals. While the traditional function of the shipbroker has been to bring traders and charterers together with the shipowners and operators, thereby finding cargoes for ships and *vice versa*, that role today is changing to include almost as much the provision of an information service to the market. Consequently, the shipbroker is becoming increasingly a major source of market intelligence, and the reporting of freight rates and analysis of shipping industry trends is illustrative of this newer role.

Regular reportage of trends in the single voyage sector in particular has come to represent a barometer for the measure of existing shipping market conditions. Freight rates tend to be at higher than average levels the closer that demand for vessel tonnage approaches total shipping supply, and *vice versa*, therefore, correspondingly lower as supply increasingly exceeds demand.

Grain's importance in determining freight market strength cannot be overstated. In the early 1980s, through 1981–1983, when the market was generally a lot stronger than throughout the rest of the last decade, over half (53 per cent) of all reported dry bulk commodity single voyage charters were accounted for by grain shipping contracts. Although that percentage has been reduced in the later 1980s and into the 1990s—due in part to a large number of steel mills foregoing their traditional use of COAs (contracts of affreightment) to take advantage of the low spot freights available for coking coal and iron ore shipments—grain's importance is nevertheless still significant.

Another indicator of the importance of the grain trades to freight market strength is the fact that consistently well over a quarter of the total seaborne grain trade is moved under single voyage trip contracts. Drewry Shipping Consultants point out that between 50 and 60 million of deadweight cargo tons (dwct) was fixed under spot terms annually throughout 1981 to 1987, compared with an average total seaborne grain trade of some 195 million tons over the period, equivalent to 28 per cent of this total in fact.

Charter payments for the single voyage market are quoted in terms of US$ per ton of cargo transported on a specified shipment route between loading port (or ports) to discharge port (or ports). The plotting of freight rate trends over time typically involves quoted rates for standard vessel sizes moving cargo on most commonly used routes. Rate trends for three of the most significant grain routes are plotted in Table 16.1.

As an example, grain shipments from the US Gulf (USG) and North Pacific (NPAC) coasts to Europe and Japan are most often cited and typically might be for, say, 55,000 tons HSS (heavy grains, sorghum and soyabeans) USG to ARA (Antwerp/Rotterdam/Amsterdam range); or 52,000 tons HSS USG to Japan; or 52,000 tons HSS NPAC to Japan.

The usual form of the spot market charter fixture will include, in order: the date the fixture was concluded or reported; the voyage route; the vessel name (if it is disclosed, which it nearly always is); the cargo tonnage; grain products carried; US$ freight rate per ton cargo; further charter specifics concerning apportionment of costs and cargo handling responsibilities between cargo seller/trader, shipowner and charterer; laytime/laydays/laydays cancelling (time allocated by the shipowner to the charterer for the completion of loading and/or discharging the cargo); other charter terms specifics; and the name of the charterer.

In the case of a spot charter for delivery of USG to Japan 52,000 tons HSS $16.50, as example, the charterer will pay in total $858,000 for the hire of the ship. Alternatively, a spot charter rate can be stipulated as a lump-sum payment, $730,000 for moving 27,300 tons grains River Plate to the West Coast of Italy, for example, otherwise equivalent to a per ton freight rate of some $30.80.

Table 16.2 (plotted graphically in Figure 16.1) shows the development of single-voyage freight rates for US Gulf to Japan 52,000 tons cargo size during 1995 to 1998 (January–May). Higher rates are paid for the longer-haul single-voyage charter to Japan, simply because the vessel is obviously on hire for a greater number of days, plus an allowance to pay for the transit charge to pass through the Panama Canal on route.

Figure 16.1 also illustrates the seasonality of the trades. Peaks are generally experienced during the Northern Hemisphere winter months (December to March) at the height of the traditional grain shipping season, slumping to low levels during the quiet summer (June and July) months with the corresponding close of the shipping season at the junction of the old and the new harvests.

While clearly there was a marked and gradual strengthening in the grain trades freight structure over 1988 to 1991 compared with 1982 to 1987, rates still had some way to go before regaining the highs of 1980–1981, as illustrated by the numbers in Table 16.1. The high rates in 1980

Table 16.1 Indicative grain freight rates 1980–1997 (US$ per tonne)

Route/Dwct	*1980*	*1981*	*1982*	*1983*	*1984*	*1985*	*1986*	*1987*	*1988*	*1989*	*1990*	*1991*	*1992*	*1993*	*1994*	*1995*	*1996*	*1997*	*1998**
USG—ARA/55,000:																			
High	23.0	21.00	11.80	9.30	11.30	11.00	8.00	12.30	15.70	16.50	15.00	16.30	13.00	14.00	17.00	19.00	14.10	13.00	10.10
Low	14.50	10.30	6.10	7.30	7.50	6.20	4.90	7.70	9.80	11.30	9.80	11.80	8.80	9.30	8.40	12.50	8.90	10.20	6.80
Average	18.60	13.90	8.60	8.30	9.10	8.40	6.40	9.50	12.80	14.00	12.40	14.10	10.30	11.70	11.60	16.10	12.50	11.40	8.20
USG—Japan/52,000:																			
High	37.00	29.50	21.00	20.30	17.00	16.10	13.20	20.00	27.00	29.00	27.10	30.00	24.30	27.00	33.50	35.20	26.80	25.50	20.20
Low	21.50	19.00	12.50	14.30	13.30	10.70	7.90	13.80	19.20	20.00	17.50	24.00	17.50	20.50	18.80	27.80	19.10	20.70	16.00
Average	27.50	23.90	16.40	16.40	15.00	13.60	10.40	16.10	22.50	25.10	22.70	25.70	20.60	23.60	23.70	32.10	23.20	22.90	18.40
USNP—Japan/52,000:																			
High	21.50	19.80	11.80	10.50	11.00	9.20	9.00	12.30	16.40	17.10	17.20	15.10	14.10	14.50	16.90	19.60	15.10	13.80	11.90
Low	16.50	10.00	6.50	8.00	9.00	6.80	5.30	7.80	10.90	12.90	9.30	12.30	9.70	12.50	12.00	14.50	10.00	11.90	8.80
Average	18.60	14.00	8.40	9.20	10.00	8.30	7.70	10.20	13.50	15.10	12.60	14.10	11.20	13.20	14.00	17.90	13.10	12.90	10.40

*January to May only.

Source: Drewry Shipping Consultants Ltd, London June 1998.

Table 16.2 Single voyage freight rates US Gulf to Japan, 50–60,000 dwct (January 1995–May 1998) (US$/tonne/dwct)

	Jan	*Feb*	*Mar*	*Apr*	*May*	*Jun*	*July*	*Aug*	*Sep*	*Oct*	*Nov*	*Dec*
1995	30.90	31.60	34.25	35.20	34.20	32.25	32.40	33.60	33.15	30.15	29.10	27.80
1996	26.75	24.65	24.35	24.50	24.65	22.55	21.00	20.60	19.10	20.95	24.20	25.40
1997	25.55	25.30	24.30	23.45	21.00	21.10	23.15	22.90	23.00	22.95	20.70	21.40
1998*	20.20	17.45	18.75	19.50	16.00							

*January to May only.

Source: Drewry Shipping Consultants Ltd, London June 1998.

Figure 16.1 Single voyage freight rates USG–Japan 1995–1998

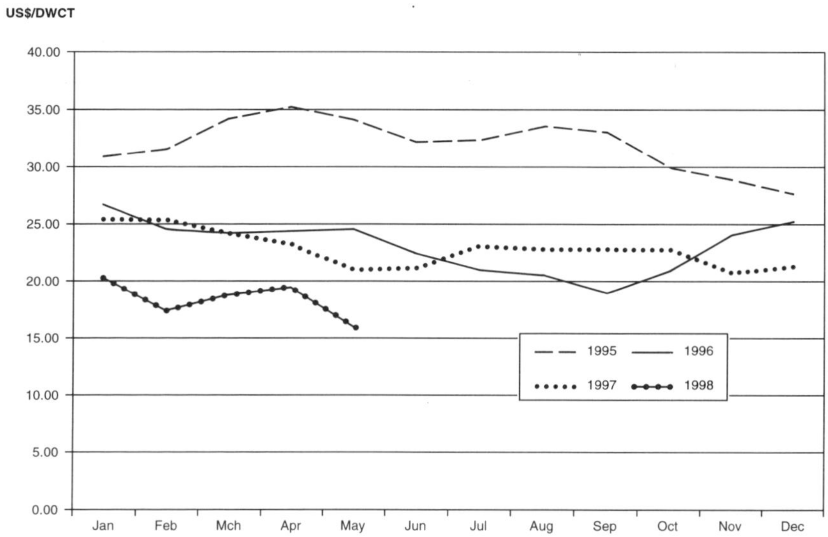

Source: Drewry Shipping Consultants Ltd, London, June 1998.

were about $9–10 per ton higher than the 1987 average rates for the USG to ARA and Japan routes, for example.

At the prevailing end-1989 levels, ocean freight rates were adding approximately 17–25 per cent to the price of North American wheat and maize delivered to Japanese ports for 52,000 ton cargoes loaded in the US Gulf, or similarly some 9–13 per cent extra on the US Gulf fob (free on board) export price for 55,000 tonnes cargoes delivered to the ARA.

Throughout most of the 1990s, however, grain freights have been largely flat, with the exception of 1995 which proved to be an exceptionally good year. Since then, though, rates have gone into free fall decline, the average for 1998 to date being the lowest level since the extremely low levels experienced during 1986. Rate trends for three of the most significant grain routes are shown in Table 16.1.

Another excellent indicator of the general trend in freight rates for grain transport by sea is the BIFFEX referred to earlier—the Baltic Freight Index, or BFI for short. Table 16.3 and Figure 16.2 show the development of BIFFEX over the last three years plus. The index itself was established at a base equivalent 1000 in January 1985. The BIFFEX is now calculated from a list of 11 different cargo trade routes, comprised of four grain routes (a combined weighting of 40 per cent), two coal (15 per cent weighting), two iron ore (15 per cent) and three round voyage timecharter routes—transatlantic round, transpacific round and Far East to North Pacific/Continent—with a combined 30 per cent weighting.

Table 16.3 Baltic Freight Index Monthly 1995–1998

	Jan	*Feb*	*Mar*	*Apr*	*May*	*Jun*
1995	2,017	1.990	2,196	2,258	2,249	2,006
1996	1,549	1,435	1,384	1,431	1,394	1,272
1997	1,461	1,440	1,471	1,380	1,279	1,273
1998	1,156	985	1,056	984	981	
	July	*Aug*	*Sep*	*Oct*	*Nov*	*Dec*
1995	1,971	1,994	2,010	1,716	1,654	1,622
1996	1,118	1,088	1,030	1,131	1,448	1,489
1997	1,340	1,294	1,297	1,324	1,237	1,235

*January to May only.

Source: Drewry Shipping Consultants Ltd, London, June 1998.

The index used to be (until just a few years ago) even more heavily weighted (65 per cent of the total) by the inclusion of five grain trades including US Gulf to North Continent (20 per cent), US Gulf to Japan (20 per cent), US North Pacific to Japan (15 per cent), US Gulf to Venezuela (5 per cent), and Antwerp to Jeddah (5 per cent). The last two routes have now been dropped from the equation and replaced by the US Gulf to Far East grain time charter route.

Because the index is still so heavily weighted by the grain rates component, its movements provide quite a close approximation to the

Figure 16.2 Baltic Freight Index 1995–1998

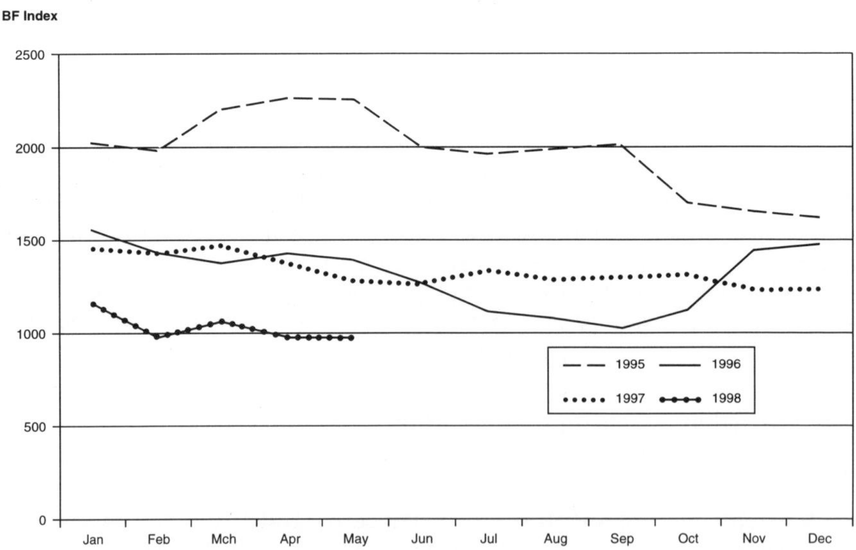

Source: Drewry Shipping Consultants Ltd, London, June 1998.

underlying trends in the grain sector overall. This key freight market indicator responds very largely to rate movements on just three primary Panamax grain routes, the first three routes on the list of 11 which alone account for 30 per cent of the BIFFEX weighting.

The index has plummeted during the past few years, reaching an 11 year low of 900 around the middle of June 1998, compared with monthly averages well in excess of 1100 throughout January 1995 to January 1998. This trend can be clearly seen in Figure 16.2.

CHAPTER 17

Inland waterways and river transport, the value and impact of waterway transportation in the Mid-west

The agricultural heartland of the United States is the world's most efficient and lowest cost producer of corn, soyabeans and other crops because of the quality of its land, its favourable climate, and its well developed production technology. Exports from this region provide the stocks to fill the world's food needs. This is true in times of stress from drought and other natural disasters, but also in ordinary times as a stable low-cost source of food and feedstuffs for consumers around the world.

Table 17.1 shows that in 1992, 82 per cent of the nation's corn, 77 per cent of its soyabeans and 32 per cent of its wheat was produced in the 10 Mid-western states that are bordered or traversed by the Mississippi, Illinois, Ohio and Missouri Rivers. The inland waterway system formed by these rivers is the major transportation route from the Mid-west grain production area to export ports on the Gulf of Mexico. Agricultural prosperity in the Mid-west absolutely depends on exporting 25 per cent of US grain and oilseed production annually. Although grain and oilseeds

Table 17.1 US production of major crops by state 1992 (million bushels)

	Corn	*Soyabean*	*Wheat*	*Total*
Iowa	1,904	364	2	2,270
Illinois	1,646	405	62	2,113
Nebraska	1,067	103	56	1,226
Indiana	877	194	23	1,094
Minnesota	741	173	140	1,054
Ohio	508	147	59	714
Kansas	260	68	364	692
Missouri	324	162	65	551
Wisconsin	307	22	3	332
Kentucky	172	44	23	239
Total Ten States	7,806	1,682	797	10,285
Total USA	9,479	2,197	2,459	14,134
Per cent Ten States	82.4	76.6	32.4	72.3
Total US Exports	1,725	770	1,340	3,835

Source: Jerry Fruin, University of Minnesota.

are also exported from the East and West Coast, the Great Lakes, and the Texas Gulf, approximately 60 per cent of the US grain and oilseed exports are shipped from Mississippi River terminals each year. Since the United States provides about 43 per cent of the grain and oilseeds moving in international trade each year, this means that over 25 per cent of the total grain and oilseed moved internationally originates far inland on this low cost waterway. The Gulf will continue to dominate US export grain origins because of international bulk trade patterns and the growing population in South East Asia and the Southern Hemisphere.

Additional quantities of grain, oilseeds and related products are moved on the inland waterway system to domestic food processors, feedlots and poultry producers. Also, large quantities of processed farm products such as vegetable oil and animal feeds are shipped by barge both to domestic users and for export around the world. For example, over 10 million tons of animal feed, primarily corn gluten feed exports to Europe, was barged in 1994. Agriculture also relies on the inland navigation system for the low cost transportation of farm inputs. Between 22 per cent and 25 per cent of all the fertilisers used in the United States each year are shipped on the Mississippi and its tributaries. Barge transportation is also important for other major farm inputs such as petroleum, petroleum products and chemicals.

Agricultural exports are very important to the US economy and the strength of the US dollar. Farm exports have been one of the few encouraging elements in the nation's balance of trade. Agricultural exports averaged over $41 billion per year from 1990 to 1994, or almost 10 per cent of all US exports. The trade balance (total agricultural exports less total agricultural imports) for the US agriculture sector averaged $17.2 billion per year over that time period. Consequently, the US foreign trade deficit would be about 15 per cent greater, were it not for agricultural exports.

But why has an effective shallow draft navigation system become so essential to a healthy agriculture in the United States Mid-west?

The heart of the corn and soyabean production area in the upper Mid-west is over 700 miles as the crow flies from the Gulf ports (and any other ocean port). The corn belt in Minnesota extends to beyond 1,200 miles from the Gulf. Table 17.2 shows the distances from important grain market and collection centres to the export elevators at the Gulf and to alternative ocean ports.

These distances from the US agricultural heartland to ocean ports are three to five times those of any of the competing agricultural production areas around the world. For instance, the prime soyabean growing areas of Brazil are all within 200 to 600 miles of the ports of Paranagua and Porto Alegre. The corn production area of Argentina is only 40 to 400 miles from Buenos Aires. South Africa's corn exporting region lies within

Table 17.2 Distances from Mid-west grain production areas to ocean ports (miles)

	New Orleans Barge	*New Orleans Rail*	*New Orleans Truck*	*Baltimore Rail*	*Seattle / Portland Rail*
Minneapolis/St Paul	1,670	1,273	1,346	1,193	1,745
St Louis	1,010	699	698	920	2,187
Peoria	1,299	864	862	796	2,141
Cincinnati	1,303	836	802	582	2,422

Source: Jerry Fruin, University of Minnesota.

120 to 450 miles from its deepwater port of Durban. All of Australia's major wheat growing areas lie within 80 to 300 miles from the ocean. The grain growing areas of the European Union are virtually all within 300 miles of a deepwater port.

Of the major grain exporters, only Canada has to move grain as far, or further, to its export ports than the United States. Historically, Canada's solution was to subsidise agricultural exports with the very low "Crow Rail Rates", followed by the Western Grain Transportation Act subsidies (Canada's subsidies of rail rates were discontinued in 1995 as a result of the GATT. This will result in substantial shifts in how Canada grain exports are managed).

Canadian shippers paid only about one-third of the actual cost of moving grains and farm products to export points until less than 18 months ago. Between 7 per cent and 30 per cent of Canada's traditional grain exports would cost less to move down the Mississippi than over the traditional routes.

One thing which should be pointed out is that the shift in demand for grain from Europe to Pacific Rim countries that has occurred over the last 30 years has greatly reduced the role of North America's other great waterway, the St Lawrence Seaway, in moving grain to international markets. Shifts in Canadian agricultural production and trade patterns will cause this decline in importance of the Seaway for agricultural products to continue.

To summarise, although the United States has an excellent land transportation infrastructure of railroads and interstate highways, and port facilities as good as or better than its competitors', the distances from the US heartland to its ports would leave US agriculture with a major transportation cost disadvantage if not for the low cost and efficiency of the shallow draught barge system.

COST COMPARISONS

One of the factors contributing to the low costs of barging grain on the inland system is volume. A typical 9 ft draught barge holds from 1,400 to

1,600 short tons of cargo, or more than 50,000 bushels of grain. Barges are combined into tows consistent with the characteristics and dimensions of the waterway. For example, tows leaving Minneapolis typically consist of 15 barges loaded with a cargo of 21,750 tons or approximately 750,000 bushels of grain. At St Louis, below the locks of the Upper Mississippi, barges will typically be placed in larger tows of 30 or more barges for the rest of the movement to the export elevators on the Lower Mississippi near the Gulf. Another major factor contributing to the low cost of barging is the energy efficiency of water movements. The low energy use also means that there are less emissions that contribute to air pollution than other modes of transportation.

Although the circuitous nature of the waterways means that barged grain will have to move more miles than that sent by rail, the barge costs, and therefore rates, are generally much lower than rail rates between similar destinations. Table 17.2 shows the mileage by mode from four major inland grain collection points to the Lower Mississippi River export elevators. It also shows rail mileage to the East and West Coast. Note that these are "short line" rail mileages which are the shortest distances possible by rail. The actual miles a train travels between two points is frequently greater than this most direct route because of terrain, interchange points, and other operational factors.

Table 17.3 shows the relative costs of shipping grain from selected points by both barge and rail to Lower Mississippi ports. Long-distance truck movements are not considered as an alternative because of cost. A very efficient long-distance grain trucking operation would have costs of 3.5 cents per ton/mile or greater.

Barge rates typically fluctuate between the 135 per cent and 175 per cent of tariff values shown in the first two columns, although rates may be as high as 300 per cent during periods of exceptional demand for barges. Rates have varied from below 100 per cent to over 300 per cent in the last 10 years due to extremes in supply/demand conditions. However, quoted rates have averaged 135 per cent to 175 per cent over the season in recent years.

The last three columns in Table 17.3 also show the probable range of rail rates between the same points for grain shipped in 50-car unit trains.

Table 17.3 Comparative rates in $/ton from Mid-west grain areas to Lower Mississippi ports

	Barge—Percent of Tariff			*Rail—Cents Per Ton/Mile*		
Tariff/Cents Per Ton/Mile:	135	175	250	1.20	1.70	2.20
Minneapolis/St. Paul	8.36	10.83	15.48	15.28	21.64	28.01
St Louis	5.39	6.98	9.98	8.38	11.68	15.38
Peoria	6.49	8.41	12.03	10.37	14.69	19.01
Cincinnati	6.33	8.21	11.73	10.03	14.21	18.39

Source: Jerry Fruin, University of Minnesota.

The rate level of 1.2 cents per ton/mile in the fourth column approximates to rail unit train variable costs for grain on long hauls. The rate level of 1.7 cents per ton/mile in the fifth column approximates to the fully allocated rail unit train costs to haul grain for long distances. Unit train rail rates typically will be between these levels. Rate levels were computed using the ICC Uniform Rail Costing System (URCS) for select origins and destinations. For example, for a 50-car unit train haul of 900 miles with no interchanges, variable costs were 1.3 cents per ton/mile and fully allocated costs were 2 cents per ton/mile. For a 50 car unit train haul of 1,344 miles with one interchange, variable costs were 1.2 cents per ton/mile and fully allocated costs were 1.7 cents per ton/mile.

The rate level of 2.2 cents per ton/mile in column six is an estimate of a rate level for non-unit trains, low volume or short distance grain movements. Note that for all four shipping points, barge rates at 175 per cent of tariff are less than rail rates at the variable cost level of 1.2 cents per ton/mile. Only at 250 per cent of tariff do barge rates exceed variable cost rail rates, but even then barge rates are substantially less than the fully allocated unit train cost level of 1.7 cents per ton/mile. In the past, it was valid to make the point that ignoring collection costs, i.e. trucking to river points and handling grain at both country and river elevators understated total barge movement costs when compared to rail. However, these days, since much grain is hauled by semis directly from farms to river terminals and grain is hauled long distances to country rail terminals, this criticism frequently is no longer valid.

Although moving grain by barge is generally the low cost method, another consideration is equipment and infrastructure capacity. Although rail capacity (car, tracks, locomotives, sidings, etc.) could be added, the magnitude of such an undertaking should not be underestimated. As noted earlier, each barge moves about 1,500 tons of grain or as much as 15 rail cars, so that each 15 barge tow carries more grain than two 100-car unit trains. If the rail system had to move all the grain and oilseeds that now move on the Mississippi River system, an additional 44,000 rail cars and over 1,000 locomotives would be required (the US grain car fleet averaged approximately 19 round trips at 90 tons per trip in 1993).

Such an investment would cost nearly $4 billion. However, because of the backhaul practices of the barge industry, this large sum actually understates the increase in equipment that would be required. The covered hopper barges used for taking grain downstream are also used for hauling products like fertiliser, salt, coal and similar products upstream so that backhauls are available for up to 50 per cent of the time. The use of rail grain hopper cars for backhauls has been insignificant in recent years.

Some rail proponents would argue that the required investment in rail equipment is irrelevant. However, $4 billion is a lot of money even in Washington and should be considered when costing alternative rehabilitation plans for the river. From a national infrastructure cash flow requirement, rail rolling stock has a 20 to 30 year life while locks and dams have 50-plus year life cycles which makes the timing of investments, as well as the amounts, important.

FUTURE IMPORTANCE

As a result of factors such as the great flood of 1993, the increase in rail competitiveness for grains and fertiliser as a result of deregulation, shifting export patterns and the federal deficit, questions have been raised whether the United States still needs all of its inland navigation system. An examination was undertaken of the recent trends and the long-range outlook for traffic volumes from the head of navigation on the Upper Mississippi and Minnesota Rivers at the Twin Cities of Minneapolis/St. Paul.

This study found the volume of commodities moved by barge on the Upper Mississippi River to and from the Twin Cities had nearly 50 years of uninterrupted growth after the completion of the locks and dams and the 9 ft channel system in the 1930s. This upward trend accelerated after tugs were switched from steam to diesel electric power in the 1950s. However, barge volumes peaked in 1983 and 1984 and were followed by unprecedented declines in the late 1980s. Annual movements in 1985 and later were sometimes less than two-thirds that of the peak. Why did this occur? Was the decline permanent or an aberration? Had commercial navigation in the region lost its competitiveness compared with other modes of transportation? Were there structural changes in the economy which reduced the need for the commodities commonly shipped by barge? If so, are these one time changes or long-term trends?

MAJOR COMMODITY MOVEMENTS

To make a long story short, the answer is coal. Unlike some types of commerce, changes in barge movement volumes tend to be lumpy. Because of the types of commodities and their uses, once a major commodity flow is committed to water, it tends to continue to be moved by water, year after year. However, once the flow stops, it probably will not be restarted. For example, a power plant or refinery located on the river will use water transportation and will require approximately the same amount of coal or crude oil year after year until expanded or retired. At that time the volume of barge traffic to that location will permanently change.

In the Twin Cities, coal movements increased from less than two million tons in 1963 (when it was the most important waterborne commodity accounting for over 25 per cent of total shipments and receipts) to over 5 million tons in 1975, when it accounted for over 38 per cent of total Twin Cities barge movements (Figure 17.1). However, from 1987 to 1994 coal has averaged well under 1 million tons a year and in 1994 accounted for less than 4 per cent of total volume.

Coal receipts in the 1960s were primarily shipments of relatively high sulphur coal from southern Illinois to local power plants. Due to environmental concerns over sulphur emissions and the increasing costs of southern Illinois coal, Northern States Power (NSP), the region's major electric utility, began to switch the fuel in its Twin Cities generating plants (which were all on rivers in the port area) to western coal. Originally, the western coal came by unit train to the Twin Cities and was transferred to barges for the final delivery to power plants that could not unload unit trains.

The drop in coal traffic after 1985 is due to the completion of unit train handling equipment at all the Twin Cities NSP plants, so that the western coal is no longer transhipped locally by barge. The only coal barged in recent years was western coal for a down-river power plant that does not have adequate unit train handling facilities and some

Figure 17.1 Twin Cities waterborne coal movement

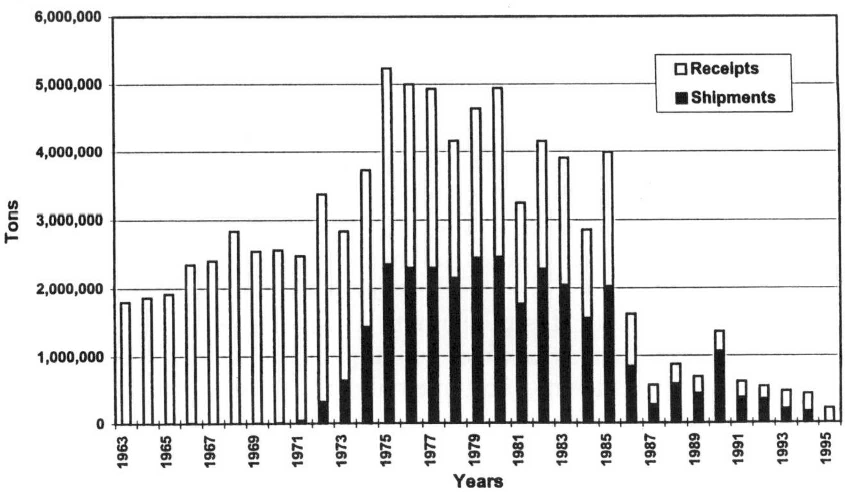

Source: Jerry Fruin, University of Minnesota.

upbound eastern coal that meets specific requirements of a few industrial users.

In conclusion, permanent reductions have occurred in the quantities of specific commodities moved to and from the Twin Cities area on the Upper Mississippi River. These are due both to changes in the source of supply (coal) and to increased competition from railways after deregulation (wheat). However, other commodities have shown continued growth and reached all time highs in the 1990s (corn shipments and cement, chemicals and fertilizer receipts). In fact, ton/miles (as opposed to tons) and the volume of long distance shipments of Twin Cities waterborne movements appear to have reached an all-time high in 1992. If coal is not included, 1992 had the third highest barge tonnage ever. Only in the peak grain shipment years of 1983 and 1984, following the drought in the eastern corn belt, were barge shipments greater.

Rail deregulation and other changes in the economy have had little effect on the competitiveness of the barge industry for the movement of bulk commodities. Commercial navigation on the Mississippi River remains very important to the economy of Minnesota and will remain so for the foreseeable future.

A healthy shallow-draft barge industry is essential to the well being of US agriculture and other barge dependent industries. Some 60 per cent of US farm grain, oilseeds and feed exports (which represents 25 per cent of the world trade in grain and oilseeds) is transported on the Mississippi River system. This low cost transportation system is also used to transport 25 per cent of US farm fertilizer and is important for other farm inputs. US farm exports are a major factor in reducing the US balance of payments deficit and maintaining the strength of the dollar. The inland navigation system provides low cost transportation that permits US agriculture to compete and prosper in world markets even though all competing agricultural regions in the world, except Canada, are much closer to export ports. To move the current barge volumes of grain and oilseeds by rail would require a $4 billion investment in rolling stock. In addition, most river export elevators would require land-side investments to handle increased quantities by rail.

This low cost system is necessary for the United States to compete with other agricultural exporting areas of the world, all of which are much closer to deepwater ports. Canada, as noted, is the exception which has relied on subsidised rail rates to compete in world markets.

Water is the low-cost method of moving bulk commodities such as grain. It is energy efficient, and contributes little to air and water pollution. We can expect barge rates to remain low because there is free entry into the industry. The equipment supply is dictated by market conditions and cannot be manipulated by limiting access to facilities or refusal to handle privately owned equipment. The shallow-draught waterway system is in place. It is a major contributor to the US national economy and to economies around the world. Therefore, it should continue to be used wisely and productively. See Figure 17.2 for a map of the main waterways of the United States.

POSTSCRIPT

Since it is not given to everybody to experience a journey by a grain-barge tow up the Mississippi River, the following account by the author of such a voyage may be of interest to students, and inspire them to repeat the trip, or a similar one, as a means of acquiring practical knowledge of the trade.

In 1985 I had the opportunity to travel the 200 miles from Prairie du

Figure 17.2 Waterways of the United States

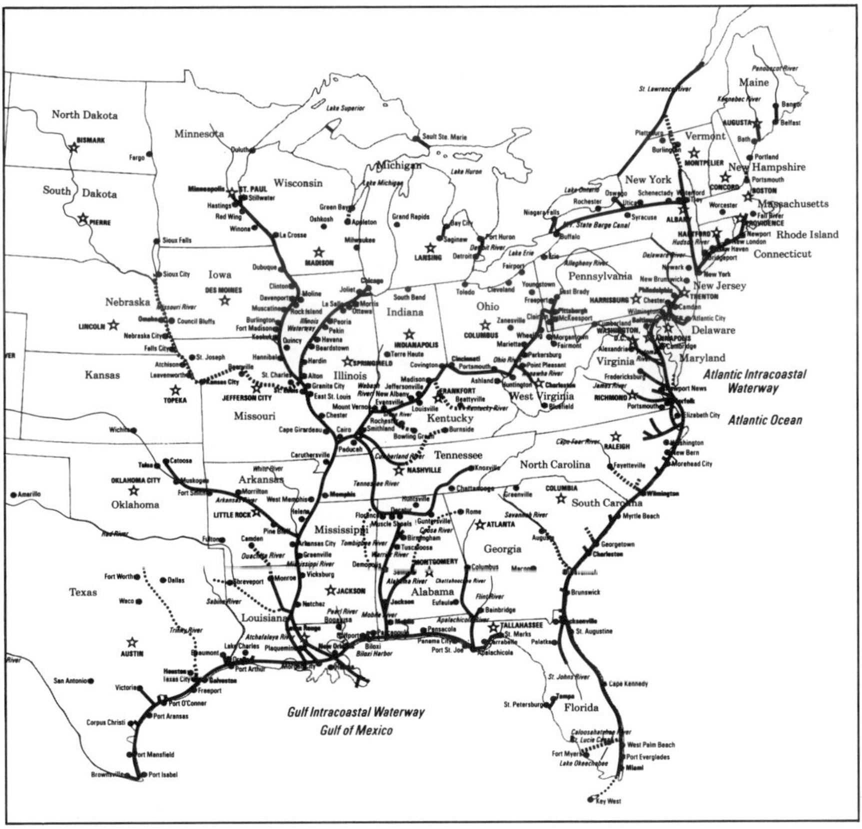

Source: The American Waterways Operators, Arlington VA 22209.

Chien in Wisconsin to the Twin Cities in Minnesota on a barge-tow the size of the ocean liner, QE2, by courtesy of the Riverway Transportation Company of Minneapolis.

Mississippi barge traffic is virtually synonymous with grain trading. Carrying cargoes of wheat, corn and soyabeans is the livelihood of the commercial waterways of North America. The river system has a vital role in distributing commodities from the areas of production to the centres of consumption and export.

The bulk of US hard wheat, suitable for breadmaking, together with most of the corn (maize) and soyabeans, is grown in the Mid-west, from Minnesota to Texas. The soft red wheats are grown in Illinois, Indiana and Iowa, and the white wheats in the western seaboard states.

The main deficit areas as far as human consumption is concerned (i.e. to which the grain must be moved), are the industrialised states of the East (human consumption), while grain and beans for animal feed go to the feedlots of Kansas, Texas and Arkansas.

The main outlets for export grain are Duluth on Lake Superior, and Chicago on Lake Michigan in the North; Baltimore on the East Coast, the Gulf ports in the South, and Portland on the West Coast.

The distances are enormous. From Minneapolis to the Gulf down the Mississippi is 1,807 miles—St Louis, which is 678 miles from Minneapolis, lies at the confluence of the Missouri and Illinois rivers with the Mississippi, and from Kansas City to this point is 373 miles and from Chicago 326 miles. The journey northward from Prairie du Chien was a perfect way of passing three days. The Mississippi is not so much a river as a flooded alluvial plain several miles wide between two low ranges of limestone cliffs. The navigation channel was painstakingly dug out by the US Corps of Engineers to a depth of 9 ft in the years to 1906 and is now maintained at between 10 and 14 ft by constant dredging. The monumental locks and dams were constructed by the same valiant Corps in the 1930s, 26 of them between St Paul and St Louis. The trees on the bank come down to the water's edge, and for long stretches the effect is not unlike that of the Amazon, down a tributary of which my wife and I once travelled by dug-out canoe.

The Mississippi was first seen by the French explorers Hennepin, Marquette and Joliet as they came down the Great Lakes in the late seventeenth century. Fifty years later the fur traders began to open it up, travelling by *pirogue* and *bâteau*, and the wide-open plain of Prairie du Chien at the junction of the Wisconsin river and the Mississippi is where the Indian tribes congregated annually to trade their pelts to the French trappers. For this used to be Indian country. Minnehaha's grave lies just north of Prairie du Chien, and a few miles beyond it a small town called Victory commemorates the decisive battle of the Blackhawk War in 1832. In the same year a young lieutenant just out of West Point prepared surveys of the river as a prelude to improved navigation. His name was Robert E. Lee.

The Sioux dominated the Mississippi Valley until pushed west by the influx of settlers in the mid-nineteenth century, and the hilly, densely wooded banks are dotted with Indian mounds and rocky outcrops bearing Indian names. Further north, the mix of place names shows the confusion of Indian and European tribes, where Buffalo City, Wabash and Red Wing alternate with small towns called Stockholm, Hastings and Fort Snelling. The twin cities of Minneapolis (predominantly Scandinavian and Lutheran) and St. Paul (German and Catholic) are situated on the St. Anthony Falls and marked the end of our journey.

The Tennessee and Cumberland Rivers flow into the Ohio at Cairo, Illinois. Pittsburgh is 981 miles and Cincinnati 470 miles from Cairo by river; Knoxville in 647 miles and Chattanooga 464 miles from Cairo; Nashville 183 miles from the same spot.

The river operations are on a commensurate scale. I used to operate a pair of traditional narrow boats on the Grand Union Canal in England, and thought that steering a 70 ft long motor-boat towing a butty-boat of similar length through locks 7 ft wide called for some skill. On the Mississippi our barge-tow was made up of 15 barge units each 195 ft long by 35 ft wide, pushed by a twin-screw diesel-engined tug only slightly shorter.

The barge units on the Mississippi were lashed together three abreast and five deep, with the tug pushing from behind. What became in effect a rigid bulk carrier thus measured 1,140 ft in length with a beam of 105 ft. Each barge had a cargo hold 14 ft deep, with a cargo capacity of 1,500 tons. Total cargo capacity of the tow was 22,500 tons. The entire unit was surprisingly manœuvrable, more so than a supertanker, and slid sweetly enough into the locks 110 ft wide. The only problem, and it was a delaying factor, was that most locks are 600 ft long, so that the tow has to lock through in two sections, making the average time to negotiate a lock about 1–1½ hours. The size of the tow becomes comprehensible if one knows for comparison that the QE2 is exactly the same width but only 963 ft long.

The tug itself is extremely powerful. Fully loaded with 105,000 gallons of fuel, the *Mary L* drew 11 ft of water, and her two General Motors E7 12-cylinder turbines generated a total of 4,300 hp.

My wife and I crewed our pair of narrow boats ourselves, with assistance from our daughter. The crew of the *Mary L* consisted of a Captain and First Officer (called the Pilot), a Chief Engineer and Second Engineer, six deck hands and a cook in the galley. Accommodation was luxurious to one accustomed to the traditional English boatman's cabin. The guest's stateroom, which I occupied, was a comfortable double-bunk cabin with desk and chairs, private bathroom with shower and WC. I was told that on the lower Mississippi, between St Louis and New Orleans, where there are no locks, the barge-tows are more than twice the size, a normal unit being made up of five lines of barges seven abreast, tugs twice the size of the *Mary L* and accommodation correspondingly grander.

Cargo carrying on the waterways should be sound business. A comprehensive study of 1984 barge rates on the Mississippi was carried out by the University of Minnesota. This included a comparison with alternative modes of transport by rail and truck, and showed that water transport was by far the most economical. To carry grain or soyabeans from a production centre such as Litchfield, Minnesota, to the Gulf cost $16.52 per ton by water via the Twin Cities. The water delivery allowed for truck (i.e. lorry) movements of 75 miles to the barge terminal, and movement of 1,723 miles by water; to move by rail alone, although over a shorter distance of 1,358 miles, cost $31.6 per ton. Moreover, out of the $16.52 per ton mentioned above the actual water movement—although accounting for by far the greater portion of the journey—accounted only for $10.52 of the total. From Marshall—a centre of corn and soya growing—to the Gulf Coast cost $19.72 per ton by the mainly water route, and $29 per ton by rail and truck.

A factor which complicates the economics of grain carrying is that downstream grain shipments dominate the traffic on the Mississippi. An inevitable consequence of this is that many dry cargo barges have to be brought empty back up the river. Rates for the backhaul journey, therefore, tend to be very low, as carrying any cargo at all in this direction is to be regarded almost as a bonus.

The anomaly in price rates is best illustrated by looking at fertiliser movement. Potassium fertiliser is carried south and nitrogen phosphate and compound fertiliser carried north. The latter is regarded as a "perfect" backhaul since the origins and destinations are exactly the opposite of the grain ones. Thus, to carry phosphate by water from the Gulf to the Twin Cities costs $4.00–$5.00 per ton; the charge for the same commodity by rail is $47.90 per ton. Even for destinations beyond the Twin Cities necessitating a transfer from barge to rail for the later part of the journey to, say, Albert Lea in North Minnesota, this mode is cheaper ($15.11–$16.11 per ton) than rail all the way (from $34.52 to $43.29 per ton, depending on the length of train used).

Downbound fertiliser rates, as, for example, potash mined in Saskatchewan which is railed from Canada to the Twin Cities, has become big business in recent years as onward barge traffic. From Twin Cities to Nashville, Tennessee, for example, a distance of 1,096 miles by barge or 842 miles by rail would cost from $9.00 to $16.00 by barge or $32.00 to $36.00 by rail. Not all barge operators rush to obtain backhaul cargoes. While to some companies it makes sense to charge such trade at a rate sufficient to defray variable costs, others regard the time spent in obtaining the business, in increased turn-around time and the added scheduling problems, as making it barely worthwhile.

In 1981 and 1982, the last years for which I was then able to obtain statistics, the total freight tonnage carried on the Mississippi system amounted to 15.5 million and 16.1 million tons respectively. Of these totals grain (including soyabeans) shipments accounted for 54.9 per cent and 48.2 per cent respectively. Of the non-grain commodities, fertilisers represented only 2 per cent and 3.5 per cent of cargoes; coal (mainly short-haul loads) 20.9 per cent and 26 per cent. Other small shipments included oats, salt, lime, sand and gravel, and milling products. No timber, cement or petroleum products were carried on the water during these years.

Since I made my journey, the Mississippi and its barge traffic have known both good and bad times. At one point in the late 1980s, drought halted barge traffic altogether, dramatically illustrating the dependence of river traffic on weather conditions. But provided the channel can be kept open and the export markets continue, the Mississippi will continue to be the lifeline of the US grain trade.

CHAPTER 18

Shipping to the developing world

Chapter 12 has emphasised the strategic importance of developing world markets to replace the diminishing outlets for the international grain trade in Russia and Eastern Europe.

The FAO in Rome has made a special study of factors which will seriously affect seaborne trade to the developing world in the next 20 years and beyond. Based mainly on a comprehensive report supplied by the firm of Ocean Shipping Consultants some far-reaching trends have emerged which will have considerable implications for the stability and security of supply to meet demand specifically in the developing world grain markets.

Trends in seaborne trade demand over the last 20 years are shown in Table 18.1. In the mid-1970s the largest market was located in the OECD, with the structure of world trade dominated by demand for wheat and feedgrain imports into western Europe and Japan. At this time there was heavy investment in shipping and port/terminal capacity, coupled with a search for scale economies by the increased use of larger bulk carriers.

Table 18.1 Long term trends in seaborne grain demand, 1975–1995

	1975	1980	1985	1990	1995
Million Tons					
OECD Markets	71.48	75.73	65.32	43.31	39.17
Centrally-Planned*	17.05	39.06	41.04	40.32	6.53
Developing Markets**	48.93	83.46	81.89	115.97	146.30
Total	137.46	198.25	188.25	199.60	192.00
Percentage					
OECD Markets	52.0	38.2	34.7	21.7	20.4
Centrally-Planned*	12.4	19.7	21.8	20.2	3.4
Developing Markets**	35.6	42.1	43.5	58.1	76.2
Total	100.0	100.0	100.0	100.0	100.0

*"Economies in Transition" in 1995.
**Includes PR China.

Source: Ocean Shipping Consultants Ltd.

Throughout the 1980s overall grain demand stagnated, despite short-term factors, but there were considerable structural changes. The Common Agricultural Policy of the EEC first cut grain imports and then expanded grain exports, accompanied by increased grain output. Demand boomed in the then centrally-planned economies, with imports into the Soviet Union outstripping the loss of EEC markets. Transport investment was expanded to meet this situation.

The position since the 1980s has completely changed. The restructuring of the former CEPs has reduced grain import demand, while Russia has changed from a large importer to a (small) exporter. At the same time demand from the developing world has accelerated sharply. In 1975 the developing world accounted for about 35.6 per cent of world seaborne grain demand, and by 1995 this figure had increased to 76.2 per cent, or 146 million tons.

Detailed consideration of the developing world is contained in Table 18.2, showing major sub-regions. The strongest growth has been in East Asia (including China), and by 1996 it was apparent that many of these markets were recording levels of wealth comparable with the OECD countries. In these cases port investment proceeded apace and grain transport systems and costs became highly efficient. There is now, in 1998, a question mark over the availability of the further investment which will be needed to keep up progress.

In the poorer countries grain demand will increase sharply and investment in infrastructure—not simply in ports but in the wider sphere of distribution—cannot be regarded as certain. Leaving aside for the moment the East Asian countries trade to the "poorer countries" sector has increased between 1985 and 1995 by 50.8 per cent, to a total of 92 million tons.

The consequent fragmentation of a large portion of world demand is underlined by the development of the market share of the major world grain trades, summarised in Table 18.3. Demand in the major trades to

Table 18.2 Developing world seaborne grain demand, 1980–1995 (million tons)

	1980	1985	1990	1991	1992	1993	1994	1995
Africa	14.7	19.8	19.8	20.0	28.2	26.1	25.3	29.3
Latin America	24.3	21.5	21.4	23.8	27.0	27.3	33.8	36.9
Middle East	3.4	10.8	4.6	5.3	4.6	5.3	4.7	6.5
Indian Sub-Continent	8.4	8.9	19.5	16.6	17.8	14.5	17.5	19.2
East Asia*	32.7	20.9	50.7	45.0	41.3	39.9	44.5	54.3
Total	83.5	81.9	116.0	110.7	118.9	113.1	125.8	146.3

*Includes PR China.

Source: Ocean Shipping Consultants Ltd.

Table 18.3 The structure of seaborne grain trade, 1986–1994 (percentage of total seaborne trade tonnages)

	1986	1988	1990	1992	1994
USA–West Europe	7.8	7.1	6.3	6.1	5.7
USA–East Europe	5.2	9.2	8.5	8.4	5.1
USA–Far East	17.2	24.5	23.4	24.0	23.5
Australia–Africa/Middle East	4.7	2.9	1.0	1.4	1.9
Australia–Far East	4.4	2.5	5.8	4.3	5.6
Australia–Europe	2.1	1.1	–	0.5	0.5
Canada–Europe	4.6	3.2	3.3	3.4	3.0
Canada–Far East	3.2	5.9	6.1	5.4	5.8
Argentina–West Europe	2.2	0.6	4.5	3.4	4.7
Argentina–East Europe	4.8	1.2	1.2	1.1	0.8
Argentina–Latin America	1.9	1.2	1.9	1.2	1.5
Total	58.1	59.4	62.0	59.2	58.1

Source: Ocean Shipping Consultants Ltd.

Europe has declined while the Far East has increased in importance. An increasing proportion is on concessional terms to the developing world—mainly from the US and the EU.

Naturally these developments have exerted their influence on the overall development of bulk shipping demand. As far as grain is concerned, and in contrast to the situation in other major bulk commodity trades, in the last ten years there have been no real moves in favour of larger vessels. In the iron ore and coal trades the drive for further scale economies has seen average ship sizes increase dramatically. This is a change from the preceding ten years (1975–1985) when the increased use of Panamax and larger bulk carriers was most noticeable.

The above slowdown has been the direct result of secondary trades where port restrictions and lack of investment has made the introduction of larger—and cheaper—vessels of debatable advantage. As the bulk fleet is modernised this is increasingly resulting in a dependence on obsolete and lower quality tonnage for the trade to the developing world.

In East Asian markets, where there has been considerable port investment, there has been a steady increase in the market share of larger vessels. The position is similar in the Middle East. But in the poorest nations of Latin America, Africa, and the Indian sub-continent there has been very little improvement in the use of larger bulk vessels. Indeed the level of demand for inefficient vessels has actually increased between 1985–1995.

In general, therefore, it may be said that despite the rapid increase in demand there has been no matching improvement in the types and sizes of vessels employed in the trade to the developing world. In fact, these vessels are now ageing rapidly and these trades are becoming increasingly dependent on a class of vessel that will become increasingly hard to charter at acceptable rates in the next few years. The net effect is that shipping investment will continue to be slanted in favour of other commercially more significant trades in the next few years.

The major constraint preventing the introduction of larger vessels into the grain trade with the developing world lies in the port sector. The position has worsened in the last few years as the level of demand has accelerated. Since the freight market began to recover in 1986–1987 the unit freight cost differentials between large and small bulk carriers (and between bulk and bagged operations) has increased dramatically. And furthermore the outlook for rates is one of generally higher levels, leading to an increase in the difficulties.

Since 1981 there has been a significant increase in the number of grain terminals but most have been designed for Handy and Panamax size vessels, and there has been little investment in larger capacity terminals.

Grain handling rates at major terminals show that ports with capacity for ship sizes of 150,000 dwt and more can load at 2575 and discharge at 2000 tons per hour, while those with capacity for ships between 50,000 and 80,000 dwt can only load at 1900 and discharge at 1650 tonnes per hour. Moreover, there are 146 grain discharge terminals in the developed world and only 64 in the developing world, and practically all the latter only cater for vessels up to 50,000/80,000 dwt capacity. There is a clear bias in favour of the lower ship size capacity terminals in this category. Most new terminal construction in the developing world since the mid-1980s has taken place in China, North Africa and the Middle East. There are only 15 terminals operating in the poorest nations.

This gives rise to the observation that the most dynamic aspect of the world grain trade is the most poorly served with efficient ports and terminals. Table 18.4 summarises the port capacity of individual Developing Nations, and highlights the difference between North Africa and Africa South of the Sahara. The latter typically uses intensive labour and slow bagged grain handling, leading to high unit freight rates, port congestion and demurrage payments. In 1986 the general demurrage costs per ton for a 20,000 dwt general cargo vessel were reckoned at $0.20 per day, so a typical three-week delay would generate a per ton penalty of approximately $8.84 per cargo ton, significantly increasing the costs of grain in those markets. As demand increases these penalties seem likely to increase further.

GRAIN STORAGE AND SHIPPING OPERATIONS.

Actual tonnage shipped and duration of voyage are the two main factors which influence the volume of grain stored at-sea (in bulk carriers and

Table 18.4 Africa: developing nations port summary

Nation	Typical Cargo Size (dwct)	Maximum Draught (metres)	Discharge Rates (t/d) Bags	Bulk
North Africa				
Morocco	30,000	15.0	–	10,000
Algeria	15,000	10.0	–	500
Tunisia	25,000	11.0	800	2,000
Libya	20,000	12.0	750	–
Egypt	35,000	14.0	1,600	8,000
Sub-Saharan Africa				
Angola	12,000	10.4	–	650
Benin	12,000	10.0	–	–
Cameroon	4,000	7.0	750	1,200
Ethiopia	5,000	8.8	400	1,000
Ghana	26,500	9.1	750	–
Ivory Coast	14,000	10.0	–	1,000
Kenya	20,000	10.0	750	1,500
Madagascar	4,000	6.7	600	–
Mauritania	3,000	7.0	500	–
Mauritius	11,000	10.0	280	1,000
Mozambique	8,000	9.5	750	1,000
Nigeria	6,000	7.5	1,000	–
Senegal	11,000	10.0	1,000	2,000
Somalia	11,000	10.0	500	–
Sudan	25,000	10.5	–	800
Tanzania	12,000	10.0	750	1,000
Zaire	4,000	7.5	750	–

Source: IWC / Ocean Shipping Consultants Ltd.

general cargo vessels). These factors have changed considerably over the past 20 years, as is illustrated in Table 18.5. This shows that while trades to the developing world have increased, as have the average voyage times, those to other destinations have shown little change. However, the average daily at-sea volumes of the trades to the developing world have trebled, as have the daily port silo volumes, while the at-sea volumes and port silo volumes of other trades (i.e., other than to the developing world) have halved or more than halved. Already some strain is being placed on port storage at the import end of the chain in some rapidly expanding markets. Further investment is required to cope with the expected increased demand.

SHIPPING AVAILABILITY AND GRAIN SUPPLY

General cargo vessels are dominant in the supply of bagged grains and small parcels of bulk grains which are typical of large parts of the developing world grain trades. There has been a steady decline in the

Table 18.5 World grain demand—shipping and stock development, 1975–1995

	1975	1980	1985	1990	1995
Average Grain Haul Length—nautical miles					
Trades to Developing World	5,210	5,300	5,400	5,410	5,450
Other trades	5,485	5,945	5,250	5,600	5,500
Average Voyage Times—days*					
Trades to Developing World	29.1	28.4	28.8	30.8	31.9
Other Trades	24.0	25.6	23.2	24.4	24.1
*Average Daily At-Sea Volumes—million tons***					
Trades to Developing World	4.07	6.77	6.74	10.21	13.33
Other Trades	6.07	8.40	7.05	5.83	3.16
Total	10.14	15.17	13.79	16.04	16.49
*Estimates Daily Port Silo Volumes—million tons****					
Trades to Developing World	2.10	3.57	3.51	4.97	6.27
Other Trades	3.80	4.92	4.56	3.59	1.97
Total	5.90	8.49	8.07	8.56	8.24

*From start of loading to completion of discharge (includes port delays).
**The methodology utilised is as follows: Each traded tonne of grain for the LDC markets is at sea for 31.9 days. Therefore, given the current demand total—146.3 m tonnes or a daily requirement of 0.418 m tonnes on a shipping year of 350 days—the overall LDC tonnage stored at-sea equates to 13.3 m tonnes.
***Average time in port silos—15 days—has remained fairly stable over the study period.

Source: Ocean Shipping Consultants Ltd.

capacity of this fleet. In 1982 it totalled 85.47 million dwt, but by 1995 this figure had shrunk to 62.10 million dwt, a decline of 27.3 per cent. This is because these ships are increasingly regarded as obsolete, and most investment is directed towards bulk carriers and cellular container vessels. The decline in the general cargo fleet has slowed somewhat since 1990, since firmer freight rates have delayed scrapping programmes. However, the delay in scrapping and the absence of new ordering has meant that the average age of this fleet of vessels has increased, 39.5 per cent of capacity having been constructed before 1979. So it is likely that before the year 2000 a high proportion will be scrapped or require heavy investment to continue trading. A further decline of some 11.4 per cent is forecast by the year 2000, and this will become more acute in the period up to 2010.

The net effect of this will be a considerable increase in freight rates for these increasingly scarce vessels, perhaps by as much as 37 per cent up to 1999 and a further 27 per cent up to 2010. It is to be expected that there will be variations around these levels, but in some cases it may be physically not possible to charter the necessary tonnage. This could put a lot of pressure on the supply chain to the developing world countries.

The FAO, through Ocean Shipping Consultants, have extended their study of the problem by a parallel analysis of the bulk carrier fleet sectors that are of most critical importance to the developing world grain trades.

At present most of the grain demand for the poorer parts of the developing world are handled either in general cargo form or in the smallest classes of dedicated bulk carriers in the 10/25,000 dwt size range. Although Handy Size vessels up to 50,000 dwt are also used these are primarily employed in the East Asian trades where port investment has been greater.

Accordingly, it is the 10,000–25,000 dwt range that is of most importance to the poorer part of the developing world. The development of this fleet between 1986 and 1996 is shown in Table 18.6. The main conclusion to be drawn from these figures is that while the Handy Size vessels have increased, the 10,000–25,000 dwt class—the part of the fleet most appropriate for grain operations—is declining. Over the period it has fallen by 11.6 per cent to 24.3 million dwt. The position is very similar to that recorded for general cargo ships. That is, the contraction has diminished as scrapping has slowed. But again there has been no notable increase in ordering, so the average age of the fleet has increased. Some 70 per cent of capacity was built before 1983 and is thus coming up for third survey assessment. This reinforces the view that the developing world grain trades are heavily dependent on a largely obsolete class of vessels.

The position for the 25,000–50,000 dwt sector is less critical, but fewer trades are optimised for these vessels and where they can be used a deadfreight penalty may be involved. Though the smaller bulk carrier

Table 18.6 Mid-year bulk carrier fleet size distribution, 1986–1996 ('000 dwt)

	10/25,000 dwt	25/50,000 dwt	Total Bulk Fleet
1986	27,499	79,170	198,786
1987	25,882	76,842	193,800
1988	25,004	76,539	193,900
1989	24,073	77,472	198,900
1990	24,442	78,575	206,843
1991	23,880	79,700	210,400
1992	24,085	80,852	215,200
1993	24,199	81,587	218,810
1994	23,670	82,185	220,845
1995	23,843	83,421	229,240
1996*	24,321	85,491	241,252

*At 1/1/96

Source: Fearnleys / Ocean Shipping Consultants Ltd.

fleet may stabilise in the near future and the larger class may slightly expand it is forecast that the demand side of the equation for these vessels will expand more rapidly. This will tighten the supply/demand balance, with an inevitable increase of freight rates, as previously noted. Time-charter rates for the smaller vessels may increase by 38 per cent to the year 2000, and the larger vessels by around 45 per cent.

The conclusions of studies presented to the FAO show that the Developing World has increased its share of global seaborne trade demand very rapidly and now accounts for 76 per cent of demand. A distinction has emerged between the East Asian markets and the rest of the developing world, where investment is less available. As a result the more efficient and larger bulk vessels are not being introduced into developing world grain trades. The lack of modern port investment in most developing markets seems likely to continue, daily handling rates are a fraction of those in the OECD countries, and in the worst ports they are half of those in the better ports and as far as bagged cargoes are concerned even worse. The physical capacity to handle existing demand does not exist, and future demand will become increasingly expensive and inefficient. The trade is increasingly dependent on stocks in transit (at-sea), and the demand for further storage will increase. Freight rates for the developing world account for 15–20 per cent of landed prices, compared with 6–8 per cent for inter-OECD trades, and as a result grain prices are significantly higher in the developing world.

This pessimistic scenario is one to exercise traders and governments alike, but in the present world economic situation there is no easy solution to it. Ocean Shipping Consultants have suggested that greater reliance might be placed on transhipment operations as a means to lower costs, despite the practical difficulties this may involve. This conclusion is not unlike that reached by myself and my co-author when we studied the contrasting situation of oversupply of grain in the developed world and famine in the developing world in the publication *Famine and Surplus* written for the Democratic Group of the European Parliament in 1982. No action was discernible following our 1982 study, but the FAO may be nearer to the scene of action now than the European Parliament appeared to be then.

CHAPTER 19

The multinational shippers and trading houses

Following the establishment of inter-continental movement of grain there emerged five predominant companies involved in this world-wide trade: the Bunge Corporation, for long based in Argentina but now in Brazil; André et Cie of Lausanne, Switzerland; Louis Dreyfus of Paris; Cargill Incorporated of Minneapolis; and Continental Grain Company of New York. These five have recently been joined by the fast-expanding Soufflet Group of Nogent, France.

Although trading in commodities worth vast financial sums, these companies have seldom been identified among the major companies of the world, for they have all been largely retained in the ownership of the successors of the founding families. Despite each having a major corporate base these companies are active in business in all countries from and to which grain flows, and where private enterprise is allowed to prosper (compared to the operations of Canada and Australia which are directed through statutory wheat and barley boards which control commercial activities).

While these companies are principally trading houses, they have in most cases, and at some time, been involved in the freight of grain from source to destination, owning or chartering vessels to carry the goods which they have traded. International trading of grain commodities requires particular skills in an industry which traditionally operates on small profits when measured in percentage terms. Involvement in the physical movement of these commodities requires further skills, for international shipping freight rates vary widely (and react quickly to local stimuli), with movements which may easily negate the profit made on the trading element of the transaction. It was largely as a result of these risks and pressures that the international grain trade became concentrated into so few hands. As the grain production of the western world rose, the requirements for the movements between countries and continents became increasingly large, with maize and wheat becoming strategic bargaining counters between the West and East political blocs. Sales of these commodities are frequently preceded by politico-economic negotiations, during which quantity parameters are defined and reciprocal requirements stated. Subsequent trade bargaining has to be made with high levels of expertise requiring the skills of the experienced traders of the major companies, who frequently effect the business (and accept the risk) which then percolates through all levels of the grain trade in many countries, eventually affecting the price paid to the individual cereal grower, be they in the American Mid-west, in Western Europe or in Argentina. These companies, now major players on the world commercial stage, have similarities in their origins, which, with their current activities, are briefly considered in the remainder of this chapter.

ANDRÉ ET CIE SA

Founded in 1877 André et Cie SA is a Swiss-based company trading in cereals, oilseeds and animal feeds worldwide. Despite early vicissitudes and setbacks, George André persevered at his business in the French-speaking cantons of Switzerland. Having been joined by his son Henri in 1905, George André built a reputation as a leading importer of cereals. In common with other fledgling "super companies" the years following the First World War proved to be a turning point for the André business, which transferred to Lausanne in 1920. It was at this time that overseas expansion began, and in 1927 it imported large quantities of Argentinian grain. This led to trade with North America, subsequently interrupted by the Second World War. The Andrés invested widely in Argentina, beginning a diversification into livestock breeding, milling, oilseed crushing and machine tool manufacturers' representation.

The years following the Second World War saw a boom in international movements of grain, upon which André was able to capitalise, having managed to maintain the shipping of supplies to Switzerland throughout the war years.

The rapidity of the increase of the international grain trade led to wide-scale expansion of business with the North and South American continents and with Western Europe. Economic and financial strictures, and the problems encountered with the "clearing" of currencies led to the establishment of a division of the company known as "Finco"—finance, compensation and commerce. This department became involved in the international handling of agricultural commodities and industrial products from many countries, leading to the recognition of André et Cie SA as a major trading house.

Its diversification led it to "departmentalise". Hence it now dominates domestic Swiss business; international commodities; industry; and shipping as well as the established "Finco". The principal participant in Swiss domestic agriculture, André et Cie SA owns and operates many of the silos and elevators which hold the grain reserves required by Swiss law. The company has offices throughout Western Europe, in the United States and South America, East China, West and South Africa, the Middle East, Singapore, Korea, Japan and Australia, through which its many trading activities are co-ordinated. The activities of Finco are ever-widening, consisting of short- and long-term project financing; special trade agreements and barter deals; collaboration with industry in the installation of new plant or the adoption of new techniques; and assisting with the economic development of new markets.

An associated company, Suisse-Atlantique SA, now operates a shipping fleet of vessels, principally carrying grain, but also carrying large tonnages of sugar, coal, ore and other dry bulk cargoes.

Now overseen by company president Henri André, the fourth generation of the André family to hold this position, the business is administered from Lausanne, where nearly 300 staff control the worldwide activities of this skilful and professional international business.

THE BUNGE GROUP

The Bunge Group has grown from the founding firm of Bunge & Born, formed in Holland in 1818. After establishing a successful trading base the company moved to Antwerp, Belgium, in 1850. Recognising Argentina as a prime source of grain, founding partner Georg Born moved to Buenos Aires to establish closer supplier links. The family connection in the business remains with the current group managing director Jorge Born, the third generation to run this multinational operation. South America remains the base, with group headquarters no longer in Argentina but at São Paulo, Brazil. A major headquarters is also based in St Louis, Missouri. During the intervening years Bunge has evolved from a primary involvement with grain trading to concentrating on the processing of primary products to sell as branded goods, frequently within the country of production. Food and food products are their principal activities, their main focus now being agribusiness.

Part of the Bunge philosophy is to be not solely export traders but to become involved with, and to develop, the products and needs of the countries in which they are based. Close to that philosophy is the ethos of involvement of public ownership in a share of the nationally established companies.

The Bunge Group is rated as one of the world's largest flour millers, with mills using more than 4 million tons of wheat annually. Integrated in this operation is the production of pasta, in which the company claims to be the world leader. With a large investment in oilseed crushing facilities, Bunge ranks third to Cargill and ADM worldwide, with a crushing capacity in excess of 7 million tonnes per year. Coupled to this, and integral to its philosophy, the company has become very involved with the refining of vegetable oils and the packaging, to supermarket shelf sizes, of oil for salads and cooking.

The opinion has been expressed by commentators that the Bunge policy is to reduce its activities in world grain trade, but still it rates third in volume behind Cargill and Continental Grain Company. Bunge's largest operations are in Brazil, Argentina and the United States, with many activities linked to grain. In Brazil the company has large investments in flour milling and oilseed crushing, with additional diversification into textiles, fertiliser and pasta production. Its operations in Argentina are very similar. In Venezuela it produces flour, pasta and animal feeds. All its South American crushing operations put the finished product into branded containers for the consumer market. The United States serves as the focal point of the Bunge worldwide grain operations. Apart from domestic and export grain it has widespread involvement in oilseed crushing, oil refining and corn milling.

Another change in the Bunge investment portfolio was the disposal in 1958–1959 of its merchant shipping fleet. As optimism faded, the virtually guaranteed profits from international grain trading that had existed to that time evaporated under the pressures of too many uncontrollable external factors. Fluctuating financial interest rates, international currency exchange rates and political instability made profitability more precarious so the fleet was sold off.

The formation of the European Economic Community brought changes to the established pattern of world grain trade. Imports to the Community were subject to levies, and an artificial price structure was determined to maintain the production levels and profitability of the farmers of the Member States. Bunge was initially widely involved with internal EC trade, but developed a strategy to withdraw from this position to concentrate upon the use and operation of silo and elevator facilities. Thus the import facilities formerly owned in Rotterdam and Antwerp have now been sold off.

On the other side of the world, the Bunge Group has spread its influence in Australia, which it entered in 1923. From initial involvement with flour milling and bread baking its interests are now pig rearing and meat packing.

The Bunge Group has a commitment to its involvement in the production of branded consumer products, particularly oil and oil products, pasta and mayonnaise, especially in South America and Australia. All the soyabean oil produced from the company mills in South America is refined into consumer products, while 40 per cent of the flour from its world mills is processed at its own baking and pasta plants.

The company's interest in the development of demand for such goods in South America follows its early developmental days in that continent. The group headquarters in Brazil is staffed by fewer than 50 people who regulate and control the vast financial implications of the Group's worldwide activities.

CARGILL INCORPORATED

Cargill Incorporated has grown from a grain trading and warehousing company founded by the MacMillan and Cargill families in Minneapolis, Minnesota, in 1865. Both families retain major ownership interests and an executive role within the present organisation which is now the world's largest trading corporation.

As with the other major companies of this type, the growth has been achieved by a planned programme of diversification, and by investment in and acquisition of interrelated businesses. Grain and commodity merchandising remains the principal activity of the now worldwide corporation, but other major involvements cover oilseed and maize processing and refining, flour milling, beef production and processing and steel manufacturing.

Cargill is a major trader of grain and oilseeds, as well as a marketer of many other agricultural and non-agricultural commodities.

Merchandising grains and oilseeds begins with Cargill's country elevators, located in North and South America, Europe and Asia. This system allows Cargill to purchase harvested grains and oilseeds directly from farmers, store them until marketing opportunities emerge, and then ship the commodities in bulk to points of demand around the globe. Cargill operates both owned and leased facilities and transport systems to ensure economical and efficient distribution.

Cargill maintains a network of trading offices throughout the United States, South America, Europe, Africa, Asia and the Pacific Rim. A close working relationship among geographic locations allows traders to share the information and resources that keep Cargill customers continuously linked to market opportunities.

Cargill trades cocoa and cocoa products. It merchandises green coffee to roasters in the United States, Europe and Asia. Together with its subsidiary, Excel, the company also merchandises meat, meat by-products, variety meats and hides in Latin America, Europe and the Pacific Rim.

Cotton is traded through two Cargill subsidiaries. Hohenberg Bros. Company of Memphis, Tennessee merchandises American, Mexican and South American cotton to textile manufacturers and other users worldwide. Ralli Bros. and Coney of Liverpool, England, trades cotton from growers in the Eastern Hemisphere.

From offices in the United States, Pacific Rim, Asia and the United Kingdom, Cargill trades sheet and block rubber, rice, palm and coconut oil. Cargill trades raw and white sugar in Minneapolis, Paris, Geneva and Hong Kong. Cargill sells fruit juice concentrates from offices in the United States, Japan, Brazil and the Netherlands. The company also merchandises apple juice from Chile and Argentina.

Cargill trades edible and non-edible tallow. It is acquired from major US meat packers and sold in Algeria, Brazil, Colombia, Egypt, Korea, Mexico, the Netherlands, Spain and Venezuela among others.

The company trades nitrogen, phosphate and potash fertiliser products worldwide.

Cargill merchandises salt for agricultural and industrial uses. Cargill's energy division trades and distributes crude and refined petroleum products, natural gas and electricity. Cargill Ferrous International trades products ranging from pig iron to finished steel.

Cargill owns and operates refrigerated bulk orange juice vessels, in addition to juice storage and distribution facilities in the United States, Brazil and the Netherlands. Greenwich Marine, a division of Cargill Marine and Terminal, meets some of the company's ocean-shipping needs by chartering vessels for Cargill entities worldwide. Cargill also brokers freight on ships either owned or chartered by Cargill to non-Cargill entities.

Rogers Terminal & Shipping, another Cargill Marine and Terminal division, provides services to both Cargill businesses and outside companies on the East and West Coasts and inland waterways in the United States. G&M Stevedoring, based in the Gulf of Mexico, also provides services to Cargill and non-Cargill businesses. Another division of Cargill Marine and Terminal, Cargo Carriers, operates jumbo dry and liquid cargo barges on inland waterways in the United States.

Cargill uses rail services to haul grain, soyabean meal, flour, salt, fertiliser and liquid commodities throughout the United States, operating a leased fleet of hopper and tank cars.

Cargill provides livestock farmers with well-balanced nutritional feeds. These animal feeds are produced at mills throughout North America, Latin America, Europe and Asia and are sold to raisers of hogs, poultry, cattle and fish.

Cargill also markets block and loose mix salt products to dairy and beef producers in the United States to meet the dietary needs of livestock.

The company markets hybrid corn, soyabeans, sorghum and sunflower seeds as well as canola, cotton and forage seeds in North America, Latin America, Europe, Asia, the Pacific Rim and Africa.

From fertiliser facilities in North and South America, Europe and the

Pacific Rim, Cargill produces, markets, stores and transports fertilizer products.

Caprock Industries, a Cargill subsidiary, operates cattle feedlots in the southwestern United States.

Cargill Central Research, located at Cargill headquarters in the United States, is dedicated to developing new agricultural products to address the needs of customers around the world.

The Financial Markets Group (FMG) supports Cargill and its subsidiaries with financial products and services that address the full spectrum of market conditions. These include financial instrument trading, emerging markets instrument trading, value investing and trade and structured finance.

Cargill Investor Services (CIS) is a futures/futures options broker and risk management consultant. The company is a clearing member of all major US and London futures and options exchanges, with the added resources to represent commercial and institutional clients on all futures and options exchanges worldwide. CIS specialises in trading futures and options for financial, agricultural, energy, metals and soft commodities. With offices in the United States, France, Japan, South Korea, Switzerland, Taiwan and the United Kingdom, CIS and its affiliated companies serve individual investors, multinational corporations, international banks, energy suppliers, agribusinesses, portfolio and fund managers and investment banking firms.

Cargill Leasing Corporation offers capital equipment leasing to help US customers expand their businesses. The company provides financing arrangements for computer, material handling, mining, construction, production, food processing and agricultural equipment, furniture, commercial aircraft, road and rail equipment and barges.

Cargill Technical Services (CTS), based in London, consults with clients world-wide regarding all phases of agricultural production, handling, transportation processing and related services. CTS also works with its affiliates, the British Cotton Growing Association and Minster Agriculture, on behalf of aid-related organisations in developing countries.

Corn wet milling plants in the United States, Europe and Brazil produce corn syrups and dry sweeteners used in canning, preserving, baking, brewing and making ice cream and candies. High fructose corn syrups, produced in the United States, provide a superior sweetening alternative to sugar for foods and beverages. Citric acid and sodium citrate, produced from refined, corn-derived liquid dextrose, are ingredients in foods and beverages, cosmetics, detergents and pharmaceuticals. Food grade cornstarch is used in a variety of food processing applications.

Cargill mills flour in the United States for sale to domestic wholesale and retail customers, as well as for export. It also mills flour in Argentina, Brazil and Venezuela and produces pasta in Venezuela.

Cargill operates malting plants in Belgium, France, Germany, the Netherlands, Spain and the United States for brewing, distilling and food processing customers around the world.

For bakers, breakfast cereal manufacturers, brewers and snack food customers, Cargill's Illinois Cereal Mills produce dry corn products such as grits, meal and flour in the USA and England. In addition, masa flour, used to make tortillas, tortilla chips and taco shells, is produced in the United States.

Gerkens Cocoa and Cargill Cacau are among the world's largest processors of cocoa and cocoa products, with processing plants in the Netherlands and Brazil. Cargill operates apple processing plants in Argentina and Chile, and orange processing plants in Brazil, Pakistan and the United States.

Through its oilseed processing activities in the United States, Latin America, Australia, Europe and Asia, Cargill processes soyabeans, sunflower seed, canola, flaxseed, corn, palm and cottonseed. Bulk and packaged oils are used in salad dressings, margarine, frying and baking by food processors and restaurants.

Cargill top grade salt is produced in the United States for food preparers and manufacturers worldwide. Protein products, including soya protein, are processed in the United States.

Cargill's rice milling operations, located in the United States, Malawi and Venezuela, mill white and brown rice, parboiled white and brown rice and rice flour.

Cargill Corn Milling produces industrial-grade starches used in the manufacture of paper and many other products. Ethanol, also derived from corn, is produced in the United States for use in reformulated gasoline.

Cargill facilities in the United States and Australia mine rock and solar salt, and process evaporated salt. Customers use the products to produce textiles and drugs, soften water, produce electrochemical energy, manufacture paper, tan leather and stabilise winter roads.

Cargill mines phosphate and manufactures phosphate fertilisers for distribution to users in North and South America, Europe and the Pacific Rim. Through a joint venture with the Province of Saskatchewan, Canada, the company also produces nitrogen fertilisers for the North American market.

CONTINENTAL GRAIN COMPANY

Although now recognised as the oldest American grain company, the roots of Continental Grain were in Belgium, where Simon Fribourg founded the company in 1813. As with most of the other major commodity trading houses the ownership and control of the business has remained in the hands of the founding families, who are still actively involved in the day-to-day decisions.

A subsidiary company was launched in Chicago in 1921 to generate grain for the European parent and to obtain a foothold in the fast-growing US domestic trade. Offices in New York and in Winnipeg followed quickly, and in 1925 a trading centre was established in Switzerland (although it was not until 1957 that the now famous Finagrain was formed in Geneva).

Trading of the expanding company was originally designed to facilitate commodity merchandising, handling and freight, but as the concept of integration grew, so the company became closer to "farm gate" business, and processing became an important factor of the operations within the United States. The company headquarters were relocated to New York in 1939, from which time expansion was rapid, spreading across the United States as its involvement with the war effort, and the movement of food supplies to Europe, increased.

Now ranking second only to Cargill in volume and financial involvement, the Continental Grain expansion has followed the pattern common to many of their competitors. Diversification included freight operations (with deep-sea vessels, owned or operated, and with their own fleet of rail wagons for the transportation of dry goods within the United States) and the processing of grains and related commodities.

The group financial demands spawned the formation in 1957 of the international clearing house, Finagrain (Compagnie Commerciale Agricole et Financière SA) in Geneva. However this operation alone does not satisfy the financial demands of this mighty international conglomerate so Continental is a borrower, on a huge scale, of currencies around the world emanating from its operations in many countries of South America, in Australia, Singapore, South Africa and Mexico. In addition, it has trading offices in most of the Western European states of the EU, as well as silo operations and processing mills in many of these countries.

THE LOUIS DREYFUS GROUP

The Louis Dreyfus Group is a worldwide organisation of companies with headquarters in Paris, supporting more than 40 offices in other countries including Singapore, London, Buenos Aires, Sao Paulo, Kiev and Rumania as well as a number located in principal cities of the United States, with a main office in Wilton, Connecticut.

The Group has been in business for 150 years, being retained in the ownership of the Louis Dreyfus family under the presidency of Gerard Louis-Dreyfus, a great grandson of the founder.

Historically, the Group's principal activity has been the trading of cereals and the development of the services allied to this activity. Latterly, frequently through its subsidiaries, the Group has become recognised as an international trader of cotton, sugar, meat, vegetable oils and crude oil. In common with many of its counterparts, ranching and cattle-raising now form part of the Dreyfus diversified activities, particularly in South America and the United States. In support of the buying and selling of commodities the Group owns and operates silo elevators, barges, rail and road tanker fleets and deep-sea vessels. With a chain of offices throughout the principal grain producing areas of the United States, Canada, Argentina, Australia, Brazil, Eastern Europe, South Africa and the EU, Dreyfus is actively involved in trading, handling and transportation of commodities in all these countries, with export a principal aim. Through its New York subsidiary the Louis Dreyfus Group owns, develops and manages property and real estate in the United States, Canada, Spain and France, concentrating on urban investment in offices and hotels.

The Group also owns and operates seed crushing mills in Brazil and Argentina, soyabean crushing mills and factories producing orange juice.

The commercial operations of Louis Dreyfus Armateurs through the CETRAGPA fleet based in France include 18 ships of Panamax and Capesize categories, as well as LNG carriers and floating cranes. As a Group, Louis Dreyfus controls 40 ships with a total deadweight of some 2 million tons.

THE J. SOUFFLET SA GROUP

A latter-day emergent as a world-scale trading house is the Soufflet Group, based in Nogent-sur-Seine in the heart of the cereal production area of France. Founded at the beginning of this century by the grandmother of the present chairman, Michel Soufflet, the company fortunes were built on the acquisition of a modest local grain business. Expansion in 1927 was accompanied by the building of a silo on the Seine and the construction of its first maltings at Nogent-sur-Seine.

The family tradition has been maintained through the intervening years but particularly since the mid-1950s when the major expansion began, as it was recognised that its geographical position gave the company a well placed base from which to spread its influence and activities throughout Europe.

While maintaining the primary activity of grain trading, the Soufflet Group developed in a way that is identifiable with many of the world's leading trading houses. Diversification saw it progress from being a buying agency to the supply of growers' requisites and the processing of commodities. In France, in 1998, the Group handled more than 2.3 million tons of farm-based cereals through more than 130 silo facilities strategically placed in the principal growing areas of that country, becoming the principal grain storage company in France. The programme of diversification has included the acquisition of businesses manufacturing and distributing fertilisers and others involved in agricultural and horticultural seed production. Purchases of maltings complemented their plant at Nogent as many of the traditional family-owned businesses yielded to the pressures of national and multinational firms. Investment in new factories has made Soufflet the largest malt producer in France, with malt production now of 570,000 tons per year from nine maltings throughout France. Construction on another is about to start in St Petersburg. Flour milling features very largely in the Group's business, and following various acquisitions the tonnage of wheat milled is now some 2 million tons in France and Belgium. The Costimax business based at Strasbourg carries out the production of maize semolina, and the manufacture of maize products for food, brewing and industrial requirements, which is now a major industry. Other involvements are with rice milling, animal feed manufacture, dried vegetables, oil products and petroleum product distribution, together with nation-wide distribution of fertilisers and sugars to the French wine industry, also ancillary equipment.

Soufflet has built a strong international trading arm dealing on the world markets. This division occupies a special place within the group, acting as a centre of information and a source of raw materials for many of the other divisions of the company. Considerable investment has been made in port-side silo facilities at La Pallice and Rouen (France), Southampton (England) and Rotterdam (Holland). For the distribution of their commodities within Europe, they have permanent trains of bulk wagons to service their trading activities. The trading arm was responsible for some 48 per cent of the financial turnover of the group in 1998, with 7 per cent of personnel employed. The company traded 12 million tons of cereals and processed products in 1997. The Dutch element of the company, based at Schiedam, near Rotterdam, provides strategic advantage for cover in Northern Europe, while from Novara (Italy) the mission is to distribute in that country the considerable tonnage of commodities arriving by train from France. There is an office in Segovia (Spain) with a trading and logistics unit handling the commodities flowing to and from Spain.

There is also a trading office in Minneapolis, while in England there has been a trading office since 1974 when the principal objective was the promotion and introduction of French grain to the United Kingdom. That objective remains, but the development of UK agriculture during the intervening years has seen Soufflet's activity spread to become involved in the trading of over 3 million tons of UK produced cereals, oilseeds and pulses, domestically as well as through export markets.

Soufflet consider that much of its success is due to the continuing control of the family and to its management style. It has endeavoured to develop international connections based on personal relationships and to ensure that its internal structure remains sufficiently manageable that a "family" atmosphere remains among the employees wherever they are working.

PART 4

Main claims arising from carriage of grain

CHAPTER 20

International Maritime Organisation legislation

Those concerned with maritime trade will be familiar with the acronym IMO, standing for International Maritime Organisation. This was formerly called the Inter-Governmental Maritime Consultative Organisation (IMCO), but changed its name in 1982.

The IMO is the only United Nations specialised agency based in Britain, the Convention establishing it being adopted in 1948, a year which saw the birth of so many international organisations including GATT (formed independently of the UN). IMO arose on the foundation of the many existing conventions governing safety of life at sea (SOLAS), of which the first was the 1914 Convention, arising out of the *Titanic* disaster in 1912.

THE SOLAS CONVENTIONS

Passenger travel by sea was then universal. There were no aircraft and vast numbers of emigrants were still being transported by ship to North and South America and Australasia. Britain was the centre of this activity, with the great ports of London, Liverpool and Glasgow, besides being the home country of the *Titanic*, and it was thus natural that Britain should have been the instigator of the 1914 conference, attended by 13 countries.

The 1914 Convention included chapters on safety of navigation, construction, radiotelegraphy, life-saving appliances and fire protection. These subjects are still dealt with in separate chapters in the current SOLAS Convention, dated 1974. The 1914 Convention, was, as the title implies, concerned primarily with the safety of human life.

Further SOLAS conferences followed, in 1929 when the Collision Regulations were agreed, and in 1948 which created IMCO, the first ever international body devoted exclusively to marine matters. The 1948 Conference covered a wider range of ships and went into greater detail than the previous conventions. It dealt with such matters as watertight subdivision in passenger ships; stability standards; the maintenance of essential services in emergencies; structural fire protection, including the introduction of three alternative methods of subdivision by means of watertight bulkheads, and the enclosure of main stairways. An international safety certificate for cargo ships of 500 gross tons and above was introduced, this being an indication of the growing importance of cargo ships relative to passenger ships.

The Collision Regulations were also revised, and regulations concerning the safety of navigation, meteorology and ice patrols were brought up to date. A separate chapter was included dealing with the carriage of grain and dangerous goods, including explosives. Developments in radio which had taken place during and since World War II were taken into account and the relevant chapter radically revised.

The first conference organised by the newly-named IMO in 1960 was concerned with marine safety. That conference adopted the International Convention on Safety of Life at Sea (again known as SOLAS) which came into force in 1965, replacing the version adopted in 1948. This conference was attended by 55 countries and took in further post-war technical progress, extending to cargo ships many safety measures previously applied to passenger ships. For example, it incorporated control provisions including requirements for various surveys and certificates for cargo ships of 300 gross tons and above making international voyages. It also included for the first time rules dealing with the carriage of grain and dangerous goods, together with revised Collision Regulations.

The 1960 SOLAS Conference set the programme for much of IMO's later technical work, particularly on the navigational and communications side. In 1973 a resolution was passed by the IMO Assembly (resolution A.264 (VIII)), which contained a major amendment consisting of a complete revision of Chapter Six of the Convention, dealing with the Carriage of Grain, and this was subsequently incorporated in the 1974 Convention.

By this time it had become increasingly apparent that the efforts being made to respond to the lessons learnt from major disasters and to keep the SOLAS Convention in line with technical developments were not proving successful. This was due to the amendment procedure adopted at the 1960 Conference. This procedure stipulated that amendments would enter into force 12 months after being accepted by two-thirds of the Contracting Parties to the parent Convention.

This procedure had worked all right in the early days when most international treaties were ratified by a relatively small number of countries. But during the 1960s the membership of the United Nations and international organisations such as IMO grew rapidly. More and more countries had secured their independence and many of them soon began to build up their merchant fleets. The number of Parties to the SOLAS Convention grew steadily. This meant that the number of ratifications required to meet the two-thirds target needed to secure entry into force of SOLAS amendments also increased. It became clear that it would take so long for these amendments to become international law that they would be out of date before they did so.

As a result IMO decided to introduce a new SOLAS Convention which would not only incorporate all the amendments to the 1960 Convention so far adopted but would also include a new procedure which would enable future amendments to be brought into force within an acceptable period of time. The result was the 1974 SOLAS Convention.

The 1974 SOLAS Conference was held in London from 21 October to 1 November and was attended by 71 countries. The Convention which was adopted is the version currently in force, and it is unlikely to be replaced by a new instrument because of the new tacit amendment procedure included in its Article VIII.

This procedure was an attempt to solve the problem of a multitude of ratifications by in effect reversing the hitherto existing process: instead it was assumed that governments were in favour of the amendment unless they took positive action to make their objection known.

Article VIII states that amendments to the chapters (other than Chapter I) of the Annex, which contains the Convention's technical provisions, shall be deemed to have been accepted within two years (or a different period fixed at the time of adoption) unless they are rejected within a specified period by one-third of the Contracting Governments or by Contracting Governments whose combined merchant fleets represented not less than 50 per cent of world gross tonnage. Although the explicit acceptance procedure was still provided for as an alternative, in practice the tacit acceptance procedure described above has proved rapid and effective and is now invariably used.

The 1974 Convention recognised ships constructed specially for the carriage of grain, and specified a method for calculating the heeling moment caused by shift of cargo in ships carrying bulk grain. Each ship was required to carry a document of authorisation, grain loading stability data and associated plans of loading.

The full contents of the important Annex to the 1974 Convention are as follows:

Chapter I General provisions, the most important of which concern surveys required for documents signifying compliance with the requirements of the Convention
Chapter II–1 Construction—subdivision and stability
Chapter II–2 Construction—Fire protection, fire detection and fire extinction
Chapter III Life-Saving appliances
Chapter IV Radiotelegraphy and radiotelephony

Chapter V Safety of navigation
Chapter VI Carriage of Grain
Chapter VII Carriage of Dangerous Goods
Chapter VIII Nuclear Ships

One subject which was not discussed at the 1974 SOLAS Conference was the revision of the Collision at Sea Regulations, which had been on the agenda of all the previous SOLAS Conferences. The reason was the decision taken some years before that the Collision Regulations should no longer form an Appendix to the SOLAS Convention but should become a separate international instrument.

The Convention on the International Regulations for Preventing Collisions at Sea was adopted by an IMO Conference in 1972 and came into force in 1977. This Convention, like SOLAS, adopted the "tacit acceptance" provision. A separate protocol due to major accidents to oil tankers about that time was also adopted in 1978.

In 1981 numerous amendments were adopted under the tacit acceptance procedure and entered into force on 1 September 1984. One of these extended the application of Chapter VI (Carriage of Grain) to ships of less than 500 gross tonnage engaged on international voyages.

Yet more amendments were made in April and October 1988, resulting from the *Herald of Free Enterprise* tragedy; in November 1988 (Global Maritime Distress), May 1990 (stability of cargo ships) and May 1991.

The latter amendments included the complete rewriting of Chapter VI, which previously covered only the carriage of grain, to cover other cargoes including bulk cargoes. The new Chapter VI is divided in three parts: Part A contains general provisions; Part B special provisions for bulk cargoes other than grain; and Part C carriage of grain. This last part deals with the carriage of grain in two general regulations, and detailed grain rules have been transferred to the International Code for the Safe Carriage of Grain in Bulk, now mandatory (other Codes are merely recommendations). The text of Part C reads as follows:

Part C
Carriage of grain

Regulation 8

Definitions

For the purposes of this part, unless expressly provided otherwise:

1. *International Grain Code* means the International Code for the Safe Carriage of Grain in Bulk adopted by the Maritime Safety Committee of the Organisation by resolution MSC.23(59) as may be amended by the Organisation, provided that such amendments are adopted, brought into force and take effect in accordance with the provisions of Article VIII of the present Convention concerning the amendment procedures applicable to the annex other than chapter I.

2. The term *grain* includes wheat, maize (corn), oats, rye, barley, rice, pulses,

seeds and processed forms thereof whose behaviour is similar to that of grain in its natural state.

Regulation 9

Requirements for cargo ships carrying grain

1. In addition to any other applicable requirements of the present regulations, a cargo ship carrying grain shall comply with the requirements of the International Grain Code, and hold a document of authorization as required by that Code. For the purpose of this regulation, the requirements of the Code shall be treated as mandatory.

2. A ship without such a document shall not load grain until the master satisfies the Administration, or the Contracting Government of the port of loading on behalf of the Administration, that the ship will comply with the requirements of the International Grain Code in its proposed loaded condition.

THE INTERNATIONAL GRAIN CODE

The International Code for the Safe Carriage of Grain in Bulk (IMO Publication IMO-240E), whose short title is "International Grain Code", is of great importance to readers of this book and a short account of its provisions follows.

The 18 paragraph headings in Part A are as follows:

1. Application
2. Definitions
3. Document of Authorisation
4. Equivalents
5. Exemptions for certain voyages
6. Information regarding ship's stability and grain loading
7. Stability requirements
8. Stability requirements for existing ships
9. Optional stability requirements for ships without documents of authorisation carrying partial cargoes of bulk grain
10. Stowage of bulk grain
11. Strength of grain fittings
12. Divisions loaded on both sides
13. Divisions loaded on one side only
14. Saucers
15. Bundling of bulk grain
16. Overstowing arrangements
17. Strapping or lashing
18. Securing with wire mesh.

Part B contains six paragraphs covering detailed instructions regarding the calculation of heeling moments. Paragraph 1 contains general assumptions of void depth in filled compartments, etc.; paragraph 2 the

Figure 20.1 Stability requirements

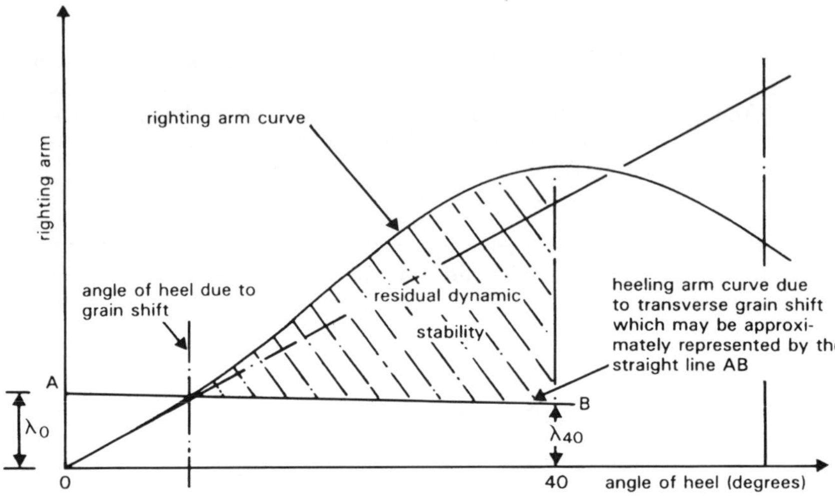

(1) Where:

$$\lambda_0 = \frac{\text{assumed volumetric heeling moment due to transverse shift}}{\text{stowage factor} \times \text{displacement}}$$

$\lambda_{40} = 0.8 \times \lambda_0$;
Stowage factor = volume per unit weight of grain cargo;
Displacement = weight of ship, fuel, fresh water, stores etc. and cargo.

(2) The right arm curve shall be derived from cross-curves which are sufficient in number to accurately define the curve for the purpose of these requirements and shall include cross-curves at 12° and 40°.

Source: IMO.

assumed volumetric heeling moment of a filled compartment, trimmed; paragraph 3, the same, untrimmed; paragraph 4 the same, in trunks; paragraph 5 the same, in a partly filled compartment, and paragraph 6, other assumptions.

Figure 20.1, which relates to paragraph 7 of Part A is an illustration of the kind of detail gone into, while Fig 20.2 is an illustration of the final void pattern after the assumed shift of grain in a compartment with two or more hatchways.

The Code applies to all ships, including those of less than 500 tons gross tonnage.

Grain has been carried at sea for thousands of years, but has always presented problems because of its tendency to shift when carried in bulk. Measures to counter this were included in the 1960 SOLAS Convention and equivalent measures adopted in 1969. The 1969 rules formed the basis of the 1974 SOLAS Convention, and were known as the IMO Grain Rules. They are based on the recognition that, in a compartment

Figure 20.2 Final void pattern after assumed shift of grain in compartment with two or more hatchways

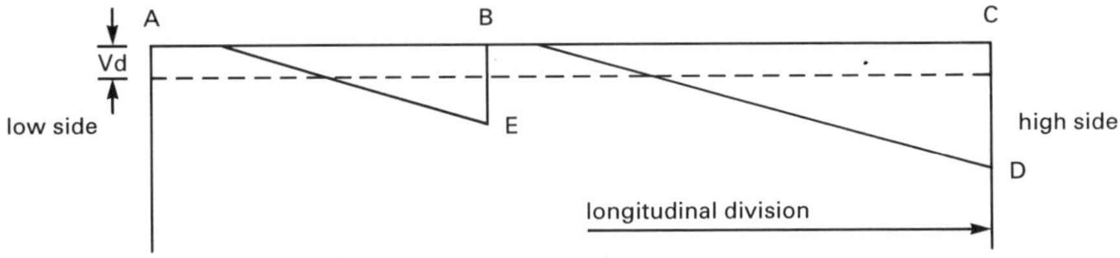

(1) If the maximum void area which can be formed against the girder at B is less than the initial area of the void under AB, i.e. AB × Vd, the excess area shall be assumed to transfer to the final void on the high side.
(2) If, for example, the longitudinal division at C is one which has been provided in accordance with A 10.9, it shall extend to at least 0.6 m below D or E, whichever gives the greater depth.

Source: IMO.

nominally filled with grain, there exists a void space between the surface of the grain and the deckhead. The Rules require demonstration by calculation that at all times during a voyage the ship will have sufficient intact stability to provide adequate residual dynamic stability after taking into account the adverse effects caused by an assumed pattern of grain movement.

Temporary fittings to reduce grain shift, such as shifting boards, depend entirely on achieving the correct relationship between the intact stability characteristics of the ship and the heeling effects of a possible grain shift within the various compartments.

The Rules require a minimum level of acceptable stability for the carriage of grain in terms of angle of heel due to assumed grain shift, residual righting energy and initial metacentric height.

The 1991 rewrite of Chapter VI was not the last time the SOLAS Convention was amended. It has since been amended almost annually, mainly relating to high-speed craft, ro-ro ferries, fire protection, liquefied gas carriers, traffic management systems in busy straits, etc. But now (1998) it is generally accepted that future amendments, saving in exceptional circumstances, will be adopted only every four years.

CHAPTER 21

The US Federal Grain Inspection Service

GENERAL

All countries which export grain set standards of quality (moisture, protein content, etc.) and cleanliness which must be checked at the time of loading. In the United Kingdom and most European countries this service is provided on a commercial basis by private firms, usually known as superintending companies. When a ship is loaded or discharged the contracting parties appoint a superintendent who issues a certificate saying what he determines, so that it can be seen whether or not the cargo conforms to the contract.

In the United States this service is provided for exporters by the Federal Grain Inspection Service (FGIS), a state agency of the US Department of Agriculture. Inspection on discharge of cargoes in the United States is done by commercial companies in the same way as superintendents in Europe and elsewhere. The contract will usually specify whether quality is to be final at loading or at discharge. GAFTA contracts, for example, are normally final at time of loading. If the quality is not met then the certificate will make it clear that the party concerned is not meeting the contractual terms.

The FGIS administers a system for officially inspecting and weighing grain and other commodities through field offices in 23 states and Canada. FGIS also oversees the work of state and private agencies which provide official services at other domestic grain markets. Eight of these state agencies are also authorised to perform official export services at ports.

Most US grain is weighed on an electronic weighing system. The system consists of a load receiving element (e.g., weigh hopper, platform, etc., with load cells), an indicating element (e.g., digital instrument), a printer and the associated material-handling equipment. The load cell senses the amount of the applied load in the load-receiving element and produces an output voltage that is sent to the digital instrument. The digital instrument converts the output voltage into a digital display. The tape printer records the digital display onto a tape or ticket for a permanent record.

Levertronic scales

There are two types of electronic scales: Levertronic and full electronic. Levertronic scales are mechanical scales that have been converted to electronic scales by inserting a load cell into the lever system. The dial used to obtain and print a weight is replaced with a digital instrument and printer.

Full electronic scales

In full electronic scales, the load receiving element is either supported by, or rests on, the load cell.

Digital instrument with printer

Digital instruments, printers, and control boards are located in the control room. The control room is the operations control centre for the export elevator. It may be located in the elevator or in a building separated from the elevator.

A digital instrument may have some sort of control that allows the operator manually or automatically to operate the gates of the garners and the scale. In the manual mode, the operator controls the operation of each scale cycle; in the automatic mode, the scale cycle repeats in succession.

Control boards are scaled-down diagrams of the elevator's grain handling systems. Elevator personnel can control bin selection, tripper movement, diversion points, legs, conveyor belts, slides and gates from this board. Official weighing personnel monitor export grain flow after weighing and sampling to ensure that all of the grain weighed and sampled is actually delivered to the vessel.

Scale tapes

During the operation of an electronic weighing system, the official weigher continually verifies that the weight value displayed on the digital instrument is the same as the printed value on the scale tape or ticket to assure proper system operation and to detect any printer malfunction.

The weight of each draft is added to determine the sublot total. The official weigher records the number of the sublot on the tape and initials the total weight. When the tape is removed from the printer, the weigher initials it, records the time, carrier identification, kind of grain, tape number and scale numbers. If this information is printed on the tape automatically, the weigher verifies the accuracy of the information and initials it.

To be officially graded, grain must be inspected according to provisions of the US Grain Standards Act. This means that the equipment and procedures used must be approved and checked regularly for accuracy and that inspectors must be tested for proficiency in carrying out their inspection duties. The US Congress has given FGIS the responsibility for carrying out this work.

There are five basic operations performed when officially inspecting and weighing grain going aboard a ship: stowage examination, sampling, weighing, inspection, and certification.

Stowage examination

A stowage examination is an inspection that determines if a carrier is fit to receive grain. To be considered fit, the carrier's stowage area must be clean, dry, free of odour and infestation, and otherwise suitable for receiving or storing grain, insofar as the suitability may affect the quality, quantity, or condition of the grain.

To determine cleanliness, the stowage space is examined for:

1. Previous cargo. If the stowage space contains fertiliser, old grain, loose cement, coal, lime, dunnage, refuse, or other debris, the space is declared unfit for loading.
2. Rust scale and paint scale. Rust scale and paint scale must be checked to see if they could become dislodged from the carrier and contaminate the grain. Loose scale will break when struck with a fist or when light pressure is applied with a knife blade under the edge of the scale. The use of safety goggles is recommended when scraping rust or similar material. Rust scale should not be confused with oxidation rust, which forms on exposed metal surfaces. Oxidation rust will not flake off when light pressure is applied.

   For ships, the area is declared unfit when a single area of loose rust scale or paint scale is more than 25 square feet (approximately 2.3 square metres) or several patches of loose rust scale or paint scale together exceed 100 square feet (roughly 9.3 square metres).
3. Unsanitary conditions. If the stowage space contains any animal filth, rodent excreta, bird excreta, decaying animal or vegetable matter, sewage or any other unsanitary conditions, the space is

declared unfit for loading. Sites close to the hatch (e.g., ship deck, top side of the hatch cover) also must be clean.

4. Unknown substances. If any unknown substances are found, the space is declared unfit for loading. All unknown substances are considered contaminating. FGIS does not try to identify them but, if possible, FGIS will take samples of the substance and show them to the supervisor for future reference.

To determine dryness, the stowage space is examined for standing water, puddles or any amount of leaking water; if any of these is present, the space is declared unfit for loading. Condensation, commonly called "sweating", can form on bulkheads or lower decks. This is unavoidable and poses no threat to the grain.

If the stowage space is contaminated with the odour of petroleum, an oil-based chemical, decaying animal or vegetable matter or any other commercially objectionable foreign odour, the space is declared unfit for loading.

Finally, the stowage space is examined for infestations of rodents and/or insects. The discovery of any live rodents or more than two live insects injurious to stored grain will result in the space being declared unfit for loading.

INSPECTION EQUIPMENT

Moisture

The moisture content in the grain is determined by a standardised Motomco Moisture Meter, an electronic capacitance meter. Moisture does not influence the numerical grade or any special grades. However, it is determined on all shipments and reported on the official certificate.

To measure the moisture, a sample must first be weighed. The balance should be accurate to at least 0.15 grams. A 1.0 gram error in weighing produces an error of 0.15 per cent in the moisture determination; therefore it is important to be precise.

After weighing, the sample is placed in an approved moisture-proof container, and a rubber-stopper thermometer is inserted.

Paper bags, fibre cartons, etc., are not used as moisture sample containers. Containers found to be the most practical for use in determining moisture are moisture-proof, plastic, 475-ml containers with openings of approximately 45 mm. Paper identification should not be inserted in the grain samples.

Temperature must be accurately determined for the moisture test. Meters are standardised for a grain temperature of 77° Fahrenheit

(25° C). For temperatures other than 77° Fahrenheit (F), correction must be applied by referring to the appropriate conversion chart.

Because of wide variations between room and grain temperatures throughout the year, it is not possible to predict exactly how long after the thermometer has been inserted into the grain that the temperature should be read. Generally, three to five minutes are sufficient to obtain an accurate temperature.

Dockage is a factor determined for barley, flaxseed, rye, sorghum, triticale and wheat, but not for other grains. Dockage consists of material which can be easily removed by machine and includes material lighter than, larger than, and smaller than the grain.

Dockage is determined with a special machine called the Carter Dockage Tester, which uses aspiration (air) and a combination of riddles and sieves to remove materials lighter or of a different size than the grain. Figure 21.1 depicts the testing process.

Figure 21.1 Carter Dockage Tester

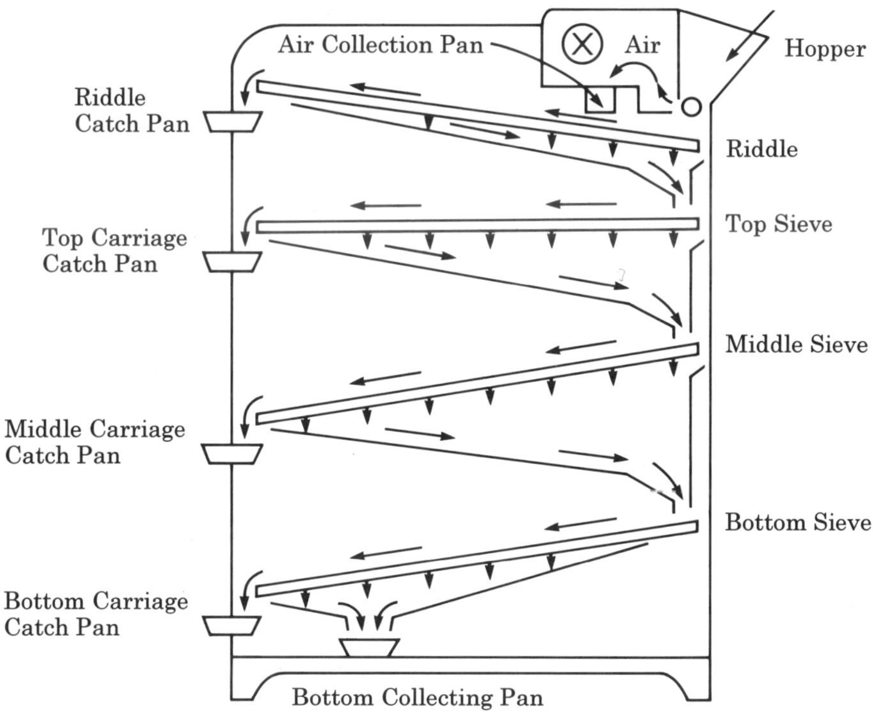

Source: FGIS.

Like moisture, dockage does not influence the numerical grade of the grain, but it always is determined and reported on the certificate. After dockage is removed, a portion of the sample is manually examined for foreign material, which is all material remaining in the sample other than the predominant grain. Foreign material includes materials which could not be separated mechanically, such as seeds and other grains similar in size and weight to the grain.

The Dockage Tester also is used to determine the percentage of broken corn and foreign material in corn. Broken corn and foreign material are a grading factor in corn.

Test weight per bushel

Test weight per bushel is the weight of the grain required to fill a level Winchester bushel measure (approximately 35.2 litre capacity). The factor "test weight per bushel" is determined using an approved apparatus which has a kettle capacity of one dry quart (approximately 1.1 litres). This determination is made on a representative portion of grain of not less than 1⅛ to 1¼ quarts (1.2 to 1.4 litres) cut from the representative sample using a Boerner divider.

Test weight per bushel is a grading factor. Generally, it is expressed in pounds per Winchester bushel, but upon request it will be converted to kilograms per hectolitre.

To determine test weight, the work sample is poured into the closed hopper which is centred over the kettle. The valve is opened to allow the grain to fill the kettle. A standard stroker held in both hands with the flat sides in a vertical position is used to remove the excess grain from the top of the kettle with three full-length, zigzag motions. The kettle is hung on the beam and the beam weights are moved until the beam is perfectly balanced. Then, the test weight per bushel is read.

BARLEY

Barley is divided into three classes based on kernel characteristics: six-rowed barley, two-rowed barley and barley. The class barley has no subclasses; six-rowed barley and two-rowed barley are divided into subclasses based on their malting qualities.

Six-rowed malting barley is divided into three numerical grades, and two-rowed malting barley is divided into four numerical grades. All classes of barley not designated as "malting" are divided into five numerical grades and US sample grade. Special grades are provided to emphasise special qualities or conditions affecting the value of barley and are added to and made a part of the grade designation. They do not affect the numerical or sample grade designation.

In general, a kernel of barley is considered damaged for inspection and grading purposes only when the damage is distinctly apparent and recognised as damaged for commercial purposes.

Blight-damaged kernels are kernels and pieces of barley kernels that are covered at least one-third or more with fungus or mould. Blight discolourations should not be confused with badly stained, weathered or water-stained kernels or kernels that have black discolouration on the tip of the germ end due to weather conditions. Barley containing more than 4 per cent of blight-damaged kernels is designated "blighted".

Malt-damaged kernels are kernels and pieces of barley kernels that have undergone the malting process and show any degree of sprout. Frost-damaged kernels are kernels and pieces of barley kernels that are badly shrunken and/or distinctly discoloured black, brown or green by frost.

Germ-damaged kernels (sick and/or mould) are kernels and pieces of barley kernels that have discoloured germ due to heat or mould from respiration. This includes barley injured by heat.

Heat-damaged kernels are kernels and pieces of barley kernels that are damaged by heat. The determination for heat-damaged kernels is made on a pearled portion.

Weevil or insect-bored kernels are kernels and pieces of barley kernels that have been bored or tunneled by insects.

Mould-infected kernels are whole kernels of barley that are covered 50 per cent or more with a mould-like substance.

Sprout-damaged kernels are kernels and pieces of barley kernels that have sprouted, that have swelling over the germ and that show sprout after examination.

Dockage (DKG) in barley is non-barley matter removed from the sample by the Carter Dockage Tester. Dockage is recorded to the nearest hundredth per cent, unless it is 1 per cent or more.

Foreign material (FM) in barley is all matter that remains in the sample after the removal of dockage. FM is determined on 25 grams of dockage-free barley and is recorded on the official certificate to the nearest tenth.

CORN (MAIZE)

Corn is divided into three classes based on colour: yellow corn, white corn and mixed corn. Each class is divided into five US numerical grades and US sample grade. Special grades are provided to emphasise special qualities or conditions affecting the value and are added to and made a part of the grade designation. They do not affect the numerical or sample grade designation.

Broken corn and foreign material (BCFM) is determined using the Carter Dockage Tester machine. Broken corn (BC) is all matter that passes through a $^{12}\!/_{64}$-inch (4.8 mm) round-hole sieve and over a $^{6}\!/_{64}$-inch round-hole sieve. Foreign material (FM) is all matter that passes through a $^{6}\!/_{64}$-inch (2.4 mm) round-hole sieve and that remains on top of a $^{12}\!/_{64}$-inch (4.8 mm) round-hole sieve. All matter other than corn remaining in the sample is removed by hand. (Sweetcorn and popcorn are considered FM.)

BC and FM are recorded to the nearest tenth on the shipping log and the total of the two, BCFM, is recorded to the nearest tenth on the official inspection certificate. This information will provide the miller with the exact amount of millable and non-millable material.

In general, a kernel of corn is considered damaged for inspection and grading purposes only when the damage is distinctly apparent and can be recognised as damaged for commercial purposes.

Blue-eye mould damage occurs when a germ is infected with blue-eye mould, regardless of the amount.

Purple plumule is a genetic or varietal characteristic which does not constitute damage and should not be confused with blue-eye mould. Cob rot is caused by a fungus that attacks weakened plants and produces a distinct colouration or rotting.

Drier-damaged kernels are kernels and pieces of kernels which are wrinkled, discoloured, blistered, puffed or swollen in appearance. They also are germ-damaged, with peeled or peeling seed coats, or a fractured or checked appearance. Drier damage should not be confused with heat damage.

Germ-damaged kernels are kernels and pieces of kernels damaged by respiration or heat but not materially discoloured.

Heat-damaged kernels are kernels and pieces of kernels that are materially discoloured by excessive respiration, with the dark discolouration extending out of the germ through the sides and into the back of the kernel.

Heat-damaged kernels (drier) are kernels and pieces of kernels that are puffed or swollen and materially discoloured by external heat caused by artificial drying methods. Insect-bored kernels are kernels and pieces of kernels with obvious insect-bored holes, tunnelling, insect webbing or insect refuse. Kernels that are partially eaten but entirely free of refuse, webbing or other types of damage are not considered damaged.

Mould-damaged kernels are kernels and pieces of kernels infected with mould on the exposed endosperm. When a kernel is cracked or broken the starch is exposed and it becomes susceptible to mould. Mould is usually blue or green in colour. If the surface mould penetrates the kernel, it is considered damaged. Kernels that have dirt on them should not be confused with kernels containing mould.

Discoloured kernels that contain a mould-like substance are considered damaged when whole kernels are 50 per cent or more covered.

Surface mould (blight) is kernels and pieces of kernels that have mould caused by corn leaf blight. While it appears to lie on the surface, it actually penetrates the seed coat.

Mould (pink Epicoccum) is kernels and pieces of kernels that have a mould-infected germ.

SORGHUM

Sorghum is divided into four classes based on colour: white sorghum, yellow sorghum, brown sorghum and mixed sorghum. There are no subclasses. Each class is divided into four numerical grades and US sample grade. Special grades are provided to emphasise special qualities or conditions affecting the value of sorghum. Special grades are added to and made a part of the grade designations. They do not affect the numerical or sample grade designation.

Broken kernels (BN) are all matter which passes through a $\frac{5}{64}$-inch (2.0 mm) triangular-hole sieve and over a $\frac{5}{128}$-inch (1.0 mm) round-hole sieve. Foreign material (FM) is all matter, except sorghum, that remains on top of the $\frac{5}{64}$-inch (2.0 mm) triangular-hole sieve. BN and FM are each recorded to the nearest tenth per cent on the shipping log and the total of the two (BNFM) is recorded to the nearest tenth per cent on the official inspection certificate.

In general, a kernel of sorghum is considered damaged for inspection and grading purposes only when the damage is distinctly apparent and can be recognised as damaged for commercial purposes.

Germ-damaged kernels are kernels and pieces of kernels of sorghum that contain dark-coloured germs after bleaching.

Ground- and/or weather-damaged kernels are kernels and pieces of kernels that contain dark stains or discolourations and have a rough, cake-like appearance. This type of damage is caused by ground and/or weather conditions.

Heat-damaged kernels are kernels and pieces of kernels of sorghum that are materially discoloured and damaged by heat. It is usually necessary to cross-section the kernels to determine whether the colour is creamy.

Mould-damaged kernels are kernels and pieces of kernels containing surface mould and should not be confused with dark stains or discolouration caused by ground and/or weather conditions.

Sorghum with a mould-like substance is considered damaged when over half of the whole kernels of sorghum or pieces of kernels are discoloured and covered with a mould-like substance.

Sprout-damaged kernels are kernels and pieces of kernels where the sprout clearly protrudes from the germ. Kernels and pieces of kernels of sorghum that have a split over the germ area but that have no sprout protruding are not considered sprout-damaged. Insect-bored kernels are kernels and pieces of kernels of sorghum that have been bored or tunneled by insects.

INTERPRETIVE FACTORS—VISUAL GRADING AIDS

The visual grading aids system was developed by the FGIS Board of Appeals and Review to assist inspectors in making subjective grading decisions and to reduce inter-market differences in inspection results. This system consists of Interpretive Line Slides and Interpretive Line Prints. Reference is made to the visual grading aids throughout the grain inspection manuals.

The Interpretive Line Slide System consists of a portable table-top viewer and photographic slide transparencies. The portable viewer uses a precisely controlled light source of desired intensity and quality. The Interpretive Line Slides are placed on the viewer at the inspection table to aid the inspector in making grading decisions. The slides are designed for use with the special viewer only. If they are used in a normal slide projector, they will become bleached by the high intensity light, rendering them unusable for the comparative purposes for which they were intended.

Interpretive Line Prints are photographs exhibiting a particular attribute. These prints allow a more uniform application of the general appearance factors. Both the Interpretive Line Slides and Prints are available for viewing at every FGIS field office, and are available for purchase from the manufacturer.

FUMIGATION AND GRAIN PROTECTANTS

A fumigant is a gas which penetrates the grain kernels and kills insects at all life stages: eggs, larvae and adults. Grain protectants are applied to the surface of grain and kill adult insects on contact, but do not kill insect eggs.

When a portion of cargo is graded “infested” the exporter can accept the official certificate with the “infested” designation, return the infested cargo to the elevator or continue to load the vessel and then fumigate it in transit following procedures specified by FGIS. If the exporter selects the last option, the "infested" designation is not reported on the certificate because the condition is considered remedied.

The fumigation of vessels in transit with aluminium phosphide fumigant formulations is a widespread practice. The fumigation is performed by a registered applicator; FGIS personnel observe the fumigation to assure that it is performed according to correct procedures. FGIS requires the applicator to sign a statement on his company's letterhead stating that the fumigant was applied according to US government regulations and the manufacturer's instructions.

UNIFORM INSPECTION PLAN/CERTIFICATION

During the loading of an export grain vessel, FGIS follows a uniform plan for sampling and inspection. A shipment or "lot" of grain is divided into "sublots" for the purpose of maintaining quality. The sublot size is based on the hourly loading rate of the elevator and the capacity of the vessel being loaded. A sublot may represent up to approximately 3,000 metric tons. The grade and factors determined on each sublot must meet, within specified tolerances, the official grades and factors requested in the applicant's load order. Sublots that do not meet specified tolerances can be removed from the shipment or certified separately. Otherwise, FGIS certificates represent the entire lot of grain based on the weighed average of sublot results at the time of loading.

The uniform inspection plan for shiplots is called the Cu-Sum Plan. It establishes statistically based tolerances known as breakpoints for accepting those occasional portions of a lot that, due to known sampling and grading variations, may grade below the desired lot quality. The Cu-Sum Plan was adopted to ensure that the entire lot is of uniform quality. The inspector uses an inspection log to record his findings for each sublot. Each log contains all of the factor results for each sublot, plus any other observations made by the sampler and inspector. It is a complete record of all inspection information concerning the lot. This record is retained by FGIS; however, a buyer can obtain a copy by requesting it in the contract.

The product of all analysing, grading and monitoring is the Official Export Grain Inspection Certificate. There are two options under which shiplot grain can be loaded and certified: "Option 1" and "Option 2". Under Option 1, the exact grade must be loaded; with Option 2, the exact grade or a better grade can be loaded. Option 2 gives the shipper more flexibility and gives the buyer a potentially better quality of grain.

While the grain standards denote a general level of quality, more stringent criteria can be requested in a contract. For example, if a buyer contracts for US No. 2 or better yellow corn and 3 per cent BCFM is excessive for the end-use, the contract can specify "US No. 2 or better yellow corn, maximum 2.5 per cent BCFM". However, more stringent criteria may command a premium price. It is also important to specify in the contract all of the optional testing services FGIS is to perform, such as "aflatoxin testing to be performed by FGIS". If FGIS is not specified to perform the test, then it may be done by a private laboratory.

FOREIGN COMPLAINTS

If a discrepancy between grain quality at origin and destination arises, an importer can register a complaint with the US Embassy's agricultural counsellor, attaché or trade officer. The embassy will then notify the USDA's Foreign Agricultural Service (FAS) in Washington, DC, who in turn will notify the FGIS International Monitoring Staff (IMS). The IMS will review the complaint, gather information about the reported discrepancy and respond. However, FGIS does not issue a new certificate, nor does it function as an arbitrator between buyer and seller.

File samples are held for 90 days after loading. If they are available when the complaint is filed, they will be re-examined during the investigation. If a receiver chooses to submit a sample from destination it, too, will be examined. The FGIS findings are sent in a report through the US Embassy to the originator of the complaint. The facts in the response are available to any person having financial interest in the grain.

GRAIN QUALITY IMPROVEMENT ACT

The Grain Quality Improvement Act of 1986 required FGIS to revise certain procedures in order to enhance the quality of US grain of 1986 exports. The Act addressed three primary areas: grain handling practices, insect tolerances and the usefulness of grain standards. Before this Act, some elevator operators removed and stored dust, dockage and foreign material during grain handling to reduce dust levels in the elevator, then recombined it before loading the vessel. This practice is no longer permitted. While the Act prohibits recombining dust that has been removed and stored, it does not require dust to be removed. More stringent insect tolerances became effective in May 1988.

Finally, FGIS is required to study the need for additional end-use value tests for grain. For further information on US grading and sampling standards, contact:

Federal Grain Inspection Service, USDA
Room 1627

South 14th and Independence Avenue, SW
Washington, DC 20250
Phone: 001 (202) 382-0226
Fax: 001 (202) 447-4628
Web site: http:\\www.usda.gov (search for GIPSA FGIS home page)

FGIS field and sub-offices are located in the following cities: Mobile, Alabama; Stuttgart and Jonesboro, Arkansas; Montreal, Canada; Savannah, Georgia; Moscow, Idaho; Chicago and Peoria, Illinois; Indianapolis, Indiana; Cedar Rapids, Iowa; Wichita, Kansas; Belle Chasse, Crowley, Destrehan, Lutcher, and Port Allen, Louisiana; Baltimore, Maryland; Saginaw, Michigan; Duluth and Minneapolis, Minnesota; Greenville, Mississippi; Kansas City and St Louis, Missouri; Omaha, Nebraska; Grand Forks, North Dakota; Toledo, Ohio, Portland, Oregon; Memphis, Tennessee; Beaumont, Corpus Christi, Galveston, Houston, Pasadena, and Plainview, Texas; and Norfolk, Virginia. Federal/state offices are located in Sacramento, California and Olympia, Washington.

CHAPTER 22

Contracts and arbitration

Until the outbreak of the Second World War the United Kingdom had relied upon the supply of many basic foodstuffs, particularly grain, from overseas sources. The major processing plants, flour mills and animal feed mills were port-side facilities in the principal cities of London, Liverpool, Birkenhead, Manchester, Southampton, Cardiff, Bristol, Hull, Glasgow and Leith. These mills relied on world supplies for wheat, maize and protein sources. In many ports there were facilities for the trans-shipment of goods, including barley from Chile and California for the malting industry. Although eastern England was developing at that time as a production area of barley, supplies were mainly imported until 1939.

It was to protect the interests of the buyers of these supplies that The Port Corn Trade Association drew up contracts to cover the imports of foreign materials. It was part of the original concept that in the event of disputes arbitration proceedings should be held in London. Because of the volume of trade being conducted with the United Kingdom the world suppliers accepted these terms, particularly as the UK arbitration system was already held in high esteem. It became the practice for traders who were not conducting business with or through the United Kingdom to accept the London Grain Contract terms, and to be bound by arbitrations held in London.

As the years passed, many trade associations in other countries developed their own contracts, using the London contracts as their models.

There were within the United Kingdom several separate port trade associations covering international and domestic trade. The London Corn Trade Association (formed in 1878) initially amalgamated with the London Cattle Feed Trade Association, founded in 1906, eventually to become in 1971 The Grain and Feed Trade Association (GAFTA), now based in the heart of the City of London at GAFTA House. GAFTA acts as the regulatory body for the majority of contracts covering the movement of grain and feedstuffs to and from the United Kingdom and for a substantial proportion of business between countries trading in world commodity markets.

Domestic trade associations within Britain experienced the amalgamation of the Seed Trade Association with the National Association of Corn and Agricultural Merchants (NACAM), and fusion with the Compound Animal Feed Manufacturers National Association (CAFMNA). The outcome of these unions was the United Kingdom Agricultural Supply Trade Association (UKASTA). Under this heading are now gathered grain merchants, seedsmen, compound animal feed millers, provender millers, agro-chemical suppliers, fertiliser merchants and many other businesses with interests in the UK domestic agricultural industry.

In 1955 NACAM decided to produce a grain contract suitable for all sectors of the internal trade—growers, traders and consumers. It took three years' work, at the end of which there was still not total unanimity but the contract was accepted by the National Farmers Union, flour millers, maltsters and animal feed manufacturers.

In the intervening years the contract has been adapted to keep in step with the demands of the UK trade, which has seen the cereal crop rise from six million tonnes to 26 million tonnes (the record harvest of 1984). In 1977 it became necessary to have one contract to govern purchases from growers, and another to cover merchant-to-merchant and merchant-to-consumer business, now known as the UKASTA grain contracts, numbers 1 and 2.

The GAFTA contracts covering export trade from the United Kingdom and Ireland are the number 79, effective from 1 February 1996, for cif trade (see Figure 22.2 on page 276), and the 79A for fob cargoes and 80 for general EC origins. The 79B was introduced in 1987 for use where grain is purchased directly from growers with the express intent of export. All UK contracts, whether under GAFTA or UKASTA terms, carry written-in details of the transaction, and the terms and conditions pertaining to it. They also contain explicit regulations concerning the use of arbitration procedures.

The arbitration requirements are governed by the UK Arbitration Acts of 1950, 1975, 1979 and 1996, and the latest Act became effective on 31 January 1997. These Acts govern the extent to which parties are free to define in their contracts the terms under which their dispute will be resolved in arbitration. All parties accepting these terms are bound to undertake conciliation by arbitration before resorting to the processes of the law to settle their differences. But there is nowadays very little access to the courts; arbitration is seen as the alternative to court action.

Under the disciplines of GAFTA and UKASTA the arbitration process provides for two stages in the proceedings. The first is undertaken by a tribunal of approved arbitrators, experienced persons with a wide knowledge of commodities, contracts and current trading practices. The proceedings are largely informal and the majority of cases are disposed of at this stage.

Lack of satisfaction by the decision of the first consideration, by either party, may result in a request for an Appeal Board hearing, conducted by five similarly qualified arbitrators, nominated by the Association under whose rules the business was conducted. Here again, proceedings are relatively informal to aid the prompt and efficient disposal of disputes.

Where GAFTA rules apply, Appeal Board members must be approved by GAFTA Appeal Committee. They are required to be "Qualified Arbitrators" as per the continuing professional development programme syllabus of GAFTA , and must have passed the appropriate examination of competency. An Appeal Board is a rehearing of the case, at which fresh evidence or new witnesses may be introduced. It is at the second stage that legal representation may be introduced, although parties resorting to lawyers are required to meet their own legal fees.

The immediate benefits of this arbitration system are that disputes are settled without the long delays that frequently accompany court hearings; the costs of the proceedings are relatively cheap and the findings are private, i.e. known only to the parties involved.

These features support the principle that any individual or company, however small, may feel able to challenge the large national and international trading companies without fear of punitive costs.

Other than by a transgression of the law of the land or by failing to provide suitable reasons for their decision, the decision of the arbitration panel is final. Dissenting arbitrators are not able to express their differing opinions on the award form. It is necessary that all arbitrators sign the award, even if it is arrived at by a majority decision.

Within Europe, commodity contracts have been developed to suit the requirements of individual states or large ports. Similarly, contracts have been raised to cover the trade from North America and Argentina as they have become major exporters. The Russians, too, have issued a contract to protect their interests as major buyers, while the Australian wheat and barley boards have contracts to cover their world trade. All bear a relationship to the original London contracts which governed international trade for so long and which did much to regulate and control the expanding activities of commodity trading around the world.

The Canadian Wheat Board has five contracts, one for each of the port areas. The accredited exporter, when he sells to his customer, utilises either the GAFTA or the North American Exporters Grain Association (NAEGA) contract. On UK sales it is basically the GAFTA contract and on others the NAEGA contract. The NAEGA contract recognises the Canadian Wheat Board in-store contract and has particular provisions covering the CWB contract.

Generally speaking, NAEGA, Canadian Wheat Board and other

similar contracts are for bringing the goods to the domstic ports, and then from there the goods are "carried" to destination on GAFTA terms. This is the case for most countries—i.e., GAFTA terms are used from point of export to importing country.

Examples of Canadian Wheat Board, GAFTA and UKASTA contracts are given in Figures 22.1, 22.2 and 22.3.

Fig. 22.1 The Canadian Wheat Board Bulk Export Grain Contract No. 3

The Canadian Wheat Board No. 3

BULK EXPORT GRAIN CONTRACT INSTORE CANADIAN ATLANTIC PORT(S)

Contract Date ―――――― 19 ――――――

Contract No. ――――――――――――――――

Winnipeg, Manitoba

Seller ――――――――――――――――

SPECIMEN

Buyer ――――――――――――――――

on the following terms and conditions:

1. **Grain sold:** ――――――――――――――――
2. **Quantity:** ―――――――――― tonnes subject to a tolerance not exceeding 5% more or less at Buyer's option, at contract price. (1 tonne = 2204.6226 lbs.). If the first delivery under this contract is for a quantity between contract minimum and contract maximum (both inclusive), no further deliveries shall be made. If this contract is to be executed by more than one vessel, the loading tolerance of 5% more or less shall apply on the difference between the mean contract quantity and the quantity that has been delivered on all prior vessels. Any further delivery which falls within this difference, plus or minus 5%, shall complete the contract.
3. **Grade (s):** ――――――――――――――――

   In Accordance with the grade(s) established under the Canada Grain Act in effect on the contract date.
4. **Quality Certification:** 'Certificates for Canadian Grain' issued by the Canadian Grain Commission at the port or ports of delivery shall be final as to grade.
5. **Definitions:** In this Contract
   - (a) **Call Period** - means the call period established pursuant to Section 12 and any extension thereof.
   - (b) **Contract Period** - means the contract period established by Section 11 and any extension thereof.
   - (c) **Delivery of the Grain** - means the delivery by the seller to the buyer of Terminal Elevator Receipts or Transfer Elevator Receipts for grain of the appropriate grade and kind issued by a licensed Elevator at the port/ports of delivery duly endorsed to the bearer or to the order of the Buyer.
   - (d) **Ports of Delivery** - means HALIFAX, Nova Scotia or SAINT JOHN, New Brunswick or both of them at the Seller's option.

SPECIMEN

6. **Seller's Option:** The Seller may deliver and the Buyer shall accept at the contract price grain of the same kind as that sold, having a level of excellence higher than that of the contract grade and if the grain is sold on a protein basis, having a protein content equal or higher than that of the contract grade.
7. **Delivery:** Instore in one or more elevator(s) licensed by the Canadian Grain Commission at one or two of the ports of delivery at the Seller's option, for each vessel nominated. The ports to be capable of handling the vessel.
8. **Price:** Canadian $ ――――――――
   per tonne, instore elevators at the port or ports of delivery.
9. **Terms of Payment:** Payment shall be net cash in Canadian Funds paid to the Seller at Winnipeg on or before the day named for delivery of the grain at a port or ports of delivery (as provided in Clause 13 (b), in exchange for delivery of the grain.
10. **Destination:** ―――――――――――――――― subject to Section 18.
11. **Period for Delivery of Grain:** Between the date of ―――――― and ―――――― both dates inclusive. This period to be known as 'CONTRACT PERIOD'.

SPECIAL PROVISIONS:

SPECIMEN

IN WITNESS WHEREOF the Buyer and the Seller have caused this contract to be executed on their behalf by this their proper officers this day of A.D. 19

THE CANADIAN WHEAT BOARD	THE ――――――――――
PER: ――――――――――	PER ――――――――――
Seller	Buyer - ACCREDITED EXPORTER

(SEE OVER) FOR CONTRACTUAL PROVISIONS OF THIS CONTRACT No. 12 TO 20

Source: The Canadian Wheat Board.

Fig. 22.2 GAFTA Contract No. 79

Effective 1st February 1996

No: 79

Gafta

CONTRACT FOR UNITED KINGDOM AND REPUBLIC OF IRELAND GRAIN

RYE TERMS - CIF TERMS

Date . . . .

SELLERS . . . .

INTERVENING AS BROKERS . . . .

BUYERS . . . .
have this day entered into a contract on the following terms and conditions.

1. **GOODS**- . . . .

. . . .

2. **QUALITY**-
SPECIFICATIONS: . . . .

NATURAL WEIGHT . . . . kilograms per hectolitre
at time and place of loading/discharge.

MOISTURE . . . . %

ADMIXTURE . . . . %

. . . .

* To be certified by . . . .
Certificate of inspection at time of loading shall be final as to quality.
* of fair average quality of the season's shipments at time and place of shipment, to be assessed upon the basis of, and by comparison with the Grain and Feed Trade Association's official F.A.Q. Standard of the month during which the bill of lading is dated. In the event of no F.A.Q. Standard being established by the Association, the arbitrator(s) shall in his/their discretion decide what is the fair average quality. An average sample of the delivery shall be taken and sealed jointly at port of discharge by the representatives of the Sellers and of the Buyers and shall be forwarded immediately to the Association for the purpose of establishing the F.A.Q. Standard. The expenses of such sampling and forwarding shall be paid half by the Sellers and half by the Buyers. Place of shipment under this contract shall be understood as the port or group of ports adopted by the appointed Standards Committee in making the Standard.
If the difference between the delivery and the F.A.Q. Standard shall not amount to 0.50% of the contract price, no allowance for quality shall be due; otherwise Buyers shall be entitled to the full difference in value.

*at time and place of shipment about as per sealed sample marked . . . . in possession

of . . . .
The word "about" when referring to quality shall mean the equivalent of 0.50% of the contract price.
In any assessment at arbitration of allowances for quality, due regard shall be given to any analyses under other guarantees. Difference in quality shall not entitle Buyers to reject, except under the award of Arbitrator(s) or Board of Appeal, as the case may be, referred to in accordance with the Arbitration Rules specified in the Arbitration Clause hereinafter appearing. The goods are not warranted free from defect, rendering the same unmerchantable, which would not be apparent on reasonable examination, any statute or rule of law to the contrary notwithstanding.
Shipment in good condition. Should the goods arrive out of condition, due allowance shall be made for the time of year in which the shipment took place. The fact of the goods so arriving shall not necessarily be sufficient proof of an improper shipment.

3. **FINALITY**- Where the natural weight, analysis for moisture and admixture or analysis for warranties/guarantees is to be determined by The Grain and Feed Trade Association or their appointed Analysts, or other accepted authority agreed by both parties, instructions to proceed shall be sent by the last Buyers to the Association, Analyst or accepted authority whichever is applicable within 21 days of final discharge of the ship at the last port of destination under this contract. The certificate

Source: GAFTA.
Note: Illustrative only. The remaining clauses 4-35 set out the normal GAFTA trading rules, and a full copy of the contract can be obtained from GAFTA.

Fig. 22.3 UKASTA Approved contract note for home grown grain

Grain No 1/91 (© UKASTA) April

APPROVED UKASTA CONTRACT NOTE FOR HOME GROWN GRAIN
Prepared by UKASTA in Consultation with the NFU of England & Wales
Suitable for Producer/First Buyer Transactions.
Issued by a Member of the United Kingdom Agricultural Supply Trade Association Limited

Date...

Buyer's Ref. .... Seller's Ref. ....

Sellers: ....

....

Buyers: ....

....

being the only two parties who have any rights whatsoever under this contract have this day entered into a contract whereby the Buyers agree to buy and the Sellers agree to sell grain not necessarily being the Sellers own produce, on the following terms and conditions:

1. **Goods sold on *Sample/*Description:** Contractual quality for each individual consignment as under:

Grain Type/ Variety	Min Specific Weight (kg/hl)	Max Nitrogen % (basis dry matter) Barley sold for Malting Clause to apply	Min/Max* Protein %	Min Germinative Capacity %	Min Hagberg Failing No.	Max Admixture (by weight) %	Max Sprouted Grains (by weight) %	Max Screenings (by weight) % (enter sieve size)	Hardness Min/Max* (Stenvert Value)

2. **Moisture:** Moisture shall not exceed ....% to be measured according to ISO 712 standard. If the Buyer's test shows moisture to be above this figure, the Buyer shall, at his option, have the right to reject the goods or to claim an allowance to be agreed. For malting barley, the scale of moisture allowances at present published by the Maltsters Association of Great Britain shall apply and this shall be varied only by mutual consent.

3. **Weighing Charge:** Weighing Charges of ....shall be for Buyers*/Sellers* account.

4. **Special Terms:** ....

....

....

5. **Drying:** Undried/dried or conditioned* ....

6. **Quantity:** About* .... tonnes OR between .... and .... tonnes*. Where the word 'about' is used in reference to quantity the Sellers shall have the option of delivering 5% more or less at contract price. Any quantity delivered in excess of 5% over the contract quantity shall be deemed a breach of contract and entitle the Buyer to reject the excess if he so wishes. If he does not so reject the price of any excess quantity, i.e. over 105%, shall be settled by mutual agreement or otherwise by arbitration. If the Seller fails to deliver 95% of the contract quantity he shall compensate the Buyer in accordance with the provisions of the Default Clause herein and calculation of damages will be against the mean contract quantity and not 95% of it (See also Intervention Clause).

7. **Price:** ....per tonne ex-farm/ex-store/delivered to* ....

.... (location)

8. **Period of Delivery:**..

9. **Payment Terms:** ....

....

THIS CONTRACT IS SUBJECT TO THE CONDITIONS ON THE BACK HEREOF SO FAR AS THEY ARE NOT INCONSISTENT WITH THE TERMS SET OUT ABOVE. (Whenever the word 'grain' is used, this is to mean goods of the contractual description).

*** Delete words which do not apply.** Signature ....

Source: UKASTA.

PART 5

Current developments and conclusions

CHAPTER 23

Forty years of the European Union grain market

The Treaty of Rome, which established the European Common Market, was signed in 1957. There were six founding members—Belgium, France, Italy, Luxembourg, Netherlands and West Germany. In 1972 they were joined by Britain, Denmark and Ireland; in 1981 by Greece, in 1985 by Portugal and Spain, and in 1995 by Finland, Sweden and Austria, making the present total of 15. Ten further countries—mainly in eastern Europe—are on the waiting list with negotiations having now (1998) just started.

A German historian, Ludwig Borne, once remarked of the Holy Roman Empire that its chief characteristics were that it was not an empire, not Roman and far from holy. One might be tempted to say of the European Union that it is not wholly European, nor is it a union, however much some of the politicians involved may desire it. But the Member States are inching along the communal road. As always in our troubled world, their failure and their problems are better publicised than their successes.

One of their first successes was the establishment of the Common Agricultural Policy. The leading plank in the policy was the regime for grain (the terms "cereals"—more usual in Europe—and "grains" are used interchangeably here). In the early hours of 14 January 1962 after nearly 200 hours of discussion the Council of Ministers approved 12 draft regulations on agricultural matters, among which was a regulation entitled "On the Progressive Establishment of a Common Market Regime for Cereals". This was the culmination of work set in train at the Stresa Conference, which had been convened under Article 43 of the Rome Treaty and took place in July 1958.

At that time the six Member States still fixed their own national grain prices—a common price was yet to come. It required the stimulus of a crisis to achieve this. The crisis was provided by the breakdown in the first negotiations for British entry into the Community: this, coupled with the need to adopt a common policy in the Kennedy Round of GATT negotiations, at which the Community for the first time spoke with one voice instead of six, made a supreme effort necessary.

There was, however, still the obstacle of a financial crisis which, in

1965, led to a walkout by the French. It was not until 1 July 1967 that the basic Regulation 120, "On the Common Market Organisation for Wheat", was adopted. It was far from perfect. French reluctance to place its reserve production in the common pool, coupled with German, Italian and Luxembourgeois resistance to lower support prices and hence lower farm incomes, made it inevitable that the common price level then adopted seems in retrospect to have been much too high. Nevertheless, at the same time, the Kennedy Round was successfully concluded, and the International Wheat Convention was signed, as well as the first International Food Aid Convention.

THE INTERNATIONAL GRAIN MARKET

Only two years of progress followed before the grains regime was threatened with breakdown owing to a devaluation of the French franc. Calamity was averted by the institution of "monetary compensatory amounts"—cross-border charges and subsidies designed to counteract the effects of currency fluctuations. This was a consequence of the lack of progress in adopting a common financial policy (Europe still does not have one) and was not due to the progress in harmonising agricultural policy.

One result of the increase in productivity which followed the setting up of the Community was an exodus from the countryside, 4.5 million people leaving the land for the towns in the decade 1958–1968. Inspired by Sicco Mansholt, the then Agricultural Commissioner, the Community took the first steps towards a socio-structural policy by which the social consequences of agricultural measures were considered as a problem in their own right.

The average size of farms in the Community was then about 10 hectares (25 acres), and over 80 per cent of dairy herds consisted of fewer than 10 cows, while half the Community's farmers were over 57 years old. Mansholt made the first efforts to control surplus production without provoking unrest and revolution.

The Mansholt Plan (Memorandum on the Reform of Agriculture in the EEC, 21 December 1968) was in advance of its time (it took another two decades for "decoupling' to become a respectable concept) and did not wholly succeed. It was not adopted because the financial outlay was considered too great. In a prophetic passage, Mansholt concluded his report: "This may seem a lot of money in absolute terms, but it must be compared with the foreseeable expansion that will occur in the overall expenditure already being incurred by the Community and the Member States unless agricultural policy is rapidly reshaped along new lines." His warning went unheeded.

In 1972–1973 two events profoundly influenced grain policy. The first was the Russian crop failure, and the massive "grain robbery" leading to expectation in the United States of a new export market almost unlimited in size and duration. The second event was the accession to the Community of the three northern members, all countries deficient in grain production. The main "sweetener" inducing the French to accept Britain into the Community was an expectation of new outlets for exports of French wheat. As a consequence of the "first enlargement" the net grain import requirement of the Community rose from 4 million tons in 1971–1972 to over 11 million tons in 1973–1974, the first full year of membership of the United Kingdom, Ireland and Denmark. Thus, the net grain import requirement increased by about 8 million tons (which cross-checks with the previous level of UK grain imports). The financial importance to the Community of being a net importer of grain is readily understood if one appreciates that a major source of Community revenue is derived from levies on agricultural imports; a major part of expenditure (when the dollar is strong) is incurred on subsidies on grain exports. Quite apart from the financial consequences of storing surplus grain, therefore, the subsequent transformation of the Community from major grain importer to major exporter has imposed an increasing strain on the Community budget.

A further development which caused problems was the success of the plant breeders in increasing wheat yields. These practically doubled—from 37.5 to 61.6 quintals per hectare—between the two extreme years of 1976, which was very dry, and 1984, when growing conditions were ideal. An additional complication was the amazing success of the Cambridge plant breeders in developing a new variety of wheat ("Maris Huntsman"), the yield of which was such that it threatened to displace the traditional varieties of French breadmaking wheats. Although a hard variety, this wheat was considered by millers to be unsuitable for breadmaking. However, the Chorleywood baking process developed by the Flour Milling and Baking Research Association (FMBRA) in Chorleywood, England, enabled a proportion of Huntsman and similar wheats to be incorporated in the bread grist suitable for loaves of the type demanded by consumers in the UK.

As a consequence of these developments a new price structure (known as the "silo system", since a graphic illustration of the respective prices resembled a grain silo) was adopted in 1977–1978 whereby the support prices for feed wheat, barley, rye and maize were placed at an identical level some 14 per cent below that for breadmaking wheat. This was the figure taken as the difference in yield between Huntsman and the bread wheats, and its purpose was to channel the lower-grade wheats into feed outlets and reduce input costs in the livestock sector. This purpose was partly frustrated by the availability of cheap imports of corn gluten feed from the United States and manioc from Thailand which substituted for grain in the animal feed ration. Using computer-based least-cost formulae, the compounders preferred such substitutes to grain. A possible outlet for Maris Huntsman in India and the Middle East, where it was ideal for making unleavened bread and chapatis, came to nothing owing to a sudden rise in Indian domestic grain production.

THE GRAIN SURPLUS PROBLEM

Production of wheat in the Community rose so fast in the years after the adoption of the higher-yielding varieties that, by 1980, for the first time the Community became a net exporter of grain. This would have occurred some years earlier had the Community not remained unable to produce more than about half its maize requirement. Self-sufficiency ratios for wheat and barley had already risen to 100 per cent by 1973–1974.

This had the inevitable effect of bringing the Community into conflict with the traditional grain-exporting nations and in particular the United States. The conflict was masked for a time by the coincidence of the grain embargo placed on the Soviet Union by the Carter Administration as a reprisal for the Soviet invasion of Afghanistan. This embargo was loyally supported by the European Community as long as it lasted (a fact for which the United States has never given sufficient credit to the Europeans), but was eventually frustrated when the Soviets switched to alternative sources of supply, particularly Argentina. The early 1980s saw a considerable expansion in EC wheat exports and a big reduction in its imports of coarse grains, particularly maize from the United States.

The resulting difficulties for US exports led to an intensification of competition for those financially viable markets which remained, mainly in North Africa. Differences of opinion arose over how to define "equitable market share" (the GATT phrase), but the situation was held for a time by an informal Community decision to limit wheat exports to 14 per cent of world trade (in all grains). After the record harvests of 1984, however, this self-denying ordinance became increasingly difficult to observe, as the United States embarked on its own Export Enhancement Programme.

In 1981–1982 the Commission moved to a new policy of setting production targets for grain, overstepping which would lead to financial penalties in the form of a reduced price for producers. At the same time, a gradual process of diminishing the gap between world grain prices and Community support prices was initiated—designed not merely to contain expenditure on export subsidies but also to lower input costs of feedingstuffs.

The exceptionally large 1984 crop (in which Community wheat

production actually exceeded that of the United States) led to fresh threats to the system, but proposals for reduced support prices were vetoed by the Germans. Increasingly restrictive proposals followed, raising the levy on producers and reducing the period during which intervention purchasing by state agencies would operate.

SUPPORT SYSTEM

The EC support system for grain production is based on three prices: (1) a target price which, like the US target price, is the notional return needed for an efficient cereal producer to give a reasonable margin of profit for his work and to encourage him to remain in production; (2) an intervention price at which government agencies will buy grain offered to them and thus provide a floor to the market; (3) a threshold price at which grain imported from non-member countries can enter the Community.

The first two prices are set by the Council of Agricultural Ministers—that is to say, by national politicians—and the third price is derived from the first by subtracting the cost of transport from Rotterdam to Duisburg (i.e. from the principal Community port to the area of greatest deficiency—it has been pointed out semi-seriously that since the enlargement of the Community the area of greatest deficiency is in fact Northern Ireland rather than Germany, but nothing has been done to alter the system). Derivation of the threshold price is considered a technical operation, performed by officials within the European Commission.

Just as non-member country imports of grain offered at world prices are raised to the threshold price by imposition of a variable import levy, so exports of Community grain are conversely subsidised down to world prices by an export restitution payment (which may approach, but never exceed, the amount of the import levy).

The progressive increases in grain production and the ever-increasing costs of disposal then caused the EC policy-makers to make it more difficult to sell grain into intervention, leaving a greater proportion of lower quality stocks to find an outlet on the domestic market at prevailing prices. Thus, grain could no longer be offered into intervention all the year round, but only for a limited number of months. The quality standards relating to moisture and other technical qualifications were also tightened up, while payment for grain delivered into intervention stores was delayed for up to 120 days instead of the normal trade terms of 28 days after the end of the month of delivery. The biggest change of all was the introduction in 1986–1987 of a co-responsibility levy, entailing a tax paid by producers when grain is first sold, on sales into intervention and on exports. This was a weapon which could be progressively used to discourage production until an acceptable balance between supply and demand was achieved. Production could also in theory be reduced by offering incentives to take land out of production, following the US example.

It may be noted, however, that despite the difficulties placed in the way of EC farmers selling grain into intervention, they managed to do so in quite large quantities in 1990–1991. Total intervention stocks at the end of that season on 30 June 1991 amounted to 18.6 million tons, including 10 million tons of wheat and 5.5 million tons of barley. Intervention stocks were expected to rise even higher during 1991–1992: the official EC forecast in autumn 1991 put them at 21.3 million tons, including 12.1 million tons of wheat and 5.7 million tons of barley.

To anyone entering the high-price EC support system from the former low-price UK system the experience was not unlike that of Alice on climbing through the Looking Glass. However, just as Alice found that in Looking Glass Land the rules of chess were always carefully observed, so too the CAP possesses a logic and symmetry of its own, eccentric though this must often seem to the observer.

An attempt to reform the Common Agricultural Policy was begun in February 1991 on the initiative of the then Commissioner for Agriculture, Ray MacSharry. He inspired a Community-wide debate based on a Commission "reflections" paper (COM(91)100) in February 1991. This concluded that production and intervention stocks were running out of control, that exports were becoming progressively more difficult, the environment was suffering, and that while budgetary expenditure was rising, farm incomes were dropping. In other words, it was a no-win situation.

In July of the same year the Commission came up with detailed proposals. As far as cereals were concerned, the prospects opened up were severe. As explained by David Roberts, Deputy Director General of Agriculture in DG VI (the Commission's Agricultural Directorate), at the Seventh International Grains and Oilseeds Conference in Brussels in November 1991, the centrepiece of the plan was a 35 per cent cut in cereal prices, compensated for by decoupled direct aids based on past yields in the region concerned. To qualify for this aid all but the smallest farmers were required to participate in a set-aside scheme covering, initially, 15 per cent of the area previously devoted to cereals, oilseeds and proteins. On proteins the same rate of compensation would be paid as for cereals. For oilseeds a higher rate would be paid so as to bring the notional total return on oilseeds to 2.1 times the return on cereals. At average Community yields the first 7.5 hectares of set-aside land would also receive the cereals compensation. The total area of each farm eligible for aid and subject to set-aside would be limited to a base area, i.e. the area previously sown to the qualifying crops and set-aside. And although this base area could be rotated around the farm, land not previously ploughed would not be eligible. For those looking for a detailed exposition of these Commission proposals the best source is a *Green Europe* paper entitled "The Development and Future of the Common Agricultural Policy", copies of which can be obtained from Directorate General X (Agricultural Information), of the European Commission in Brussels.

The proposals, which contained some elements of thinking reminiscent of the neglected Mansholt Plan, were seen as so radical a departure from the past thinking, inasmuch as they represented a switch from market support to direct subsidies and a reduction of Community prices to world levels, that they provoked a wide variety of reaction, ranging from the anguished British complaint that they discriminated against the large and efficient farmers who provide the greater part of UK production, to the German reluctance to contemplate price reductions. Others objected that essentially what was involved was simply a matter of replacing a hidden subsidy by an open one (if that were all that were involved it should have appealed to certain sections of British opinion, since that is very much what happened in the days before Britain joined the EC). The MacSharry Reforms, as they became known, were a step in the right direction, but it soon became clear that scientific and technical developments were going to increase production at a rate that outstripped the restraints imposed, and were quite inadequate to prepare the Community (or Union, as it became following the Maastricht Treaty) for the Fifth Enlargement due to be completed early in the twenty-first Century.

In consequence the European Commission was instructed by the Council of Heads of Government held in Madrid in December 1995 to submit opinions on the individual applications and to embark on a composite paper on enlargement, taking into account the budgetary implications. As a result the paper, known as Agenda 2000, was produced in July 1997, the main provisions of which are summarised in the following chapter.

CHAPTER 24

The fifth and final enlargement

To many, the European Union already seems large enough. It has been enlarged four times, and each time there are more headaches.

The European Union started as the European Economic Community in 1958 with six members. The United Kingdom and Denmark joined in 1972; Greece in 1981; Spain and Portugal in 1985; and Sweden, Finland and Austria in 1995.

Legislation has to be written in 11 languages. Taking decisions is laborious, and revising a decision already made is next to impossible. Why add more complications?

The driving force is politics, not agriculture. With the collapse of communism, no time must be lost in tying Central and Eastern Europe into a democratic capitalist framework. Politicians in Europe consider 10 more countries as candidates: Poland, Hungary, the Czech Republic, Slovakia, Slovenia, Romania, Bulgaria, Lithuania, Latvia and Estonia. Cyprus, Malta and Turkey are on another waiting list. Maybe one day, the states that make up the former Yugoslavia might want to enter. And it has to be remembered that the EU-15 now has a common frontier with Russia.

A European Union containing 25 members would create the most important economic body in the developed world, with 475 million inhabitants and a gross domestic product of 6,100 billion ECUS (1993 figures), or 126 per cent of the population and 102 per cent of the GDP of North American Free Trade Agreement members.

Enlargement was a topic in the EU Intergovernmental Conference in Amsterdam (known for convenience as Maastricht II). At a previous Heads of Government meeting in Madrid, the decision was taken that negotiations with the 10 countries of Central and Eastern Europe (CEEC-10), Cyprus and Malta should start six months after the conclusion of Maastricht II, which ended in mid-1997.

In Europe, it is envisaged that the negotiations will be finished in time for the transition to start in 2000, and total integration for all the CEEC will be completed by 2010. For agriculture total integration would consist of complete alignment of prices, deficiency payments, set-asides and quotas for milk and sugar. Nobody has forgotten that the next agricultural negotiations under the General Agreement on Tariffs and Trade are scheduled to begin in 2000.

Although from the viewpoint of existing members agriculture is a reluctant partner in the process, the European Commission under Franz Fischler has shown courage in adopting a positive attitude to enlargement. For their part, the CEEC-10 countries have shown themselves desperate to join, proving the truth of the old French adage "[t]here is always one who kisses while the other offers the cheek".

In 1994, the European Union commissioned from well known academics four reports on agriculture policy in the EU and Central and Eastern Europe and followed these up with a White Paper known as Agenda 2000, published in Strasbourg in July 1997. Other experts, including Claude Villain and Brian Gardner, have produced useful studies. These are the key documents for anyone wishing to analyse the situation. Part One of Agenda 2000 deals with the reform of the Common Agricultural Policy (CAP) in Section III, while Part II deals extensively with the Challenge of Enlargement.

ECONOMIC INDICATORS AND AGRICULTURAL PROBLEMS

If enlargement is to be successful, the current differences between the EU-15 and the CEEC-10 must be reduced. Otherwise, the pressures generated could lead to disaster.

Based on 1993 figures, the combined GDP of the CEEC-10 was only 3 per cent of the EU's, and *per capita* income was only 11 per cent. The CEEC-10 showed a sharp drop in production in the first years of transition from communism—production fell by 6.2 per cent in 1990—but production now is recovering, with a 3.6 per cent increase in 1995. Indeed, this growth rate is greater than the EU-15's 3.2 per cent increase. Agenda 2000 contains a table (reproduced here as Table 24.1) comparing basic data on the applicant countries of Central and Eastern Europe (CEEC-10) and the 15 EU Member States.

The Vienna Institute of Comparative Economics has estimated that by 2010 the most dynamic "newcomers" might outdo the "least performing" of the EU-15. Nevertheless, it is clear that the transition to a free market economy in the CEEC is operating at a different pace in the various states and that there is still a long way to go to catch up. The main structural problems result from disruption of production, switch in trade to the West from the former Soviet bloc economic system and the need to create proper financial, banking, administrative and judicial systems on Western lines.

In agriculture, the greatest difficulty probably consists of low

Table 24.1 Applicant countries of central and eastern Europe and EU Member States. Basic data, 1995.

	Area	*Population density*		*GDP at current market prices*			*GDP at purchasing power standards*			*Agriculture*	
	(1000 km²)	(millions)	(inh./km²)	(billion ECU)	(in ECU per head)	(in ECU per head as % of EU average)	(billion ECU at PPP rates)	(in ECU per head at PPP rates)	(in ECU per head as % of EU average)	(% of total Gross Value Added)	(% of empl.)
	1	2	3	4	5	6	7	8	9	10	11
Hungary	93	10.2	110	33.4	3,340	19	64.6	6,310	37	6.2	8.0
Poland	313	38.6	123	90.2	2,360	14	203.3	5,320	31	7.6	26.9
Romania	238	22.7	95	27.3	1,200	7	94.3	4,060	23	20.5	34.4
Solvak Rep.	49	5.4	110	13.3	2,470	14	38.0	7,120	41	6.3	9.7
Latvia	65	2.5	38	3.4	1,370	8	7.9	3,160	18	9.9	18.5
Estonia	45	1.5	33	2.8	1,850	11	5.9	3,920	23	8.1	13.1
Lithuania	65	3.7	57	3.5	930	5	15.3	4,130	24	9.3	23.8
Bulgaria	111	8.4	76	9.9	1,180	7	35.4	4,210	24	13.9	23.2*
Czech Rep.	79	10.3	130	36.1	3,490	20	97.2	9,410	55	5.2	6.3
Slovenia	20	2.0	100	14.2	7,240	42	20.1	10,110	59	5.0	7.1
CE-10	1,078	105.3	98	234	2,220	13	582.0	5,530	32	8.6	22.5
—in % of EU-15	*33*	*28*	*85*	*4*	*13*		*9*	*32*		*358*	*425*
Belgium	31	10.1	332	205.9	20,310	118	196.0	19,340	112	1.7*	2.7
Denmark	43	5.2	121	132.1	25,260	146	104.4	19,960	116	3.7*	4.4
Germany	357	81.5	228	1,845.2	22,600	131	1,556.8	19,070	110	1.0*	3.2
Greece	132	10.4	79	87.4	8,360	48	118.4	11,320	66	14.7*	20.4
Spain	506	39.2	77	428.1	10,920	63	518.8	13,230	77	3.7*	9.3
France	544	58.0	107	1,174.3	20,200	117	1,076.5	18,520	107	2.5*	4.9
Ireland	70	3.6	51	49.2	13,740	80	57.4	16,020	93	7.5*	12
Italy	301	57.3	190	831.4	14,250	83	1,036.8	17,770	103	2.9*	7.5
Luxembourg	3	0.4	157	13.3	32,370	187	11.9	29,140	169	1.5*	3.9
Netherlands	42	15.4	371	302.5	19,570	113	284.3	18,390	107	3.6*	3.8
Austria	84	8.0	96	178.4	22,180	128	155.5	19,320	112	2.4*	7.3
Portugal	92	9.9	108	77.1	7,770	45	115.2	11,620	67	5.1*	11.5
Finland	338	5.1	15	95.6	18,720	108	84.5	16,550	96	5.2*	7.8
Sweden	450	8.8	20	176.3	19,970	116	153.5	17,390	101	2.1*	3.3
United Kingdom	244	58.5	240	844.8	14,410	83	971.7	16,580	96	1.6*	2.1
EU-15	3,236	371.6	115	6,441.5	17,260	100	6,441.5	17,260	100	2.4*	5.3

* 1994

Notes:
- Exact compatibility of CEEC Statistical Institutes data with EU standards on statistics cannot be guaranteed.
- For calculating the per capita GDP data, the populations according to national account definition are used.
- Purchasing power parity (PPP) exchange rates are commonly used in place of official exchange rates to estimate relative standards of living. They therefore take into account cost differences between countries.

Sources: CEECs (Col. 1–10: Eurostat, based on data from the CEEC Statistical Institutes; col. 11: Statistical Yearbooks from the CEEC Statistical Institutes). EU Member States (Eurostat).

production rates and the inefficient use of resources in the CEEC-10. For example, although CEEC farmland is 44 per cent of that of the EU and the CEEC employs more agricultural workers than the EU (9.5 million or 26.7 per cent of the total workforce compared with 8.19 million or 5.7 per cent of the workforce), CEEC agricultural production in real value terms only amounts to 7 per cent of EU production. These figures may be slightly varied in the Agenda 2000 table, and will no doubt evolve as circumstances change and fresh surveys are produced during the course of entry negotiations.

These figures illustrate the chronic overmanning in CEEC farms, as well as the social problem of what will become of the surplus labour if farms are brought up to Western standards of efficiency; this problem would be especially acute if other economic sectors do not expand fast enough to absorb those displaced from agriculture. This indication of low living standards is most apparent in Poland, Romania and Bulgaria, while the Czech Republic and Slovenia more greatly resemble the West.

Another important problem consists of the absence or slowness of establishment of a proper system of land tenure and facilities for the transfer of land ownership. The disappearance of large collective farms (or their transformation into co-operatives), the end of consumption subsidies (raising prices and reducing demand) and changes in consumption (less livestock products) are additional complications.

PRODUCTION AND PRICES

Commodity forecasts of production and use for the EU-15 and CEEC-10 have been produced by the European Commission as a table in its White Paper. It must be emphasised that these projections. as far as the EU-15 is concerned, are based on a continuation of the current Common Agricultural Policy—described as the "*status quo*" option.

As seen in Table 24.2, the projections based on current trends show the CEEC grains deficit of nearly three million tonnes in 1959 will turn into a surplus of 11 million tonnes in 2010, with average grain yields in the CEEC at three tonnes per hectare compared with 4.9 tonnes per ha in the EU. Meanwhile, the EU's current exportable surplus of 29 million tonnes would almost double by the same year. This is a powerful argument for further reform of the CAP. Tables 24.3 and 24.4 show the relationship between wheat and maize prices in the EU-15 and CEEC-10. Only Slovenia has higher prices than the EU, although Latvia, and to a lesser extent Poland, were above world price levels in 1994. Support prices for wheat in Poland, Hungary, and the Czech and Slovak Republics ranged between 56 per cent and 73 per cent of those in the EU.

The European Commission's White Paper does not minimise the

Table 24.2 Grain supply balances (in million tonnes)

	1989	1994	2000	2000*	2005	2010
Production						
EU-15	188.5	171.3	187.5	–	202.0	217.6
CEEC-10	88.3	74.0	85.7	80.7	89.6	96.7
Domestic Use						
EU-15	159.3	154.5	157.5	–	160.4	163.2
CEEC-10	91.0	72.7	79.6	–	82.4	85.7
Ending balance						
EU-15	29.2	16.8	30.0	–	41.5	54.4
CEEC-10	–2.8	1.3	6.1	0.5	7.2	11.0

*Applying 15% set-aside.

Source: European Commission.

problems for the future and makes it clear that the CAP reforms have not gone far enough. It poses three possible lines of strategy for the EU, called Options 1, 2 and 3.

Option 1 is leaving the CAP as it is—the "*status quo*" mentioned above, which is dismissed for the reasons explained. Option 2 is radical reform of the CAP, including abolition of all supply management measures; this option is not favoured because of the social and environmental risks it would pose and the huge sums of additional public expenditures that would be needed.

The third option is to develop further CAP reforms in the direction of higher competitiveness, an integrated rural policy and simplification—for example, switching from yearly price support negotiations to a five-year framework on the lines of US farm legislation. Speaking in London

Table 24.3 CEEC-10 wheat prices compared with EU and world prices in 1994

	Domestic price ecu/tonne	*As per cent of EU price*	*As per cent of world price*
Poland	98	73	104
Hungary	75	56	80
Czech Republic	88	66	94
Slovak Republic	81	63	63
Slovenia	175	131	186
Romania	81	60	86
Bulgaria	54	40	57
Lithuania	60	45	64
Latvia	121	90	129
Estonia	75	56	80
EU	134	–	143
World	94	70	–

Source: European Commission.

Table 24.4 CEEC-10 maize prices compared with EU and world prices in 1994

	Domestic price ecu/tonne	*As per cent of EU price*	*As per cent of world price*
Poland	N/a	N/a	N/a
Hungary	72	52	97
Czech Republic	100	72	135
Slovak Republic	93	67	126
Slovenia	123	89	166
Romania	75	54	101
Bulgaria	71	51	96
Lithuania	N/a	N/a	N/a
Latvia	N/a	N/a	N/a
Estonia	N/a	N/a	N/a
EU	138	–	186
World	74	34	–

Source: European Commission.

in February 1996, Mr Fischler, the European Commissioner for Agriculture, made it clear that this is the preferred option.

Specific problems that will surface in the negotiations include the question of compensatory payments to producers, the so-called "arable aid" measures, by which EU farmers are currently paid large sums to make up for the reduction in support prices flowing from the GATT Uruguay Round. CEEC countries would dearly like their farmers to get this too, but the EU is adamantly saying "no way". No doubt, large sums in the end will have to be paid over to the CEEC countries on the ground of assisting restructuring and rural development. Mr Fischler, in an interview published in June 1998 in *World Grain* magazine in the USA made it clear that such payments would not be justified for farmers in accession countries who, unlike the EU-15 producers, would encounter price rises. Moreover, he said, direct payments to farmers in the candidate countries would involve the possibility of creating negative impact on the other socio-economic groups.

Lastly, debate remains in the EU-15 over whether the CEEC-10 are to be seen as customers or competitors. There is much anxiety among EU farmers at the prospect of being out-produced and out-sold by a restructured, low-wage agriculture in Central and Eastern Europe, which those with long memories recall used to be the "breadbasket of Europe". The Commission plays down those fears, pointing out that the European Union now exports more agricultural produce to Central and Eastern Europe than it imports from them.

Such consolation ignores the fact that much of the favourable EU balance is based on superior processing facilities, technology, sanitary and phytosanitary levels in the West and that the CEEC countries eventually will catch up—ironically enough, with EU financial help.

Moreover, the CEEC is only now beginning to return to 1989 production levels and has yet to achieve its full potential.

All in all, negotiations, when they take place, seem likely to contain bitter battles before they bring eventual accommodations.

CHAPTER 25

The US Farm Act

The 1996 US Farm Act, generally known by the acronym FAIR Act, from the full title "Federal Agriculture Improvement and Reform Act" was hailed as marking a fundamental reform of the US agricultural support system, in the eyes of US commentators. To understand the significance of this it is necessary to look back at a few decades of American agricultural history.

Much of US agricultural commodity policy dates back to programmes established in the Agricultural Adjustment Act of 1938, the Commodity Credit Corporation Charter Act of 1948, and the Agricultural Act of 1949 (the so-called permanent legislation). Originally, the programmes were designed to stabilise and boost farm income as a means of economic recovery and development in the Depression and post-War eras. Agricultural policies have been amended since then to address additional objectives, such as export promotion and environmental quality.

When the permanent legislation was enacted, one quarter of the US population lived on farms and agriculture employed almost 40 per cent of the labour force. Agriculture's direct contribution to GDP averaged around 7 per cent in the 1930s. Farm household incomes averaged about one third of non-farm household income. Farms were generally small and owner-operated. Most farms were mixed, or in American terms diversified, and produced some of a small number of principal crop and livestock commodities. In the 1930s, about 60 per cent of US farms produced corn and 40 per cent produced milk. Programme benefits were dispersed widely throughout the sector, even though supports were tied to only a few commodities.

In 1996, when the current Act was passed, agriculture contributed less to the general economy and even to rural America. And now only about 2 per cent of the US total population lives on farms. Production agriculture's direct contribution to GDP is around 1.5 per cent. Farm households, on average, have generally achieved income parity with all US households, primarily through off-farm employment. Farm households depend more on income from off-farm sources than on income from farming. Farms are now larger and more specialised, with 20 per cent of farm operations producing 80 per cent of total US agricultural output. Today, 26 per cent of US farms produce corn, while 7 per cent produce milk. Farmers now compete directly with non-farmers for inputs such as capital. They also compete directly with farmers in other countries, with over 25 per cent of the value of agricultural production exported and the equivalent of 8 per cent of US consumption imported. This may sound familiar to those who have studied the evolution of agriculture in Britain since the 1930s and even in other Member States of the EU since World War II.

Many farmers and policymakers felt that planting restrictions during the 1980s were particularly limiting. Programme acreage bases and deficiency payments were based on historical plantings, creating an incentive for farmers to maintain historical production patterns. Some farmers wanted to change the mix and level of crops they produced in order to comply with conservation requirements and to respond to market conditions. Legislation enacted in 1985 began to address this concern. In addition, many argued that the annual acreage reduction programmes, which idled US farmland and thereby reduced US crop production, provided an incentive for foreign competitors to expand their production, reducing US agricultural exports.

Increased concern over the Federal budget deficit strengthened pressure for agricultural policy reform. Farm programme costs were high and benefits were concentrated both geographically and among large-scale producers. Federal commodity programme outlays were also highly variable, ranging during the past decade from $7 billion in fiscal year 1995 to a record $26 billion in fiscal year 1986. As part of the effort to balance the Federal budget, these agricultural outlays were targeted for a seven-year cut of $13 billion from a 1995 Congressional Budget Office (CBO) forecast of 1996–2002 outlays that assumed a continuation of past programmes. This legislation was vetoed by the President in December 1995 and did not become law. Nonetheless, many features of the commodity programme provisions of the vetoed legislation remained largely intact in the 1996 Act.

The 1995–1996 market setting also contributed to the reform effort. High commodity prices weakened the case for continuing price and income support programmes. Many called for less government intervention to free producers from government regulations, particularly planting restrictions, and to allow them to respond to market signals.

Economic conditions in the US agricultural sector in the early 1980s led to a new direction in agricultural programmes, beginning with the Food Security Act of 1985 (the 1985 Farm Act). Previous farm legislation had been too rigid to allow US producers and exporters to adjust to changing world market conditions. Relatively high US loan rates in the early 1980s provided a floor for US and world market prices, which led to mounting grain surpluses in the United States, escalating programme costs, increasing foreign production and trade competition, falling exports and increased farm financial stress. I was myself engaged in research and lecturing at the University of Minnesota at the time, and well remember the crisis atmosphere in agricultural circles. Many farmers were in difficulty. Those in most difficulty were the medium-sized farms, some 40 per cent of the total, though accounting for only 20 per cent of production.

The medium farms were family-owned, reliant on their production for survival. Many of them had expanded in the prosperous 1960s and 1970s, borrowing to buy additional land at inflated prices and investing in buildings and machinery. The banks were happy to accept land as collateral.

But after reaching a peak in 1981 land values declined by 37 per cent over the next three years. Land values had remained extraordinarily stable over the long period between 1910 and 1970, but the bubble rapidly inflated after 1975, bursting suddenly in 1982. Small rural banks were obliged to foreclose on their debts to ensure their own survival, and many grain farms virtually ceased work for a year. Continental Illinois Bank recorded record losses of $1.1 billion in the second quarter of 1984 and was spectacularly bailed out by the US Government. This was the background to the 1985 Act.

The Act, in response, moved toward a more market-oriented farm policy that would enable farmers better to respond to market signals. The legislation inaugurated marketing loan provisions for upland cotton and rice lowered loan rates and provided discretionary authority for their adjustment, reversed upward trends in target prices, and generally froze programme yields.

The Export Enhancement Programme (EEP) was included in the 1985 Act as a means of competing with export subsidies of other countries, particularly those of the European Community. EEP was initiated in early 1985 under existing Commodity Credit Corporation (CCC) authority to promote US agricultural exports, and then was included in the 1985 Act.

The 1985 Act revived long-term land retirement by implementing the Conservation Reserve Programme (CRP), with a goal of protecting fragile cropland and improving water quality by retiring 40–45 million acres of highly erodable and environmentally sensitive cropland from production for 10–15 years.

The Food, Agriculture, Conservation, and Trade Act of 1990 (1990 Act), as well as the Omnibus Budget Reconciliation Act of 1990, built on the market-oriented foundation laid by the 1985 Act. By 1990, conditions in the agricultural sector had improved. Broader initiatives were under way to promote freer trade and to move US and world agriculture toward greater market orientation. Pressure to cut the Federal budget deficit also played an important role.

The main goals of 1990 farm legislation were to further market orientation, reduce government spending on agricultural programmes, help maintain farm income through expanding exports and protect the environment, to lower budget expenditures and introduce planting flexibility. Producers could respond to market signals in their planting decisions because they could plant alternative crops on the new 15 per cent normal flex acres that were not eligible to receive income support payments. This resulted in a further reduction in the portion of production covered by government payments, continuing the trend started in the 1985 Act. Marketing loan provisions were extended to wheat and feed grains, starting in 1993 under GATT trigger provisions of 1990 farm legislation. EEP was retained to help counter the export subsidies of other countries.

The 1996 Act fundamentally changed US agricultural programmes by eliminating supply management, increasing planting flexibility, and changing income supports for "contract crops" (wheat, corn, grain sorghum, barley, oats, rice, and upland cotton).

The 1996 Act changed income supports by replacing the target price/deficiency payment programme, which had been in place since the early 1970s, with a new programme of decoupled payments for seven years that are not related to most farm-level production decisions or market prices.

To receive payments and be eligible for loans on contract commodities, a producer would enter into a production flexibility contract for 1996–2002. That contract would require the participating producer to comply with conservation, wetland and planting flexibility provisions, as well as to keep the land in agricultural uses. Land eligible to enter into a contract includes land enrolled in acreage reduction programmes for any of the crop years 1991 to 1995, land considered planted under programme rules (certified acreage), or land that had been enrolled in the CRP that had a crop acreage base associated with it. Farmers would receive production flexibility contract payments for seven years. Payments would be based on enrolled contract acreage and not related to current plantings.

Cumulative outlays for 1996 Act contract payments for the fiscal years 1996–2002 are capped at $36 billion. Total contract payments would be lower, reflecting payment limitations. Payment levels are allocated among contract commodities according to percentages specified in the 1996 Act. These percentages are based on commodity shares of projected total deficiency payments for 1996–2002 from an early 1995 CBO baseline.

Annual contract payments under the 1996 Act are limited to $40,000 per person, a $10,000 reduction from the previous $50,000 limit on deficiency payments. Limits on marketing loan gains and loan deficiency payments are unchanged at $75,000 per person per crop year, and the three-entity rule is retained.

Also, planting flexibility was increased under the 1996 Act. Under past law there was a 15 per cent limit on planting flexibility without affecting deficiency payments. A producer's deficiency payments were reduced if more than 15 per cent of the farm's base acreage for a crop were planted to other crops, with an overall limit on flexibility of 25 per cent of base acreage. Additionally farmers were often required to idle a portion of their cropland under the annual ARP as a condition for receipt of deficiency payments.

An important provision of the 1996 Act was the expiry of the Acreage Reduction programme. Participating producers are now permitted to plant 100 per cent of their contract acreage plus any other cropland acreage on the farm to any crop with no loss in payments, as long as the producer does not violate conservation and wetland provisions.

The 1996 Act retained non-recourse commodity loans, in a modified form. Farmers could receive a loan from the government at a designated rate per unit of production (loan rate) by pledging and storing a quantity of a commodity as collateral. Loan rates for most crops continued to be based on 85 per cent of the preceding five-year average of farm prices, excluding the high- and low-price years. Maximum loan rates were specified in the new law for wheat, corn, upland cotton, soyabeans and minor oilseeds. The rice loan rate was set at $6.50 per cwt, its 1995 level. Corn, wheat and upland cotton loan rates were capped at their 1995 levels, while soyabean loan rates could vary between $4.92 (the 1995 loan rate) and $5.26 per bushel. Corn and wheat loan rates could be further reduced based on stock-to-use ratios. Loan rates for barley, sorghum, and oats were to be set taking into account their feed values relative to corn. Marketing loan provisions, allowing repayment of loans at the lower level of the loan rate plus accrued interest or market prices were retained, thus continuing some income protection at relatively low prices for the contract commodities and helping to limit accumulation of government-owned stocks as a result of collateral forfeited through defaulted loans.

The above summarises the provisions of the FAIR Act. Although it is less than two years old at the time of writing (1998) it is already possible to discern some of the consequences of the legislation. Speaking at the fortieth Anniversary congress of the European Grain Traders Association in 1998 Carroll Brunthaver gave some interesting insights.

He pointed out that as a result of the legislation there had been a significant shift in US crop acreages over the past three years. US corn acreage increased by 16 per cent, mainly due to the elimination of set-aside and stronger prices, but also because the US farmer has comparative advantages in corn production and continued to plant corn on former set-aside acreage although he had the option of shifting to other crops.

On the other hand US wheat acreage decreased by 11 per cent from 1996. Soyabean acreage, like corn, increased by 16 per cent, indicating that government schemes had been holding down soya acreage in favour of deficiency-paying programme crops. When farmers were allowed to plant soyabeans on previous programme crop acreage without losing benefit of government payments they compared net income from soya with net income from other crops rather than comparing net income from soya with net income from other crops that included government payment income.

It also became evident that some farmers had been planting wheat only to receive government deficiency payments, and with the freedom of the new legislation they turned to soya and sorghum. An Ohio State University study concluded that the acreage planted to Soft Red Winter Wheat in the US eastern corn belt would reduce by 50 per cent in the following 10 years. Another major finding is that rotation of crops as a consequence of the FAIR Act was assuming greater importance: enhanced fertilisation with higher yields was being reported on soyabeans planted following corn and on corn following soyabeans. Better weed control, better use of labour, and greater discretion to vary and delay planting intentions until the weather implications could be better assessed were also reported as substantial gains from the Act.

Brunthaver was emphatic in his conclusion from this brief experience of "freedom to farm"—namely, that government had no role to play in determining resource allocation in agriculture.

CHAPTER 26

Environmental considerations and biotechnology

Everyone will be familiar with the dustbowls of the Mid-west of America created in the 1930s by continuous cultivation, and publicised in John Steinbeck's *The Grapes of Wrath*. In the UK first stirrings were evoked by Richard Llewellyn's *How Green was my Valley*, which appeared in 1951 and was directed at the destruction of the South Wales countryside by the mining industry. Industrial detritus caused by mining and the decay of river banks (by the transition from water power for the textile mills to machinery in Yorkshire and Lancashire) caused criticism from those concerned with the countryside, but environmental questions concerning agriculture did not become a burning issue until the implications of the Common Agricultural Policy began to become evident in the 1970s.

In the UK the debate surfaced when "traditional" hedgerows began to be rooted out in the great cereal areas of East Anglia and Hampshire under the influence of mechanisation (which made the small enclosed fields of the mixed farms difficult to work with wide machinery). After entry into the European Common Market the rapid rise in cereal prices during the five-year period of transition from pre-1972 prices to full Community levels made intensive production of wheat and coarse grains a profitable occupation, and the environmental lobby denounced the profit motive as the cause for turning the fields of England into prairies reminiscent of the American Mid-west. That the hedgerows themselves only dated from the Enclosure Acts of the nineteenth century was not given much weight in this argument.

Nevertheless environmental issues attracted so much publicity with industrial pollution leading to the destruction of forests by acid rain—usually carried by the wind across frontiers and thus becoming an international problem—that the International Policy Council on Agriculture (IPC) devoted a series of conferences from 1992 onwards to the problem as it concerned agriculture.

The IPC is Washington-based, and its Council comprises members from 22 major agricultural countries of the world. It meets infrequently, but when it does Governments pay attention to its opinions. It is a major honour to be invited to speak at such gatherings, and scarcely less of an honour to be privileged to attend its sessions as a participating delegate. Attendance is not vast—but the mix is prestigious and the Chairman is Lord Plumb, formerly President of the European Parliament.

The first such conference, held in the Netherlands in 1992, dealt with the environment and agricultural trade, and whether the two faced conflict or could co-operate. Naturally the emphasis was on finding ways of co-operating. The problem seemed to present different aspects in developed and developing countries. In rich countries environmental problems arose through intensification and attempts to improve productivity; in poor ones they were the by-products of inadequate technology and population explosion. The Sahara desert, it was said, expanded annually by an area three times the size of the area of the Netherlands. This difference called for different solutions—in rich countries by a policy calling for "sustainable development" as defined by the 1986 Bruntland Commission and in poor countries by birth control, technology transfer and easier access to world markets.

In rich countries the principle of "polluter pays" seemed to be accepted, with a suggestion that farmers should be rewarded for taking positive care of the countryside. In poor countries, if the example of Zimbabwe was any guide, the question of pollution was simply not recognised as a problem for the foreseeable future. However there was a general recognition in developed countries that conflict over environmental questions was a real risk, and steps had to be taken to minimise it.

The second conference, held in France in 1995, posed the blunt question—"Is Agriculture a Threat to the Environment?". There was general acknowledgement that a risk existed, but it was thought that it must and could be controlled. It was pointed out that the fundamental task of agriculture was to provide food. It had done this with much benefit to the consumer. For example, in France 34 per cent of the household budget was spent on food in 1960, but only 18 per cent in 1990. It had to be remembered that in the next 30 years 50 per cent more food had to be produced to feed the increased world population and to relieve existing hunger. Agriculture also had to act as a source of renewable raw material for industry. The farmer's interest was to preserve the soil, and this had to be done without creating pollution. In France there were numerous research organisations covering water purity, chemical fertilisers, experimental farms all devoted to improving production while limiting pollution. The French Ministry of Agriculture advocated the maintenance of farmers through income support, relieving the necessity of intensive methods. They pointed out that an EEC regulation awarded a "grass premium", encouraged extensification and conversion of arable into pasture, etc.

In Japan the 2,000-year-old system of rice cultivation in paddy fields had been threatened by the discharge and accumulation of harmful metals and chemicals following the industrialisation of the 1970s and 1980s, coupled with an "inappropriate discharge of livestock manure". Measures were being taken to promote sustainable agriculture through soil management and fertilisation, planting and pest-control technologies. Problems of ageing farmers, depopulation of remote communities and neglected forests were being counteracted, not least by the promotion of "green tourism".

Some positive efforts by the non-food use of vegetable oils could be demonstrated by the production of "diester"—bio-fuel constituted from rapeseed esters. In France the inclusion of 5 per cent diester in conventional fuels was authorised by law, and the product exempted from payment of the gasoil tax. Many advantages were claimed—including the reduction of emissions of sulphur, carbon dioxide, hydrocarbons, and particles; reduction of the greenhouse effect and of acid rain, and prevention of the exhaustion of non-renewable resources.

In the EU the Single European Act of 1986 added a new "Title" on the environment; the Maastricht Treaty of 1992 contained an Article on agriculture and the environment; and the Agenda 2000 policy paper envisaged major changes in the structural funds, with greater emphasis on rural development and the rural environment. In the WTO the Marrakesh decisions of April 1994 included a declaration to begin a comprehensive world programme on trade and environment. But in resolving conflicts of interest in the developed world there was a need to recognise honestly the differences between agricultural production and the perceptions of the majority of the populace (who did not suffer from hunger), and hence great efforts should be made to inform public opinion.

A fresh source of controversy with environmental implications arose in 1998 with a debate on genetic engineering. This first attracted public attention with the cloning by British biologists of a sheep: the emotions awakened by this soon spread to the application of genetic modification to plants. At government level this became a live issue with the question of permitting the importation into the EU of US-produced sugar beet, maize and soya. In June 1998 the US Under-Secretary for Agriculture proclaimed that 10 per cent of the US corn (maize) crop was produced by biotechnology, and 14 per cent of the soya crop. These figures he said would rise to 20 per cent and 30 per cent in the following year.

Genetically modified organisms (generally known as GMOs) are plants, animals, and other biological agents altered by gene manipulation to improve performance or resist challenge. In the United States there appears to be more public acceptance than in Europe of genetic engineering where agriculture is concerned. There is of course a vast amount of money involved in securing popular acceptance of this process. Much publicity accompanied the launch in 1998 by the US firm

Monsanto of a £1 million campaign to persuade the British housewife that genetically-modified food products are what she wants.

The case for acceptance rests on the assertion that this is a process which started some time ago, that a number of food products such as courgettes, nectarines, tomato paste, etc., have been consumed without attracting attention or adverse effect, and all that is being done is to accelerate by a "one shot" technique evolution which could have occurred naturally over generations. In this way there is scope for improving the content of oilseed rape, the characteristics of wheat flour, or the starch in potatoes to make a better potato crisp. Also—and this is perhaps the most controversial point—plants can be modified to improve tolerance to herbicides and resistance to insects, viral disease, or fungal pathogens.

Proponents of GMO technology argue that the only way to feed future generations and save the world from hunger is by the accelerated approval of GMO crops with their improved yields and better resistance to disease and tolerance of herbicides. According to this view, weedkiller-resistant crops require less herbicide than conventional crops and make possible low-tillage or no-tillage systems of agriculture. Some enthusiasts are already hailing it as the basis for the third agricultural revolution.

Opponents, numbering amongst their ranks the Prince of Wales, who is concerned that GM oilseed rape and sugar beet are tolerant of Roundup (the herbicide marketed by Monsanto, which leaves fields sterile for wildlife), and the international Greenpeace movement, base their case on the need to wait until thorough testing has shown that there are no unexpected side-effects from the use of GMOs, no transgenic risks, etc. They argue that it is a qualitative and moral leap into the dark with unknown consequences for human health and the ecological balance. There may be little risk of a major problem, they say, but the feeling is that not enough is known and that if something does go wrong we will be faced with the problem of clearing up a kind of pollution which is self-perpetuating. There is also a fear of big-business dominance of the market-place.

A great deal rests on the adequacy of scientific techniques proposed for screening the processes. In the UK, GMOs must undergo a well-established regulatory system with official ramifications which are extensive and often, to the layman, bewildering. The system's existence is the essential prerequisite to public health and environmental security, but its very complexity makes for a large degree of public uncertainty. The Austrian and Luxembourg Governments have refused to accept GMOs in any form—and there is a certain suspicion of such developments in France, Germany and, to some extent, Britain. The Labour Government, when in opposition, took a negative attitude to imports of GM maize because of fears of transmission of antibiotics resistance via animal feed to humans. On the opposing side, some Heads of

Government have already been in action. Opening the 1997 ANUGA food fair in Cologne, German Chancellor Helmut Kohl pronounced definitely upon GMOs: "[t]he prejudice of the EU public against food products containing GMO material must", he said, "be overcome".

Almost simultaneously the international environmental pressure group Greenpeace was telling the British press that Doomsday results of genetic engineering were already loose and uncontrollable in the environment. It made some small stir in the newspapers. Food, its price, supply and quality, is always news. At the same time the then UK Minister of Agriculture, Dr Jack Cunningham, was insisting upon the safety of GMOs, whilst suggesting that the final consumer be allowed to choose between products produced with GMO and non-GMO techniques. In many cases however this would be a practical impossibility, as the US demonstrated when mixed soya meal from GMO/non-GMO sources was released.

Under such circumstances someone has to sort out scientific fact from public perception, let alone fiction and, in the UK, that task largely falls to the number of small groups of experts, inevitably highly qualified in a wide range of scientific disciplines, working under a variety of acronyms and abbreviated titles. Their activities are rarely reported and their names are generally unknown outside their own close professional circles.

The most immediately involved with biotechnology and GMOs are the Advisory Committee on Genetic Modification (ACGM), the Advisory Committee on Releases to the Environment (ACRE), the Advisory Committee on Novel Foods and Processes (ACNFP), the Food Advisory Committee (FAC) and the Advisory Committee on Pesticides (ACP). All are independent bodies, their members chosen from among top people in their respective disciplines. Their advice and recommendations are available interdepartmentally, but their secretaries are provided by individual ministries.

In the case of ACGM, administration is done by the Health and Safety Executive which, via the Health and Safety Commission, answers to the Secretary of State for the Environment on matters concerning the "contained" development of GMOs; ACRE has a somewhat wider remit, advising the Department of the Environment, Transport and the Regions (DoETR) direct on the deliberate release into the environment of GMOs for scientific or commercial purposes.

The debate is presented by those in favour of GMOs as one of scientific progress against emotional reaction. Their opponents plead for caution and more extensive trials before, as they put it, "letting the genie out of the bottle" with irreversible consequences.

CHAPTER 27

Future trends and the demographic time-bomb

Forecasts can only look forward some five years with any validity: to peer further into the future is crystal-gazing.

Even forecasts can go horribly wrong through unexpected contingencies, usually stemming from unreasonable behaviour by the weather or world politicians. How has El Niño influenced harvests this year, and what startling changes will result from its action in future years? And who, to give another example, could have foreseen the winterkill in the Soviet Union in 1963–1964 which forced the Russians to slaughter much of their livestock and caused them to resolve on the astutely managed "great grain robbery" next time the harvest failed a decade later? Or the droughts in 1976–1977 which concealed the transformation of the United Kingdom into an important grain exporting country, the same weather in 1980 which impelled the United States to place an export embargo on soyabeans—an act which they still find hard to live down—or the droughts of the late 1980s which did more to reduce overhanging stocks of corn and soya than any government action?

More significant still, the invasion of Afghanistan on Christmas Day 1979, ordered by Brezhnev, which provided an illustration of the (unsuccessful) use of grain as a strategic weapon by the United States, and resulted in a far-reaching diversification of their sources of supply by the Russians. Finally, the apocalyptic events of 1989–1991, which included the measures to transform the economies of Eastern Europe from a system of central planning to one of the free market; the Gulf War, which disrupted the pattern of grain trading in the Middle East; and the disintegration of the Soviet Union and the banning of the Communist Party, with consequences which cannot still be predicted with certainty. One does not even know whether some of these recent events may yet be reversible.

Basically, the early chapters of this book show how grain production has been on a rising trend over the last two decades, and stocks have shown a cyclical pattern with successively higher peaks, followed by even greater declines, so that by the end of 1996 we saw the lowest level of stock-to-use ratio and the highest levels of prices since 1961. Since then stocks have recovered while prices have declined again with the withdrawal of the former Soviet Union from the market and the introduction of the FAIR Act in the USA.

Trade expanded extremely quickly in the 1970s (it doubled) and subsequently entered a period of erratic variations. See Tables 27.1 and 27.2. Much the same can be said of rice, though the fluctuations are greater.

As far as grain is concerned, world prices have for the greater part of the time been disastrously low, placing a heavy burden of subsidy on the treasuries of exporting nations while stultifying the growth of domestic agriculture in developing importing countries. Officials have swung from predictions of famine to preoccupation with surplus disposal. Internally, governments have fought a losing battle to preserve the economic viability of their own farmers, while placing the blame for failure at the door of obstinate or aggressive foreigners. Externally, this resentment has manifested itself in barely concealed antagonism in international negotiations.

The problem of bringing supply and demand into balance and thus restoring a reasonable grain price can of course be solved in two ways either by increasing effective demand, or by restraining production. The first is a matter for the finance ministers of the world, who have up to the present shown very little capacity for dealing with it: in Europe the finance ministers of the Fifteen cannot even agree on a common financial policy or common financial institutions—if they were ever to do so we should hear less about the high proportion of the Eurobudget appropriated by the only existing common policy, that of agriculture.

The second can only be dealt with in the immediate future by some more sophisticated system of supply management than exists at present: this is of course anathema to liberally-minded governments and parsimonious treasuries, who much prefer to exercise policy through prices since it costs them less in terms of administration and manpower. Set-aside or acreage reduction has worked tolerably well in the United

Table 27.1 World wheat production, consumption, ending stocks and prices, 1966–1998

Period	*Production*	*Consumption*	*Ending Stocks*	*Prices ($/t)*
Average 1966–75	328	325	90	95
Average 1976–85	449	441	133	147
Average 1986–95	536	542	134	144
1974	355	356	81	161
1995	536	552	99	185
1998	592	599	127	127

Source: IGC.

Table 27.2 World coarse grains production, consumption, ending stocks and prices, 1966–1998

Period	*Production*	*Consumption*	*Ending Stocks*	*Prices ($/t)*
Average 1966–75	583	581	90	80
Average 1976–85	743	732	144	116
Average 1986–95	804	814	149	107
1974	623	613	90	128
1995	778	819	95	152
1998	905	901	135	103

Source: IGC.

States, though they understandably feel that the more land they take out of production the greater the opportunity for their rivals to usurp their place. It works less well in Europe, due to the higher population density and the environmental difficulties resulting from its all too visible effect. At some stage it may be necessary to introduce quotas for grain production—a most unpopular word. Nobody likes the idea of quotas, which must be saleable to work, and hence create an artificial asset, but after the initial trauma of installation they have restored a semblance of prosperity to the dairy sector in Europe. Modern satellites have made surveillance a simpler matter than employing an army of inspectors (aerial photography has long been used in France for measuring cereal yields): the late John Cherrington, whose wisdom introduced agricultural common sense into the pages of the *Financial Times*, accepted that they were probably inevitable. It is essential to recognise in farming that though there is a continuous process of change, things cannot be changed too fast. But unless production and effective demand can be reconciled we could face the awkward situation of a world "awash with grain", in the words of an American writer, but awash in some places while others are left high and dry, not through lack of demand but through lack of the wherewithal to finance its importation.

The major preoccupation in external relations has been the outcome of the Uruguay Round. Negotiations were unduly protracted because the United States started with unrealistic demands for the total abolition of agricultural subsidies over 10 years: the EU position can best be summed up by saying that it wished everyone else would go away. The problem for the United States is to preserve an export trade which grew up on the back of the events of 1972–1973, coupled with unwise exhortations to plant "from fence-post to fence-post", and over-investment in export capacity in the belief that the expansion of exports would never stop. For the EU the difficulty has been to reform the Common Agricultural Policy and get away from the high-price structure with which they were saddled for political reasons at its inception without ruining their farmers in the process.

Though this is now forgotten, the CAP was immensely successful in its early years, not only in restoring production after the years of war but in helping to preserve political stability in countries where there was a risk of Communist takeover. Lorenzo Natali, speaking in Stresa in October 1983, talked of the "miracle" of the CAP. From the social point of view there are probably more reasons for explaining why the CAP cannot be reformed than for saying how it can be. It went wrong when expenditure ran out of control, and when its export successes provoked the envy and antagonism of more extensive producers and exporters. The Americans constantly assert that they are not out to destroy the CAP: none the less their success in spending the Russians into the ground in defence matters must give them cause to believe that the same tactic could have advantages in agriculture, and the aggressive use of the Export Enhancement Programme and the introduction of the FAIR Act has shown that they mean business.

There will eventually be an agreement, or an agreement to disagree, in the next WTO Round, negotiation of which is due to start in 1999. To achieve agreement there must be far greater contact at the professional and at the informal level, as well as strengthening the existing system of official exchanges. European farm organisations should talk more to American farm organisations, check figures together and discuss what the target is. They should assess what threats are genuine and what are not. The first point to recognise is that what divides us is of less importance than what unites us. In CAP Reform, though not in WTO negotiations, time is on our side. Farming pressures will ease in Europe as the older farmers retire and as the younger ones diversify and supplement their income from other sources. It used to be said of General Franco that he only kept two trays on his desk—one labelled "problems that time will solve", and the other "problems that time has solved", and periodically he would transfer files from the first tray to the second.

The grain exporting nations will then have to worry about the likely consequences now that the Russian demand for imported grain has collapsed, and if the Western will to finance continuing exports to developing countries who cannot afford to pay for it were to evaporate. They will also have to worry about the possibility that the East European countries, once let into the EU, could turn over the years from clients to competitors, and whether the interests of domestic producers, whether of grains, beef or soft fruit, take precedence over the need to allow these democratic countries the opportunity to earn hard currency and develop their own market economies.

As regards rice, the most important issue is whether or not Japan can be prevailed upon to allow substantial imports of rice. Were the Japanese Government to permit this fully it could open up a completely new world market. Japanese rice prices are hugely inflated to support a very large number of part-time farmers, and there was great pressure from the United States in particular to liberalise trade in the context of the Uruguay Round. This pressure proved partly successful, and a tentative attempt was made by Japan to allow limited rice imports. Were the gates to be opened fully, quantities of rice would pass from California and Australia to Japan, and Japanese traders have already been buying into Californian companies in anticipation of this (buying into Australian businesses is not so easy since they are largely controlled by co-operatives). Thailand does not stand to benefit to the same extent, since the Japanese do not eat long grain Thai rice. However, the resistance to such a development is perhaps stronger than realised, since, in Asia rice is regarded as almost sacred. A Chinese colleague tells me that in China, especially in the south, the words "Have you eaten rice today?" are commonly used as a greeting, where Westerners might say "How are you?".

Further developments to look out for are the progress of the fight over genetically modified seed (see the previous chapter) and a further phase in the green revolution. The problem here is of insect damage and plant disease and their prevention. The traditional varieties of rice had over time developed resistance to disease and to extremes of temperature, whereas the new and higher-yielding varieties are more susceptible. Furthermore the new varieties are more prone to damage by insects (especially brown hoppers). Nobody can at present say whether a breakthrough will come in finding a solution to these difficulties, still less whether any solution would be permanent.

In the long run the most critical problems facing the world grain economy may well be the result of demographic factors.

Since Thomas Malthus wrote his *Essay on Population* a century and a half ago (when the world population was about 1,000 million), it has been impossible to ignore the risk that the race between growth in population and growth in food production might end in extensive famine. The United Nations has addressed the question of population growth and economic development seriously and continuously through its Population Division since World War II. Milestones in their studies were the World Population Conference at Bucharest in 1974 and the International Conference on Population at Mexico City in August 1984.

Although some countries (e.g. Afghanistan and Ethiopia) have never held a census, the broad figures of population growth and future projections are not in dispute. According to UN statistics, world population, which stood at 1,600 million in 1900 and 2,400 million in 1950, grew to 3,700 million in 1970, 4,400 million in 1980, and 5,176 million in 1995. Projections are for it to increase to 6,000 million in the year 2000 and over 8,000 million by 2025 (i.e. less than 40 years on). The figure may be stabilised at around 10,000 million by the end of the twenty-first century but this hypothesis depends on the drop in the birth-rate in China achieved by methods which may not be possible elsewhere.

However these figures conceal variations. It is estimated that 92 per cent of population growth over the years 1975 until 2000 will take place in developing countries, and this will raise their populations from 3,000 million in 1980 to 5,000 million in 2000. Examples comparing 1995 with 2025 include Kenya rising from 28 million to 63 million, Ethiopia from 55 million to 127 million, Malawi from 11 million to 28 million, Nigeria from 111 million to 238 million, Haiti from 7 to 11 million, Brazil from 162 million to 230 million, India from 936 million to 1392 million, Pakistan from 140 million to 284 million. Can our planet support these increases, and if not what is to be done?

A definitive method of assessing the earth's carrying capacity has not yet been agreed. The simple figure of dividing total land area (150 million square kilometres including Antarctica) by total population gives about 30 persons per square kilometre. But this is not a very significant guide. The FAO method—in collaboration with the World Health Organisation—takes the minimum calorie requirement for a working male as 2,380 calories per day. A formula of calculating the food production potential of arable land in calories gives a rough index of carrying capacity at three levels of input technology (low, intermediate and high) ranging from hand labour to complete mechanisation. Applying this formula to the five regions of the globe and assuming that there would be unrestricted movement of food surpluses, the FAO found that with the exception of South West Asia, all regions could meet the food needs of their people in the year 2000 using intermediate inputs (i.e. pesticides, fertilisers and improved crop varieties).

But if it were assumed that there was no movement of food from one country to another but only within each country, it was found that with low-level inputs (e.g. as at present in much of the developing world), 65 countries with a total population of 441 million people would have domestic food shortages by the year 2000. The World Population Plan of Action arising out of the 1974 Bucharest Conference placed its faith in economic development as the best contraceptive. By the Mexico City Conference of 1984, however, it was recognised that a mere transfer of technology from the developed to the developing world would not resolve the problem of shortages. The fact is that poverty and rapid population growth reinforce each other, and unless the demographic factors receive more attention the problem—with all due deference to crystal-gazing—may outstrip the capacity of the world grain economy to meet the needs of humanity. One should not forget, moreover, that ecological considerations—particularly restrictions on the use of fertilisers and chemicals—could soon limit the world's production capacity for grain. Even countries like India and Pakistan now use large amounts of fertiliser to maintain their yields, and consume a great deal of energy (oil) in agricultural operations, irrigation systems, grain drying, etc. Oil prices are currently (1998) as low as they have been for years, but should oil prices rise seriously it could be a critical problem to keep up with world food demand.

APPENDIX 1

World grain export terminals

COUNTRY/ PORT	TERMINAL NAME	PHONE	FAX	BERTH/DOCK LIMITATIONS
ARGENTINA				
Bahia Blanca	Cargill Saci Berth	(54) 91 573 299	(54) 91 573 299	Length 270m, Draft 13.7m, spout outreach 30m
Bahia Blanca	Glencore/Toepfer UTE	(54) 91 72 332	(54) 91 72 360	Length 360m, Draft 13.7m, spout outreach 30m
Bahia Blanca	Moreno Brothers	(54) 91 553 631	(54) 91 553 631	Length 270m, Draft 12.2m, spout outreach 20m
Bahia Blanca	Pier Nos 5/6 and 7/8	(54) 91 573 035	(54) 91 71728	Length 300m, Draft 9.1m, spout outreach 20m
Bahia Blanca	Pier No 9	(54) 91 573 035	(54) 91 71728	Length 294m, Draft 13.7m, spout outreach 20m
Buenos Aires	ENCYM Berth	(54) 1 313 0347	(54) 1 313 1341	Length 250m, Draft 9.1m, spout outreach 20m
Buenos Aires	Terbasa Basin D	(54) 1 311 3598	(54) 1 311 8031	Length 770m, Draft 9.8m, spout outreach 22m
Diamante	Puerto Diamante Elevator	(54) 43 981 378	(54) 43 981 645	Length 160m, Draft 9.1m, maximum Loa 260m
Necochea	ACA Elevator	(54) 262 37980	(54) 262 37985	Length 260m, Draft 11m, spout outreach 13m
Necochea	Terminal Quequen SA Piers 4/5	(54) 262 26158	(54) 262 26159	Length 300m with dolphins, Draft 11m, spout outreach 13m
Necochea	Terminal Quequen SA Pier 6	(54) 262 26158	(54) 262 26159	Length 180m, Draft 11m, spout outreach 13m
Ramallo	Puerto Ramallo Elevator	(54) 407 42273	(54) 407 41245	Length 57m between two 20m wide outriding dolphins providing maximum 145m Loa, Draft 7.7m, spout outreach 20m

EQUIPMENT AND HANDLING RATES	LARGEST VESSEL/CARGO	STORAGE FACILITIES	OPERATOR/ OTHER DETAILS
Three loading spouts, total 1000tph capacity	MEGA HILL, 35,000 tonnes	60,000 tonnes silo capacity	New facility built 1994, Cargill
Four loading spouts, total 650tph capacity	CAPTAIN VENIAMIS, 89,100 tonnes	120,000 tonnes silo	Glencore/Toepfer
Four loading spouts, total 600tph capacity	TOMIS FUTURE, 30,400 tonnes	150,000 tonnes silo capacity	Oleaginosa Moreno Anos
Eight loading spouts, total 600tph capacity	Not indicated	120,000 tonnes silo capacity	Terminal Bahia Blanca SA
Five loading spouts, total 1000tph capacity	POINT CLEAR, 85,000 tonnes	Not indicated	Terminal Bahia Blanca SA
Five loading spouts, total 1000tph capacity	Less than Panamax, up to 45,000 tonnes	14,000 tonnes for grain and by-products	ENCYM
Six shipping lines with 27 loading spouts and 10 bagging lines, total 2000tph bulk loading capacity	Not indicated	175,000 tonnes silo capacity	Terminal Buenos Aires SA
Two loading belts feeding any two of six fixed position loading spouts, total 1000tph capacity	AKOBA, 24,000 tonnes	50,000 tonnes silo capacity	Puerto Diamante SA/ Continental
Three loading spouts, total 750tph capacity	LINDA, 42,000 tonnes	80,000 tonnes silo capacity	Terminal modified 1994, Asociacion de Cooperativas Argentinas CL
Four loading spouts, total 1200tph capacity	EL ADJAR, 40,000 tonnes	80,000 tonnes silo capacity	Terminal modified 1993, Terminal Quequen SA
Seven loading spouts, total 1200tph capacity	EL ADJAR, 40,000 tonnes	80,000 tonnes silo capacity shared with Piers 4/5	Terminal modified 1993, Terminal Quequen SA
Two loading belts and rotating loading spouts, total 500tph capacity	PATMOS, 32,780 tonnes	18,000 tonnes silo capacity	Puerto Ramallo SA

COUNTRY/ PORT	TERMINAL NAME	PHONE	FAX	BERTH/DOCK LIMITATIONS
Rosario	Genaro Garcia Elevator	(54) 30 1530	(54) 30 1530	Length 140m, Draft 9.1m, spout outreach 22m
Rosario	General Lagos Elevator	(54) 402 90182	(54) 402 90185	Length 140m, Draft unrestricted, spout outreach 25m
Rosario	Punta Alvear SA Berth	(54) 92 1964	(54) 92 1965	Length 250m, Draft 9m, spout outreach 25m
Rosario	Elevator Unit III	(54) 39 3198	(54) 39 3198	Length 200m, Draft 9.1m, spout outreach 20m
Rosario	Elevator Unit VII	(54) 82 4695	(54) 82 4695	Length 287m, Draft 8.8m, spout outreach 21m
Rosario	FACA Unit I	(54) 30 8111	(54) 30 8111	Length 170m, Draft 7m, spout outreach 15m
San Lorenzo/San Martin	ACA Berth	(54) 476 22225	(54) 476 22225	Length 184m, Draft 13.1–13.7m, maximum Loa 290m, spout outreach 25m, access channel limited to 11m
San Lorenzo/San Martin	Dempa Berth	(54) 476 29048	(54) 476 22045	Length 190m with four fendered dolphins, Draft unlimited, spout outreach 15m
San Lorenzo/San Martin	El Transito Berth	(54) 476 29130	(54) 476 29166	Length 150m, Draft unlimited, spout outreach 20m
San Lorenzo/San Martin	Nidera SA Berth	(54) 476 29147	(54) 476 29162	Length 150m with four fendered dolphins, Draft 13m, spout outreach 22m
San Lorenzo/San Martin	Quebracho Elevator	(54) 476 29049	(54) 476 29057	Length 150m, Draft 9.1m, spout outreach 25m
San Lorenzo/San Martin	Terminal 6 Berth	(54) 476 29038	(54) 476 29011	Length 170m, Draft 12m, spout outreach 30m

EQUIPMENT AND HANDLING RATES	LARGEST VESSEL/CARGO	STORAGE FACILITIES	OPERATOR/ OTHER DETAILS
Two loading belts feeding any two of five loading spouts, total 1600tph capacity	UNITED VENTURE, tonnage not indicated, Loa 244m	70,000 tonnes silo capacity	Terminal modified 1996, Genaro Garcia SA, leased to Cargill
Three telescopic loading spouts fed by one 1000 tph loading belt	AKOBA, Loa 255m	103,000 tonnes silo capacity	Terminal modified 1992, operator Louis Dreyfus
Loading gallery with two inclined belts and three telescopic spouts, total 2000tph capacity	MEGADDLE, Loa 268m, 26,250 tonnes	250,000 tonnes silo capacity	Productos Sudamericanos SA/La Emiliana
Two loading belts feeding two spouts, total 1600tph capacity	Not indicated	88,000 tonnes silo capacity	Servicios Portuarios SA
Seven vertical silos each has individual telescopic loading spout, total 1200tph capacity	EPTALOPHOS, Loa 262m	80,000 tonnes silo capacity	Servicios Portuarios SA
Three loading belts and spouts, total 1000tph capacity	Loa 242m	18,000 tonnes silo capacity	Federacion Argentina de Cooperativas Agrarias
Two belt loaders feeding four spouts, total 2000tph capacity	VAPOUR LEADER, Loa 263m, 38,400 tonnes	240,000 tonnes silo capacity	Asociacion de Cooperativas Argentinas CL
One loading belt and fixed position spout, total 500tph capacity basis heavy grains	Loa 250m	90,000 tonnes silo capacity	La Plata Cereal SA
One loading belt feeding three spouts, total 1000tph capacity	30,000 tonnes	60,000 tonnes silo capacity	Alfred C Toepfer
One loading belt feeding four spouts, total 1200tph capacity	Loa 256m, 30,400 tonnes	266,000 tonnes silo capacity	Nidera SA
One loading belt feeding three spouts, total 1000tph capacity	Loa 275m, 39,800 tonnes	540,000 tonnes silo capacity	Cargill Saci
Two loading belts feeding four spouts, total 1000tph capacity	Loa 276m, 40,000 tonnes	400,000 tonnes silo capacity	Consortium of six operating companies

COUNTRY/ PORT	TERMINAL NAME	PHONE	FAX	BERTH/DOCK LIMITATIONS
San Lorenzo/San Martin	Vincentin Elevator	(54) 476 22612	(54) 476 22612	Length 140m, Draft 12.2m, spout outreach 25m
San Nicolas	San Nicolas Elevator	(54) 415 60002	(54) 415 60002	Length 163m, Draft 12.2m, spout outreach 17m
San Pedro	San Pedro Elevator Pier 1	(54) 329 23535	(54) 329 25279	Length 220m, Draft 9.8m, spout outreach 16m
Santa Fe	Elevator Terminal No 1	(54) 42 539804	(54) 42 554393	Length 240m, Draft 7.9m, spout airDraft 18.7m basis at MLW
Villa Constitucion	Servicios Portuarios Unit No 2	(54) 461 74404	(54) 461 74404	Length 250m, Draft 8.2m, spout airDraft 21.6m basis zero MLW
AUSTRALIA				
Adelaide	SACBH Adelaide Berth 27	(61) 8 211 8087	(61) 8 211 8087	Length 204m, Draft 10.7m, spout outreach 18m
Albany	Albany Grain Terminal	(61) 9 322 3677	(61) 9 322 3942	Length 227m, Draft 11.5, spout airDraft 15m
Ardrossan	SACBH Ardrossan Terminal	(61) 8 211 8087	(61) 8 211 8087	Length 409m, Draft 9.2m, spout outreach 12.1m
Brisbane	Grainco Queensland Fisherman Island Terminal	(61) 7 638 2440	(61) 7 638 2440	Length 240m, Draft 13m
Brisbane	Grainco Queensland Pinkenba Terminal	(61) 7 638 2440	(61) 7 638 2440	Length 256m, Draft 10.5m
Esperance	Esperance Grain Terminal Berth 1	(61) 9 322 3677	(61) 9 322 3942	Length 244m, Draft 12.8m, spout outreach 17.5m
Fremantle	Kwinana Grain Terminal	(61) 9 322 3677	(61) 9 322 3942	Length 291m, Draft 16.8m
Geelong	Grain Elevators Board Terminal	(61) 52 785 755	NA	Length 201m, Draft 11m. Two Berths: No 1 Berth 235m Loa, No 2 Berth 192m Loa, spout outreach 24m

EQUIPMENT AND HANDLING RATES	LARGEST VESSEL/CARGO	STORAGE FACILITIES	OPERATOR/ OTHER DETAILS
One loading belt feeding three spouts, total 1200tph capacity	Loa 275m, 36,000 tonnes	270,000 tonnes silo capacity	Vincentin SA
Two loading belts feeding any two of six spouts, total 1500tph capacity	Not indicated	67,000 tonnes silo capacity	Direccion Provincial Actividades Portuarias
Seven rotating loading spouts, total 700tph capacity via one loading belt feeder	NEW HORIZON, 34,000 tonnes soyabeans	138,000 tonnes silo capacity	Terminal Puerto San Pedro SA
Three loading belts feeding eight spouts, total 900tph capacity	Loa 217m, 24,000 tonnes	55,000 tonnes silo capacity	Santa Fe Port Administration
Seven loading spouts, three on north berth and four on south berth, total 700tph capacity through any two spouts combined	Not indicated	55,000 tonnes silo capacity	Servicios Portuarios SA
Two travelling shiploaders, total 1500tph capacity	30,000 tonnes	30,000 tonnes silo capacity	South Australia Cooperative Bulk Handling
Three shiploaders, total 1600tph capacity	67,000 tonnes	50,000 tonnes silo capacity	Cooperative Bulk Handling
One 900tph belt conveyor loader	Not indicated	283,000 tonnes silo capacity	South Australia Cooperative Bulk Handling
One 2200tph belt conveyor loader	80,000 tonnes	60,000 tonnes silo capacity	Grainco Queensland Cooperative Association
One 1200tph mobile gantry loader	50,000 tonnes	62,000 tonnes silo capacity	Grainco Queensland Cooperative Association
One 1000tph link belt conveyor loader	Loa 200m, Beam 32m	50,000 tonnes silo capacity	Cooperative Bulk Handling
Four spout loaders, total 5000tph combined	Up to 100,000 tonnes	128,500 tonnes silo capacity	Cooperative Bulk Handling
One 154m long loading gantry with four feeder belts and nine spouts each side, total loading capacity 1600tph to two berths	FAVORITA, 44,540 tonnes	825,000 tonnes silo and warehouse (three) capacity	Grain Elevators Board of South Victoria

COUNTRY/ PORT	TERMINAL NAME	PHONE	FAX	BERTH/DOCK LIMITATIONS
Geraldton	Geraldton Grain Terminal Berth 3	(61) 9 322 3677	(61) 9 322 3942	Length 203m, Draft 9.4m, spout outreach 13.1m
Gladstone	Grainco Queensland Gladstone Terminal Berth 2	(61) 7 638 2440	(61) 7 638 2440	Length 251m, Draft 11.3m
Mackay	Grainco Queensland Mackay Terminal Berth 5	(61) 7 638 2440	(61) 7 638 2440	Length 150m, Draft 12.5m
Newcastle	NSW Graincorp Newcastle Terminal	(61) 249 691 855	(61) 249 611 059	Length 229m, Draft 11.6m
Port Giles	Port Giles Grain Terminal	(61) 8 211 8087	(61) 8 211 8087	Loa maximum 206m, Draft 11.6m, spout outreach 19.8m
Port Kembla	Port Kembla Grain Terminal	(61) 249 691 855	(61) 249 611 059	Length 315m, Draft 16.2m
Port Lincoln	Port Lincoln Grain Terminal	(61) 8 211 8087	(61) 8 211 8087	Length 330m, Draft 15m, boom outreach 35.5m
Port Pirie	Port Pirie Grain Terminal Berth 2	(61) 8 211 8087	(61) 8 211 8087	Length 190m, Draft 8.2m, spout outreach 17.2m
Portland	KS Anderson Berths 1 and 2 Grain Terminal	(61) 55 231 544	NA	Length 396.2m overall, Draft 12.2m
Thevenard	Thevenard Grain Terminal	(61) 8 211 8087	(61) 8 211 8087	One 396m long jetty with two bulk berths each side of Length 198m, Draft 9.8m
Wallaroo	Wallaroo Grain Terminal Berth 2	(61) 8 211 8087	(61) 8 211 8087	Length 290m, Draft 9.5m, spout outreach 20.1m
BELGIUM				
Antwerp	Northern Shipping Terminal	(32) 3 204 7901	(32) 3 323 9985	Berths 154 and 156, Length 300m, Draft 12m, Beam 32.2m, Loa 260m
BRAZIL				
Paranagua	Port Administration Berth 1	(55) 41 432 1413, Port Administration	(55) 41 422 5324, Port Administration	Length 210m, Draft 10.7m

EQUIPMENT AND HANDLING RATES	LARGEST VESSEL/CARGO	STORAGE FACILITIES	OPERATOR/ OTHER DETAILS
Two wharf gantries of total 1000tph loading capacity	Loa 233m, Beam 32.3m	Not indicated	Cooperative Bulk Handling
Two mobile gantry loaders, total 1600tph capacity	Panamax	82,000 tonnes silo capacity	Grainco Queensland Cooperative Association
One 1000tph mobile gantry loader	30,000 tonnes	34,800 tonnes silo capacity	Grainco Queensland Cooperative Association
Four 1000tph travelling gantry shiploaders	Panamax up to 60,500 tonnes	150,000 tonnes silo capacity	New South Wales Graincorp Operations
Five slewing loading booms, total 1000tph combined	40,000 tonnes	150,000 tonnes silo capacity	South Australia Cooperative Bulk Handling
Two 2500tph gantry shiploaders	Loa 290m, Beam 45m, vessels to 120,000 tonnes	260,000 tonnes silo capacity	New South Wales Graincorp Operations
Two 2000tph belt conveyor travelling gantry loaders	80,000 tonnes	Not indicated	South Australia Cooperative Bulk Handling
Five slewing shiploading booms fed by single 800tph belt conveyor feeder	Not indicated	Above 200,000 tonnes silo capacity	South Australia Cooperative Bulk Handling
One 1200tph laterally transversing shiploader	80,000 tonnes	60,000 tonnes silo capacity	Grain Elevators Board of Victoria
One 500tph travelling gantry shiploader	35,300 tonnes, Loa 184m, Beam 28m	200,000 tonnes silo capacity	South Australia Cooperative Bulk Handling
Five shiploading booms fed by single 800tph belt conveyor feeder	Loa 230m, Beam 30m	30,000 tonnes silo capacity	South Australia Cooperative Bulk Handling
Two telescopic spiral chute shiploaders for bulk and bagged cargoes, grab crane barge unloaders	78,000dwt	Grain stored in covered, contamination free warehousing	Northern Shipping Terminal
One 300tph shiploading tower, travelling 150m	Loading Draft restricted to 9.1m	10,000 tonnes silo capacity	Administracao dos Portos de Paranagua e Antonina—Port Administration

COUNTRY/ PORT	TERMINAL NAME	PHONE	FAX	BERTH/DOCK LIMITATIONS
Paranagua	Socopar Berth 2	NA	NA	Length 210m, Draft 10.7m
Paranagua	Gransol Berth 4	NA	NA	Length 210m, Draft 9.5m
Paranagua	Sanbra Berth 6	NA	NA	Length 204m, Draft 9.5m
Paranagua	Cargill Grain Berth 12	NA	NA	Length 230m, Draft 11.3m
Paranagua	Berth 13, New Terminal	NA	NA	Length 225m, Draft 11.3m
Porto Alegre	Samrig (Bunge) Terminal	(55) 51 224 5733, Port Administration	(55) 51 224 3103, Port Administration	Loa 235m, Beam 35m, Draft 5.2m
Porto Alegre	Cesa Terminal	NA	NA	Loa 235m, Beam 35m, Draft 5.2m
Porto Alegre	Ciagran (Fecotrigo) Terminal	NA	NA	Loa 235m, Beam 35m, Draft 5.2m
Rio Grande	Cotrijui Grain Terminal, Rio Grande Super Port	(55) 532 323 366, Port Administration	(55) 532 323 857, Port Administration	Length 200m, Draft 14m
Rio Grande	Termasa (TTS) Grain Terminal, Rio Grande Super Port	NA	NA	Length 450m providing simultaneous loading for two vessels, Draft 14m
Rio Grande	Samrig Terminal, Rio Grande New Port	NA	NA	Length over 170m, Draft 8.8m
Rio Grande	Cesa Terminal, Rio Grande New Port	NA	NA	Length over 150m, Draft 8.8m

EQUIPMENT AND HANDLING RATES	LARGEST VESSEL/CARGO	STORAGE FACILITIES	OPERATOR/ OTHER DETAILS
One 300tph shiploading tower, travelling 110m	Loading Draft restricted to 9.1m	64,000 tonnes silo capacity	Socopar
One 400tph shiploading tower, travelling 150m	Loading Draft restricted to 9.1m	10,000 tonnes silo capacity	Gransol
Two 100tph fixed loading spouts and two 100tph partly moveable loading spouts	Loading Draft maximum of 12.8m possible by use of pontoons	12,000 tonnes silo capacity	Sanbra
One 500tph shiploading tower, travelling 172m	Loading Draft maximum of 12.8m possible by use of pontoons	20,000 tonnes silo capacity	Cargill
Two 1500tph mobile shiploading towers, travelling 162m	Loading Draft restricted to 10m	164,000 tonnes silo capacity	New terminal, additional two 110,000 tonnes silos available for shared usage
One 300tph soyabeans (200tph soyameals) shiploader fed by 120m long dock belt conveyor	Loa 245m, Draft 5.2m	24,000 tonnes silo for soyabeans plus 100,000 tonnes facility located 25km from port	Samrig, Administracao do Porto de Porto Alegre – Port Administration
One 200tph soyabeans (100tph soyameals) shiploader fed by 90m long dock belt conveyor	Loa 245m, Draft 5.2m	18,750 tonnes silo for soyabeans	Cesa
One 250tph soyabeans (150tph soyameals) shiploader fed by 80m long dock belt conveyor	Loa 245m, Draft 5.2m	50,000 tonnes silo for soyabeans	Ciagran
Two 1000tph wheat and soyabeans (400tph soyameals) belt conveyors feeding eight shiploading spouts	80,000 tonnes following berth dredging from 12.2m to 14m	Eight 25,000 tonnes capacity storage sheds, total 200,000 tonnes for wheat and soyabeans/ meals	Incobrasa (Bunge Bjorn/Sanchista), Administracao do Porto de Rio Grande—Port Administration
Two 1500tph soyabeans (750tph soyameals) shiploaders	Two 85,000 tonnes vessels simultaneously	220,000 tonnes capacity in eight horizontal storage sheds, plus 150,000 tonnes in two additional horizontal sheds	Termasa, largest Grain Terminal in South America
One 300tph soyameals belt conveyor travelling shiploader	Draft limitation of 8.8m	35,000 tonnes warehouse storage for soyameals	Samrig
Two 300tph capacity pneumatic loading/ unloading towers	Draft limitation of 8.8m	50,000 tonnes soyabeans storage	Cesa

COUNTRY/ PORT	TERMINAL NAME	PHONE	FAX	BERTH/DOCK LIMITATIONS
Rio Grande	Bianchini Terminal, Rio Grande New Port	NA	NA	Length over 140m, Draft 8.8m
Rio Grande	DNPVN Grain Terminal, Rio Grande New Port	NA	NA	Length over 215m, Draft 8.8m
Santos	Macuco Novo Quay	(55) 13 233 6565, Port Administration	(55) 13 233 3080	Length 280m, Draft 11m
São Francisco do Sul	Cocar Berth 1 Terminal	(55) 474 440 200	(55) 474 440 115	Length 225m, Draft 10m
Vitoria	Capuaba Quay Grain Terminal	(55) 272 221 311	(55) 272 227 360	Overall Length 600m shared with container and general cargo terminals, Draft 7.5–12m
CANADA				
Baie Comeau	Cargill Terminal	(1) 418 296 2233	(1) 418 648 7980	Two piers and three berths. Two berths of 178m Length and one of 212m Length, Draft alongside of 12.2m, 11.6m and 8.4m respectively
Churchill	Hudson Bay Port Co Terminal	(1) 204 675 8823	(1) 204 675 2550	Berths 1 and 2 of 211.5m Length, Draft between 9.4–10m
Goderich	Goderich Elevators No 1	(1) 519 524 7367	(1) 519 524 7995	Not indicated
Halifax	Halifax Grain Elevator	(1) 902 421 1714	(1) 902 420 0343	Length 174m, Draft 12.2m, unloading berth Length 168m, Draft 11.2m
Montreal	Port Grain Elevator	(1) 514 283 6948	(1) 514 283 1502	Length 394m, Draft 11m

EQUIPMENT AND HANDLING RATES	LARGEST VESSEL/CARGO	STORAGE FACILITIES	OPERATOR/ OTHER DETAILS
One 400tph capacity soyabeans belt conveyor travelling shiploader	Draft limitation of 8.8m	40,000 tonnes soyabeans storage	Bianchini
One 800tph capacity soyabeans belt conveyor travelling shiploader	Draft limitation of 8.8m	56,000 tonnes soyabeans storage	DNPVN
One 3000tph belt conveyor shiploader for cereals	Draft limitation of 11m	Two horizontal silos, total 68,500 tonnes capacity	CODESP, Compania Docas do Estado de São Paulo—Port Administration
Two shiploading spouts with 800tph belt conveyor feeder	Draft limitation of 10m	Two storage silos of total 115,000 tonnes capacity	Cocar, Administracao do Porto de São Francisco do Sul—Port Administration
Two 600tph pneumatic shiploaders/unloaders for soyabeans	Not indicated	30,000 tonnes silo, increasing to 90,000 tonnes	CODESA, Companhia Docas do Espiritu Santo—Port Administration
Loading gantries on North pier Berths 1 and 2	Not indicated	440,000 tonnes silo capacity	Cargill
Four belt conveyor feeders and 23 loading spouts, can load three vessels up to 15,000 tonnes simultaneously, or two vessels above 15,000 tonnes at 1680tph	Not indicated	140,000 tonnes silo capacity	Canada Ports Corp
Not indicated	Not indicated	Not indicated	Goderich Elevators
One 1000tph shiploading gallery on Berth 28, unloading facilities for self unloaders and Lakes bulkers via receiving hoppers/marine leg on Berth 26	Marshall Class bulkers	144,000 tonnes silo capacity	Halifax Grain Elevator
Three 1500tph fixed towers with telescopic spouts, total 4500tph capacity	75,000 tonnes	260,000 tonnes silo capacity	Port of Montreal

COUNTRY/ PORT	TERMINAL NAME	PHONE	FAX	BERTH/DOCK LIMITATIONS
Port Cartier	Les Silos Port Cartier	(1) 418 766 2515	(1) 418 766 4136	Loa 442m, Draft 15.2m
Port Colborne	Port Colborne Grain Terminal, Wharf 19	(1) 416 834 3644	(1) 905 682 4525	Length 503m, Draft 8.2m
Prescott	Prescott Grain Elevator	(1) 613 925 4228	(1) 613 925 5022	Dock A length 281.6m, Dock B Length 394.6m, Seaway Draft 8.2m
Prince Rupert	Ridley Island Grain Terminal	(1) 250 627 8777	(1) 250 627 8541	Length unrestricted, Draft 14.5m
Quebec	Bunge of Canada Elevator	(1) 418 892 3761	(1) 418 692 0182	Length unrestricted, Draft restriction of 15.2m at high tide and 21.3m at low tide due to airdraft under shiploaders
Quebec	Berth 107 Elevator	(1) 418 688 7504	(1) 418 687 3143	Length 173m, Draft 11.3m
Sarnier	Cargill Sarnier Elevator	(1) 519 337 5428	(1) 519 337 9997	Length 274.3m, Draft 8.5m at Seaway maximum
Sorel	Les Elevators Sorel	(1) 514 743 3893	(1) 514 743 7566	Five Docks; Berth 11 Length 152.4m, Draft 7.3m; Berth 12 Length 106.7m, Draft 7.3m; Berth 13 Length 76.2m, Draft 7.3m; Berth 14 Length 187.5m, Draft 8.3m; Berth 15 Length 189.6m, Draft 10.7m
Trois Rivieres	Trois Rivieres Elevators, Berth 16 Terminal	(1) 819 374 6203	(1) 819 374 3675	Length 175m, Draft 10.7m
Thunder Bay	Canada Malting	NA	(1) 807 345 2682	Length 305m

EQUIPMENT AND HANDLING RATES	LARGEST VESSEL/CARGO	STORAGE FACILITIES	OPERATOR/ OTHER DETAILS
Six loading spouts averaging 2800tph, plus two marine legs unloading at 2240tph	FINIX, 110,623 tonnes soyabeans in 1996; LEON, 123,556 tonnes wheat in 1992	181,500 tonnes silo capacity, plus eight storage tanks totalling an additional 112,000 tonnes	Les Silos Port Cartier
Shiploader of 2800tph capacity at Wharf 20	Not indicated	63,000 tonnes silo capacity at Wharf 19, another 84,000 tonnes silo at Canada Ports Wharf 20	Port Colborne division of Goderich Elevators
Nine loading spouts, any four providing 2000tph total at one time	PATTERSON, Loa 224.5m, Beam 23.1m, Draft 12.8m	154,000 tonnes silo capacity	Canada Ports Corp, facility available for sale
Three tower mounted shiploaders, total 4000tph capacity	140,000 tonnes	210,000 tonnes silo capacity	Prince Rupert Grain
Two marine towers at Berth 18 with 1250tph bucket elevators for unloading; Berth 29 reception for self unloading Lakers at 2500tph; Berth 28 shiploading totalling 5000tph via three booms	PROSPEROUS, Loa 270.3m, Beam 43m, 149,490 tonnes cargo	224,000 tonnes silo capacity	Bunge of Canada
Single 600tph shiploader	Not indicated	76,000 tonnes silo capacity	Cargill
Two 2500tph loading spouts	PATTERSON, 27,000 tonnes cargo	76,000 tonnes silo storage, 75,000 tonnes flat storage	Cargill
3600tph loading rate	Not indicted	138,000 tonnes steel and concrete silo capacity	Sorel Elevators
2150tph loading capacity, two marine legs each of 1000tph unloading capacity	Not indicated	110,000 tonnes silo capacity	Trois Rivieres Elevators
600–1000tph loading rate, malt and barley	Seaways maximum	62,800 tonnes silo capacity	Canada Malting

COUNTRY/ PORT	TERMINAL NAME	PHONE	FAX	BERTH/DOCK LIMITATIONS
Thunder Bay	Cargill Thunder Bay Elevator	(1) 807 623 6743	(1) 807 623 8559	Length 182.9m, Draft 9.1m
Thunder Bay	Manitoba Pool Elevators	(1) 807 345 7351	(1) 807 346 4018	Length 328m, Draft 9m
Thunder Bay	Parrish & Heimbeckker Terminal	NA	(1) 807 345 8713	Length 305m, Draft 8.2m
Thunder Bay	Richardson Terminals	(1) 807 343 5570	(1) 807 345 0522	Length 365.7m, Draft 8.2m
Thunder Bay	Saskatchewan Wheat Pool Elevator	(1) 807 346 3377	(1) 807 346 3358	Berths 4A and 4B, Length 414m; Berth 7A, Length 518m; Berth 7B, Length 341m
Thunder Bay	United Grain Growers Elevators A and M	(1) 807 345 4425	(1) 807 345 7421	Berth A, Length 452m; Berth M, Length 377m
Thunder Bay	Western Grain By-Products Storage	(1) 807 623 8500	(1) 807 622 0482	Length 300m
Vancouver	Alberta Wheat Pool Elevator	(1) 604 684 5161	(1) 604 684 7106	Length 274m, Draft 15.2m
Vancouver	Pacific Elevators	(1) 604 895 5220	(1) 604 864 7106	Berth 1, Length 160m, Draft 12m; Berth 2, Length 225m, Draft 14m; Berth 4, Length 220m, Draft 10m
Vancouver	Pioneer Grain Terminal	(1) 604 669 2520	(1) 604 688 4598	Length 180m, Draft 14.3m
Vancouver	Saskatchewan Wheat Pool Elevator	(1) 604 990 2553	(1) 604 990 2559	Two shipping berths, Lengths 380m, Draft 15.2m at outer berth and 12.2m at inner berth
Vancouver	United Grain Growers Elevator	(1) 604 254 4145	(1) 604 254 3212	Two berths: East Berth Draft 13.7m, West Berth Draft 11.6m, Airdraft 21.3m subject to tides
FRANCE				
Bordeaux/Bassens	Blaye Grain Terminal	(33) 57 420 307	(33) 57 423 918	Draft 10.5m

EQUIPMENT AND HANDLING RATES	LARGEST VESSEL/CARGO	STORAGE FACILITIES	OPERATOR/ OTHER DETAILS
Three electric mechanical loaders totalling 3700tph capacity	PATTERSON, Loa 233.6m, Beam 22.9, 29,016 tonnes cargo	140,000 tonnes silo capacity	Cargill
Six loading spouts of 2000tph capacity	PATTERSON, 29,000 tonnes wheat cargo	167,400 tonnes silo capacity	Manitoba Pool Elevators
1000tph loading capacity	Seaways maximum	40,000 tonnes silo capacity	Parrish & Heimbeckker
Four fixed loading spouts of 2200tph capacity	Seaways maximum	210,000 tonnes silo capacity	James Richardson International
3200tph at Berths 4A and 4B; 3400tph at Berth 7A; 1200tph at Berth 7B	Seaways maximum	Berths 4A and 4B 208,000 tonnes silo capacity; Berths 7A and 7B 362,650 tonnes silo capacity	Saskatchewan Wheat Pool
Loading capacities: 1900tph at Berth A, 2300tph at Berth M	Seaways maximum	Berth A 231,000 tonnes silo capacity; Berth M 91,000 tonnes silo capacity	United Grain Growers
1200tph loading capacity	Seaways maximum	30,000 tonnes silo capacity	Western Grain By-Products
Seven loading spouts of 1600tph each	120,000 tonnes	286,000 tonnes silo capacity	Alberta Wheat Pool
Berth 2, gallery with seven loading spouts of 1500tph each; Berth 4, one travelling ship loader of 1500tph	70,000 tonnes, Loa 225m	199,000 tonnes silo capacity	Pacific Elevators is managed by Alberta Wheat Pool
Two ship loaders of 1000tph each	Not indicated	108,000 tonnes silo capacity	Pioneer Grain Terminals
Loading gallery with two 1200tph belt conveyors feeding five loading spouts at both outer and inner berths	AMOCO KIRO, 130,000 tonnes	235,000 tonnes silo capacity in 311 bins	Saskatchewan Wheat Pool
Seven mechanical shipping spouts each berth, one conveyor belt feeder each berth of 500tph	70,000 tonnes, Loa 232m, Beam 32m	102,000 tonnes silo capacity	United Grain Growers

Two 700tph ship loading gantries	CYPRUS STAR ONE, 17,420 tonnes cargo, 22,300dwt	130,000 tonnes silo capacity	Semabla

COUNTRY/ PORT	TERMINAL NAME	PHONE	FAX	BERTH/DOCK LIMITATIONS
Bordeaux/Bassens	Ste Aquitaine du Silo de Bordeaux-Bassens	(33) 556 385 570	(33) 556 316 994	Draft 10m
Dunkerque	Silonor	(33) 328 249 010	(33) 328 249 015	Draft 13.8m
Le Havre	Le Havre Grain Centre	(33) 232 747 400	(33) 232 747 429	Quay Joannes Couvert, Length 300m, Draft 10.6–13.5m, vessels to 110,000dwt; Quay Hermann du Pasquier, Length 550m, Draft 9–11m, vessels to 30,000dwt
Nantes	Port Atlantique—Roche-Maurice Terminal	(33) 40 442 020	(33) 40 442 181	Six berths, Length 747m overall, Draft 8.5m
Nantes	Quai des Grand Puits/ Quai des Darses	(33) 40 442 020	(33) 40 442 181	Length 850m overall, Draft 8.5m
Rouen	Simarex Villette	(33) 35 681 015	(33) 35 672 993	NA
Rouen	Ucacel	(33) 235 183 030	(33) 235 183 033	Three loading berths, Lengths 250m each
SOUTH AFRICA				
Durban	Island View Terminal Berth 3	(27) 31 466 1331	(27) 31 466 1783	Loa 255m, Draft 12.5m, Beam 36m
Durban	Maydon Wharf Berth 5	(27) 31 301 9201	(27) 31 304 6794	Length 210m, Draft 9.6m
East London	East London Grain Terminal	(27) 43 144 2300	(27) 43 144 2302	Loa 245m, Draft 10.5m
UK				
Hull	Humberside Grain Terminal	(44) 1482 701 281	(44) 1482 784 891	Loa 198m, Draft 10.4m, Beam 25.5m

EQUIPMENT AND HANDLING RATES	LARGEST VESSEL/CARGO	STORAGE FACILITIES	OPERATOR/ OTHER DETAILS
Two 450tph ship loading gantries	ALLEGRAF, 35,000dwt	80,000 tonnes silo capacity	Sica du Silo Portuaire de Bordeaux-Bassens
One 800tph ship loader	TIGRIS, 88,000dwt fully laden	120,000 tonnes flat storage	Silonor
1800tph loading capacity at Quay Joannes Couvert since 1997, barge/coaster discharge at Quay Hermann du Pasquier	110,000 tonnes	80,000 tonnes silo capacity, plus 380,000 tonnes flat storage capacity	Ucaspor
Two 700tph ship loading gantries	MUSASHI, 54,400 tonnes maize cargo	120,000 tonnes silo capacity, plus 30,000 tonnes flat storage	Port of Nantes/St Nazaire
One 700tph gantry ship loader	Not indicated	10,000 tonnes silo capacity, plus 20,000 tonnes flat storage	Port of Nantes/St Nazaire
500tph loading capacity	Not indicated	60,000 tonnes silo capacity, plus 20,000 tonnes flat storage	Simarex
First berth, three loading spouts of 1000tph each; Second berth, two spouts of 800tph each; Third berth, two spouts of 300tph and one spout of 600tph	Loa 275m	500,000 tonnes of silo and flat storage capacity	Ucacel
One 1500tph belt conveyor ship loader, two 580tph pneumatic ship unloaders for imports	ULTRA MAX, Loa 274m; FEAX, 62,994dwt	69,500 tonnes silo capacity	Durban Bulk Shipping
Belt conveyors loading shore to ship, one continuous ship unloader for imports	36,000 tonnes cargo	35,000 tonnes silo capacity	Rennies Terminals
Ten ship loading spouts, any four operating together at 6000tph	CAPT WJ CARGELL, loaded 40,440 tonnes	76,000 tonnes silo capacity, 8,000 tonnes shipping bins	Portnet
One 1200tph mobile loading tower	GALEA, 30,375dwt	60,000 tonnes silo capacity	Cargill

COUNTRY/ PORT	TERMINAL NAME	PHONE	FAX	BERTH/DOCK LIMITATIONS
Immingham	Immingham Grain Silos	(44) 1469 577 747	(44) 1469 571 305	Loa 223m, Draft 10.4m
Newcastle	Tyne Grain Terminal	(44) 191 489 9932	(44) 191 428 5202	Loa 220m, Draft 10.5m
Tilbury	Tilbury Grain Terminal	(44) 1375 852 342	(44) 1375 852 250	Main Berth: Loa 230m, Draft 12m, 60,000dwt; Inner Berth: Loa 137m, 10,000dwt
Southampton	Continental UK	(44) 1703 639 033	(44) 1703 330 227	Draft 10.5m, Beam 23m
Southampton	Soufflet Grain Terminal	(44) 1703 334 433	(44) 1703 330 657	Loa 220m, Draft 9.9m
URUGUAY				
Montevideo	Nueva Palmira Terminal	(598) 2 956 509	(598) 2 962 874	Loa 240m, Draft 8.5m, Beam 32.2m
USA				
Albany	Cargill Elevator	(1) 518 465 2120	(1) 518 449 4762	Length 228.6m, Draft 9.5m, Air Draft 41.1m
Baltimore	Countrymark Cooperative Locust Point Elevator	(1) 410 685 6410	(1) 410 685 0233	Length 304.8m, Draft 12.2m
Baton Rouge	Cargill Port Allen Elevator	(1) 504 383 5221	(1) 504 388 9455	Length 165.5m, Draft 13.7m, Air Draft 22.9m
Beaumont	Continental Grain Elevator	(1) 409 838 6251	(1) 409 892 8127	Length 305m, Draft 12.2m, Air Draft 13.7m
Brownsville	Port Elevator	(1) 210 831 8245	(1) 210 831 7181	Length 122m, Draft 11m, Air Draft 14.6m
Burns Harbour	Burns Harbour Elevator	(1) 219 787 8613	(1) 219 787 8613	Length 222.5m, Draft 8m, Beam 22.9m
Charleston	South Carolina Farm Bureau Elevator	(1) 803 744 0441	(1) 803 747 4284	Length 111.3m, Draft 11.6m, Air Draft 18.3m
Chicago	Cargill Elevator	(1) 219 787 8613	(1) 219 787 9465	Length 222.5m, Draft 8m, Beam 22.9m
Chicago	Continental B and C Elevators	(1) 312 207 5100	(1) 312 207 5233	Both Elevators, Length 222.5m, Draft 8m, Beam 22.9m

EQUIPMENT AND HANDLING RATES	LARGEST VESSEL/CARGO	STORAGE FACILITIES	OPERATOR/ OTHER DETAILS
One ship loader, capacity 5,000 tonnes/day	30,000dwt	8,000 tonnes silo capacity, 4,000 tonnes flat storage	Agroceres/Lingrain
One 1000 tonnes ship loader with trimmer	40,000 tonnes	60,000 tonnes silo capacity	Tynegrain
One 1000tph ship loader on Outer Berth, six loading spouts at Inner Berth, any two combined at 2000tph	EL AMAAN, 75,484dwt, Loa 242m, Beam 32m, loaded 52,500 tonnes cargo	100,000 tonnes silo capacity	Port of London
One ship loader, capacity 8,000 tonnes/day	60,000 tonnes	16,000 tonnes silo capacity, plus outside country flat storage	Continental UK
One 1000tph ship loader with 13m outreach from quayside	54,000 tonnes	28,000 tonnes silo capacity	Soufflet Grain
Single point 800tph shuttle conveyor ship loader	GUISEPPE D'AMATO, 75,348dwt	150,000 tonnes storage capacity in four horizontal silos	Corporacion Navios Sucursal Uruguaya
One 800–1000tph ship loader	32,000 tonnes cargo loaded, Loa 229m	300,000 tonnes silo capacity	Cargill
Four 750tph loading spouts	45,000 tonnes	55,000 tonnes silo capacity	Countrymark Cooperative
Five ship loading spouts totalling 1100tph	Not indicated	170,000 tonnes silo capacity	Cargill
Three ship loading spouts totalling 1200tph	68,000 tonnes	90,000 tonnes silo capacity	Continental Grain
Two 600tph ship loading spouts	Not indicated	75,000 tonnes silo capacity	Port of Brownsville
One 950tph ship loading spout	Not indicated	137,500 tonnes silo capacity	Cargill
Five 800tph ship loading spouts	35,000 tonnes	37,500 tonnes silo capacity	South Carolina Farm Bureau Marketing Association
Five loading spouts totalling 8150tph	25,000 tonnes	575,000 tonnes silo capacity	Cargill
B Elevator, five loading spouts of 900tph; C Elevator, eight loading spouts of 900tph	FEDERAL FRASER, loaded 25,000 tonnes	175,000 tonnes silo capacity at B and 125,000 tonnes silo capacity at C Elevators	Continental Grain

COUNTRY/ PORT	TERMINAL NAME	PHONE	FAX	BERTH/DOCK LIMITATIONS
Corpus Christi	Public Elevator	(1) 512 882 1456	(1) 512 882 1998	Length 274.3m, Draft 13.7m, Air Draft 16.8m
Duluth	Cargill B1 Elevator	(1) 218 727 1581	(1) 218 727 8718	Length 274m, Draft 82.m, Beam 22.8m, Air Draft 15.2m
Galveston	Elevator B	(1) 409 765 9321	(1) 409 766 6107	Length 243.8m, Draft 12.2m, Air Draft 16.2m
Galveston	Farmland Elevator G	(1) 409 763 6447	(1) 409 763 8608	Length 243.8m, Draft 12.2m, Air Draft 16.8m
Hampton Roads	Cargill South Elevator, Chesapeake	(1) 804 545 8461	(1) 804 545 8460	Length 259m, Draft 11.3m, Air Draft 12.2m
Hampton Roads	Cargill North Elevator, Norfolk	(1) 804 545 8461	(1) 804 545 8460	Length 289.5m, Draft 12m, Air Draft 14m
Houston	Cargill Elevator	(1) 713 457 7000	(1) 713 457 3002	Length 243.8m, Draft 12m, Air Draft 18.3m
Houston	Public Elevator No 2	(1) 713 671 7100	(1) 713 670 2564	Length 243.8m, Draft 12m, Air Draft 16.8m
Kalama	Harvest States Elevator	(1) 360 673 2011	(1) 360 673 5101	Length 182.9m/222.5m with dolphins, Draft 12.2m, Air Draft 12.8m
Kalama	Peavey Elevator	(1) 360 673 3900	(1) 360 673 3910	Length 163.7m, Draft 12.2m, Air Draft 25m
Milwaukee	Continental Grain Elevator	(1) 414 482 1900	(1) 414 482 1733	Length 222.5m, Draft 8m, Air Draft 12.2m
Mobile	Alabama State Docks Public Grain Elevator	(1) 334 441 7343	(1) 334 441 7344	Length 259m, Draft 12.2m, Air Draft 19.8m
New Orleans	Continental Westwego Terminal	(1) 504 436 5800	(1) 504 436 5812	Two Docks, total Length 610m, Draft 14.6m, Air Draft 15.2m
Plaquemines	HSPV/LLC Myrtle Grove Elevator	(1) 504 656 2212	(1) 504 656 7394	Length 165.2m/229m with dolphins, Draft 14.6m, Air Draft 16.5m
Portland	Columbia Grain Elevator	(1) 503 224 8624	(1) 503 241 0296	Length 136.2m, Channel Draft 12.2m, Depth alongside 13.7m, Air Draft 55.3m
Portland	Louis Dreyfus Elevator	(1) 503 243 1133	(1) 503 243 5079	Length 137.5m/256m with dolphins, Draft 12.2m

EQUIPMENT AND HANDLING RATES	LARGEST VESSEL/CARGO	STORAGE FACILITIES	OPERATOR/ OTHER DETAILS
Five loading spouts of 1500tph, plus two spouts of 1800tph	65,000 tonnes	125,000 tonnes silo capacity	Port of Corpus Christi
Five loading spouts of 1900tph	20,000 tonnes	Total grain storage in Port of Duluth amounts to 1,880,000 tonnes	Cargill
Three loading spouts of 1600tph	55,000dwt	125,000 tonnes silo capacity	Port of Galveston
Four loading spouts of 1875tph	60,000dwt	150,000 tonnes silo capacity	Farmland
Three loading spouts of 800tph	Not indicated	75,000 tonnes silo capacity	Cargill
Two loading spouts of 1000tph	Not indicated	17,000 tonnes silo capacity	Cargill
Four loading spouts of 1800tph	60,000 tonnes	162,500 tonnes silo capacity	Cargill
Two loading spouts of 1600tph	55,000 tonnes	150,000 tonnes silo capacity	Pour of Houston
Two 600tph loading belts feeding seven loading spouts totalling 1200tph maximum	Maximum Loa 274.3m, Beam 32m	175,000 tonnes total capacity, of which 64,000 tonnes in vertical cells	Harvest States Cooperatives
Four loading spouts totalling 3000tph	CHESNUT HILL, 68,380dwt	50,000 tonnes silo capacity	Peavey Company
Six loading spouts of 950tph	CAPTIN HENRY JACKSON, 27,107 tonnes	75,000 tonnes silo capacity	Continental Grain
Two loading spouts of 750tph	GOLDEN ENDEAVOUR, 55,000 tonnes	77,500 tonnes silo capacity	Alabama State Docks
Four loading spouts on Dock 1, two loading spouts on Dock 2, 1500tph cach	MANHATTAN, 87,000dwt	100,000 tonnes silo capacity	Continental Grain
Four loading spouts of 1500tph	BARTHOLEMEW DIAZ	150,000 tonnes silo capacity	HSPV/LLC
Three loading towers, 45.7m apart, 2200tph total loading capacity	OCEAN CHALLENGER, 246,000dwt	110,000 tonnes silo capacity	Columbia Grain
Six loading spouts of 1200tph	Loa 250m, 50,000 tonnes	37,500 tonnes silo capacity	Louis Dreyfus

COUNTRY/ PORT	TERMINAL NAME	PHONE	FAX	BERTH/DOCK LIMITATIONS
Portland	Cargill Irving Dock	(1) 503 286 0678	(1) 503 286 9033	Length 121.9m/335.3m with dolphins, Draft 12.2m, spout height 11.3m above dock level when raised
Portland	Cargill T-4 Dock	(1) 503 286 0678	(1) 503 286 9033	Length 155.8m/311.5m with dolphins, Draft 12.2m, spout height 16.5m above dock level when raised
Sacramento	Cargill West Elevator	(1) 209 466 5443	(1) 612 742 7587, Cargill Minneapolis	Length 182.9m, Draft 9.6m
Seattle	Cargill Elevator	(1) 206 284 4851	(1) 612 742 7587, Cargill Minneapolis	Length 182.9m, Draft 21.3m
South Louisiana Port	ADM Gromark AMA	(1) 504 431 8245	(1) 504 431 7275	Length 165.5m, Draft 13.7m, Air Draft 17.7m at MLW
South Louisiana Port	Zen-Noh Convent	(1) 504 867 3500	(1) 504 867 3508	Length 243.8m, Draft 13.7m, Air Draft 24.4m
South Louisiana Port	ADM Gromark Destrehan	(1) 504 764 7586	(1) 504 764 1888	Length 194.8m, Draft 13.7m, Air Draft 18.3m
South Louisiana Port	Bunge Destrehan	(1) 504 764 6516	(1) 504 725 8245	Length 365.7m, Draft 13.7m, Air Draft 17.8m at MLW
South Louisiana Port	ADM Gromark Reserve	(1) 504 536 1151	(1) 504 536 1152	Length 255.7m, Draft 13.7m, spout Air Draft 18.3m at MLW
South Louisiana Port	Cargill Terre Haute Reserve	(1) 504 536 1500	(1) 504 536 1515	Length 204.5m, Draft 13.7m, Air Draft 19.8m
South Louisiana Port	HSPV/LLC St Elmo	(1) 504 869 4405	(1) 504 869 4517	Length 152.4m, Draft 12.2m, Air Draft 18.3m at MLW
Stockton	Continental Elevator	(1) 209 466 5443	(1) 209 466 5817	Length 221m, Draft 11.6m maximum/10.5m average fresh water
Tacoma	TEMCO	(1) 503 228 9222	(1) 503 323 6298	Length 137.2m/228.6m with dolphins, Draft 18.3m, spout height 24.4m above dock level when raised

EQUIPMENT AND HANDLING RATES	LARGEST VESSEL/CARGO	STORAGE FACILITIES	OPERATOR/ OTHER DETAILS
Five loading spouts of 1200tph	EQUINOX CORPORATION, nine hatch bulker	37,500 tonnes silo capacity	Cargill
Two loading spouts of 2250tph	Not indicated	200,000 tonnes silo capacity	Cargill
One loading belt and spout of 600tph	Not indicated	31,250 tonnes silo capacity	Cargill
Five loading spouts of 3000tph	OCEAN CHALLENGER, 200,000 tonnes	105,000 tonnes silo capacity	Cargill
Four loading spouts of 1250tph	THEODORE A, 96,798 tonnes	137,500 tonnes silo capacity	ADM Gromark
Four loading spouts of 3000tph	Not indicated	100,000 tonnes silo capacity	Zen-Noh Corporation
Seven loading spouts of 1350tph	MEGA DALE, 98,294 tonnes	156,250 tonnes silo capacity	ADM Gromark
Eight loading spouts of 1450tph, marine leg barge unloader	140,000dwt	171,000 tonnes silo capacity	Bunge
Three loading spouts of 1800tph	ISTANBUL, 88,914 tonnes	87,500 tonnes silo capacity	ADM Gromark
Three travelling loading spouts of 1800tph	BROOKLYN, 108,663 tonnes	150,000 tonnes silo capacity	Cargill
Two travelling loading spouts of 1200tph	FRONT LEADER, 111,584 tonnes	50,000 tonnes silo capacity	Peavey Company
Two loading spouts with 0.33m diameter telescopic spouts of 800tph and two loading belts	Not indicated	162,500 tonnes silo capacity	Continental Grain
Three loading spouts of 1100tph	OCEAN CHALLENGER, 200,000 tonnes including top off at Seattle	50,000 tonnes	Port of Tacoma

COUNTRY/ PORT	TERMINAL NAME	PHONE	FAX	BERTH/DOCK LIMITATIONS
Toledo	Anderson Elevator	(1) 419 893 5050	(1) 419 891 6513	Length unrestricted, Draft 7.9m, Air Draft 13.7m
Toledo	Cargill	(1) 419 241 2143	(1) 419 893 3662	Length unrestricted, Draft 7.9m, Air Draft 13.7m
Toledo	Country Mark Elevator	(1) 419 691 5703	(1) 419 691 1951	Length unrestricted, Draft 7.9m, Air Draft 14m
Vancouver	United Grain Elevator	(1) 360 693 1521	(1) 360 694 1986	Length 217.3m, Draft 12.2m

EQUIPMENT AND HANDLING RATES	LARGEST VESSEL/CARGO	STORAGE FACILITIES	OPERATOR/ OTHER DETAILS
Seven loading spouts of 1000tph	Maximum Laker	175,000 tonnes silo capacity	The Andersons
One loading spout of 1000tph	Maximum Laker	152,500 tonnes silo capacity	Cargill
Twelve loading spouts of 1000tph	Maximum Laker	Total silo storage 245,000 tonnes	Country Mark Elevator
Travelling 2000tph gantry loader	OCEAN CHALLENGER, 115,000 tonnes/ 135,000dwt	Silo 100,000 tonnes plus 18,750 tonnes flat store	United Grain

APPENDIX 2

World grain import terminals

COUNTRY/ PORT	TERMINAL NAME	PHONE	FAX	BERTH/DOCK LIMITATIONS
ALGERIA				
Algiers	Agha Basin Terminal, Berth 25	(213) 2 579 021	NA	Loa unrestricted, Draft 9.8m
Annaba	Quai Nord Grain Berth	(213) 8 823 131	NA	Loa 200m, Draft 11.8m
Ghazaouet	Berth 15 Grain Facility	(213) 7 321 232	(213) 7 321 255	Length 289m, Draft 12m
BAHRAIN				
Mina Sulman	Bahrain Grain Terminal	(973) 222 602	(973) 210 925	Length unrestricted, Draft 9m
BELGIUM				
Antwerp	Sobelgra, 6th Harbour Dock	(32) 3 545 0415	(32) 3 542 0582	Length 620m, Draft 14.6m
Antwerp	Samga Lefebvre Dock	(32) 2032 3711	(32) 3 225 0080	Quays 48–50, Total Length 850m, Draft 12.8m for unloading/ 9.7m for loading
Ghent	Euro-Silo	(32) 9 251 2141	(32) 9 251 6074	Total Quay length 480m, Discharge berth: Length 270m, Draft 12.2m, Loading berth: Length 210m, Draft 12.2m
Ghent	Ghent Grain Terminal	(32) 9 345 9611	(32) 9 345 5778	Length 800m, Draft 12.2m fresh water Terneuzen Locks, Draft 13m Rodenhuizendok
Zeebrugge	CTO Bulk Terminal	(32) 50 542 488	(32) 50 545 281	Quay Length 800m, Draft 13.5m
CHINA				
Dalian	Berths 8 and 9	(86) 411 263 7873	(86) 411 280 7148	Berth 8: Length 232m, Draft 11m, Berth 9: Length 246m, Draft 12.5m
Guangzhou	Xinggang No 1	(86) 20 227 9412	(86) 20 227 8303	Length 220m, Draft 11m, access channel depth 10.5m

EQUIPMENT AND HANDLING RATES	LARGEST VESSEL/CARGO	STORAGE FACILITIES	OPERATOR/ OTHER DETAILS
Not indicated	25,000dwt	30,000 tonnes silo capacity	Enterprise Portuaire d'Alger, wheat imports terminal
Grain discharged at 400tph	20,000dwt	16,000 tonnes silo capacity	Enterprise Portuaire d'Annaba
Not indicated	Loa 185m, Draft 8.5m	30,000 tonnes silo capacity	Enterprise Portuaire de Ghazaouet
Two 750tph mobile pneumatic wheat unloaders	25,000 tonnes	25,000 tonnes silo capacity	Bahrain Flour Mills
Five 400tph pneumatic elevators	OBO BAZAK, 103,000dwt	106,000 tonnes vertical silo capacity, 60,000 tonnes flat store capacity	Sobelgra
One 600tph pneumatic elevator, one 350tph grab crane, 1500tph belt conveyor loading capacity	Loa 250m	105,000 tonnes vertical silo capacity, 15,000 tonnes flat store capacity	Samga
Two 700tph screw ship unloaders, two 500tph pneumatic elevators, five 1000tph barge loading towers	Panamax	131,050 tonnes vertical silo capacity, 114,000 tonnes flat store capacity	Euro-Silo
One 1500tph grab crane, one 700tph mobile pneumatic ship unloader, one fixed 800tph barge loader	Loa 265m, Beam 34m (Terneuzen Locks limit)	170,000 tonnes vertical silo capacity, 240,000 tonnes flat store capacity	Ghent Grain Terminal
Grab cranes ranged between 8–40 tonnes lifting capacity	Not indicated	Not indicated	Combined Terminal Operators
Ships gear used for unloading, Two 500tph loading spouts, one each at Berths 8 and 9	Not indicated	80,000 tonnes silo capacity	Dalian Port Authority
One pneumatic ship unloader	35,000dwt	37,000 tonnes silo capacity	Guangzhou Port Affairs Bureau

COUNTRY/ PORT	TERMINAL NAME	PHONE	FAX	BERTH/DOCK LIMITATIONS
Shanghai	Ming Sheng Stevedores Nos 2, 3 and 4	(86) 216 329 0660	(86) 216 329 0202	Dock Lengths 169m, 171m and 213m, Draft 8.6–9.6m, Dock height 5.3m
Shekou	Shekou No 9 Terminal	(86) 755 669 1135	(86) 755 668 5859	Length 300m, Loa 280m, Draft 12m
Tianjin	Terminal No 13	(86) 22 570 7540	(86) 22 570 9747	Length 251m, Draft 11.5m
Xiamen	Dongdu No 2	(86) 592 601 3616	(86) 592 601 0034	Length 254m, Draft 11.7m, access channel limited to 8m depth
Zhanjiang	Zhanjiang Berth No 404	(86) 759 225 4011	(86) 759 228 0814	Loa 240m, Beam 32m, Draft 11.5m, access channel limited to 9.6m depth
CYPRUS				
Limassol	Limassol Grain Terminal	(357) 5 365 246	(357) 5 365 597	Not indicated
DENMARK				
Kalundborg	Kalundborg Bulk Terminal	(45) 5351 1901	(45) 5351 1752	Loa 235m, Draft 12m
EGYPT				
Alexandria	Kamaria Grain Terminal	(20) 3 483 1640	(20) 3 445 8397	Length 365m, Draft 10m
Damietta	Mina Damyut Terminal	(20) 57 325 940	(20) 57 325 930	Length 600m, Draft 14.5m, Loa 250m
Port Said	Asswan and Observer Grain Terminal	(20) 66 223 892	(20) 3 445 8397	Length 590m, Draft 11.6m
Safaga	Grain Berth No 1	(20) 62 227 375	(20) 62 227 375	Length 289m, Draft 14m

EQUIPMENT AND HANDLING RATES	LARGEST VESSEL/CARGO	STORAGE FACILITIES	OPERATOR/ OTHER DETAILS
Six pneumatic ship unloaders of 150–200tph each	25,000dwt	Around 50,000 tonnes warehousing	Ming Sheng Stevedores
Nineteen grab cranes of 10–35 tonnes lift capacity	45,000dwt	Not indicated	Port Authority of Shekou
Two floating grab cranes of 120tph and 200tph, one pneumatic spout unloader	20,000dwt	60,000 tonnes silo capacity	Tianjin Port Authority
Three 10 tonnes shore grab cranes	25,000dwt	Around 50,000 tonnes silo capacity	Xiamen Port Affairs Bureau
Shore grab cranes	45,000dwt	Around 50,000 tonnes silo capacity	Zhanjiang Port Authority
Three pneumatic ship unloaders	25,000dwt	30,000 tonnes silo capacity	Cyprus Ports Authority, silo expansion project to 70,000 tonnes storage capacity to be completed during 1998
Two portal grab crames	AMADEUS, 66,916dwt	50,000 tonnes in four flat stores	Kalundborg Bulk Terminal
Two mobile pneumatic ship unloaders	40,000dwt	Two silos, one each of 100,000 tonnes and of 48,000 tonnes capacity	Alexandria Port Authority
Two 350tph pneumatic ship unloaders	80,000dwt	100,000 tonnes silo capacity	Damietta Port Authority
Floating discharge utilising mobile Vacuvators through converted bulk carriers (ASSWAN and OBSERVER) to shoreside facilities	45,000dwt	80,000 tonnes silo capacity	Port Said Port Authority
Two mobile pneumatic ship unloaders	Loa 220m, 12.2m Draft maximum	100,000 tonnes silo capacity	Ports and Lights Administration, Safaga

COUNTRY/ PORT	TERMINAL NAME	PHONE	FAX	BERTH/DOCK LIMITATIONS
ESTONIA				
Tallin	Tallin Grain Terminal	(372) 6 319 502	(372) 6 319 544	Three Berths, Nos 7, 8 and 9: Lengths 302m, 280m and 330m; Drafts 14.5m, 14.5m and 17.4m
FINLAND				
Helsinki	Munkkisaari Quay, Berth LHA	(358) 9 172 331	(358) 9 1733 3232	Length 196m, Draft 7.4m
Loviisa	South Quay Grain Terminal	(358) 19 515 163	(358) 19 515 055	Length 141m, Draft 8.5m
Naantali	Grain Terminal	(358) 2 755 111	(358) 2 751 727	Length 370m, Draft 13m
Rauma	Petajas Quay Facility	(358) 2 834 4710	(358) 2 822 6369	Length 315m, Draft 10.5m
FRANCE				
Brest	Quai 6th Sud	(33) 98 46 2380	(33) 98 46 2380	Length 230m, Draft 12m
Brest	Quai 6th Est	(33) 98 46 2380	(33) 98 46 2380	Length 165m, Draft 10m
Le Havre	SHGT Multibulk Centre	(33) 2 32 74 2480	(33) 2 35 21 3815	Length 251m, Draft 17.1m at main berth, Length 110m, Draft 7m at coaster/barge berth
Lorient	Port de Commerce Lorient	(33) 97 87 7600	(33) 97 37 2219	Three quays: one of Length 568m, Draft 10m; one of Length 150m, Draft 8m; one of Length 120m, Draft 9m
Nantes	Port Atlantique, Montoir Agribulk Terminal	(33) 40 44 2020	(33) 40 44 2181	Four berths, total Length 820m, Draft 8.5–9.5m maximum
Sète	Multibulk Berth	(33) 4 67 46 2828	(33) 4 67 74 2701	Length 200m, Draft 13m

EQUIPMENT AND HANDLING RATES	LARGEST VESSEL/CARGO	STORAGE FACILITIES	OPERATOR/ OTHER DETAILS
Not indicated	Loa 280m, Draft 16.5m	300,000 tonnes silo storage capacity	Port Authority of Muuga, Tallin
One pneumatic grain unloader owned by State Granary	Not indicated	Not indicated	Port of Helsinki
Not indicated	Not indicated	60,000 tonnes silo capacity	Port of Loviisa, Grain and Coal imports quay
Two 250tph pneumatic unloaders	70,000dwt	Not indicated	Port of Naantali, Grain and Coal imports quay
Not indicated	Not indicated	125,000 tonnes silo capacity	Port of Rauma Authority
One 30 tonnes grab crane, two 8 tonnes grab cranes	80,000dwt	32,000 tonnes vertical silo capacity, one 25,000 tonnes flat store linker via conveyor and one 30,000 tonnes flat store not linked to berth	Chambre de Commerce et d'Industrie
Three 8 tonnes grab cranes	50,000dwt	Same as for Quai 6th Sud	Chambre de Commerce et d'Industrie
Two gantry grab cranes, one each of 1200tph and 500tph	150,000dwt at main berth, 8000dwt at coaster berth	45,000 tonnes flat store	SHGT Centre de Commerce International
Grab cranes	Loa 270m, Draft 11m (part laden)	13,000 tonnes transit silo capacity, 180,000 tonnes of private warehousing and 120,000 tonnes flat stores	Chambre de Commerce et d'Industrie du Morbihan
Two continuous ship unloaders of 1200tph each, five 15 tonnes (250tph) grab cranes and one 20 tonnes (500tph) grab crane	KLEON, 68,430dwt	400,000 tonnes warehousing capacity	Port of Nantes/St Nazaire
Three grab cranes	Loa 180m	20,000 tonnes silo capacity	Chambre de Commerce et d'Industrie Sète

COUNTRY/ PORT	TERMINAL NAME	PHONE	FAX	BERTH/DOCK LIMITATIONS
GERMANY				
Brake	Karl Gross Silo	(49) 4401 1081	(49) 4401 10832	Discharging: Loa 275m, Draft 11.8m; Loading: Loa 260m, Draft 11m
Brake	J Muller Terminals	(49) 4401 9140	(49) 4401 914229	Discharging: Loa 275m, Draft 11.8m; Loading: Loa 260m, Draft 11m
Bremen	Bremen Lagerhaus Gesellschaft	(49) 421 398 3942	(49) 421 398 3865	Discharging: Loa 270m, Draft 106m; Loading: Loa 220m, Draft 8.5m
Bremen	AJ Muller Terminals	(49) 421 389 960	(49) 421 381 298	Loa 170m, Draft 8.5m
Emden	Emder Lagerhaus	(49) 49 2120 311	(49) 49 2180 0225	Length 450m, Draft 8.5m
Hamburg	GTH	(49) 40 751 060	(49) 40 751 0633	Length 270m, Draft 12.5m discharging/ 11.3m loading, Beam 42m
Hamburg	NHG Terminal	(49) 40 752 7070	(49) 40 752 2512	Loa 285m, Draft 13.8m, Beam unrestricted
Kiel	Nordhafen Grain Terminal	(49) 431 30932	(49) 431 94477	Length 1068m, Draft 9.5m
Nordenham	Midgard Terminal	(49) 473 1810	(49) 473 88564	Loa 270m, Draft 24m
Rostock	Port of Rostock Terminal	(49) 381 350 3500	(49) 381 350 3505	Berth 16: Length 210m, Draft 7.3m; Berth 17: Length 210m, Draft 11.3m; Berth 18: Length 210m, Draft 1.3m
GREECE				
Thessaloniki	Port of Thessaloniki Grain Terminal	(30) 31 593 911	(30) 31 510 500	Length 160m discharging/120m loading, Draft 9.3m
INDONESIA				
Panjang	Berths A, B, C and D	(62) 721 31447	(62) 721 3115	Lengths: A 172m, B 210m, C 138m, D 486m; Drafts A 7m, B 7m, C 8m, D 11m

EQUIPMENT AND HANDLING RATES	LARGEST VESSEL/CARGO	STORAGE FACILITIES	OPERATOR/ OTHER DETAILS
One 600tph elevator, one 600tph ship loader	Loa 275m	80,000 tonnes silo capacity	Grain and Feedstuffs Terminals – River Weser
One 800tph ship unloader, one 600tph ship loader	Loa 275m	150,000 tonnes silo capacity	Grain and Feedstuffs Terminals – River Weser
Three 1200tph elevators, two 400tph ship loaders	Loa 270m	150,000 tonnes silo capacity	Grain and Feedstuffs Terminals – River Weser
One 200tph elevator, two 250tph ship loaders	Loa 170m	120,000 tonnes silo capacity	Grain and Feedstuffs Terminals – River Weser
Two shore elevators, 5000 tonnes/day discharge	92,600dwt	150,000 tonnes silo capacity	Outer Harbour Terminal
Five ship unloading elevators, seven ship loading spouts	Loa 270m	250,000 tonnes silo capacity, 30 tonnes flat store	Getreide Terminal Hamburg
Two 330tph pneumatic ship unloaders, one 1000tph mechanical ship unloader, one 1200tph mechanical ship loader	87,000 tonnes	187,000 tonnes silo capacity	Neuhof Hafengesellschaft
One 200tph travelling elevator	Loa 245m	77,000 tonnes silo capacity	Kiel Lagerhaus Gesellschaft
One 400tph elevator, one 300tph elevator	Loa 270m	28,000 tonnes silo capacity	Midgard
Berth 16: Two grab cranes; Berth 18: Two pneumatic unloaders	50,000dwt	80,000 tonnes silo capacity, plus 165,000 tonnes other capacity available from three private companies	Seehafen Rostock Umschlagsgesellschaft
One tower pipe, 2000 tonnes daily discharge rate (roughly 250tph)	Not indicated	20,000 tonnes silo capacity	Thessaloniki Port Authority
Unloading and loading through ships gear	40,000dwt	145,000 tonnes silo capacity	Panjang Port Administration

COUNTRY/ PORT	TERMINAL NAME	PHONE	FAX	BERTH/DOCK LIMITATIONS
Tanjung Perak	Bogasari Flour Mills Terminal	(62) 31 329 3082	(62) 31 329 1843	Length 180m, Draft 9.7m
Tanjung Priok	Bogasari Flour Mills Berth	(62) 21 430 1048	(62) 21 491 677	Length 180m, Draft 9.8m
IRAQ				
Basrah	Basrah Grain Terminal	(964) 7711	NA	Length 213m, Draft 8.8m
IRELAND				
Cork	Ringaskiddy Deepwater Terminal	(353) 21 273 125	(353) 21 276 484	Length 335m, Draft 13.4m
ISRAEL				
Haifa	Haifa Grain Quays 8 and 9	(97) 4 851 8111	(97) 4 867 4853	Length 281m, Draft 13.5m
ITALY				
Genoa	Santa Limbania Terminal	(39) 10 2411	(39) 10 241 2382	Draft 10.3m
Genoa	Ponte Parodi Terminal	(39) 10 2411	(39) 10 241 2382	Draft 12.8m
Livorno	New Port, Stabilimento dei Silos Berth	(39) 586 893 362	(39) 586 884 578	Length 246m, Draft 8.7m
Savona	Savona Silos	(39) 19 821 295	(39) 19 821 462	Length 128m, Draft 10.6m
Savona	Cereol Silos	(39) 19 880 695	NA	Length 150m, Draft 11m
Venice	Venice Grain & Feedstuff Terminal	(39) 41 533 4484	(39) 41 533 4577	Porto Marghera Pier B: Berth Lengths 350m, 420m and 300m; Draft 10m throughout, Beam 35m
IVORY COAST				
Abidjan	Grands Moulins D'Abidjan, Berth No 1 North Quay	(225) 242 640	(225) 242 328	North Quay Berths 1 to 5: Total Length 775m, Draft 10m

EQUIPMENT AND HANDLING RATES	LARGEST VESSEL/CARGO	STORAGE FACILITIES	OPERATOR/ OTHER DETAILS
Three sets of ship unloading spouts, 2000tph combined	65,000dwt, 55,000 tonnes	126,000 tonnes silo capacity	Bogasari Flour Mills
Three sets of mobile ship unloading spouts, 4500 tonnes daily discharge rate	60,000 tonnes	150,000 tonnes silo capacity	Bogasari Flour Mills
NA	Loa 183m	65,000 tonnes silo capacity	State Organisation for Iraqi Ports
Two 400tph grab cranes	60,000dwt fully laden	Three privately owned silos, totalling 100,000 tonnes capacity	Port of Cork
Three 600tph mobile ship unloaders	66,000dwt	100,000 tonnes silo capacity	Dagon-Batey Mamguroth Le-Israel
600tph grain discharge capacity	Not indicated	65,000 tonnes silo capacity	Port of Genoa
450tph grain discharge capacity	Not indicated	45,000 tonnes silo capacity	Port of Genoa
200tph grain discharge	Not indicated	12,000 tonnes silo, plus flat storage capacity	Port of Livorno
Two 250tph mobile pneumatic ship unloading towers (two 125tph pipes each tower)	50,000dwt, maximum Loa 220m	Approximately 60,000 tonnes silo capacity	Porto de Savona
Two 850tph slewing grab unloaders	50,000dwt, Loa 193m	50,000 tonnes silo capacity	Porto de Savona
Four 300tph pneumatic elevators, one 600tph Siwertell screw unloader, two 330tph bridge grab crane unloaders, plus four 30 tonnes grab cranes	GEORGIOS P, Loa 255m	Approximately 135,000 tonnes grains silo capacity, 100,000 tonnes flat store for feedstuffs	TMB SRL, Venice
150tph grain discharge	Loa 260m	30,000 tonnes silo capacity	Port Autonome d'Abidjan

COUNTRY/ PORT	TERMINAL NAME	PHONE	FAX	BERTH/DOCK LIMITATIONS
JAPAN				
Chiba	Chiba Ocean Terminal Berth	(81) 43 242 5541	(81) 43 247 4925	Length 160m, Draft 11.9m
Chiba	Kyodo Silo Berth	(81) 43 246 3737	(81) 43 247 8882	Length 150m, Draft 11.9m
Chiba	Nihon Silo Berth	(81) 43 242 3011	(81) 43 243 1410	Length 160m, Draft 11.9m
Hakata	Hakozaki No 12 and 13 West	(81) 92 282 7164	(81) 92 291 2101	Berth 12: Length 294m, Draft 10.8m; Berth 13: Length 240m, Draft 10.8m
Hakata	Suzaki No 2 and 4 West	(81) 92 282 7164	(81) 92 291 2101	Berth 2: Length 184m, Draft 9.8m; Berth 4: Length 186m, Draft 9.8m
Kagoshima	Pacific Grain Terminal	(81) 99 268 8291	(81) 99 269 5553	Length 170m, Draft 12m
Kashima	Kanto Grain Terminal	(81) 299 92 6531	(81) 299 92 6548	Length 280m, Draft 11.9m
Kashima	Showa Sangyo Pier	(81) 299 92 8952	(81) 299 92 0289	Length 206m, Draft 11.9m
Kashima	Zen-Noh Silo Pier	(81) 299 92 1173	(81) 299 92 6450	Length 210m, Draft 11.9m
Kawasaki	Mitsui Wharf Terminal	(81) 44 333 5315	(81) 44 333 5962	Length 225m, Draft 12m
Kawasaki	Nisshin Seifun Berth	(81) 44 333 5315	(81) 44 333 5962	Length 225m, Draft 11.8m
Kawasaki	Toyo Futo Wharf	(81) 44 333 3521	(81) 44 366 0166	Length 230m, Draft 12m

EQUIPMENT AND HANDLING RATES	LARGEST VESSEL/CARGO	STORAGE FACILITIES	OPERATOR/ OTHER DETAILS
Two 300tph pneumatic ship unloaders with 23.5m pipe outreach	50,000dwt, 40,000 tonnes discharged	174,000 tonnes silo capacity	Chiba Ocean Terminal/ Sanpo Unyu Company
Three 800tph pneumatic ship unloaders with 20m pipe outreach	50,000dwt, 40,000 tonnes discharged	152,000 tonnes silo capacity	Kyodo Silo/Ogawa Unyu Company
Three pneumatic ship unloaders of 1000tph combined capacity	50,000dwt, 43,000 tonnes discharged	120,000 tonnes silo capacity	Nihon Futu Soko
Two ship unloaders serving both berths, approximately 200–350tph each unloader	63,000dwt, 55,000 tonnes discharged		Hakata Futo Company
Four ship unloaders serving both berths, approximately 200–350tph each unloader	63,000dwt, 55,000 tonnes discharged		Hakata Futo Company
Two 400tph and one 1000tph pneumatic ship unloaders, one 800tph mechanical unloader, two barge loaders, one each of 200tph and 400tph	C FYLYOS, 71,733dwt and PACIFIC PROSPECTOR, 72,800dwt, ships to 80,000dwt possible with maximum Loa 250m	236,260 tonnes silo capacity	Pacific Grain Terminal
One 400tph pneumatic ship unloader and two 400tph mechanical ship unloaders	NORD MORITZ, 72,610dwt, 57,607 tonnes discharged	193,000 tonnes silo capacity	Kanto Grain
Three 600tph ship unloaders	60,000 tonnes	270,000 tonnes silo capacity	Showa Sangyo
Two 600tph ship unloaders, 16.7m outreach	60,000 tonnes	214,000 tonnes silo capacity	Zen-Noh Silo Company
One 180tph ship unloader for handling soyabeans only	Not indicated, but approximately 60,000dwt	Not indicated	Mitsui Wharf & Company, terminal handles mainly coal, iron and steel, and cement
Two 640tph pneumatic ship unloaders	Approximately 60,000dwt	100,000 tonnes silo capacity	Nisshin Seifun
One 600tph ship unloader, 22m outreach	Approximately 60,000dwt	170,000 tonnes silo capacity	Toyo Futo Wharf and Warehouse Company

COUNTRY/ PORT	TERMINAL NAME	PHONE	FAX	BERTH/DOCK LIMITATIONS
Kinuura	Itochu Dolphin Wharf	(81) 566 42 1521	(81) 566 42 1523	Length 195m, Draft 11.8m
Kinuura	Nakanipon Dolphin	(81) 566 42 0321	(81) 566 42 0512	Length 162m, Draft 11.8m
Kobe	Hanshin Silo, Eastern No 3 Sector	NA	NA	Length 246m, Draft 12.5m
Kobe	Konan Futo Terminal, Eastern No 4 Sector	(81) 78 451 1141	(81) 78 451 8023	Length 214m, Draft 10.8m
Kobe	Kobe Futo Terminal, Shinko Pier No 7	NA	NA	Length 200m, Draft 10m
Kobe	Showa Sangyo Terminal	(81) 78 841 4481	(81) 78 841 6405	Length 213m, Draft 10.4m
Kobe	Tomen Silo	(81) 78 811 0911	(81) 78 811 0914	Length 215m, Draft 10.4m
Kobe	Zen-Noh Silo	(81) 78 811 3562	(81) 78 843 1002	Length 171m, Draft 10.4m
Nagoya	Chita Futo J-5	(81) 562 54 0018	(81) 562 56 0161	Length 185m, Draft 12m maximum
Nagoya	Nisshin Flour Milling G-1 Terminal	(81) 562 32 4135	(81) 562 32 2169	Length 150m, Draft 12m
Nagoya	Rinoru Oil Mills BH2	(81) 562 11 9789	(81) 562 12 6730	Length 182m, Draft 10m
Nagoya	Toyo Grain Terminal J-T	(81) 562 32 5571	(81) 562 33 2357	Length 200m, Draft 12m
Nagoya	Zen-Noh Silo J-S	(81) 562 32 5207	(81) 562 33 5709	Length 190m Draft, 12m
Yokohama	Daikoku Pier L-8 Chugai Soku	(81) 45 502 8371	(81) 45 502 6742	Length 230m, Draft 12m
Yokohama	Government Silo Berth	(81) 45 441 7755	(81} 45 453 3292	Length 175m, Draft 10m

EQUIPMENT AND HANDLING RATES	LARGEST VESSEL/CARGO	STORAGE FACILITIES	OPERATOR/ OTHER DETAILS
Two 600tph ship unloaders, 20m outreach	70,000dwt, 50,000 tonnes discharged	48,000 tonnes silo capacity	Itochu Kinuura Marine Terminal
Two 750tph pneumatic ship unloaders, 18m outreach	70,000dwt, 50,000 tonnes discharged	75,500 tonnes silo capacity	Central Japan Grain Terminal Company
Not indicated	50,000dwt	Not indicated	Hanshin Silo
Three pneumatic ship unloaders, 1000tph combined capacity	75,000dwt	120,000 tonnes silo capacity	Konan Futo Company
Not indicated	40,000dwt	Not indicated	Kobe Futo Company
Three ship unloaders, 2000tph capacity	Not indicated, approximately 50,000dwt	135,000 tonnes silo capacity	Showa Sangyo
Three pneumatic ship unloaders, 2000tph capacity	50,000dwt	67,000 tonnes silo capacity	Tomen Silo Company
Two ship unloaders of 2500tph, 18m outreach	72,000dwt, 47,900 tonnes discharged	89,160 tonnes silo capacity	Zen-Noh Silo Company
Two grab cranes, one continuous ship unloader, combined discharge rate 1200tph	70,000dwt, 55,000 tonnes discharged	113,500 tonnes silo capacity	Chita Futo Company
Three 250tph pneumatic ship unloaders, 25m outreach	HERCULES BULKER, 60,682dwt, 53,700 tonnes discharged	111,450 tonnes silo capacity	Nisshin Flour Milling Company
Two 1000tph continuous ship unloaders, 28.2m outreach	77,000dwt maximum, 23,600 tonnes discharged	60,000 tonnes silo capacity	Rinoru Oil Mills Company
Two 750tph pneumatic ship unloaders, 20m outreach	50,000 tonnes	54,430 tonnes silo capacity	Toyo Grain Company
One mechanical continuous ship unloader and one pneumatic ship unloader	55,000 tonnes	152,000 tonnes silo capacity	Zen-Noh Silo Company
Two 520tph pneumatic ship unloaders	50,000dwt, Loa 197m	80,000 tonnes silo capacity	Chugai Warehouse & Transportation Company
Two 400tph pneumatic ship unloaders	Storage limitation of 20,000 tonnes	20,000 tonnes silo capacity	Japanese Government

COUNTRY/ PORT	TERMINAL NAME	PHONE	FAX	BERTH/DOCK LIMITATIONS
Yokohama	Kokusai Futo Berth	(81) 45 625 7024	(81) 45 621 5126	Length 282m, Draft 17.3m
Yokohama	Nippon Seifun Berth	(81) 45 453 5711	(81) 45 453 5245	Length 175m, Draft 9m
Yokohama	Nisshin Seiyo Terminal	(81) 45 757 5060	(81) 45 757 5065	Length 230m, Draft 12m
KUWAIT				
Shuwaihk	Kuwait Flour Mills Berth 1	(965) 243 4752	(965) 243 6752	Length 186m, Draft 9.6m
MALAYSIA				
Penang	Prai Bulk Cargo Terminal	(60) 4 380 2200	(60) 4 380 397 0605	Length overall totals 588m ranging from 140–250m, Draft alongside ranges from 10.2m at Berths 1, 2 and 3, and 7m at Berth 4
Port Klang	South Port Bulk Terminal	(60) 3 376 7411	(60) 3 376 4895	Length 176.7m, Draft 10m
Port Klang	North Port Bulk Terminal	(60) 3 376 7411	(60) 3 376 7411	Two Berths: Length 213m, Draft 11.5m, Quay Width 15.85m for both berths
MALTA				
Valletta	Kordin Grain Terminal	(356) 696 977	(356) 800 085	Two Berths: Magazine Wharf Length 252m, Draft 13.7m for unloading; Laboratory Wharf Length 191m, Draft 12m for loading
MOROCCO				
Casablanca	Mole du Commerce, Berths 20–24 and T3–T4	(212) 2 317 111	(212) 2 313 501	Length 240m, Draft 9.5m
Safi	Silo Quay	NA	NA	Length 270m, Draft 9.2–10.3m

EQUIPMENT AND HANDLING RATES	LARGEST VESSEL/CARGO	STORAGE FACILITIES	OPERATOR/ OTHER DETAILS
Three 600tph shoreside grab cranes, 29.5m outreach	Not indicated	140,000 tonnes silo capacity	Kokusai Futo Company
Two pneumatic discharge pipes, 550tph capacity	23,000dwt, Loa 175m	80,000 tonnes silo capacity	Nippon Flour Mills
Two 800tph pneumatic ship unloaders, 21m outreach	65,000dwt	110,000 tonnes silo capacity	Nisshin Seiyo Company
One 400tph ship unloader, 20m outreach	40,000dwt, Loa 175m	Silo and flat storage available	Kuwait Flour Mills
Two rail mounted grab cranes of 12.5 tonnes lift capacity	LUCKY BULKER, Loa 233m	Approximately 100,000 tonnes storage capacity in thirteen different port and privately owned warehouses	Penang Port Sdn Bhd
Three pneumatic pipes, three quayside hoppers and belt conveyors to storage	AGHIA SOPHIA, around 23,000dwt, Loa 182.5m	Private warehousing and silos	Klang Port Management
Two 12 tonnes high speed grab cranes, two belt conveyor lines from quay to warehousing	MAITZ TRAMP, Loa 293m	Four warehouses with 54,000–83,000 tonnes flat store capacity depending on product density	Klang Port Management
1100tph unloading capacity, 1250tph loading capacity	70,000 tonnes	86,000 tonnes silo capacity	Kordin Grain
Three 200tph grab gantry cranes	Not indicated	30,000 tonnes silo capacity	Office d'Exploitation des Ports
Two 100tph pneumatic unloaders	Loa 185m without shifting vessel at berth	24,000 tonnes silo capacity	Office d'Exploitation des Ports

COUNTRY/ PORT	TERMINAL NAME	PHONE	FAX	BERTH/DOCK LIMITATIONS
NETHERLANDS				
Amsterdam	IGMA Bulk Terminal	(31) 20 580 8111	(31) 20 682 3267	Length 366m, Draft 15m
Amsterdam	OBA Grain Terminal	(31) 20 587 3750	(31) 20 611 8215	Length unrestricted, Draft 16.5m
Rotterdam	EBS Europoort	(31) 181 262 988	(31) 181 258 125	Terminal No 1. Outside Pier: Length 580m, Draft 18m; Inside Pier: Length 370m, Draft 18m. Terminal No 2. Length 230m, Draft 16m
Rotterdam	EBS Botlek	(31) 181 262 988	(31) 181 258 125	Length 490m, Draft 12.8m at Pier, Length and Draft unlimited for floating anchorages
Rotterdam	Meneba Meel/ Latenstein Silo Excelsior	(31) 10 423 8911	(31) 10 423 8626	Loa 250m, Draft 8m
NORWAY				
Stavanger	Stavanger Havnesilo	(47) 51 891 045	(47) 51 890 440	Length 165m, Draft 15m

EQUIPMENT AND HANDLING RATES	LARGEST VESSEL/CARGO	STORAGE FACILITIES	OPERATOR/ OTHER DETAILS
Two 700tph Siwertell screw ship unloaders, two 16 tonnes (500tph) floating grab cranes with weighing tower, two 25 tonnes (1250tph) floating grab cranes with weighing tower, one 350tph floating elevator, and one each 350tph shore and floating elevators	110,000 tonnes fully laden	52,000 tonnes silo capacity, plus 50,000 floating storage	Internationale Graanoverslag
Two 30 tonnes travelling gantry cranes, one 16 tonnes floating grab crane	MEGA DALE, 99,000dwt	Approximately 90,000 tonnes top loading warehouse storage	OBA Group
Three 1000tph shore based pneumatic ship unloaders at Terminal No 1; Two 1000tph shore based pneumatic ship unloaders at Terminal No 2; One 36 tonnes gantry grab crane, additional floating pneumatic and grab ship unloaders as necessary	Vessels from 20,000–120,000 tonnes at Terminal No 2; vessels from 60,000–200,000 tonnes at Terminal No 1	Two silos with 210,000 tonnes total capacity	European Bulk Services
Two shore based 600tph pneumatic ship unloaders, seven floating grab cranes between 12–36 tonnes lift capacity, four 750–1500tph capacity floating weighing towers, one 800tph floating pneumatic ship unloader	Vessels from Panamax to 150,000 tonnes at Pier Terminal, vessels up to 120,000 tonnes at floating anchorages	60,000 tonnes silo capacity, 32,000 tonnes flat storage	European Bulk Services
Grab and pneumatic ship unloaders	30,000dwt	120,000 tonnes silo capacity	Meneba Meel
Two pneumatic ship unloaders, one mechanical Simporter ship unloader, 2000tph combined discharge capacity	Not indicated	30,000 tonnes molasses silo, 195,000 tonnes grain silo capacity	Stavanger Havnesilo

COUNTRY/ PORT	TERMINAL NAME	PHONE	FAX	BERTH/DOCK LIMITATIONS
OMAN				
Port Sultan Qaboos	Port Sultan Qaboos, Berth 3	(968) 701 291	(968) 797 994	Length 228m, Draft 10.5m, Air Draft 13m
PHILIPPINES				
Mariveles	Asia Terminals Berth	(63) 42 935 4930	(63) 42 935 4338	Length 220m, Draft 14.5m
POLAND				
Gdynia	India Quay Berth	(48) 58 274 002	(48) 58 275 601	Total Quay Length 1009m, Draft 11m
Szczecin	Zbozowe Berth	(48) 91 308 999	(48) 91 624 842	Length 220m, Draft 9.1m
PORTUGAL				
Lisbon	Beato Terminal	(351) 1 3859 658	(351) 1 3859 614	Length 200m, Draft 8m
Leixoes	Silopor Leixoes	(351) 1 3859 658	(351) 1 3859 614	Length 200m, Draft 9m
Trafaria	Silopor Trafaria	(351) 1 3859 658	(351) 1 3859 614	Two discharge berths: Lengths 230m and 250m, Drafts 13.2m and 15m. Two loading berths: Lengths 150m and 200m, Drafts both 13.7m
QATAR				
Umm Said	Qatar Flour Mills	(974) 457 457	NA	Length 213m, Draft 11.6m
ROMANIA				
Constantza	Port Grain Terminal			Berths No 17, 18, 24, 31, 32 and 33; Lengths from 112–230m, Drafts from 7–10.6m

EQUIPMENT AND HANDLING RATES	LARGEST VESSEL/CARGO	STORAGE FACILITIES	OPERATOR/ OTHER DETAILS
One 250tph pneumatic ship unloader	27,000dwt	120,000 tonnes silo capacity	Oman Flour Mills
Four 750tph Siwertell screw type ship unloaders, fully mobile along whole of quay length	Can accommodate two 80,000dwt vessels simultaneously	50,000 tonnes warehouse storage capacity	Asia Terminals Inc, adjacent San Miguel Corp Terminal discharges malt for brewing via 2200tph rated Buhler Portalino ship unloader
Shore based and floating elevators providing up to 1000tph	Loa 247m	Two silos, one of 12,200 tonnes and one (new) of 14,400 tonnes capacity	Port of Gdynia
Not indicated	Loa 210m	75,000 tonnes silo capacity	Port of Szczecin
One 600tph Siwertell screw ship unloader, one 600tph Hartmann pneumatic ship unloader	30,000dwt fully laden	120,000 tonnes silo capacity	Silopor
Two 15 tonnes (350tph) grab cranes	30,000dwt fully laden	100,000 tonnes silo capacity, 15,000 tonnes mechanised flat store	Silopor
Three 1000tph pneumatic ship unloaders	80,000 tonnes fully laden	200,000 tonnes vertical silo capacity	Silopor
Two mobile Vacuvators connecting to six discharge points	Not indicated	Not indicated	Qatar Flour Mills
Five 150tph mobile pneumatic elevators, two 250tph quayside pneumatic elevators, two 300tph floating pneumatic elevators	Draft limit of 10.6m	90,000 tonnes silo capacity	Constantza Port Authority

COUNTRY/ PORT	TERMINAL NAME	PHONE	FAX	BERTH/DOCK LIMITATIONS
SAUDI ARABIA				
Dammam	Grain Silos and Flour Mill Organisation	(966) 3 859 1171	(966) 3 589 1174	Length 240m, Draft 13m
Jeddah Islamic Port	Jeddah Grain Facility	(966) 2 647 1200	(966) 2 647 7411	Loa 250m, Draft 14m
Jubail	Grain Silos and Flour Mill Organisation	(966) 3 859 1171	(966) 3 589 1174	Length 250m, Draft 13m maximum/12.6m permissable at all times
SLOVENIA				
Koper	Port Grain Terminal	(386) 66 456 100	(386) 66 34028	Pier No 1: Length 183m, Draft 13.5m
SOUTH KOREA				
Busan	Woosung Industries Pier 5	(82) 51 634 3151	(82) 51 644 4405	Length 371m, Draft 12m, Air Draft 20m
Inchon	Korea Silo Company Pier 7	(82) 32 763 3211	(82) 32 763 9178	Two berths, both: Length 301m, Draft 12.5, Width 14.4m, Loa 250m, Beam 32.2m
Ulsan	Silo Tae Young Chemical Corporation	(82) 522 77 0621	(82) 522 77 4141	Length 187m, Draft 12m, Air Draft 18m
SPAIN				
Barcelona	Contradique Wharf, East Side Terminal	(34) 3 150 011	(34) 3 173 042	Length 241.5m, Draft 13.1m

EQUIPMENT AND HANDLING RATES	LARGEST VESSEL/CARGO	STORAGE FACILITIES	OPERATOR/ OTHER DETAILS
Two pneumatic ship unloaders plus seven mobile pneumatic/ mechanical Vacuvator type unloaders	50,000 tonnes	80,000 tonnes silo capacity	Arabian Agricultural Services, Operator and Stevedores
Total of 21 mobile Vacuvator type pneumatic unloaders	DERIANDROS OF KORINTHOS, discharged 99,376 tonnes barley	Direct bulk delivery to consignees, bagged cargoes to warehousing	Jeddah Islamic Port
Four pneumatic discharge units at Berths 11 and 12	47,000 tonnes	None	Arabian Agricultural Services, Operator and Stevedores
Grab cranes discharge	Approximately 50,000dwt	60,000 tonnes silo capacity	Lucka Koper
Four 200tph unloading pneumatic pipes, 35m spout outreach	ELPIS, 55,200 tonnes maize discharged	103,000 tonnes silo capacity	Woosung Industries
Two 400tph pneumatic ship unloaders, one 750tph mechanical ship unloader	FAREAST VICTORY, 57,225 tonnes	Two silo groups. Group A: 75,000 tonnes capacity, Group B: 100,000 tonnes vertical silo capacity, 50,000 tonnes steel bins capacity, plus 75,000 tonnes flat store warehousing	Korea Silo Company
Two 350tph mobile ship unloaders, 32m outreach	Not indicated	Not indicated	Tae Young Chemical Company
Pneumatic ship unloaders, two pipes of 200tph each, one mobile unloader with two 200tph pipes, one mobile unloader with one 400tph pipe	75,000 tonnes	145,000 tonnes vertical silo capacity	Ergransa

COUNTRY/ PORT	TERMINAL NAME	PHONE	FAX	BERTH/DOCK LIMITATIONS
Gijon	Port of Gijon Grain Terminal	(34) 85 354 945	(34) 85 359 917	Three Berths. Muelles de la Osa Outer Berth: Length 371m, Draft 11.5–12m; Inner Berth: Length 198m, Draft 9m; Muelle del Moliner: Length 310m, Draft 14m
La Coruna	La Coruna Multiport	(34) 81 227 402	(34) 81 205 862	Length 540m, Draft 16.5m
Tarragona	Silos de Tarragona	(34) 77 231 213	(34) 77 223 115	Length unrestricted, Draft 11.9m
SUDAN				
Port Sudan	Berth No 15	(249) 2910	(249) 2127	Length 205m, Draft 10.7m
SWEDEN				
Helsingborg	Port of Helsingborg Grain Terminal	(46) 42 106 300	(46) 42 135 483	Length 400m, Draft 10.5–13.5m
TAIWAN				
Kaoshiung	Wharf No 44	(886) 7 811 8490	(886) 7 561 1694	Length 200m, Draft 10.4m, Air Draft 12m
Keelung	Wharf West No 30	(886) 2 420 8499	(886) 2 423 5664	Length 213m, Draft 10.5m
Taichung	Wharf No 1	(886) 4 656 4211	(886) 4 656 8069	Length 250m, Width 20m, Draft 13.5m, Air Draft 16m
Taichung	Wharf No 3	(886) 4 656 4211	(886) 4 656 8069	Length 250m, Draft 13m, Air Draft less than 13.5m
TANZANIA				
Dar es Salaam	Port Grain Terminal	(255) 51 21212	(255) 51 32066	Elevan Berths: Total Length 2016m, Drafts 8–10.2m
TUNISIA				
Bizerte	Quai Cerealier	(216) 2 431 139	(216) 2 433 688	Length 200m, Draft 9.8m

EQUIPMENT AND HANDLING RATES	LARGEST VESSEL/CARGO	STORAGE FACILITIES	OPERATOR/ OTHER DETAILS
Six 12 tonnes grab cranes, two 30 tonnes grab cranes	Not indicated	Three enclosed flat stores, combined area 18,000sqm	Gijon Port Authority
Eight 16 tonnes grab cranes, two 32 tonnes mobile cranes	AMAZON, 77,000dwt	200,000sqm flat store capacity	Port Authority of La Coruna
Three 16 tonnes and two 12 tonnes shore grab cranes	Loa 275m	45,000 tonnes silo capacity, 135,000 tonnes flat store capacity	Silos de Tarragona, SITSA
Not indicated	Not indicated	50,000 tonnes silo capacity	Seaports Corporation of Sudan
One 250tph ship unloader	Panamax to 60,000dwt	250,000 tonnes silo capacity	Port of Helsingborg Authority
Two 350tph mobile pneumatic ship unloaders, 25m pipe outreach	40,000 tonnes	32,000 tonnes silo capacity	Kaoshiung Harbour Bureau
Three mobile pneumatic unloaders, two of 160tph and one of 220tph capacity	37,000 tonnes	50,000 tonnes silo capacity	Keelung Harbour Bureau
Two 300tph mobile pneumatic unloaders, one 550tph mechanical ship unloader	TOMIS HOPE, 58,000 tonnes discharged	90,000 tonnes silo capacity	Far Eastern Silo Company
Two 450tph mobile mechanical ship unloaders	BOBILNA, 60,409 tonnes discharged	61,290 tonnes silo capacity	Far Eastern Silo Company
Portal grab (24) cranes of 7 tonnes capacity each	Not indicated	30,000 tonnes silo capacity	Tanzania Harbours Authority
Three fixed grain ship unloaders	Not indicated	Not indicated	Office des Ports Nationaux

COUNTRY/ PORT	TERMINAL NAME	PHONE	FAX	BERTH/DOCK LIMITATIONS
Sfax	North West Quay Grain Terminal	(216) 4 225 040	(216) 4 225 107	Length 550m, Draft 10.5m
TURKEY				
Akatlar-Istanbul	Toros Terminal	(90) 212 278 5639	(90) 212 268 6259	Platform with two Berths. Main Pier: Length 187m, Draft 14–16m; Central Pier: Length 155m, Draft 12m
Mersin	Berths Nos 7, 14 and 15	(90) 324 231 1267	(90) 324 231 1350	Berths 7, 14 and 15: Lengths 158m, 275m and 275m; Drafts 10m, 11m and 14.5m
Tekirdag	TMO Terminal	NA	NA	One Berth, Length 150m
UKRAINE				
Odessa	Berth No 7 Grain Terminal	(380) 482 226 631	(380) 482 223 919	Not indicated
UNITED ARAB EMIRATES				
Jebel Ali	Gulf Import & Export Company	NA	NA	Length 460m, Draft 13.2m
Mina Zayed	Berth No 19	NA	NA	Length 190m, Draft 11.5m, Air Draft 13.5m
UNITED KINGDOM				
Belfast	Port of Belfast Grain Terminal	(44) 1232 554422	(44) 1232 554411	Draft 10.2m
Bristol	Bristol Bulk Terminal	(44) 117 820000	(44) 117 825000	Length 600m, Draft 14.5m, Lock Dimensions: Length 365.7m, Width 42.7m

EQUIPMENT AND HANDLING RATES	LARGEST VESSEL/CARGO	STORAGE FACILITIES	OPERATOR/ OTHER DETAILS
Not indicated	Not indicated	Not indicated	Office des Ports Nationaux
Main Pier: Two 400tph grab cranes, one 300tph pneumatic unloader, one 300tph chain unloader; Central Pier: one 300tph grab crane	105,000 tonnes	60,000 tonnes flat store in four chambers, 50,000 tonnes bulk warehouse, four 5,000 tonnes intermediate grain storage bunkers	Toros Terminal Services
Grab cranes	Not indicated	70,000 tonnes silo capacity	TCCD, General Directorate of Turkish State Railways
One 50tph pneumatic ship loader/unloader	Not indicated	70,000 tonnes silo capacity	TMO, Turkish Grain Office, other grain storage/import facilities at Iskenderun (60,000 tonnes silo), Haydarpasa (four silos totalling 70,580 tonnes), Izmir (76,000 tonnes silo) and Samsun (34,000 tonnes silo)
Two 300tph pneumatic ship unloaders	Not indicated	Not indicated	Port of Odessa Authority
Two 800tph travelling ship loaders/unloaders, 22.5m spout outreach	80,000 tonnes fully laden	120,000 tonnes silo capacity in twelve bins	Gulf Import & Export Company
One 240tph pneumatic ship unloader, 32m spout outreach	70,000dwt	60,000 tonnes silo capacity	Abu Dhabi Flour Mill and Animalfeeds
300tph (12 tonnes) travelling grab cranes equipped with dust aspirated hoppers and suction	30,000dwt	125,000 tonnes silo capacity in four units adjacent to berth, plus 100,000 tonnes flat store	Belfast Harbour Commissioners
Two 2000tph continuous ship unloaders, one 1200tph Simportex, one 250tph Vacuvator	CAPTAIN VENIAMIS, 122,544dwt	200,000 tonnes flat store at Portbury and 100,000 tonnes flat store at Avonmouth	Agricultural Bulk Services (Bristol)

COUNTRY/ PORT	TERMINAL NAME	PHONE	FAX	BERTH/DOCK LIMITATIONS
Edinburgh	Leith Docks Imperial Grain Silo	(44) 131 554 4343	(44) 131 555 1212	Length 197m, Draft 9.2m, Beam 28m
Liverpool	Royal Seaforth Grain Terminal	(44) 151 949 6450	(44) 151 949 6461	Loa 250m, Draft 12.8m
Teesport	Cleveland Potash General Bulk Terminal	(44) 1642 457131	(44) 1642 454184	Length 365m, Loa 230m maximum, Draft 10.9m
Southampton	Continental UK Import Terminal	(44) 1703 222655	(44) 1703 330603	Draft 10.5m, Beam 23m

EQUIPMENT AND HANDLING RATES	LARGEST VESSEL/CARGO	STORAGE FACILITIES	OPERATOR/ OTHER DETAILS
Three pneumatic travelling tower unloaders, up to 400tph each	20,000 tonnes	55,880 tonnes silo capacity	Forth Ports
Two marine unloading towers with bucket elevators and pneumatic pipes plus one pneumatic unloader	80,580dwt, part laden	133,000 tonnes silo capacity	Mersey Docks and Harbour Company
1000tph unloading capacity	60,000 tonnes wheat and barley	7,000 tonnes silo capacity	Cleveland Potash (CPL)
Four grab cranes	Not indicated	Not indicated	Continental UK

Glossary

ABTA	Allied Brewery Traders Association
ADAS	Agricultural Development and Advisory Services
ADF	African Development Fund
AFMM	Association of Fish Meal Manufacturers
AFRC	Agricultural and Food Research Council
AMC	Agricultural Mortgage Corporation Ltd
AMUFOC	Association des Etablissements Multiplicateurs des Semences Fourragères des Communautés Européennes (Association of Fodder Seed Multipliers in the EC)
ARP	Acreage reduction programme
ASSINSEL	Association Internationale des Séléctionneurs pour la Protection des Obtentions Végétales (International Association of Plant Breeders for the Protection of Plant Varieties)
ATB	Agricultural Training Board
AWB	Australian Wheat Board
BAFSM	British Association of Feed Supplement Manufacturers Ltd
BAGCD	British Association of Green Crop Driers Ltd
BCPC	British Crop Protection Council
BEPA	British Edible Pulse Association
BGIDA	British Grain Importers Defence Association Ltd
BIFFEX	Baltic International Freight Futures Exchange
BO&BMA	British Oat & Barley Millers Association
BES	Brewers Society
BSC	British Seeds Council
BSPB	British Society of Plant Breeders Ltd
CAP	Common Agricultural Policy
CBA	Cost benefit analysis
CCFF	Compensatory and Contingency Financing Facility
CELCAA	Comité Européen de Liaison des Commerces Agro-Alimentaires (European Liaison Committee of the Agricultural Trades)
CFCs	Chlorofluorocarbons
CIAT	International Centre for Tropical Agriculture
CIMMYT	International Centre for Maize and Wheat Improvement
COCCEE	Comité des Organisations Commerciales des pays de la Communauté Economique Européenne (EEC Committee of Commercial Organizations)

COCERAL	Comité du Commerce des Céréales et des Aliments de Bétail de la Communauté Economique Européenne (EEC Committee of Traders in Cereals and Animal Feeds)
COGECA	Comité Général de la Coopération Agricole de la Communauté Economique Européenne (General Federation for Agriculture Cooperation in the EC)
COPA	Comité des Organisations Professionnelles Agricoles (Committee of Professional Agricultural Organizations)
COSEMCO	Comité des Semences du Marché Commun (Common Market Seeds Committee)
CWB	Canadian Wheat Board
DAFS	Department of Agriculture and Fisheries for Scotland
DANI	Department of Agriculture for Northern Ireland
DES	Dietary energy supply
DIESA	Department of International Economics and Social Affairs (UN)
DOE	Department of the Environment
EC	European (Economic) Community
ECA	Economic Commission for Africa
ECGD	Export Credit Guarantee Department
ECLAC	Commission for Latin America and the Caribbean
ECLO	Emergency Centre for Locust Operations
ECU	European Currency Unit
ECUK	European Committee of the United Kingdom
EEC	European Economic Community
EEP	Export Enhancement Programme
EEZ	Exclusive Economic Zone
EFF	Extended Fund Facility
EIA	Environmental impact assessment
ELGA	European Liaison Group for Agriculture
EMU	European Monetary Union
ESCAP	Economic and Social Commission for Asia and the Pacific
EUROMALT	Working Party of Maltsters in the EC
FAC	Federation of Agricultural Co-operatives (UK) Ltd
FAC	Food Aid Convention
FBS	Food balance sheets
FEFAC	Fédération Européenne des Fabricants d'Aliments Composés pour Animaux (European Federation of Animal Feed Manufacturers)
FEFENA	Fédération Européenne des Fabricants d'Adjuvants pour la Nutrition Animale (European Federation of Feed Supplement Manufacturers)
FEOGA	Fonds Européens de Garantie et d'Orientation Agricole (European Guidance and Guarantee Fund)
FIS	Fédération Internationale du Commerce des Semences (Federation of International Seed Traders)
FOSFA	Federation of Oils, Seeds and Fats Associations Ltd
FOWCIS	Forest and Wildlands Conservation Information System

FTA	Freight Transport Association
GAFTA	Grain and Feed Trade Association
GATT	General Agreement on Tariffs and Trade
GDP	Gross domestic product
GIS	Geographical Information System
GNP	Gross national product
GSP	Generalized System of Trade Preferences
HGCA	Home Grown Cereals Authority
HYVs	High-yielding varieties
IBAP	Intervention Board for Agricultural Produce
IDA	International Development Association
IDB	Inter-American Development Bank
IEFR	International Emergency Food Reserve
IFAD	International Fund for Agricultural Development
IGC	International Grains Council
IGOs	Intergovernmental organizations
IMF	International Monetary Fund
IPC	International Policy Council on Agriculture and Trade
IPM	Integrated pest management
ISTA	International Seed Testing Association
ITTO	International Tropical Timber Organization
IUCN	International Union for the Conservation of Nature
IWC	International Wheat Council
LDCs	Least developed countries
MAFF	Ministry of Agriculture, Fisheries and Food
MAGB	Maltsters Association of Great Britain
NABIM	National Association of British and Irish Millers Ltd
NFU	National Farmers Union of England & Wales
NFUS	National Farmers Union of Scotland
NGOs	Non-governmental organizations
NIAB	National Institute of Agricultural Botany
NIAE	National Institute of Agricultural Engineering
NIGTA	Northern Ireland Grain Trade Association
NMP	Net material product
OCDE	Organisation de Coopération et de Développement Economiques
OECD	Organization for Economic Co-operation and Development
ONIC	Office National Interprofessionel des Céréales (National Interprofessional Office for Cereals) (France)
OPEC	Organization of the Petroleum Exporting Countries
PBI	Plant Breeding Institute
PLA	Port of London Authority
PLD	Paid land diversion
PPP	Polluter pays principle
PVRO	Plant Variety Rights Office
RASE	Royal Agricultural Society of England
RMB	Renminbi-yuan (Chinese currency)
SAF	Structural Adjustment Facility

SCOPA	Seed Crushers and Oil Processors Association
SDR	Special drawing rights
SMS	Safe minimum standard
SNAs	System of National Accounts
TFAP	Tropical Forestry Action Plan
UCEPCEE	Union du Commerce des Engrais des Pays de la Communauté Economique Européenne (Union of Fertiliser Traders in the EEC)
UKAFIS	United Kingdom Association of the FIS
UKASTA	United Kingdom Agricultural Supply Trade Association Ltd
UKSE	United Kingdom Seeds Executive
UNCLOS	United Nations Convention on the Law of the Sea
UNCTAD	United Nations Committee on Trade and Development
UNDP	United Nations Development Programme
UNEP	United Nations Environment Programme
UN-PAAERD	UN Programme of Action for Africa's Economic Recovery and Development
UPOV	Union for the Protection of New Plant Varieties
USDA	United States Department of Agriculture
WCARRD	World Conference on Agrarian Reform and Rural Development
WCED	World Commission on Environment and Development

Source: UKASTA/FAO.

Bibliography

Agra-Europe Conference "World grain trade to the year 2000", November 1995, Brussels.

Ajmera, S., Wailes, E. J., Holder, S. H. and Dixon, B. L. *Green revolution, impacts on US rice exports*.

Arnold, R and Villain, C., *New directions for European agricultural policy*, CEPS Paper, Brussels: CEPS, 1990.

Asian Development Bank, *Evaluating Rice Market Intervention Policies: Some Asian Examples*, Manila: ADB, 1988.

Bailey, Adrian, *The Blessings of Bread*, New York, Paddington Press, 1975.

Baltic Code, The, *A Guide for Dry Cargo Brokers* (includes Laytime Definitions 1980). Henry Jaffé Ltd., London, 1989.

Barker, R., Herdt, R. W. and Rose, B., "The rice economy of Asia" in *Resources for the Future*, Baltimore: 1985.

Barty-King, H., *Food for Man and Beast—The Story of the London Corn Trade Association, the London Cattle Food Trade Association and the Grain and Feed Trade Association, 1878–1978*: London: Hutchinson Benham, 1978.

Barty-King, H., *The Baltic Exchange*, Quiller Press Ltd., London, 1994.

Bastin, G. and Ellis, J., *International Trade in Grain and the World Food Economy*. The Economist Intelligence Unit Ltd, London, September 1980.

Bernado, A. and Jouve, M., *Triticale: un cereal de origen citogenico*. Ministerio de agricultura, Madrid, 1990.

Bernard, G. et Claude, W., *Les industries de première transformation des céréales*. Paris: Technique et Documentation—Lavoisier, 1991.

Besant, L. (ed.), *Grains—Production, Processing, Marketing*. Board of Trade of the City of Chicago, 1973.

Besant, L., *Commodity Trading Manual*. Board of Trade of the City of Chicago, 1973.

Buergel, Oliver. *Auswirkungen der europäischen Exportsubventionspolitik im Agrarbereich auf die Weltmaerkte*. Reutlingen, 1994.

Butler, N., *The International Grain Trade: Problems and Prospects*. Royal Institute of International Affairs, London: Croom Helm, 1986.

Byerlee, D., *Avoiding the wheat trap: how inappropriate policies change dietary habits*. FAO Review on Agriculture and Development (FAO): Ceres, September 1985.

Carter, C. A. and Zhong Funing, *China's Grain Production and Trade: an economic analysis*. Boulder, Col., Westview Press, 1988.

Charvet, J.-P., "Les greniers du monde", *Collection-économie agricole et agro-alimentaire*, Paris, Economica, 1985.

Chinese grain and oilseeds sectors: major changes under way. OECD, Paris, 1995.

Ciba Geigy, "Wheat", *Documenta*, Ciba Geigy, Basle, 1980.

Cook, E. and Hill, B., *Economic aspects of cereals production in the EC*. EC Statistical Office, Brussels, 1994.

Curry Foundation, *Confrontation or Negotiation: United States policy and European Agriculture*. Associated Faculty Press, 1985.

de Courcy Ling, J. and Sewell, T., *Famine and Surplus*. London: European Democratic Group, European Parliament, April, 1985.

Drewry Shipping Consultants, *Grain—Seaborne Trade and Transport*. London, 1988.

Echanges mondiaux de céréales: quel rôle pour les pays en développement? OCDE, Paris, 1993.

Economic Research Service, *Embargoes, Surplus disposal and US Agriculture*. Agricultural Economic Report No. 564, Washington, DC, December, 1986.

Elz, D. (ed.), *Agricultural Marketing Strategy and Pricing Policy*. Based on papers from a seminar held in Washington, DC, 6-17 May 1985, IBRI7, Washington, DC, World Bank, 1987.

Ender, G., *Food security policies of six Asian countries*. Foreign Agricultural Economic Report (USA), No. 190, Washington, DC, USDA, Economic Research Service, 1983.

European Commission. *Agenda 2000. Vols I–III*. Docs 97/6, 97/7, and 97/8. Strasbourg/Brussels, 1997.

European Commission. "The Outlook of World cereal markets", CAP Working Notes special issue, *A critical evaluation of recent forecasts 1996–2000*. Brussels, 1996.

European Commission. *Cultures arables: céréales, oléagineux, protéagineux, lin non textile: edition 1996/97*. Luxembourg, 1997.

European Commission. *Preliminary Draft Budget of the EC for 1999*. COM(98)300. June, 1998.

European Commission. *Proposal for a Council Regulation establishing agrimonetary arrangements for the euro*. COM(1998)367 final. Brussels, 1998.

Eurostat. *The effects of a worldwide liberalisation of the markets for cereals, oilseeds and pulses on agriculture in the European Union*. Luxembourg, 1997.

Euro Times. Quarterly. MATIF, London.

FAO Committee on Commodity Problems, *The cereal economy of the USSR—Trends and prospects*. Intergovernmental Group on Grains, Rome, February, 1980.

FAO Commodities and Trade Division, *Review of the results of the Tokyo round of multilateral trade negotiations under the General Agreement on Tariffs and Trade and their implications for the grains sector. New protectionism and attempts at liberalization in agricultural trade: selected working papers*. FAO Economic and Social Development Paper (FAO), No. 27, Rome, FAO, 1983.

FAO Committee on Commodity Problems, *Feed utilization patterns and implications for international trade in grains*. Intergovernmental Group on Grains, Rome, 1984.

FAO Committee on Commodity Problems, *Government-to-government trade in rice*. Intergovernmental Group on Rice, Rome, May, 1985.

FAO Committee on Commodity Problems, *The rice policy of Egypt*. Intergovernmental Group on Rice, Rome, May, 1985.

FAO Committee on Commodity Problems, *The rice policy of Thailand: recent changes*. Intergovernmental Group on Rice, Rome, May, 1985.

FAO Commodities and Trade Division, *Impact of national grain policies on world grain supplies and prices*. FAO Economic and Social Development Paper (FAO), No. 56, Rome, 1985.

FAO Committee on Commodity Problems, *Rice policy in Mexico*. Intergovernmental Group on Rice, Rome, March, 1986.

FAO Committee on Commodity Problems, *Rice policy of the Philippines*. Intergovernmental Group on Rice, Rome, March, 1986.

FAO Committee on Commodity Problems, *The rice trade situation in China (including the Province of Taiwan)*. Intergovernmental Group on Rice, Rome, March, 1986.

FAO Committee on Commodity Problems, *Rice policy of Nigeria*. Intergovernmental Group on Rice, Rome, March, 1987 (West African Rice Development Association, Monrovia (Liberia)); FAO, Rome (Italy), Commodities and Trade Division, January, 1987.

FAO Committee on Commodity Problems, *Rice policy in Panama*. Intergovernmental Group on Rice, Rome, March, 1987.

FAO Committee on Commodity Problems, *Rice policy of the EEC: recent developments*. Intergovernmental Group on Rice, Rome, March, 1987.

FAO Committee on Commodity Problems, *Rice policy of the United States: recent developments*. Intergovernmental Group on Rice, Rome, March, 1987.

FAO Committee on Commodity Problems, *Exports of rice by destination and imports by origin in 1986 and 1987*. Intergovernmental Group on Rice, Session 31, Rome, March, 1988.

FAO Committee on Commodity Problems, *Tariff and non-tariff measures affecting international trade in rice*. Intergovernmental Group on Rice, Rome, March, 1988.

FAO Committee on Commodity Problems, *Recent developments in grains policies of exporting countries*. Intergovernmental Group on Grains, Rome, November, 1988.

FAO Committee on Commodity Problems, *Structure and characteristics of the world sorghum economy*. Intergovernmental Group on Grains, Rome, November, 1988.

FAO Commodities and Trade Division, *Global Information and Early Warning System on Food and Agriculture*. Food Outlook (FAO), No. 4, Rome, April, 1989.

FAO Commodities and Trade Division, *A comparison of the cost of producing rice in selected countries*. FAO Social and Economic Development Paper (FAO) No. 101, Rome, 1991.

FAO Commodites and Trade Division, *Demand prospects for rice and other foodgrains in selected Asian countries*. FAO Social and Economic Development Paper (FAO), No. 97, Rome, 1991

FAO *Commodity Market Review 1997–8*. (Annual) Commodities and Trade Division FAO, Rome, February, 1998.

FAO, *Compendium of Demographic and Macro-Economic Assumptions: Trends and Projections, 1970–2005*. Rome, July, 1997.

FAO, *Food Outlook: Statistical Supplement 1996*. FAO, Rome, January, 1997.

Fearnley A/S., *World Bulk Trades*, Oslo, published annually.

Fornari, H., *Bread upon the Waters, a History of United States Grain Exports*. Nashville, Tennessee, Aurora Pub., 1973.

GATT, *Basic Instruments and Selected Documents*. Vol. IV. Text of the General Agreement, 1969, Geneva, March, 1969.

Hillman, J. S. and Schmitz, A. (eds.), *International Trade and Agriculture: theory and policy*. Boulder, Colorado, Westview Press, 1979.

Home-Grown Cereals Authority, *Cereals Surpluses in the EEC: Further Examination of Policy Options*. London, August, 1985.

Huddleston, B., Gittinger, J. P., Leslie, J., and Hoisington, C., (eds.), *Trends in Trade and Food Aid. Food policy: integrating supply, distribution and consumption*. IBRD, Washington, DC, Baltimore, MD, Johns Hopkins University Press, 1987.

International Bulk Journal, monthly since 1981. Regular articles by Sewell, T. on grain market and policy analysis, and by Phillips, K. on shipping and port facilities.

International Grains Council (IGC). *World Grain statistics 1996/7*. (Annually), March, 1998 (1 Canada Square, Canary Wharf, London E14 5AE).

IGC. *Grain Market Report*. (Monthly) new style, June 1998. As above.

IGC. *International Grains Agreement 1995*, As above.

International Policy Council on Agriculture, Food and Trade (IPC). Policy Briefs (periodic). (IPC, 1616 P Street, NW, Suite 100, Washington, DC 20036, USA.)

International Trade Centre UNCTAD/GATT. *Rice: A survey of selected markets in the Middle East*. Geneva, ITC, 1985.

International Wheat Council, *International Wheat Agreement, 1971*, London, IWC, 1971.

International Wheat Council, Secretariat Paper, *Wheat Support Policies and Export Practices in Five Major Exporting Countries*. London, IWC, 1988.

Josling, Timothy, *The US-EC Agricultural Trade Dispute: A Framework for Progress*. Curry Foundation, Washington, DC, November, 1985.

Kainth, G. S., *Foodgrain Marketing System in India; its structure and performance*. New Delhi, Associated Pub. House, 1982.

Kalmbach, P. M., Sharp, J. W. and Walker, F. E., "The Japanese food and feed grain economy", *Research Bulletin*, Ohio Agricultural Research and Development Center, Wooster, June, 1981.

Klugkist, J., Luteijn, P., Oppewal, J. and Renkema, D., *Hunger in Abundance. The influence of surplus production within the EC on agricultural development in the Third World*. International Coalition for Development Action, Brussels; New International Order, Amsterdam, Brussels, 1987.

Liu, K. and Roningen, V. D., *The World Grain-Oilseeds-Livestock (GOL) Model, a Simplified Version*. Washington, DC, US Dept of Agriculture, Economic Research Service, 1985.

Lloyd's Maritime Directory, Vols I and II, 1997. LLP Ltd., 69–77 Paul St., London EC2A 4LQ.

MAFF. *Cereals Deficiency Payments Scheme*. HMSO, 1973.

McElvoy R. *et al.*, *Costs of Production for Major US Crops, 1975–87*. Washington, DC, US Dept. of Agriculture, 1989.

Mielke, Myles J., *Argentine agricultural policies in the grain and oilseeds sectors*. USDA Economic Research Service, 1984.

Morgan, D., *Merchants of Grain (the power and profits of the five giant companies at the center of the world's food supply)*. New York, Viking Press, 1979.

Morris, M. L., *Rice marketing in the Senegal River Valley: research findings and policy reform options*, MSU International Development Paper (USA), No. 8, East Lansing, MI, Michigan State University, Dept. of Agricultural Economics, 1987.

Murphy, M. C., *Report on Farming in the Eastern Counties*. Department of Agricultural Economy, Cambridge, 1988.

Neville-Rolfe, E. and Thomson, K., *Cereal supply control in the European Community*, Agra Europe Special Report 25, Agra Europe, June, 1985.

Neville-Rolfe, Edmund, *The Politics of Agriculture in the European Community*. London, Policy Studies Institute, 1984.

Petit, Michel, *Determinants of Agricultural Policies in the United States and the European Community*. International Food Policy Research Institute, November, 1985.

Porter, R. B., *The US-USSR grain agreement*. Cambridge University Press, 1984.

Prachak, Charoen, and Ito, S. (Overseas Merchandise Inspection Co. Ltd., Bangkok (Thailand)), *Quality control procedures in rice exporters' warehouse in Thailand, the role of Inspection (Survey) Company. Warehouse management of bag storage of grains. Proceedings*, Regional Workshop Management of Bag Storage of Grains, New Delhi, 8–17 September, 1986; FAO, Rome; UNDP, New York; Ministry of Food and Civil Supplies, New Delhi, 1986.

Ravallion, M., *Markets and Famines*, Oxford, Clarendon Press, 1987.

Roberts, I., Love, G., Field, H. and Klijn, N., *US grain policies and the world market*, Policy Monograph No. 4, Australian Bureau of Agricultural and Resource Economics, Canberra, 1989.

Roberts, G. (ed.), *Guide to World Commodity Markets*. 4th edn, London, Kogan Page, 1985.

Root, Waverley, *Food*. New York, Simon & Schuster, 1980.

Runge, C. F. (ed.), *The Future of the North American Granary: Politics, Economics and Resource Constraints in North American Agriculture*. Iowa, Iowa State University Press, 1986.

Sewell, T., *The World Grain Trade*. Woodhead Faulkner Ltd., Simon & Schuster International Group, 1992.

Stanton, B. F., *Production Costs for Cereals in the European Community: Comparisons with the United States, 1977–1984*. Cornell University, March, 1986.

Stephens, D. G. (ed.), *Grains and Oilseeds—Handling, Marketing, Processing*. 3rd edn, Winnipeg, Canadian International Grains Institute, 1982.

Suh, K. W., *The supply-demand situation of food grains and its prospects in Korea*. Report, Regional Seminar on Food Security and Marketing Policies in Asian Countries, Seoul, June 1987; FAO, Bangkok; Regional Office for Asia and the Pacific; Association of Food Marketing Agencies in Asia and the Pacific, Bangkok, August, 1988.

SS&Y Research Services, Monthly Shipping Reviews. London, December 1989 and January 1990.

SS&Y Annual Shipping Review, London, March, 1990.

Swaminathan, M. S., *Terminology for Rice Growing Environments*. International Rice Research Institute, Los Banos, Laguna, Philippines, 1984.

Swaminathan, M. S., *Progress in Upland Rice Research* (Report of 2nd International Upland Rice Conference). International Rice Research Institute, Los Banos, Laguna, Philippines, 1986.

Syndicat Français de la Meunerie. *Exportations mondiales de farine 1981–90*. Paris, 1991.

Tealdo, A., "The arguments for protectionism: the case of Peru", Ceres, *The FAO Review* (FAO), July–August, 1987.

Thomson K. J. and Warren, R. M. (eds.), *Price and Market Policies in European Agriculture*. Proceedings, Newcastle upon Tyne, University of Newcastle upon Tyne, Dept. of Agricultural Economics, 1984.

Tracy, M., *Agricultural Policy in the European Union and other market economies*. 2nd ed. 1997. Agricultural Policy Studies, Genappe, Belgium.

Trezise, P. H., *Rebuilding Grain Reserves; toward an international system*. Brookings Institution, Washington, DC, 1976.

Ulrich, H., *The Practical Grain Encyclopedia*, Commodity Center Corporation, Grand Forks.

United Nations World Food Conference, *Assessment of the world food situation—present and future*. Rome, November, 1974.

USDA, *Usual Planting and Harvesting Dates, for US Field Crops*. United States Department of Agriculture, 1984.

USDA, *Oilseeds: World Markets and Trade*. Foreign Agricultural Service, May, 1998.

USDA, *The Basic Mechanisms of Japanese farm policy*. Economic Research Service, 1990.

USDA, *Average costs of production for Major Field Crops*. Economic Research Service, 1991.

USDA. FAS Reports (periodic). FAS Website home page (http:/www.fas.usda.-gov).

du Vivier, F. R., *Agriculture Européenne et Environnement- Un Avenir Fertile*. Paris, Editions Sang de la Terre, 1987.

Winchell, E. H. and Dahl, R. P., *Wild Rice: Production, Prices and Marketing*. University of Minnesota, 1984.

Wibberley, E. J., *Cereal Husbandry*. Farming Press, Ipswich, 1989.

World Trade Organisation, *Focus* (monthly Newsletter). WTO, Centre William Rappard, 154 rue de Lausanne, 1211 Geneva 21, Switzerland.

Yap, C. L., *World rice situation and outlook 1987–88*, International Rice Commission Newsletter (FAO), 1988.

Yotopoulos, P. A., *Competition for cereals: the food-feed connection* (Stanford Univ., CA Food Research Inst.), Ceres. FAO Review on Agriculture and Development (FAO), September, 1984.

Yu Chen Liang, Buckwell, A., *Chinese grain economy and policy*. Wallingford, CAB International, 1991.

Zeller, A., *L'imbroglio agricole du Marché commun*. France, Calmann-Levy, 1970.

Zoubek, J., *Russia and CIS Agriculture in mid-1992*. Brussels East-West Research and Advisory, 1992.

Index